ROUSSEAU IN THE SPANISH WORLD BEFORE 1833

A Study in Franco-Spanish Literary Relations

By

JEFFERSON REA SPELL

1969

OCTAGON BOOKS

New York

TABLE OF CONTENTS

PREFACE

It is the purpose of this study to show the extent to which Rousseau was known and read in Spain and Spanish America before 1833 and to indicate in a general way the impress made on Spanish thought by his works and those of his most direct imitators.

In tracing the infiltration of Rousseau's ideas, the writer has made little attempt to show minute resemblances of expression, such as line by line or phrase by phrase comparisons, but rather to indicate the extent to which his works were known by outstanding thinkers and writers; to present such of their general ideas as show strong resemblance to those of Rousseau; and to point out the intellectual movements which seem to result from his teachings. To attempt a more detailed survey of so vast a field for a period of almost a century would only be evidence of a failure to comprehend the immensity of the task. It should also be undertsood, at the outset, that the writer realizes that it is impossible to isolate entirely the work of such a man as Rousseau, who gathered ideas on all sides and scattered them at random. In Rousseau were the ideas of his age; they were not his except that he gave them expression; the feelings he voiced were not alone his, but he made them known; and the ideals he exalted were not personal but general.

No general survey of the teachings of Rousseau is offered in this study, but since the trend of thought in Spain in the period under discussion was mainly in two general directions, it is only fair that these be indicated in advance. On the one hand, the teachings of Rousseau led to direct and beneficial reforms which had for their general purpose the increase of intellectual and political liberty, the leveling of social barriers, and the more equitable distribution of goods and opportunity—all generally grasped under the term democracy; on the other, they led to the encouragement of subjective expression and to an increased emphasis upon the feelings and emotions of the individual which, combined first with certain elements and conditions, led in turn to forms of artistic expressions generally known as romanticism. To trace Rousseau is to follow the evolution of these two movements, although he was neither their sole originator nor their only nor final exponent. Perhaps the same general development would have taken place had Rousseau never lived; but while he did, he thundered forth the demands of genuine democracy, and then turned for relief to the mournful portrayal of his own feelings. These two subjects—himself and democracy—he frequently interwove as in a form of development, returning over and over again to a repetition of his main themes. It was the magic of these themes, so different in tone and meaning, that touched the Spanish heart—sometimes one, sometimes the other, often both at once—and it is the echoes of these themes that we shall hear in Spanish lands.

The evolution of this study has been slow. The subject was suggested by Dr. J. P. W. Crawford of the University of Pennsylvania in 1930, while the writer was pursuing graduate work in that institution. In the preparation of the first rough draft completed early in the following year, many fascinating problems presented themselves. The later discovery of a thesis on "Rousseau in Spain," submitted at Columbia University by Francis C. Hayes in 1930, aroused hope that someone else had solved them; but that work, while revealing laudable industry, showed little grasp of the problems presented.

As a step toward their solution, a tentative bibliography of the Spanish translations of Rousseau was prepared, published,[1] and distributed to the more important libraries for corrections and additions. A first-hand study of the *Discursos mercuriales,* located in Spain through the kindness of Professor R. H. Williams of Brown University, led to the long search which terminated with the discovery of the original of the supposed Rousseau discourse therein published.[2] Papers on "Rousseau in Spain" and "Rousseau

---

[1]*Hispanic Review,* II (1934), 134–152.
[2]"Rousseau's 1750 *Discours* in Spain," *ibid.,* 334–344.

in Spanish America," read before the Modern Language
Association in 1931 and 1932,[3] brought valuable comments
and collaboration from various scholars, especially Dr.
Marden of Princeton University. A study of the translations, performances, and influence of *Pygmalion* was read
in 1933.[4] After this much of the work had been published
and reviewed in various journals, Angel del Río of Columbia University, who had suggested the Hayes thesis of
1930, read a paper on "Rousseau in Spain" before the
American Association of Teachers of Spanish in which he
stated that the subject had not as yet "incitado la curiosidad de ningún crítico." Yet references to all these articles
are in the footnotes.[5]

A trip to South America in 1937 made possible personal
examination of much pertinent material in the main
libraries and archives.

And yet, no one is more aware than the writer that the
surface has still barely been scratched, and that intensive
study of special fields will yield further rewards to the
student of Rousseau. As an approach to such detailed
studies, this general survey may point the way.

The writer wishes to express his thanks to Dr. Crawford
for the suggestion which initiated this study; to him,
Dr. Albert Schinz, and Dr. Miguel Romera Navarro of
the University of Pennsylvania and to Dr. Aaron Schaffer
and Dr. A. B. Swanson of The University of Texas for careful reading of the manuscript at various stages of its
preparation; to Professor R. H. Williams, who placed the
writer under deep obligations when he collected in Europe
much bibliographical data and located copies of rare and
indispensable volumes; to Professor E. H. Hespelt, who
collected items from New York libraries; to Mr. B. Burstein
of Madrid, who furnished important excerpts from the
Archivo Histórico Nacional and other manuscript sources;
to Srta. Juana Manrique de Lara in Mexico City, Sr. Jorge

---

[3]The last named was published in the *Hispanic American Historical Review*, XV (1935), 260–267.
[4]*Romanic Review*, XXV (1934), 395–401.
[5]*Hispania*, XIX (1936), 105–116.

Basadre of Lima, Peru, and the librarians of the national libraries in Chile and Colombia, who furnished data concerning the copies in their respective institutions; to Dr. Ricardo Donoso, who generously placed at the disposal of the writer the resources of the National Archives of Chile; and to Miss Julia Harris, reference librarian of The University of Texas, who has been untiring in locating and borrowing needed periodicals and books. The kindness of the editors of the *Hispanic Review, Romanic Review,* and the *Hispanic American Historical Review* as well as their publishers, the Columbia University Press and Duke University Press, in permitting reprinting of the portions originally published therein is gratefully acknowledged.

J. R. SPELL

The University of Texas
Austin, Texas

February 1, 1938

BOOK I

THE DISSEMINATION, 1743–1793

CHAPTER I

ROUSSEAU'S IDEAS ENTER SPAIN

In spite of his visionary and impracticable ideas, often expressed in obscure and self-contradictory terms, no single individual of the eighteenth-century thinkers in France exerted such a wide and varied revolutionizing influence as Jean-Jacques Rousseau. Indeed, it has been said that "the world has not seen more than once or twice in all the course of history a literature which has exercised such prodigious influence over the minds of men as that which emanated from Rousseau between 1749 and 1762."[1] It was he who first awakened an abiding interest in the proletariat; who paved the way for democracy, socialism, and communism; who destroyed ancient educational systems; who taught his own and succeeding generations to see and love the beauties of Nature; and who broke down restraint and encouraged free subjective expression in literature—no small accomplishment for one individual. So fiery were his denunciations of older philosophies and so vigorous his enthusiasm for the views he championed that even before his death constructive work had begun. During the next half century the ideas he scattered were to take root in new soil; in the century that followed they were to become known as native products.

That the influence of Rousseau in France, Germany, and England was both direct and wide in application has become an accepted fact. Of this the speeches and writings of the leaders of the French Revolution are evidence; in the writings of Saint-Pierre, Chateaubriand, de Staël, and George Sand is Rousseau's admiration for Nature; Lessing, Schiller, Goethe, Kant, and Herder transmitted his ideas to the German people; while Goldsmith, Byron, Shelley, and George

---

[1]Maine, Henry, *Ancient Law* (New York, 1871), 87.

Eliot were all fired by his enthusiasm.[2] Spain alone, of the neighboring countries of Europe, is unmentioned by writers on Rousseau as affected; apparently she remained entirely aloof from his influence.[3] The acceptance of this impression has been made easy by the knowledge that Rousseau's works were prohibited from circulating in Spain—a prohibition which is generally assumed to have been effective. Another ground for the omission of reference to Spain in Rousseau literature is that few who have specialized in that field were familiar with either the language, the history, or the literature of the Iberian peninsula. Added to these facts is the very real difficulty of tracing the early influence of such a man through the works of Spaniards, many of whom did not dare, except in brief intervals, such as from 1810 to 1814 and from 1820 to 1822, to express openly their real views or to acknowledge publicly the actual sources of their ideas. That the works of Rousseau were nevertheless known in Spain and Hispanic America almost as fast as they were written, and that they made an impress on Spanish life no less marked than in the other countries mentioned, it will be the purpose of this study to show.

Contacts between Rousseau and the Iberian peninsula were established before his fame as a writer penetrated there. As early as 1743, while he was serving as secretary to the French Ambassador at Venice, the Genevan became acquainted with several Spaniards. Among these was a

---

[2]Mornet, D., "L'influence de J.-J. Rousseau au XVIIIe siècle"; Höffding, Harald, "Rousseau et le XIXe siècle"; Benrubi, I., "Rousseau et le mouvement philosophique et pédagogique en Allemagne"; Gosse, Edmund, "J.-J. Rousseau en Angleterre au XIXe siècle," in *Annales de la Société J.-J. Rousseau*, VIII (1912), 33–160. [Hereafter referred to as *Annales*.]   See also Warner, J. H. "The Reaction in Eighteenth-Century England to Rousseau's Two *Discours*," in *Publications of the Modern Language Association*, XLVIII (1933), 475–487, and to the *Nouvelle Héloïse*, in LII (1937), 803–819. [Hereafter referred to as *PMLA*.]

[3]L'influence de Rousseau ne fut, semble-t-il, profonde qu'au début du XIXe siècle avec les traductions de Marchena."—Mornet, *op. cit.*, 65.   Since the publication of the writer's bibliography and articles on Rousseau in Spain other references have been made. Cf. Mérimée, Paul, *L'influence française en Espagne au dix-huitième siècle* (Paris, 1936), 72–74.

young Basque, Manuel Ignacio Altuna, through whom Rousseau's ideas were first transmitted directly to Spain. The two men met in Venice, where Altuna made a short stay on his return from an Italian tour which had thoroughly convinced him that, beyond the taste for the fine arts he had acquired, nothing more in the way of knowledge remained. Rousseau, however, thought differently. "Je lui dis que les arts n'étoient que le délassement d'un génie comme le sien, fait pour cultiver les sciences; et je lui conseillai, pour en prendre le goût, un voyage et six mois de séjour à Paris. El me crut et fut à Paris."[4] There Rousseau found him when he himself returned to the Capital in 1744, and together the friends passed almost a year in happy association. That the Genevan felt great admiration for Spain is shown by his description of Altuna as "un de ces hommes rares que l'Espagne seule produit, et dont elle produit trop peu pour sa gloire," and he credited the Spaniard with moderation, toleration, and an open mind, in spite of the fact that he was a devout Catholic.

> Nous nous liâmes si bien, que nous fîmes le projet de passer nos jours ensemble. Je devois, dans quelques années, aller à Ascoytia pour vivre avec lui dans sa terre. Toutes les parties de ce projet furent arrangées entre nous la veille de son départ. . . . Les événements postérieurs, mes désastres, son mariage, sa mort enfin, nous ont séparés pour toujours.[5]

Another version of the miscarriage of their plans is that when Rousseau later asked permission of the Spanish authorities to visit his friend in Guipúzcoa, they demanded that he retract what he had written; and, and upon his refusal to do so, the matter was left in abeyance.[6]

The interest in science and scientific progress, which Rousseau awakened in his Basque friend, was to prove a source of great inspiration in Guipúzcoa. Altuna returned there in 1745; in the following year he was the mayor of

---

[4]*Les Confessions*, in *Oeuvres complètes*, VIII, 232.
[5]*Ibid.*, 233 ff. A letter from Rousseau to Altuna, dated Paris, January 30, 1748, is included in the *Correspondance générale*, I, 282–284.
[6]Ferrer del Río, Antonio, *Historia del reinado de Carlos III* (Madrid, 1856), IV, 38.

Azcoitia and later an alderman. In 1749 he married; of the two children born to him, one bore the father's name. The intimacy with Rousseau continued through correspondence; but the letters to the Spaniard were later destroyed by some pious soul.[7] Altuna soon associated himself with two other residents of Azcoitia, Joaquín de Eguía, later the Marquis of Narro, and Francisco Munibe y Idiáquez, Count of Peñaflorida; and from the frequent meetings of this congenial group, who performed various scientific experiments in the well equipped laboratory of Peñaflorida and exchanged news and views of general progress, grew an academy of natural sciences, which did much to arouse an interest among the Basques in scientific progress. Nor did this interest diminish with the years, for Father Isla, the satirist of the bombastic cleric, had only to make an attack on science, in one of the early chapters of *Fray Gerundio de Campazas*, to bring forth from this trio a prompt and cutting reply.[8] So well known were their views that Isla had little difficulty in recognizing under the pseudonym of "D. Roque Antonio de Cogollor" the real authors, whom he referred to as the "triunvirato de Azcoitia."[9] The death of Altuna in 1762 put an end to this triumvirate, but its influence far outlived him, as we shall see later.

Another Spaniard with whom Rousseau became intimate in Venice was Francisco Carrión, one of the secretaries in the Spanish embassy there. To this gentleman Rousseau attributes his connections with certain members of the demi-monde. Although he entertained toward the worldly Carrión little of the profound respect he felt for Altuna,

---

[7]For the facts connected with Altuna's life in Spain, I am indebted to Julio de Urquijo, who generously provided me with copies of his studies, *Menéndez y Pelayo y los caballeritos de Azcoitia* (San Sebastián, 1925) and *Los amigos del país* (San Sebastián, 1929).

[8]*Los Aldeanos críticos, o Cartas críticas sobre lo que se verá*, dadas a luz por D. Roque Antonio de Cogollor. Impreso en Evora, año de 1758, in *Biblioteca de autores españoles*, XV, 367–386. [Hereafter referred to as *B.A.E.*] See also the correspondence which follows and Isla's letter of January 18, 1759, p. 492.

[9]Isla to Peñaflorida, Villagarcía, January 13, 1759, *ibid.*, 387.

the friendship endured for many years. After Carrión was transferred to the Spanish legation in Paris, the earlier intimacy was renewed. In 1759, Rousseau tells us,

Il me vint surprendre à Montmorency, lorsque je m'y attendois le moins. Il étoit décoré d'un ordre d'Espagne dont j'ai oublié le nom, avec une belle croix en pierreries. Il avoit été obligé, dans ses preuves, d'ajouter une lettre à son nom de Carrio, et portoit celui de chevalier de Carrión. Je le trouvai toujours le même, le même excellent coeur, l'esprit de jour en jour plus aimable. J'aurois repris avec lui la même intimité qu' auparavant, si Coindet, s'interposant entre nous à son ordinaire, n'eût profité de mon éloignement pour s'insinuer à ma place et en mon nom dans sa confiance, et me supplanter à force de zèle à me servir.[10]

In spite of Coindet, the friendship continued. In 1760 Rousseau suggested to the interloper that "si nous pouvions former entre le cher Carrión, vous et moi une petite société exclusive ou nul autre mortel au monde ne fût admis, cela seroit trop délicieux. Mais je ne puis me corriger de mes châteaux en Espagne."[11] In each of his lists of those to whom copies of his works were to be presented he included the name of Carrión. In October, 1758, he ordered the *Lettre à d'Alembert* sent; in January, 1761, the *Nouvelle Héloïse;* the *Préface* on February 9; the *Projet de paix perpétuelle* on March 4; the *Recueil d'Estampes pour la nouvelle Héloïse* on the 10th; and in 1762 a copy of *Émile.*[12] In acknowledgment of the receipt of the last of these, Carrión wrote a most sympathetic letter to Rousseau, but regretted that he could not express an opinion of the work, as he had not yet had time to read it.[13] They were in touch with each other in 1763, through the Marshal of Luxembourg, who wrote in May that he had just seen Carrión; he had talked of Rousseau, and promised to send a letter that very day to be forwarded

[10]*Les Confessions*, in *Oeuvres complètes*, VIII, 364. Concerning their relations in Venice, see *ibid.*, 214–215, 221, 223, 232.

[11]Rousseau à Coindet [December, 1760], in *Annales*, XIV (1922), 35–36.

[12]*Correspondance générale*, IV, 73; V, 328, 365; VI, 88, 106; and VII, 219.

[13]*Ibid.*, VII, 260–261.

to his old friend.[14]   Ten years later, the Genevan, back in
Paris, was still corresponding with Carrión at Madrid,
through the Duke of Alba.[15]

Rousseau's acquaintance with Spaniards, even before his
fame was established as a writer, was not limited to incon-
sequential people.   Instead he showed himself able to win
the friendship of those whose influence and power meant
much.   While in Venice, he was on an intimate footing
with the Spanish ambassador, the Marquis of Mari, whom
he describes as an "homme adroit et fin," capable of leading by the nose the French diplomat, Count Montaigu.   It
was through the Spanish mail that Rousseau sent his letters
to Madame de Warens,[16] and through friends at the Spanish
court that he hoped to secure financial aid for her.[17]
Through these friends—Mari, Turrieta, Altuna, and Carrión[18]—Rousseau had early opened channels of contact with
Spain, some of which were later to provide avenues for
the introduction of his ideas.

With the publication of the essay that was awarded the
prize by the Academy of Dijon in 1750 Rousseau became
widely known in the world of letters, for his attack on the
arts and sciences furnished a subject for arguments and
controversies during many years.   A review of the work
appeared in the *Mercure* for January, 1751; in February
the *Journal de Trévoux* followed with its comments; and
these alone would have been sufficient to transform a spark
into a blaze.   During the year it was kept well before the
public: Raynal's comments were in the *Mercure* for June;
on the 22d of that month Charles Borde delivered an address against it before the Academy of Lyons; in August

---

[14]*Ibid.*, IX, 277–278.
[15]*Documentos escogidos del archivo de la casa de Alba* (Madrid,
1891), 561–563.
[16]*Correspondance*, I (58A, Venice, October 5, 1743), 192–193.
[17]"Je puis avoir quelques facilités de plus du côté de la Cour
d'Espagne ayant plusieurs amis qui pourroient nous servir de ce côté.
J'ai entre autres icy le M[ís] de Turrieta qui est assez ami de mon ami
pour être un peu le mien; je me propose à son départ pour Madrid,
où il doit retourner de Printems, de lui remettre un mémoire relatif à
votre Pension. . . ."—*Ibid.*, I (93 bis, Venice, March 1, 1745), 267.
[18]Among his casual acquaintances was a certain Fagoaga.

Professor Le Roy attacked it in Latin in the presence of a large audience at the Sorbonne;[19] Le Cat of Rouen published, shortly after, a refutation under the pseudonym of "Un académicien de Dijon," a title the Dijon body soon publicly disavowed;[20] the refutation of the King of Poland appeared in September;[21] and that of Gautier, an academician of Nancy, in October.[22] The replies Rousseau made to all of these except Le Roy were printed during 1751 and 1752; and before the end of the following year the *Discours* and documents relating to it, to the number of nineteen, had been published in two volumes at Gotha.[23] Reviews and extracts of the various articles appeared both in French and in foreign publications.

Scarcely was the Dijon prize essay off the press before news of it was circulated in Spain through a government organ. In February, 1751, there appeared in Madrid, among the news items from Paris, the following paragraph—unquestionably the first with reference to Rousseau in a Spanish periodical:

Aquí corre un Discurso, que ha logrado el premio en la Academia de *Dijon*, sobre la cuestión propuesta, es a saber, *si el restablecimiento de las Ciencias, y de las Artes ha contribuído a expurgar las costumbres.* El Autor prueba con mucha fuerza, que han sido más perjudiciales que útiles; y apoya su dictamen en un gran número de exemplos sacados de la Historia. Este Discurso, que causa aquí mucho ruido, se prohibió a los principios; pero después se ha permitido publicarlo, y muchos Sabios se disponen a impugnarle.[24]

---

[19]"Discours de M. Le Roi, Professeur de Rhétorique au Collège du Cardinal le Moine, prononcé le 12. Août 1751, dans les Ecoles de Sorbonne, en présence de MM. du Parlement, à l'occasion de la distribution des prix fondés dans l'Université. Traduit en François par M. B. Chanoine Régulier," *Recueil de toutes les pièces qui ont été publiées à l'occasion du Discours de M. J.-J. Rousseau sur cette question proposée par L'Académie de Dijon pour le Prix de l'année 1750* (Gotha, 1753), I, 200–237. [Hereafter referred to as *Recueil.*]
[20]The introductory letter [*Recueil*, II, 7–9] is dated August 15, 1751; the disavowal, June, 1752 [*Recueil*, II, 161–163].
[21]This date is cited in a "Réfutation des Observations de M. J.-J. Rousseau . . . sur une Réponse qui a été faite à son Discours" [*Recueil*, I, 113].
[22]Rousseau states in his reply, dated November 1, 1751, that Gautier's work had been printed in the *Mercure* for October.
[23]See note 19 for title and bibliographical details.
[24]*Mercurio histórico y político.* Compuesto del Mercurio del Haya y de otras noticias, LXXIII (February, 1751), 69.

Nor was the subject dropped. In the August issue of the same periodical appeared an account of the annual distribution of the Le Gendre funds to promising students of the University of Paris. The news item further stated that the address of the occasion was delivered in Latin by "Mons. Le Roy, Professor de Rhetórica en el Colegio del Cardenal le Moine"; in this he attempted to show *"lo mucho que la Virtud debe a las Letras."*[25]

The close intellectual contact between France and Spain at the middle of the eighteenth century is evidenced by the fact that before the last of Rousseau's replies had been published at Paris a refutation of the *Discours* was written in Spain. In contrast with those that came to Rousseau's notice in France, which were all written by laymen or seculars, the Spanish refutation was from the pen of a Benedictine. This work,[26] which appeared as the eighteenth letter of the fourth volume of the *Cartas eruditas y curiosas* of Feijóo, although undated, was certainly written before the twenty-fifth, which bears the date of October 20, 1752; it was probably drafted in the spring of that year. The author, Benito Feijóo y Montenegro (1676–1764), was a scholar, who had been laboring since 1726 to awaken Spain from her lethargy and to infuse her people with the investigative spirit. The bulk of his work appeared in *El Teatro crítico universal* (1726–1739) and in the *Cartas eruditas y curiosas* (1742–1760). The fact that Feijóo knew of and promptly devoted himself to a refutation of Rousseau's first work is of considerable interest, but of even greater assistance in tracing the dissemination of Rousseau's views in Spain is a knowledge of the channel by which Feijóo came in contact with the work of the Genevan whose name was still, apparently, unknown to him. This information he himself gives in the opening paragraph of the letter in

---

[25]*Ibid.*, LXXIX (August, 1751), 77.
[26]"Impúgnase un temerario que a la cuestión propuesta por la Academia de Dijón, con premio al que la resolviese con más acierto, si la ciencia conduce, o se opone a la práctica de la virtud, en una dissertación pretendió probar ser más favorable a la virtud la ignorancia que la ciencia."

question, which is addressed to his provincial. In it he recalls that some months earlier that dignitary had written him of an author who had tried to show that learning had corrupted rather than encouraged virtue, but that he had almost forgotten the incident when he received the *Memorias de Trévoux* issued in 1751, which contained both a review of the original *Discours* and an extract of the reply of the author to a refutation of his work. "Y uno y otro me dan bastante luz para conocer de qué armas usa, y del rumbo por donde navega.[27]

Although Feijóo based his refutation on these reviews and not on the original, his reply was none the less vigorous, as may be seen from the following summary:

No hallaba en Rousseau más que 'un estilo declamatoria y visiblemente afectado; una continua sofistería, basada, sobre todo, en el paralogismo *non causa pro causa*, y una inversión y uso siniestro de las noticias históricas. . . .' No le entusiasma *la virtud espartana*, que tan pomposamente encarecía Rousseau: al contrario, tiénela por *suprema y asquerosa barbarie*, sobre todo puesta en cotejo con la cultura ateniense. No concede de ligero que los romanos de la decadencia valiesen menos moralmente que los de los primeros tiempos de la república, porque no en un solo vicio consiste la *nequicia*, ni en una sola virtud la santidad; y, sobre todo, niega rotundamente que entre los hombres de ciencia sean más los viciosos que los virtuosos, porque, antes al contrario, la continua aplicación al estudio desvía la atención de todo lo que puede perturbar la serenidad del ánimo o excitar el apetito. Respírase en todas las cláusulas de este discurso el más simpático amor al cultivo de la inteligencia: truena el P. Feijóo contra quien osa buscar ejemplos de perfección en el siglo X, siglo de tinieblas, y se indigna contra los que establecen parentesco entre la herejía de Lutero y el Renacimiento de las letras humanas. Sólo se equivoca en creer que Rousseau buscaba únicamente notoriedad de ingenioso con su sofística paradoja. . . .[28]

---

[27]Edition of Blas Roman (Madrid, 1781), IV, 247–248. The references of Feijóo to the *Journal de Trévoux* have been verified in the file in the John Carter Brown Library through the kindness of Professor R. H. Williams, as follows:
"Article XXIX. Discours qui a remporté le Prix à l'académie de Dijon en l'année 1750, sur cette question proposée par la même Académie; Si le rétablissement des sciences & des arts a contribué à épurer les moeurs. Par un citoyen de Genève . . . 8°. pag. 66" [February, 1751, pp. 504–526].
"Article CXXVII. Observations de Jean Jacques Rousseau de Genève, sur la réponse qui a été faite à son discours, in 8°. pag. 62" [December, 1751, pp. 2538–2565].
[28]Menéndez y Pelayo, M., *Historia de los heterodoxos españoles* (Madrid, 1930), VI, 95–96.

This attack, far from the intent of the writer, proved to be one of the most effective means of making Rousseau and his views known in the Spanish world. Feijóo's works were eagerly read and widely circulated in his day, and his influence on the succeeding generations was scarcely less, according to the testimony of such radicals as Marchena and Blanco White, although the one regarded him as a defender of the Inquisition and despotism,[29] while the other declared that Feijóo's works were to him at the age of fifteen as an Aladdin's lamp which led him "to reason, to argue, and to doubt," and thus opened for him a new intellectual world.[30] Nor should the importance of Feijóo's source, the *Journal de Trévoux*, be overlooked as a means of circulation of Rousseau's ideas. This periodical, entitled *Mémoires pour l'histoire des sciences et des beaux arts*, but commonly known as the *Mémoires* or *Journal de Trévoux*, was a Jesuit organ of renown, long the best informed and best written journal in France. The extent of its circulation in Spain is suggested by the fact that from 1752 to 1754 a Spanish edition was issued in Madrid by José Vicente de Rustant under the title of *Memorias para la historia de las ciencias y bellas artes*, for the benefit of those who had not followed Feijóo's advice to familiarize themselves with the French language.[31] Both French and Spanish versions circulated in the New World, especially among churchmen.

But the reviews of the *Discours* and of Rousseau's replies to Grimm and to the King of Poland, published by the Jesuit organ, and Feijóo's reply were not all that Spain was to know of the first essay of the Genevan. In 1755 and 1756 there appeared in Madrid a periodical entitled *Discursos mercuriales*, edited by Juan Enrique de Graef, a

---

[29]*Lecciones de filosofía moral* (Burdeos, 1820), I, 131.

[30]Doblado Leucadio [pseud.], *Letters from Spain* (London, 1822), 99–100.

[31]In Vol. I (January–February, 1752), 100–102, is the announce-ment: "De Ginebra, Papel in 8°. Pag. 31 de Mr. Rousseau Ciudadano de Ginebra a Mr. Grimm sobre la refutación de su discurso por Mr. Gautier." In the discussion it is stated that a review of the *Discours* had appeared the previous year and that the controversy promised to last as long as the siege of Troy.

foreigner by his own statement and probably a Dutchman. In the first issue, dated October 1, 1755,[32] Graef sets forth at length the purposes of the publication, and states that the articles presented will be translations of those of greatest interest from abroad. In the second issue appears a translation, forty-eight pages in length, of the address Le Roy had delivered at the Sorbonne on August 12, 1751.[33] This is entitled "Desagravio de las ciencias contra el atentado de la Academia de Dijon, premiando el Discuro del Señor Rousseau," and follows the original exactly except for the omission of one paragraph. In the introduction, the Spanish editor states that the award has aroused men of letters everywhere and given rise to numerous replies.

El señor Le Roy, Professor (Cathedrático) Real de Rhetórica, animado de un noble estímulo y zelo, para revindicar el honor de las Letras, se aprovechó zelosamente de la presencia del Parlamento, que con una multitud de Príncipes, y Sabios asistían en la Sorbona a la distribución annual de los premios literarios. Pronunció con este motivo un elegante discurso, en que, impugnando el systema del señor Rousseau, asseguró y probó, que tan lexos está, el que las Artes y Ciencias fuessen estorvo a la virtud, que al contrario son sus más firmes apoyos, y seguras columnas. Su oración es sólida y elegante, y la materia de que habla tan importante y decorosa, que por el honor y la gloria de los doctos y apasionados a las Letras, no podemos, sin manifiesta injusticia, negarla a nuestro idioma, e insertarla traducida al principio de estos Mercuriales.[34]

Following the translation of the address are several paragraphs of editorial comment; the first of these reads as follows:

---

[32]Hartzenbusch, Eugenio, *Apuntes para un catálogo de periódicos madrileños* . . . (Madrid, 1894), 7, says that a volume was issued in 1752, but the file in the writer's library extends from No. 1, dated October 1, 1755, to No. 18, 1756. The approval is dated August, 1755, and the long "Discurso preliminar" makes no mention of an earlier issue. Sempere y Guarinos [*Ensayo de una biblioteca española de los mejores escritores* (Madrid, 1785), III, 55] gives the date of the initial issue as October 1, 1755.

[33]This was probably translated from the French version published in the *Journal Economique*, IV (November, 1751), 108–155, for Graef drew extensively from that publication.

[34]*Discursos mercuriales*, 4–5.

La Dissertation del señor Rousseau ha sido refutada por varios ilustres Literatos, cuyas obras se han publicado en el *Jornal* [*sic*] *Económico*, en el *Mercurio* de París, y en otros papeles sueltos, a los que Rousseau ha respondido con el título de patricio de Ginebra, y que al fin han interessado al mismo cuerpo Académico de Dijón. El que más fuertemente ha combatido por la verdad, y por el honor de las Letras, es el señor Le Cat, Secretario perpetuo de la Academia de las Ciencias de Ruben [*sic*], el qual sólidamente ha respondido a todas las razones en que el señor Rousseau funda su Heregía Literaria, tomando la defensa de la verdad, y del buen gusto, con las armas del gusto mismo. Y todos los apassionados a las Letras tienen especial obligación a los fuertes campeones, que han procurado arruinar un systema tan pernicioso, como lo es el que intentó abatir las Letras, y quiso entronizar a la ignorancia.[35]

No further reference to Rousseau occurs until the sixth issue, dated December 17, 1755; in this the first article is entitled "Discurso que empató los votos de la Académia de Dijón para el Premio del año de 1750, en que se examina, si el establecimiento de las ciencias y artes ha contribuído a mejorar las costumbres." The subject matter covers thirty-three octavo pages, and consists of seventy-three paragraphs, four of which, written by the editor, are of an introductory nature. In the first, he states that since many of his readers have desired to read the *Discurso* which gave rise to that of Le Roy, he is gratifying them by publishing its translation in this issue. The *Discurso* opens with a discussion of the primitive Greeks, whom the writer compares with those of the age of Pericles, to the detriment of the latter; he then considers the Romans before and during the age of Augustus, with similar results; he extols the morals of the people during the age of Leo X, and condemns emphatically those of the reign of Louis XIV. After reviewing the deplorable moral conditions prevailing in England under Charles II, he retraces briefly the history of Spain, and finds in her backward state evidence that a country can preserve herself and the most desirable qualifications in her citizens without the cultivation of the sciences and arts. After surveying the evil consequences everywhere of these agencies of culture,

---

[35]*Ibid.*, 46–47.

the author concludes with the following stanza, extracted, according to a note, from "Rousseau. Od." :

> Philosofos altivos
> Dexad essa apariencia;
> Y si del beneficio
> De vuestra Ciencia, y Arte
> Quisiesseis darnos prueba,
> Decid: Desde Pandora
> El vicio aborrecible
> Mejor establecido
> Se vío, ni más amado,
> Que en el siglo ilustrado.

Here we have a curious contribution to Rousseau literature which at once gives rise to questions. In spite of the fact that the topic treated is that proposed by the Academy of Dijon, and the point of view advanced is that of Rousseau, there is not a single paragraph in this work which corresponds completely with any in the 1750 *Discours*. There is not even a mention of its most famous section, the épopée of Fabricius. The primitive Greeks and Romans are praised and their successors found less virtuous; but in this work there is none of the fire or the eloquence which won the prize for the Genevan. Clearly the writer had no intention of palming his work off as that of Rousseau. Was it, perhaps, an essay actually submitted to the Academy of Dijon in 1750? Was the vote really tied, as the title of this article suggests? The published records of that body state that fourteen essays were submitted; the seventh, that of Rousseau, was awarded the prize. The tenth, which was awarded the "premier accessit," bore the name of M. de Chasselas of Troyes; the fourth, that of M. l'abbé Talbert of Besançon, received the "second accessit."[36] Clearly there was no tie; but the question as to whether this *Discurso* was one of those receiving awards remains yet to be answered. The poetry with

---

[36]Dufour, Théophile, *Recherches bibliographiques sur les œuvres imprimées de J.-J. Rousseau* (Paris, 1925), I, 22, quoting from the *Notes* included in *Lettres inédites de Buffon, J.-J. Rousseau, Voltaire, Piron, de Lalande, Larcher et autres personnages célèbres, adressées à l'Académie de Dijon;* accompagnées de notes historiques . . .; publiées par C.-X. Girault (Paris & Dijon, 1819), 13–15.

which the work concludes, a stanza from the ode "A
l'impératrice Amélia" by J. B. Rousseau, suggests that the
composition was the work of a Frenchman. The periods
selected for criticism bear a curious resemblance to those
cited in the introduction of Le Siècle de Louis XIV by
Voltaire, who terms the ages of Pericles, of Augustus, of
Leo X, and of Louis XIV the periods of greatest cultural
progress; but Voltaire exalts culture, while this article
condemns it. It seems improbable that Graef attempted
to summarize Rousseau, for the Spanish version contains
too much that is extraneous to the original. Besides, in a
note added on the last page of the issue, the editor dis-
claims all responsibility.

> Estoy agradecido al Curioso, que me ha honrado con el Discurso
> primero de este Tomo; y aunque hasta aquí no he tenido la fortuna
> de saber quien me lo ha mandado entregar, advierto sin embargo
> que no es mío, y que deseo con mucha ansia poder participar al
> público el primer favorecedor de mis Discursos, à fin de estimular
> à otros muchos Literatos sigan este exemplo, el qual no tiene otros
> visos sino el adelantamiento de la Literatura y de los Artes.

In the ninth issue of the same publication, dated February 4, 1756, is an accurate translation of the whole of the
Réfutation by Stanislaus Leszczynski, and it is definitely
stated that this is an answer to the "Discurso primero
del número VII"; in the index at the end of the eighteenth
issue the reply of the King of Poland is described as
"Respuesta al Discurso I del número VI. sobre la Dissertación de Rousseau"; in both of which statements the
editor gives the impression that the work published in the
sixth issue was that of Rousseau. In the nineteenth issue,
that of July 7, 1756, is a letter to the editor of the periodical from Dr. Antonio Jacobo del Barco, professor of philosophy at the University of Huelva, "sobre el Discurso
del Mr. Rousseau, premiado en la Academia de Dijon,
acerca del influxo de las letras en la depravación de las
costumbres." In it he states that he has no intention of
refuting Rousseau's principal arguments, as Feijóo, Le
Roy, and "el anónimo" of the February-fourth issue have
done; but he does intend to defend Spain against the

charge that she has existed and flourished without culti-
vating the arts, and has taken precautions to guard against
such a pernicious influence. In his twenty-page letter, he
claims that Spain has always promoted culture, and
expresses surprise that the facts are not better known in
France than Rousseau's statement would suggest.

After a tedious search through the most probable
French publications, the original of the Spanish article
attributed to Rousseau was finally identified in the June,
1752, issue of the *Mercure de France*. In reality the essay
published in Spain as that of Rousseau was the discourse
bearing the name of M. de Chasselas, which was awarded,
not the prize, but the "premier accessit," by the Dijon
Academy in 1750. Not even in the French periodical does
it bear the name of its real author, for "les Mémoires sur
la vie de Grosley, page 21, nous apprennent que Grosley
en était l'auteur."[37] The *Discurso* Rousseau wrote appears
not to have been published in Spain, even in condensed
form, for over half a century; instead he was credited with
and held responsible for the misstatements of Grosley.

Until this time, as the articles already mentioned clearly
show, while there was antagonism to Rousseau's views in
Spain as there was in France, no attempt had been made
to bar his writings from circulation in either country.
The year 1756 saw the first step in that direction. The
publication of the second essay in 1755 brought forth such
a storm of criticism from both France and Switzerland
that the Inquisition in Spain felt it could afford to take
no chances; the circulation of such a work must be stopped.
Accordingly, the "Discours, ou Dissertat. sur l'origine et
les fondements de l'inégalité parmi les Hommes. A Dresde
1755. 1 tomo" went on the *Index* in 1756,[38] a fact that
was given due publicity. A visitor in Madrid four years
later who found a list of prohibited books posted on the
church gates noted: "Few of Voltaire's or Rousseau's

---

[37]Dufour, *op. cit.*, I, 22, quoting Girault.
[38]*Indice último de los libros prohibidos y mandados expurgar para
todos los reynos y señorios del católico rey de las Españas . . .*
(Madrid, 1790), 236.

works have escaped the catalogue, and I am told that their names are growing no less terrifying in this country than those of Luther and Calvin."[39]

While the prohibition of this essay may have had the effect of discouraging articles or references to Rousseau in Spanish publications for a time, their absence is more probably due to the fact that he himself had withdrawn from the Paris limelight. During the years of his retirement, he kept up his personal contacts with Spain through Carrión, who visited him at Montmorency; through correspondence with Altuna; and he also established new ones through Prince Salm-Salm, an officer later in the Spanish army, who, Rousseau recounted, "a été mon voisin et qui me venoit voir quelques fois."[40]

Although little was heard of Rousseau in Spain, at least through the press, during the period in which he was busiest with his pen, the year 1762 brought him again sharply to public attention, and at the same time severed the first link that had bound him to Spain. Less than a week after *Émile* was put on sale in Paris, Altuna was dead;[41] but Rousseau, fleeing from persecution and imprisonment, seeking a refuge on foreign soil, did not know of his loss until much later. Meanwhile the press carried to the most remote parts of the Spanish world news of his publications and the verdict rendered by church and state against him. In the *Mercurio* of June, 1762, the subject is circumspectly broached, in the news from Paris:

El Parlamento ha mandado quemar por mano del verdugo un libro, que mete mucho ruido, y se ha impreso con el título de: "Emile, ou de l'Education," su autor "Juan Jacobo Rousseau," vecino de "Ginebra." Temiendo éste que se le prendiesse, se ha refugiado a Holanda; y allí se ha reimpresso la referida obra.[42]

---

[39]Baretti, Joseph, *A Journey from London to Genoa, through England, Portugal, Spain, and France* (London, 1770), II, 318–319.
[40]Rousseau to D. Rougin [September 17, 1764], in *Correspondance*, XI, 288. For a full account of this German prince and his Spanish friends, see Morel Fatio, A., "Grands d'Espagne et petits princes allemands au XVIIIe siècle," in *Études sur L'Espagne*, deuxième série, Paris, 1906.
[41]Urquijo, *Menéndez y Pelayo*, 40.
[42]*Mercurio histórico y político*, June, 1762, pp. 111–112.

From The Hague came further particulars. The verdict of the *Parlement* of Paris ordering the book burnt and its author imprisoned was published in full, thereby giving Spanish readers a good opportunity to acquaint themselves with the contents of the work.[43] In July the same periodical brought the news that "los Estados de Holanda y Westfrisia han condenado el libro intitulado: *Emile*, su autor 'Juan Joseph Rousseau,' ciudadano de Ginebra, . . . y otra obra del mismo autor intitulada: *Le Contrat Social* o *Principes du droit public*."[44] The issue for the following month contained an item from Brussels stating that all pains were being taken to prevent the introduction of *Émile*

. . . por ser obra impía, escandalosa, y perniciosa. Dícese que el autor no pudo volver a su patria, ni estar en los Cantones Suizos. Informado el Gobierno de Berna de que se había refugiado allí, le pidieron se fuesse a otra parte; y se halla al presente en el Principado de Neufchatel, propio del Rey de Prusia, en donde el Lord Marshal le da todo lo necesario. El dicho J. J. Rousseau es un hombre de gran talento; pero abusa de él.[45]

It was also recorded that *Émile* had been prohibited at The Hague by an edict of July 30 and at Paris by one issued by the Archbishop.[46]

In spite of these various prohibitions, there is some evidence that reforming spirits in Spain were both aware of Rousseau's existence and beginning to diffuse his ideas. One of the former type was Miguel Antonio Gándara, who brought out at Madrid in 1762 his *Apuntes sobre el bien y el mal de España*.[47] That he knew of the Genevan and classed him among the great French thinkers is shown by a statement that "los Fenelones, Racines, Fontenelles, Masillones, Montesquieus, Wolteres [*sic*] y Roseaus . . .

---

[43]*Ibid.*, 158–163.
[44]*Ibid.*, July, 1762, p. 275.
[45]*Ibid.*, August, 1762, pp. 381–382.
[46]*Ibid.*, September, 1762, p. 30.
[47]Reprinted in *Almacén de frutos literarios inéditos de los mejores autores* (León de Francia, 1804), 155–156. A summary of the reforms proposed is given by G. Desdevises du Dezert, "Un réformateur au dix-huitième siècle, Don Miguel Antonio de la Gándara," in *Revista de archivos, bibliotecas y museos*, XIV (1906), 274–293.

han escrito en su idioma poco ó nada menos que los Homeros, Demóstenes y Cicerones en los suyos"; and that he had something of Rousseau's spirit is shown by his appeal for greater educational opportunity for all classes, greater social equality through the abolition of the nobility, and for improved economic and literary conditions by the concession of more liberty of thought and action to both writers and statesmen.

Copies of *Émile* reached Spain shortly after its publication, and very soon evidence was at hand that not only the work on education but also the prohibited *Inégalité* had been furnishing Spanish writers food for thought. In August, 1762, permission to issue a periodical entitled *El Pensador* was granted to José Clavijo y Fajardo,[48] later the protagonist of Goethe's *Clavijo*. About the middle of December appeared the sixteenth weekly number of this periodical, entitled "De la crítica sobre las leyes en general" and devoted to a consideration of the origin of law; it is clearly a reverberation of the work published in Paris but a few months before, for its second paragraph opens with these well-known words: "Todo es bueno, dice un autor famoso, cuando sale de manos de la naturaleza; todo es mal, después, que pasa por la de los hombres."

Clavijo knew more of Rousseau than merely the opening lines of *Émile*, for he proceeds, following the *Discours sur l'Inégalité*, to picture primitive man as an individualist when he existed in the natural state, and to set forth hypothetical reasons for the formation of civil society. One of the first steps toward this state, he says, was the institution of property, which through developing the passions of men, brought about rivalries and dissensions.

Empezaron las voces del tuyo y del mío . . . Las pasiones irritadas, perdiendo el freno, perdieron de su vista aquellas preciosas luces que dió a cada mortal su Criador . . . El hombre fué el mayor enemigo del hombre, manchó sus manos con la sangre de su semejante, turbó su reposo, deslustró su honor, y la sociedad, que se

---

[48]His identity was concealed by the pseudonym of Álvarez de Valladares. Cf. Hartenbusch, *op. cit.*, 7. The journal was also reprinted at Barcelona under the title of *El Pensador matritense*.

instituyó para su comodidad y sosiego, se cambió en su tormento y opresión.

Here is much the reasoning of Rousseau, who maintained that men in the natural state "n'avoient pas la moindre notion du tien et du mien"; civil society resulted from property holding—"Le premier qui ayant enclos un terrain s'avisa de dire *Ceci est à moi* . . . fut le vrai fondateur de la société civile"; and that close contacts resulted in rivalry and strife. It was to the machinations of some rich man who wished to protect his property rights that Rousseau attributed the enactment of law and the creation of the state; Clavijo explains the development in a similar manner, but he does not state, as did the Genevan, that it was a means of enslaving the greater part of mankind.

Era preciso ocurrir al remedio de tan funesto desorden; y de aquí nacieron otros establecimientos, en que valiéndose la legislación del natural instinto con que los hombres aman su vida, su libertad, y todo lo que es suyo puso diferente penas de muerte, prisión y multa a proporción de los delitos . . . Esto dió causa a las leyes . . .

The magistrates chosen after the enactment of law, Rousseau claimed, abused their power to further their own ends; Clavijo follows the same argument but does not state expressly that the first magistrates acquired supreme control of the state.

Pero no bastaba fijar derechos ni hacer leyes: era preciso nombrar alguno que las hiciese ejecutar . . . Así fué indispensable nombrar personas que cuidasen de su administración. . . . Aquellos fueron los primeros magistrados . . . Así por lo mismo que el magistrado atento y vigilante es el más respetable de los hombres, el flojo y corrompido es el más abominable de todos.

He then sums up the entire situation as follows:

Ve aquí, pues, los remedios que encontraron los hombres para sus males, que introdujo en la sociedad el desorden de las pasiones, leyes y jueces; pero el mayor de los males es, que manejados estos remedios por los hombres mismos, los han hecho más nocivos que aquellos.[49]

[49]Cf. "Discours sur l'Inégalité," in *Oeuvres complètes* (Paris, 1898), I, 100, 105, 109, 113–114, 121–122.

Traces of Rousseau's ideas appear in other issues. Clavijo idealizes the American Indian and puts into his mouth the proclamation of the superiority of tribal over European society. Here the Spaniard not only echoes a contention of Rousseau,[50] but he makes his Indian a mouth-piece for the Genevan by having him set forth two of the theories expounded in *Émile:* that a mother should nurse her children, and that a father should himself take charge of their education rather than send them away to school or entrust them to paid tutors.[51]

In regard to the theater, in which he was especially interested, Clavijo expresses views that seem to echo Rousseau's condemnation, in his *Lettre à d'Alembert,* of the theater as a corrupter of public morals, and of the productions of *Molière,* the most perfect writer of comedies, as "une école de vices des mauvaises mœurs," of which the worst example was *Georges Dandin.*[52] For Clavijo felt that the Spanish theater was a "manantial de máximas falsas y perjudiciales," in which "la obscenidad y malos ejemplos . . . inficionan la juventud." In regard to Molière and *Georges Dandin,* he states that he respects the genius of Molière, who produced in *Les Femmes Savantes* "un perfecto modelo de la buena comedia," but that he sees in *Georges Dandin* only "una escuela de maldades."[53] While

---

[50]Pensamiento XXXII, "Diálogo entre un cavallero Europeo y un canadiense criado suyo."

[51]"Si vuestros padres hubiesen tenido cuidado de vosotros, y vuestras madres os hubiesen alimentado, sería justo darles estos títulos; pero dar nombre de padre a un hombre que apenas os ve nacer, permite que os arrojen de su casa y de su presencia, y que cuando debía ayudaros con sus luces y formaros con su ejemplo, os entrega a hombres alquilados, que no os tienen amor ni se interesan sino sólo en su ganacia; y llamar madre a la que, con un duro corazón como un perdenal, os niega el sustento, téngolo por necedad y aun por locura." In Clavijo's sixth discourse entitled "Visita de los locos, the reason given for the classificación of one woman as crazy is: "No quiere amas para sus hijos . . . y los cría ella misma." In the twelfth he reiterates the necessity of mothers' nursing their children.

[52]Quel est le plus criminel d'un paysan assez fou pour épouser une demoiselle, ou d'une femme qui cherche à déshonorer son époux? Que penser d'une pièce où le parterre applaudit à l'infidélité, au mensonge, à l'imprudence de celle-ci, et rit de la bêtise du manant puni?"—*Oeuvres complètes,* I, 200.

[53]*El Pensador matritense,* V, 268–270.

he did not urge the abolition of the theater as a form of public amusement, he demanded reforms: "El teatro más corregido, aquel que inspire mejores costumbres, sea griego, latino, francés, o inglés . . . aquel es mi teatro."[54]

El Pensador won great popularity, passed through several reprintings in Barcelona and other cities, and became a model for many imitations both in Spain and in Spanish America. The passages here cited are, it is believed, sufficient evidence that Clavijo knew and was beginning to disseminate, through this periodical, Rousseau's views, although in a mild form.

Meanwhile further news of the Genevan was coming into Spain from other countries. One long article concerning him opened with the following words:

Mr. Juan Jayme Rousseau, cèlebre en Europa por sus obras, y sus desgracias, publicó el año pasado una obra sobre la educación de los jóvenes, que metió mucho ruido, por la naturaleza de las críticas a que dió lugar. La firmeza de su alma, y la pureza de sus intenciones le hicieron despreciar estas censuras, a términos, que por ellas no dexó de publicar después otra obra intitulada: *Del Contrato social* que por lo vidrioso del asunta debía exponerle indefectiblemente a mayores persecuciones. Y en efecto el Consejo de Ginebra condenó ambos escritos, y pronució su sentencia de un modo, que dió motivo a Mr. Rousseau de escribir la carta siguiente al Magistrado de la República.

Thereupon followed Rousseau's letter of May 12 of that year renouncing his citizenship, and the protest, dated June 18, of the citizens of Geneva who felt he had been unjustly and illegally treated.[55] In the news from Switzerland two months later was further comment on the uproar caused by the treatment meted Rousseau by the Genevan authorities.

La patria del señor Juan Jaime Rousseau, si puede llamarse así después que la renunció, se halla por él en un desorden, que parece una guerra civil. Las representaciones, que publicamos en el Mercurio del mes de Julio, son una prueba, de que este hombre, que se intitulaba gustoso Ciuda[da]no de Ginebra antes que tuviesse ninguna quexa contra esta Ciudad, es no sólo reconocido por tal por

---

[54]*Ibid.*, V, 269. Cf. IV, 95 ff.
[55]*Mercurio histórico y político*, July, 1763, pp. 261–268.

una gran parte de sus Conciudadanos, mas tambíen de que tiene muchos parciales; y que una gran parte del pueblo está acérrima por él, clamando, que el Consejo no tenía derecho de juzgarle, ni de castigarlo. Tal vez la pacífica philosophía de este amigo del género humano, le haría considerar con dolor esta disensión, si no experimentara en sí otra, que no consiente que esta novedad llegue a su noticia, o que la escuche con atención. Escriben de Zurich, que este philósopho está enfermo en Moitie Travers, cerca de Neufchatel, donde se ha retirado, y que está de cuidado.[56]

While the storm aroused by *Émile* and the *Social Contract* was breaking over Europe, a new attack against the first *Discourse* was being launched in the far distant viceroyalty of Mexico. Late in 1763 there was published in Puebla de los Angeles an *Oración vindicativo del honor de las letras*,[57] the product of the pen of a Cuban Dominican, Christoval Mariano Coriche, rector of the College of St. Louis of that city. In the introductory pages of this work, generally credited with being the first Rousseau item published in Spanish on the American continent,[58] the censor, to whom the work had been submitted for ecclesiastical approval, states that he had read the various articles concerning *Émile* and its author published in the *Mercurio* during 1762, before seeing the present work, whose purpose is to defend "el honor de las letras públicamente vulnerado por el famoso Mr. Rousseau en un Discurso que esparció ante los Académicos de Dijón." Coriche, in his "Prólogo," states frankly the sources of his knowledge concerning the work he proposes to refute.

Aunque días ha que havía leído en el muy ilustre Feyjóo una carta en que impugna con la solidez y erudición que acostumbra la opinión, que pretendió establecer Monsieur Rousseau, que la Ciencia se opone a la práctica de la virtud, no havía yo leído el Discurso de este Francés, hasta que el presente año lo leí en el primer tomo de los Discursos Mercuriales, en donde tambíen leí la impugnación de Monsieur Le Roi; allí se da juntamente la noticia, que otros

---

[56]*Ibid.*, September, 1763, pp. 85–86.
[57]*Oración vindicativo del honor de las letras y de los literatos.* Su autor el M. R. P. Fr. Christoval Mariano Coriche. . . . En la imprenta del Colegio Real de San Ignacio de la Puebla. Año de 1763.
[58]Medina, J. T., *La Imprenta en la Puebla de los Angeles* (Santiago de Chile, 1908), 740.

sabios franceses han impugnado dicho discurso injurioso a la sabiduría, los que tampoco he leído.

The Mexican refutation covers fifty-five closely printed
quarto pages; twenty-two of these are devoted directly
to the statements of the "Discursista," as the author terms
Rousseau, whom he attacks openly by name. Like Feijóo,
Coriche believed that the prize was awarded the essay for
its erudition and style rather than for the conclusions
reached by the false logic of *non causa por causa*. Man's
desire for knowledge, he argued, is both natural and com-
mendable; that which is acquired by study becomes a part
of one's spiritual being and cannot be productive of vice.
Were Rousseau right, the man best endowed mentally
would have most cause to complain of his Maker. To the
contention that it is better to practice virtue than to
preach it, Coriche replied that virtue itself is determined
by understanding; that only a cultivated mind is able to
distinguish between right and wrong; and that the vice
pointed out as existing in spite of learned men would, but
for them, be infinitely greater. All corruption from the
fall of man to the deluge Coriche ascribes to the lack of
the arts and sciences; to him Rousseau's models of virtue—
the primitive Greeks and Romans—were both barbarous
and cruel. The shortcomings of the Greeks under Pericles
were due, he thinks, to the primitive barbarity which had
not been completely effaced, and he contradicts with statements from Socrates and other philosophers the allega-
tion that philosophy had its seat in houses of ill fame. He
offers evidence to prove that the statements regarding certain Roman emperors, especially Trajan and Vespasian,
the culture of Europe in the age of Leo X, conditions in
France under Louis XIV and in England under Charles
II, as well as the general lack of culture in Spain, are all
false and misleading. The remarks of Erasmus disparag-
ing to letters Coriche dismisses on the ground that that
scholar was a very lukewarm Catholic.

From all these statements it can readily be seen that
Coriche was attacking the source he admitted at the outset—
the *Discurso* published by Graef in the sixth issue of the

Discursos mercuriales, and had never seen Rousseau's
work. Here, then, were two refutations circulating in the
Spanish world before 1764 whose writers, a Benedictine
and a Dominican, had never read the essay they thought
they were attacking. Feijóo based his on reviews in a
Jesuit organ; Coriche, on an article which purported to
be the *Discourse* of Rousseau, but was not.

That there was need for refutations of Rousseau's ideas
such a prolific journalist as Francisco Nipho, who was in
close touch with French thought, testifies. "Por efecto de
muchos libros perniciosos que ha adoptado la Moda, como
los de Voltaire, Rousseau, Helvetius, se experimenta mucha
frialdad de fe en estos reinos," he frankly admits.[59]

The news of the repeated prohibitions of *Émile* and the
Social Contract had already set in motion the special pro-
tective machinery of the Catholic Church in Spain—the
Inquisition. When copies of both works began to circulate there, drastic action was felt to be necessary to prevent the Spanish mind from being contaminated. After
the usual slow but steady revolutions of the inquisitorial
wheels, from the mill was ground out the prohibition,
applicable throughout the Spanish dominions, of all the
works of Rousseau. As a warning and an example, a copy
of *Émile* was ordered publicly burned.[60]

All in vain. The action of the Inquisition came too late,
and was but little heeded by certain classes. Every one of
Rousseau's important works was already in circulation,
and had aroused too general discussion for the Inquisition
to have the power to bar them from the more enlightened
thinkers in Spain. Although all the means by which the
Church could express its disapproval were employed, and
many ecclesiastics directed their eloquence and influence
against Rousseau, the efforts were largely futile. Then,
too, some church dignitaries were really liberal at heart;

---

[59]*Diario extranjero. Noticias importantes y gustosas para los verdaderos apasionados de artes y ciencias.* Por D. Francisco Mariano
Nipho. Madrid, imp. de Gabriel Ramírez, 1763. Menéndez y Pelayo,
M., *Ideas estéticas en España*, V (Madrid, 1923), 263, notes that this
publication is devoted largely to translations from the French.
[60]*Indice último de los libros prohibidos*, 236.

and others were cautious souls who realized, since the powers of the Inquisition were already being threatened with limitations, that discretion in regard to denunciations of influential persons was clearly advisable.

Before the Church had awakened to a realization of the full danger of the ideas of Rousseau, they had been scattered abroad in the land; all it could hope to do was to try to eradicate the poisonous weeds as they cropped up. The futility of such efforts was long not fully grasped.

CHAPTER II

THE LIBERALS AT THE SPANISH COURT

The effect of the prohibition of Rousseau's works to all classes of readers in the Spanish world in 1764—a prohibition which both state and church were supposed to enforce—was slightly different from that contemplated by the officials of the Inquisition, although they should have known, had they been wiser, that contraband would be in Spain, as everywhere else, the natural substitute for free trade. In France the hawkers

. . . issued pirated editions . . . and . . . to their craft or courage the public owed its copies of works whose circulation was forbidden. Rousseau's *Emilius* and *Heloïsa* . . . were in every library, both public and private. The *Social Contract*, printed over and over in endless editions, was sold for a shilling under the vestibule of the king's own palace. . . . A prohibition by the authorities would send a book up within four-and-twenty hours from a half a crown to a couple of louis. This only increased the public curiosity, quickened the demand, led to clandestine reprints, and extended the circulation of the book that was nominally suppressed. . . . There was no favor that an unknown author could have asked from the magistrates so valuable to him as a little decree condemning his work.[1]

That conditions in Spain were not entirely dissimilar is strongly suggested by a choice bit of news contained in a letter to Rousseau from a Lausanne bookseller who had lately made several business trips through the peninsula:

Ne sourirez-vous pas, mon très honoré compatriote, lorsque vous apprendrez que j'ai vu brûler à Madrid, dans l'église principale des Dominicains, un dimanche, à l'issue de la grand'messe, en présence d'un très grand nombre d'imbéciles, et *ex catedra*, votre *Émile*, sous la figure d'un volume in-quarto: ce qui engagea précisément plusieurs seigneurs espagnols et les ambassadeurs des cours étrangères à se le procurer à tout prix et à le faire venir par la poste.[2]

As *Émile* was published only in octavo and duodecimo volumes, the quarto that was sacrificed was probably only

---

[1]Morley, John, *Diderot and the Encyclopaedists* (London, 1886), I, 299–300.

[2]François Grasset, Lausanne, April 8, 1765, to Rousseau. First published in the *Tribune de Genève*, October 24, 1884, and later this excerpt with comments of E. Ritter appeared in *Annales*, I, 138.

some dull old tome, while the new and much sought after
work of Rousseau found its way safely to the library of
some official or bibliophile. That prohibited works continued to be more generally in demand even twenty years
later is brought out pointedly by Samaniego's epigram
directed at Iriarte:

> Tus obras, Tomás, no son
> Ni buscadas ni leídas,
> Ni tendrán estimación
> Aunque sean prohibidas
> Por la Santa Inquisición.[3]

The publicity involved in the prohibition was to be desired
by an author rather than dreaded, even in the land of the
Inquisition.

The contempt of the more enlightened Spanish thinkers
for that ecclesiastical institution which attempted to regu-
late their reading is clearly in evidence in a reply of the
Spanish representative at the Vatican, Nicolás Azara, to
the Duke of Villahermosa, who had requested permission
from the Pope to read prohibited books.

> Estoy dispuesto a mandar a vuestra merced cuantos pergaminos
> quiera; pero debo decirle que el permiso del Papa para leer libros
> prohibidos no es posible alcanzarlo en el pontificado de este *Tartufo*.
> Felizmente, no nos incomodará much tiempo, porque está muy próx-
> imo a tender el vuelo a su paraíso; y su sucesor, que según la regla
> general, hará todo lo contrario que éste, nos dará bonitas dispensas.
> Mientras tanto, podré enviar a vuestra merced cuando quiera el
> despacho de la Congregación general del Indice, que para el efecto
> es lo mismo, pues esta congregación es superior a todas las Inquisi-
> ciones, y aun al Tribunal de Roma.

Later he referred again to the matter:

> He pedido el permiso del Indice que deseaba vuestra merced, y
> me lo han prometido para uno de estos días; en cuanto lo reciba
> cuidaré de enviárselo, para que salga cuanto antes del mal estado
> en que se encuentra por haberse comido tantas excomuniones. Yo
> me he tragado tantas como vuestra merced, y, a pesar de todo, me
> encuentro muy bien; sin duda, la fuerza y la actividad de los ácidos
> del estómago es lo que hace mejor o peor la indigestión.[4]

---

[3]Cueto, L. C., *Poetas líricos del siglo XVIII*, in *B.A.E.*, LXI, 395.
[4]Unpublished letters of June and September, 1766, in the archives
of Villahermosa, quoted by Luis Coloma, *El Marqués de Mora* (Madrid, n.d.), 41–43.

Channels had already been opened, too, for the freer circulation of French books in Spain. In 1755 François Grasset made his first trip there in the interest of the publishing house of Bousquet, which had its headquarters at Paris and at Lausanne. After establishing contacts with booksellers in Valencia, Grasset spent two years visiting the larger Spanish and Portuguese cities and placing the works his house published.[5] As the business proved profitable, he was again in Spain on a similar mission when he chanced to see the burning of the supposed copy of the treatise on education. It is not unlikely that he himself received some of the orders for *Émile* from Spaniards and foreign ambassadors, to which he refers in his letter to Rousseau.[6]

From the date of the publication of *Émile* interest in educational reform in Spain is to be traced. Although no one was daring enough to propose a Spanish translation, its imitations were not slow in becoming known. The work of Ballexerd on the physical education of the child,[7] which was published in Paris shortly after *Émile*, appeared in Madrid in 1765,[8] and other editions of the work followed in 1787[9] and in 1806. This treatise, which Rousseau claimed was "tiré mot à mot de mon premier volume, hors quelques platises dont on avoit entremêlé cet extrait,"[10] was translated into Spanish, according to the title page,

---

[5]Gaullier, E. H., *Études sur l'histoire littéraire de la suisse française, particulierèment dans la seconde moitié du XVIII° siècle* (Genève, 1856), 104. Gaullier mentions [p. 215] that Grasset left in the hands of his family his manuscript *Mémoires*. His interest in Spanish literature is shown by his translation, published at Lausanne in 1770, of Saavedra Fajardo's *República literaria*.

[6]*Annales*, I, 138.

[7]*Dissertation sur l'éducation physique des enfants depuis leur naissance jusqu'à l'âge de puberté* (Paris, 1762).

[8]*Crianza física de los niños desde su nacimiento hasta la pubertad y método el más seguro de robustecer la especie humana contra los insultos de las enfermedades.* Disertación que ganó el premio de la Sociedad holandesa de las Ciencias, año 1762. Por N. Ballexerd, ciudadano de Ginebra. Puesta en castellaño por D. Patricio de España. Madrid, imp. de D. Gabriel Ramírez, 1765. 114 p. 8°.

[9]Madrid, Antonio Espinosa, 1787. 234 p. 8°. The copy of this edition owned by the writer was found in an old book shop in Mexico City.

[10]*Oeuvres complètes*, IX, 23.

by "D. Patricio de España"; in reality it was the work of
Eugenio de Llaguno y Amírola,[11] a member of the court
group, a close friend of Jovellanos and Meléndez Valdés,
and later a cabinet minister under Charles IV. His text
became well known both in Spain and in her colonies, and
undoubtedly served to eradicate some of the foolish ideas
of Spanish parents concerning the treatment of the infant
and the young child.

There is evidence from other sources that the general
prohibition of the Genevan's works did not prevent either
their enthusiastic reception in Spain or the circulation of
news concerning their author. Earl Marischal Keith, who
knew Spain well, having served in her army for many
years,[12] wrote to Rousseau from Berlin before the end of
1764 that he had received from a friend in Spain, whom
he believed to be an official of the Inquisition, a letter voicing great enthusiasm for the work on education. "Il faut
de la force pour percer les barrières de la bigoterie en
Espagne; *Émile* l'a fait."[13] News of other works by the
man whose ideas were disturbing the intellectual world
continued to be published in Madrid.

Escriben de *Paris*, que el famoso Juan Jaime Rousseau ha dado a
luz una Obra nueva, que ha hecho estampar en Holanda, cuya título
es: Cartas del hombre de la Montaña, que un Librero de *París* ha
presentado dos juegos de esta Obra a Mr. Sartine, Corregidor, el
qual ha encargado a dos Revisores la examinen; y que conforma
d:eren su dictamen, dicha Obra se venderá o prohibirá en Francia.
Se dice también, que Mr. Rousseau ha dado a luz otra Obra, titulada Los Príncipes.[14]

A month later came news from The Hague of the prohibition of the work in Holland;[15] in April, from Paris, the
verdict of its prohibition in France. With this is printed

[11]The 1806 edition bears the real name of the translator. See the
Gaceta de Madrid, May 9, 1806.
[12]Morel Fatio, A., *Études sur l'Espagne* (2nd Series, Paris, 1906),
118–119.
[13]George Keith, Potsdam, November 24, 1764, to Rousseau, in *Correspondance générale*, XII, 84–85.
[14]*Mercurio histórico y político*, December, 1764, pp. 344–345.
[15]*Ibid.*, January, 1765, p. 94.

a full translation of Joly de Fleury's denunciation of all Rousseau's works, especially the last.

El autor procura . . . hacer la apología de sus demás escritos, y en particular de su *Emilio*, contra la censura que de él hizo la República de Ginebra. Defiende con tal terquedad el sistema que ha abrazado, que lejos de aprovecharse de las críticas que le han hecho, de confesar los errores, que le han probado, y abominarlos, renueva todos sus principios impíos y abominables contra la Religión Católica y contra J. C. su Autor, contra la Relevación, y la Sagrada Escritura, contra los Milagros, y todos los demás errores, que han exasperado los ánimos de cuantos han leído el *Emilio*. A estas impiedades ha añadido nuevas blasfemias, que no nos atrevemos a repetir, y de las cuales se indicia uno de aquellos filosophos soberbios, que oponen sus ilusiones a la verdad, hombres de entendimiento depravado, y ciego, que no harán los progresos que discurren, porque todos conocerán su locura.[16]

In the following year Spaniards learned of the declaration from Geneva that

. . . las imputaciones hechas al Consejo de los Veinte-Cinco, y al de los Doscientos, en el Libro intitulado Cartas escritas desde la Montaña son calumnias atroces; y que no se debe dar el menor crédito a esta obra, inspirada por el espíritu de venganza.[17]

Once this work reached Spain, the Inquisition lost no more than the usual time in determining its status; in December, 1766, the *Lettres écrites de la montagne* was added to the list of prohibted works.[18]

In the meantime the Spanish press followed Rousseau's career with interest. News of the projected constitution for Corsica was received from Florence.

Escriben que en Liorna hay algunas copias de un nuevo Codigo de leyes para aquellos Isleños, y que lo ha formado el Sr. Rousseau, que de este modo entra con Licurgo y Solon a la parte de la gloria de los Legisladores. Estas leyes se hacen admirar por la cordura y acierto con que están formadas. Ya nos hacemos cargo de que al escribirlas el Sr. Rousseau no habrá teñido en sangre la pluma como hizo Dracón. No se habrá propuesto más objeto que el bien del género humano. Es de creer que estas leyes harán mucho honor a la Filosofía.

---

[16]*Ibid.*, April, 1765, p. 288.
[17]*Ibid.*, August, 1766, p. 322.
[18]*Indice último de libros prohibidos* (Madrid, 1790), 236.

Hay sin embargo una especie de fanatismo del cual dudamos que el Legislador de los Corsos se haya podido libertar.[19]

With the opening of 1766 came news of the arrival of Rousseau in London.

El 13 de Enero de 1766 es un día muy grande para la Inglaterra. Si Mr. Rousseau muriese en Londres, después de muchos años de vida, tendría sin duda lugar senalado, donde lo tienen los Reyes en Westminster.[20]

By August Spaniards were reading of the rupture between him and his erstwhile friend Hume;[21] in November Rousseau was reported to have been awarded a pension by the King of England;[22] in the following June his departure for some unknown destination was chronicled;[23] and a month later his arrival in the vicinity of Paris.

El famoso J. Rousseau . . . se halla actualmente en las inmediaciones de París recibiendo visitas de sus apasionados, pues los tiene en todas partes, y algunos lo son tan fuertes, como lo es él mismo en sus sistemas. Hay sugetos que hablan demasiado mal de este filósofo; pero tampoco falta quien le estime con exceso.

A translation of the letter of Count Orloff inviting Rousseau to St. Petersburg[24] and the reply are printed in full in the same issue. A month later came news that Rousseau had retired to the home

. . . de un sugeto de distinción en Aubernia, que se compadeció de su miseria. Este generoso acogimiento hará sin duda mucho honor al que lo hizo, y le grangeará elogios de los mismos enemigos del filósofo, si, no obstante el deplorable estado en que éste se advierte, no se procura más contrarios de los que la enbidia la puede suscitar.[25]

That Clavijo, whose sympathy with Rousseau's ideas we have already seen in *El Pensador,* was the editor, may account for the generous attitude toward the philosopher shown by the Spanish official organ carrying these items.

---

[19]*Mercurio histórico y político,* September, 1765, p. 21.
[20]*Ibid.,* January, 1766, p. 84.
[21]*Ibid.,* August, 1766, p. 325.
[22]*Ibid.,* November, 1766, p. 259.
[23]*Ibid.,* June, 1767, p. 163.
[24]*Ibid.,* July, 1767. The original, dated January 2, 1767 (new style), is printed in *Correspondance,* XVI, 325–326.
[25]*Ibid.,* August, 1767, p. 301.

While his name, movements and works were thus made familiar to Spanish readers through the press, and the Catholic Church was thundering threats of dire punishment to any who should own or read them, the first traces of Rousseau's influence in Spain may be followed in the Basque provinces. Within a year after the death of Altuna, whom he had introduced to the sciences, a plan which the "triumvirate"—Altuna, Eguía, and Peñaflorida —had drawn up was presented to the *juntas forales* of Guipúzcoa for approval, and in 1764 there came into existence an organization called "Los Amigos del País," whose object was to encourage scientific progress, and to promote all that directly concerned the improvement and usefulness of the human race. Its regulations were printed in 1766 with the authorization of Grimaldi, a member of the cabinet of Charles III. Into this society came the flower of the Basque provinces, many leading men of other districts, and numerous ecclesiastics of broad culture.[26] In 1768 Altuna's son, Manuel Ignacio, then eighteen years old, was received as a member.[27] This Basque organization became the model for many others which rapidly came into existence in various parts of Spain under the direction of such men as Campomanes in Madrid, Olavide in Sevilla, and Cabarrús in Cadiz. Through these, scientific investigations were encouraged and the study of political economy introduced into Spain; the *Social Contract* was not slow in following as a textbook, even though it was found, at that epoch, best adapted to private consumption.

The scientific spirit and French thought were further disseminated in Spain by this same group of liberal thinkers through a school established in Azcoitia but soon transferred to Vergara; to this institution, which became the Royal Seminary in 1776, the Basque aristocracy sent their children rather than to Bayonne or Toulouse as

---

[26]Menéndez y Pelayo, *Historia de los Heterodoxos*, VI, 269.
[27]Urquijo, *Menéndez Pelayo*, 39, gives this date, but the list of members published in 1790 gives the date of his entry as 1778. See *Extractos de las juntas generales celebradas por la Real Sociedad Bascongada de los Amigos del País, en la villa de Bilbao por Julio de 1790*. Victoria, 1790.

formerly; and among its teachers and students were many
not only familiar but deeply imbued with the spirit of
Rousseau. Of special interest for this study were Vicente
M. Santibañez, who has been credited with translating the
Social Contract; Valentín Foronda, who issued a Spanish
version of that work; and José Marchena, who was to
make *Julie* and *Émile* available to the whole Spanish-
speaking world. Of these we shall hear more later. It was
for the pupils of this Basque school that one of its direc-
tors, Félix Samaniego, wrote the fables on which his claim
to literary fame rests.[28] In the prologue to that work,
he himself confesses the influence of Rousseau, for it was
to *Émile* that he referred when he said that a modern
author, in his *Treatise on Education,* had commented that
in the whole collection of La Fontaine there were not
more than five or six fables in which childlike simplicity
was paramount, and that many passages were entirely
inappropriate to the intelligence of children. "This criticism has served me as a lesson,"[29] he added.

Through members of the Basque society close contacts
between France and Spain were maintained. It is said
that in Guipúzcoa alone, and principally in Vergara,
Azpeitia and Azcoitia, there were fifteen subscribers to
the *Encyclopédie*—more than in all the rest of Spain.
Among these were certainly Peñaflorida, Narros, and
Samaniego.[30] We do not know whether Peñaflorida was
personally acquainted with or corresponded with Rousseau; at least he followed the prescription for Émile when
he sent his own son, Ramón Munibe, on a tour through
Europe as a part of his general education. The tutor
selected to accompany Ramón must have been quite
familar with the teachings of the educational treatise, for
when corresponding with the father of his charge concerning the expenses of the tour, the Abbé Cluvier wrote:

---

[28]Cf. review of the fables in *Correo de Madrid,* No. 318, December
12, 1789.
[29]*B.A.E.,* LXI, 357. Cf. Rousseau, *Émile, in Oeuvres complètes,*
II, 82.
[30]Lasala y Collado, Fermín, *La separación de Guipúzcoa y la paz
de Basilea* (Madrid, 1895), 141.

Si l'on suivait le conseil de Rousseau de voyager à pied et d'aller de même dans les capitales, on ne verrait que la canaille, à moins qu'on n'eût comme lui la reputation d'un trés bel esprit et du 1ᵉʳ fou de l'universe.[31]

Ramón spent three years on this tour, visiting scientific organizations as the representative of the Basque society, and reported to it his observations. In the excerpts available to the writer, he makes no specific reference to Rousseau; but in the account of his visit to England, probably in the summer of 1772, some traces of Rousseau's style and thought appear.[32]

---

[31]Cluvier to Peñaflorida, quoted in Urquijo, *Menéndez Pelayo y los caballeritos de Azcoitia*, 27.

[32]Especially is this true of a descriptive passage with reference to a visit to a cave, which reads as follows:

"En ella parece que están hermanadas la industria y la naturaleza. Inmediato a la boca hay un espacio a donde se retiran las gentes del lugar para poder trabajar guarnecidos del calor y del frío. Al verlos me parecía que entre estos montes, duraban aun aquellos felices tiempos en que el hombre era Señor de su trabajo, sin ser esclavo de sus pasiones ni de sus semejantes. Toscos y mal formados tornos daban hilazas groseras, pero fuertes a las manos que parece comenzaban a aprender de la necesidad a servirse de los bienes de la Naturaleza, de que tanto se ha abusado después; no se oía entre ellos aquel ruido que hoy mete la industria agitada del luxo y que no deja oir los lamentos de quien le da el ser. La simplicidad reinaba y el sosego. Ninguno se afanaba ni gemía oprimido del trabajo, mas todos trabajaban. Adelantóse uno y haciendo encender luz, abrió una puerta que daba entrada a lo interior de un lóbrego y estrecho callejón que nos condujo a una espaciosa morada. Parece que veíamos a la Naturaleza que con noble majestad nos recibía en su seno. Silencioso un arroyuelo se deslizaba por los huecos de las peñas que amontonadas formaban sin orden el pavimento. En otro tiempo estas peñas habían formado el techo de la gruta; pero desgajadas de lo alto, son ahora tristes monumentos de las alteraciones que en esta parte ha padecido la Naturaleza. Su desigualdad y su desorden forman varias y majestuosas perspectivas que iban iluminando las pobres gentes que nos conducían: entrábamos de estancia en estancia y las erizadas piedras que se oponían a nuestro paso parece que lo habían para obligarnos a contemplar cuanto se ofrecía de nuevo a cada uno que dábamos. Ya muy lejos de la boca descubrimos otro arroyo que fluía tranquilo en el cauce que lo había recogido al nacer y a quien los furiosos vientos no habían agitado aun; pero quien tampoco había gozado de los rayos con que el sol hermosea las aguas de los otros. Una barquilla tan pequeña que en ella no cabía sino un hombre, nos fué pasando a una nueva estancia. De repente oímos dulces cantos que nos suspendieron; en otros tiempos esto hubiera parecido misterioso y dado lugar a que el error abusase de la credulidad. Vimos que los hombres, mugeres y niños que nos acompañaban con luces, habían subido a un arco o bóveda que forma una de las naves en la gruta y que desde lo alto formando un coro, cantaban cánticos que nos elevaban, sean que las

While such similarities of thought, which seem to link the Basque society and the Genevan philosopher barely a decade after Altuna's death, may be only casual, other statements reveal that the promoters of the society were familiar with Rousseau's teachings. There is no conceal-ment of this fact on the part of the fabulist Samaniego; both in satirizing Iriarte's poem "La Música"[33] and in a letter on the theater,[34] he referred openly to "aquel gran Filósofo Ginebrino." As a result of such freedom of speech, he was denounced to the Inquisition as a reader of prohibited books, as were also Peñaflorida, Narros, and other leading thinkers of the day, but these three escaped with either warnings or comparatively light punishment. Their trend of mind was unmistakably liberal and hetero-dox, although attempts have been made to clear them of this charge.[35] And while it is quite possible that both the organization of cultured Basques and the school at Ver-gara might have come into existence had Altuna never known Rousseau, it is at least of interest that, as a result of this intimacy, one intelligent Basque carried into Spain a personal sympathy for the philosopher and an appreci-ation of scientific thought which seems to have played some part in the foundation of the Basque society, whose activities were directed along lines Rousseau approved. The friendship between the Genevan and the Spaniard, begun in Venice and ripened in Paris, was at least one stone in the foundation upon which was to rise the

---

voces fuesen de suyo melodiosas sea que las concavidades de la gruta les diese todo el valor haciéndolas más sonoras."—Urquijo, *Los Amigos del País*, I, 94–95.

[33]*Carta apologética al señor Masson* (Bayona, 1777). Reprinted in *Obras críticas de Don Félix María de Samaniego* precedidas de unos estudios preliminares escritos por Julián Apráiz (Bilboa, 1898), 113–114.

[34]"Si un buen Teatro es un mal: diría yo que debía tolerarse como un mal necesario; como un remedio saludable para evitar otros mayores males. Aquel gran Filósofo Ginebrino, tan declarado enemigo de la escena, solía decir que los teatros eran indispensables en las Ciudades populosas; y es menester no conocer a los hombres, o intere-sarse poco en su tranquilidad, para pensar de otro modo."—"Carta sobre el teatro por Cosme Damián," in *El Censor*, IV (January, 1786), 430. Also reprinted in *Obras críticas*, 81–102.

[35]Urquijo, *Menéndez Pelayo y los caballeritos de Azcoitia.*

"Friends of the Nation," whose influence upon Spain during the next half-century proved to be both deep and far-reaching.

The activity in Guipúzcoa was only the prelude to that in other parts of Spain, for the decades that followed the prohibition of the works of Rousseau and the establishment of the Basque society were marked by a rapid advance of liberalism at the Spanish court. In 1767 the suspected machinations of the Jesuits were halted by the suppression of that order in all the Spanish dominions; in 1768 the autocratic power of the Inquisition to prohibit books was curbed through its re-subjection to royal approval; in the following year the educational system was infused with fresh life through various reforms which menaced scholasticism; and in 1778 new contacts abroad were made possible through the removal of restrictions upon colonial commerce. Statesmen, diplomats, and foreigners coöperated in effecting these reforms; but strong opposition came persistently from three sources: the church—always zealous in defense of its privileges; the authorities in the universities and large administrative bodies—always conservative; and the masses of the people—easily incited to fanaticism through ignorance. The middle class was not as yet articulate. The leaders in the reform movement—all members of the court circle—were almost without exception friends and admirers of Rousseau; how far his ideas were therein operative we shall soon see.

Among the ministers of the king of Spain in this period of sweeping reforms the most influential was the Count of Aranda, a liberal in the fullest sense of the word, perfectly at home with the French language and French thought, and intimate with Voltaire, d'Alembert, Raynal, and Rousseau. A descendant of a wealthy and aristocratic family, Aranda entered the army in 1740; during the next two decades he traveled widely and spent much time in Paris; in 1765 he was placed in command of the Spanish army in Portugal; and the following year he became the governor of Valencia. As president of the Council of Castile from 1766 to 1773 he wielded great power; as Spanish ambassador at the court of France from that time until 1787 he played a part destined to determine the trend of events on the American continent; and through his personal contacts and literary interests he was able to exert considerable influence in the Spanish world of letters.[36]

While the intimacy of Aranda with Rousseau grew out of many common interests, one bond especially united them—hatred of the Jesuits. "Les jésuites ne m'aimoient pas," wrote the philosopher, "non-seulement comme ency-clopédiste, mais parce que tous mes principes étoient encore plus opposés à leurs maximes et à leur crédit que l'incrédulité de mes confrères, puisque le fanatisme athée et le fanatisme dévot se touchent par leur commune intol-érance."[37] It was the Jesuits, Rousseau believed, who caused the condemnation of *Émile* and the order for his arrest. Naturally the work of Aranda in effecting the expulsion of the order from Spain aroused the whole-hearted admiration of all the philosophic group, with many of whom the Spanish minister maintained close communication, but especially of Rousseau, who predicted to Aranda that if Spain continued her progress and did not try to imitate other nations, she would lay down the law to all.[38] When asked of what nation he had the highest opin-ion, he answered, "The Spanish," and gave as his reason, "parce qu'ils croyent." Saint-Pierre explained this prefer-ence by adding that Spain had character, and, if not rich, preserved her pride and self-respect in the midst of her poverty. Then, too, she was animated by a single spirit, for she had not been scourged by the conflicting opinions

---

[36]Morel-Fatio, *Études sur l'Espagne*, 143–184.

[37]*Les Confessions*, in *Oeuvres complètes*, IX, 17.

[38]Aranda to Floridablanca, June 7, 1786, quoted in Ferrer del Río, *Historia del reinado de Carlos III*, IV, 43–44. "Rousseau me dice que, continuando España así, dará la ley a todas las naciones, y aunque no es ningún doctor de la Iglesia, debe tenérsele por conoce-dor del corazón humano, y yo estimo much su juicio" is the version Menéndez y Pelayo [*Hist. de los Het.*, VI, 242] gives to the state-ments made by Ferrer del Río.

of philosophy.[39] Aranda, for his part, esteemed Rousseau highly as a "conocedor del género humano," even though he was forced to admit that the Genevan was "ningún doctor de la iglesia."[40] While we do not know whether Rousseau regarded the statesman as "el único hombre de quien puede envanecerse al presente la monarquía española; el único español de nuestros días, cuyo nombre escribirá la posteridad en sus libros," as did one of his countrymen,[41] Aranda himself admitted the formulation of drastic plans that miscarried. After finishing with the Jesuits, he had intended "to put an end to the Saint Office, but imprudently confided his intention to Voltaire who . . . boasted of his knowledge of the secret, which excited such a sensation in Spain that he was compelled to drop his project." Aranda often said, if Voltaire had known in advance of his intention to suppress the Jesuits, they would still have been in existence.[42]

This Spanish diplomat, however, stopped at nothing, once his enthusiasm was fired. It was he who furnished part of the material for Raynal's *Histoire philosophique et politique des établissements et du commerce des Européens dans les deux Indes*,[43] which carried directly to the people of Spain and Spanish America Rousseau's message of liberty, justice, and individual rights. For this work, of which more than twenty editions were published before the Revolution, "told of everything in the world; how to make conquests, missions, blunders, settlements, bankruptcies, fortunes, etc." The real source of its popularity, however, lay in the hatred and contempt for religion and the passion for justice and freedom which it voiced. In many respects the most vigorous and sustained

[39]Morley, John, *Rousseau* (London, 1886), II, 325; Saint-Pierre, B., *La Vie et les Ouvrages de Jean-Jacques Rousseau* (Paris, 1907), 118.

[40]Ferrer del Río, *op. cit.*, IV, 43–44.

[41]*Voyage de Figaro en Espagne* (Saint Malo, 1784), 224–225.

[42]*The Spanish Journal of Elizabeth Lady Holland* (London, 1910), 85.

[43]*Mémoires pour servir à l'histoire ecclésiastique* . . . (Paris, 1855–1857), VII, 352; Mancini, J., *Bolívar y la emancipación de las colonias españolas desde los orígenes hasta 1815* (Paris, 1914), 51.

of all the literary expressions that were given to the great
social ideas of the century, "it wholly lacked the strange
and concentrated glow that burned in the pages of the
Social Contract; on the other hand, it was more full of
movement, of reality, of vivid and picturesque incident.
It was popular, and it was concrete. Raynal's story went
straight to the hearts of many people, to whom Rousseau's
arguments were only half intelligible and wholly dreary."[44]

More than any single work published in the last half of
the eighteenth century, the *Philosophical History* awakened public opinion against the Spanish monarchy. In it
Spain's whole policy was flaunted and the Church held up
to scorn as an accessory in the mistreatment of the colonists and the enslavement of the natives. Extolling the
original nature of man and the advantages of a social
state with equal privileges for all, Raynal decried despotism of church or state. He told the story of the downfall
of great nations and of debasement through wealth and
luxury; in a sense he foretold the events of the next century in his warnings and prophecies. Although Raynal's
work was prohibited in Spain,[45] the Spanish version prepared by the Duke of Almodóvar[46] escaped that distinction
because he deliberately omitted all portions which reflected
directly upon either the Spanish government or the
Catholic Church. Despite its prohibition, the *Philosophical
History* of Raynal quickly became one of the works best
known in the whole Spanish world, especially the colonial.

While Aranda, through his contribution of material to
Raynal, helped to scatter some of Rousseau's political and
economic ideas, he was at the same time encouraging the
first of Spanish romanticists, José Cadalso. This aspirant
for literary honors had been educated in Paris and had
had the advantage of extensive travel; in the year *Émile*
was published he returned to Spain and entered the army.
When Aranda's attention was called to the young man's

---

[44]Morley, *Diderot,* II, 225.
[45]*Indice de libros prohibidos,* 133.
[46]*Historia política de los establecimientos ultramarinos de las
naciones europeas* (Madrid, 1784–1790). Published under the pseudonym of Eduardo Malo de Luque.

linguistic ability and literary interests, he made him his
aide-de-camp. Cadalso began verse making at Saragossa
and continued it at Alcalá, where he became acquainted
with Jovellanos, and at Salamanca, where he proved an
inspiration to Meléndez Valdés. For a time he was a member of the group composed of Moratín the elder,[47] Tomás
Iriarte, Muñoz, and other men of intellectual interests
that assembled at the San Sebastian restaurant in
Madrid.[48]

Generally admitted as the first literary *afrancesado*,
Cadalso was also the first Spanish romantic both in life
and work. While in Madrid he fell madly in love with an
actress whose sudden death drove him to such a state of
despair that he conceived the wild idea of disenterring the
body—an act regarded in that day as sacriligeous. In
Noches lúgubres, not published until after his death, and
generally but wrongly supposed to be an imitation of
Young's *Night Thoughts*,[49] Cadalso gave expression, as
does Rousseau in the *Nouvelle Héloïse*, to his own mad
passion. Wild-eyed, disheveled, beside the tomb, awaiting
only the moment to clasp again his beloved to his breast,
he sobbed out his agony, his despair—the first frank
expression by a Spaniard of the secrets of his own heart.
Aranda saved him from the punishment which awaited
him by exiling him from court; and a bomb at Gibraltar,
while he was on duty for a friend, suddenly ended his
career in 1782.[50]

Any doubt concerning the acquaintance of Cadalso with
the ideas of Rousseau is set at rest by the following lines
from the *Cartas marruecas*, which he read to the *tertuli-
anos* of San Sebastian:

Hay nación en Europa (y no es la Española) . . . [cuyos] sabios
se empeñaron en sostener . . . que lo de *tuyo* y *mío* eran delirios

---

[47]Mérimée, E., *A History of Spanish Literature*, translated, revised
and enlarged by S. G. Morley (New York, 1930), 422–423.
[48]Cueto, in *B.A.E.*, LXI, cv–cviii, 243–248.
[49]See Peers, A. E., "The Influence of Young and Gray in Spain,"
in *Modern Language Review*, XXI (1926), 404 ff.
[50]Cueto, in *B.A.E.*, LXI; Cejador y Frauca, J., *Historia de la
lengua y literatura castellana* (Madrid, 1917), VI, 177–179.

formales. Que en la igualdad de los hombres es vicioso el establecimiento de gerarquías. Que el estado natural del hombre es la sole-
dad, como el de la fiera en el monte. . . .[51]

Neither does Cadalso fail to introduce one of Rousseau's
favorite themes—the failure of mothers in their duty
toward their children.

Nos niegan el alimiento de la leche que la naturaleza las dió
para esté único y sagrado fin; nos vician con su mal exemplo, nos
sacrifican a sus intereses, nos hurtan las caricias que nos deben,
y las depositan en un perro o en un pájaro. . . .[52]

But Rousseau contributed more than subject matter to
Cadalso; in the work of the Spaniard there is much of
the style, the melancholy, and the individualism of the
author of the *Nouvelle Héloïse*. Without restraint he pours
out his heart in the opening dialogue of the "Second
Night."

Qué triste me ha sido este día: igual a la noche más espantosa
me ha llenádo de pavor, tedio, aflicción, y pesadumbre. Con qué
dolor han visto mis ojos la luz del astro, a quien llaman benigno los
que tienen el pecho menos oprimido que yo: El sol, la criatura que
dicen menos imperfecta, imagen del Criador, ha sido objeto de mi
melancolía. El tiempo que ha tardado en llevar sus luces a otros
climas, me ha parecido tormento de duración eterna. . . . Triste de
mí! Soy el solo viviente a quien sus rayos no consuelan. Aun la
noche, cuya tardanza me hacía tan insufrible la presencia del sol,
es menos gustosa, porque en algo se parece al día. No está tan
obscura como yo quisiera la luna: ah luna! Escóndete: no mires
en este puesto al más infeliz mortal.[53]

Cadalso in such passages has generally been recognized
as the personification of the romantic: some have seen in
him a direct contributor to the romanticism of Espronceda.[54]

---

[51]*Cartas marruecas* (Isla de León, 1820), 284–285.
[52]*Noches lúgubres*, in *Obras del Coronel Don Joseph Cadalso*
(Madrid, 1803), IV, 153–154.
[53]*Ibid.*, 163–164.
[54]"Sus diálogos con el sepulturero, su ida al cementerio para
visitar la tumba de su amada, sus desesperantes reflexiones sobre la
vanidad de todos los afectos, a excepción del que le domina, el momento tan fúnebre como repugnante en que se resuelve a contemplar
los restos de la que amó, todo forma un conjunto de sensaciones ex-
trañas, sorprendentes, macabras, que no se comprenderían en un
escritor del siglo XVII, que parecen peregrinas en uno del siglo XVIII
y que desentonan del conjunto general de la literatura de su época.
O mucho me engaño, o las *Noches lúgubres* debieron de ser uno de

The importance of Cadalso as a disseminator of ideas was great. He had had intimate contact with foreign thought and literature; he lived in an age seething with a growing spirit of revolt; as the result of a personality that attracted young and old, he knew intimately most of the thinkers of his day, and corresponded frequently with them and others; and through his own work he aroused and encouraged the spirit of inquiry, of independence, and also that characteristic of Rousseau which made him a forerunner of the Spanish romanticists—unrestrained expression of his own feelings and emotions. That Cadalso did not publish *Noches lúgubres* and *Cartas marruecas* during his life is evidence of the intolerant spirit of the Spain in which he lived—a spirit which he and his friends did much to combat. Through *Noches lúgubres* alone Cadalso furnished romantic inspiration for Spain and Spanish America in the early nineteenth century.[55]

A close friend of Aranda at court and another Rousseau admirer in Spain was Pablo Olavide, a Peruvian by birth, rich by marriage with a Spanish widow, and a littérateur by taste. Thoroughly imbued with French ideas through years spent in Paris, the Peruvian was personally acquainted with Rousseau[56] and thoroughly familiar with his indictments of the prevailing educational system. After his return to Spain, where he became very influential at court, Olavide drew up a plan for the reform of the University of Seville in which he handled scholasticism without gloves and, as a result, aroused the ire of many churchmen. His university reforms, which were initiated by the cédula of March 4, 1769, became the basis of the plan approved at Salamanca in 1771.[57] The Peruvian further contributed to the dissemination of Rousseau's

---

los libros favoritos del autor de *El Estudiante de Salamanca*."— Bonilla y San Martín, Adolfo, "El Pensamiento de Espronceda," in *La España moderna*, CCXXXIV (1908), 69.

[55]Cf. Chapter X.

[56]Rousseau, F., *Règne de Charles III d'Espagne* (Paris, 1907), II, 46 ff.

[57]Gil y Zárate, Antonio, *De la Instrucción pública en España* (Madrid, 1855), I, 59–62; and Altamira y Crevea, Rafael, *Historia de España* (Barcelona, 1911), IV, 324.

ideas through his encouragement of the "sociedades económicas," his promotion of the study of political economy,
and also through his influence upon Jovellanos, whom he
induced to study modern languages and science.[58]

But Olavide, brimming with success, had not yet learned
caution, and consequently made many enemies who eventually wrought his downfall. Through his intimacy with
Aranda he was made the superintendent of a colonization
project in the Sierra Morena, peopled by immigrants from
Germany and central Europe. The regulations concerning
the establishment were drawn up by Múzquiz and Campomanes at the very moment that the banishment of the
Jesuits was imminent; Olavide was charged with enforc-
ing them. But the fact that no religious foundations of
any description were permitted in the colony, that the
schools were placed under the control of the laity with
compulsory primary and vocational education, as advocated by the leaders of the Basque society, and that no
provision was made for spiritual instruction other than
that of the village curate, brought upon the whole undertaking, and especially upon the administrator, the condemnation of certain clericals. Had complaints not emanated
from this circle, Olavide's administration might have been
a success; instead it proved disastrous both to him and
to the colony. His liberal views and literary contacts had
already furnished a basis for denunciations to the Inquisition in 1766 and in 1768; then Aranda was at hand to
protect him.[59] But when he was charged again in 1775
with being a heretic, atheist, and materialist, who read
prohibited books and had corresponded with Voltaire and
Rousseau,[60] Aranda was in Paris and could no longer use
his influence; instead, Olavide was arrested without warning and confined in the secret cells of the Inquisition until
1778, when forty persons of different rank were invited

[58]Nocedal, Cándido, "Discurso preliminar," in *Obras . . . de Jovellanos*, in *B.A.E.*, XLV, viii.
[59]Rousseau, F., *Règne de Charles* III, II, 50. See also Danvila
y Collado, *Reinado de Carlos III*, IV, 3–71, and *El Poder Civil en
España* (Madrid, 1886), VI, doc. 1365, pp. 572–580.
[60]Ferrer del Río, *op. cit.*, III, 46 ff.

to hear sentence pronounced. In the course of this proceeding, Olavide gave a circumstantial account of his
whole life and confessed among his many sins that in his
travels he had frequented the society of such free thinkers as Voltaire and Rousseau.[61] As punishment, his property was confiscated, and he himself was condemned to
indefinite imprisonment and to permanent exile from the
court and from Lima.[62] He accepted the verdict with
apparent contrition, but at the first opportunity to escape
from the clutches of the Church he fled to France, where
he was enthusiastically welcomed by the philosophic group.
There he lived, except for a short period in Geneva, until
1798, when he was permitted to return to Spain.[63] While
hailed by some as a "filósofo desengañado," there can be
small doubt that this Peruvian, especially before the
French Revolution, was an effective disseminator of the
doctrine of the rights of man; and in 1797, little anticipating return to Spain, he is said to have been engaged
in attempting to bring about the independence of her
colonies through English aid.[64]

Another influential Spaniard intimate with Rousseau
was the Duke of Alba, who, as the Duke of Huéscar, had
been the Spanish ambassador in Paris from 1746 to 1749.[65]
That the acquaintance between the grandee and the Genevan was more than a passing one is clearly shown by
extant correspondence, for in writing from Spain in 1772
directly to Rousseau, Alba boldly declared "que personne
ne vous estime, ne vous admire, et ne vous aime plus que

[61]Bourgoanne, Chevalier de, *Travels in Spain, containing a new,
accurate, and comprehensive view of the present state of that country*. Translated from the French of the 3rd edition, Paris, 1803. In
Pinkerton, John, *A General Collection of the Best and Most Interesting Voyages and Travels in all Parts of the World* . . . (London,
1809), V, 411.
    [62]Ferrer del Río, *op. cit.*, III, 55.
    [63]Alcázar Molina, Cayetano, *Los Hombres del reinado de Carlos
III, Don Pablo de Olavide* (Madrid, 1927).
    [64]Robertson, W. S., *The Life of Miranda* (Chapel Hill, 1929), I,
167–168.
    [65]A good sketch is given by Morel Fatio, *Études sur l'Espagne*,
78–81.

moi."[66] When they first became acquainted is not clear, but before Alba left Paris, Rousseau expressed a wish for some Spanish botanical specimens, and later the grandee asked him for a list of his preferences. In replying, the Genevan confessed:

> Je suis trop ignorant pour savoir celles qu'on trouve par pré-férence dans les vastes États de la monarchie Espagnole. . . . D'ailleurs la fantaisie de cette collection s'attiédit à mesure que je pense à la folie de me faire encore des amusemens sur cette terre où je suis si étranger, et dont le tems et les hommes me détachent tous les jours.[67]

A collection was made up, however, and sent to Paris, much to the delight of the author of the *Lettres élémentaires sur la Botanique.*

In 1773 Alba asked Rousseau to have a complete set of his works sent to Madrid. After they had been shipped, the author discovered, to his dismay, that the edition was spurious. He at once wrote Alba enclosing a printed "declaration" concerning the unauthorized edition.[68] The duke then begged Rousseau to get him a complete authoritative set regardless of price, and at the same time mocked at the folly of would-be imitators.

> Des additions ou changemens aux chefs-d'œuvres de Jean Jacques Rousseau? Eh qui est le téméraire qui s'avise de les publier? Votre réputation est faite, et plût à Dieu que pour votre repos vous n'en eussiez jamais eu aucune; vous y auriez perdu à la verité des admi-rateurs, mais vous auriez aussi moins d'ennemis acharnés à vous tourmenter. . . . Tout ce qui part de votre main porte une empreinte qu'il n'est point d'homme capable de contrefaire. Quiconque vous aura lu avec un peu d'attention distinguera aisément les morceaux originaux des malignes altérations d'un imposteur aussi malhabile que criminel.[69]

When it is remembered that the writer of these words was from 1754 until his death in 1776 the director of the Spanish Academy, it is easy to surmise the influence he exerted in behalf of Rousseau and his ideas in Spain.

---

[66]*Documentos escogidos del archivo de la casa de Alba* (Madrid, 1891), October 26, 1772.

[67]*Ibid.*, 554.

[68]February 10, 1774. Printed in *Oeuvres complètes*, IX, 401.

[69]Alba to Rousseau, Minuta, 1774, in *Documentos escogidos*, 562–563.

In the Alba-Rousseau correspondence some details are revealed of the termination of the intimacy between the Genevan and George Keith. The Earl Marischal was an exiled Scotchman whose colorful career included a rollicking life in Constantinople, service in the army of Spain, and the close friendship of Frederick the Great, who made him governor of Neuchâtel, a position he was holding when Rousseau went there in 1763 seeking refuge. The two proved very congenial; and Keith recounted to Rousseau many tales of Spanish life and his Spanish friends, of whom Alba was one. So devoted was Keith to Rousseau that he offered to share his home in Scotland with the author of *Émile*. In writing to Alba, who had inquired about Keith, Rousseau sadly admitted that all communication between him and "l'homme que j'honore, respecte et chéris le plus au monde" had ceased.[70] He did not add that it was because the Earl Marischal, unable to reconcile Rousseau and Hume, had requested that the former's correspondence with him be abridged.

There were other Spanish contacts during Rousseau's last years. In close touch with Alba was Carrión, who had been appointed to a good post in Madrid in 1764.[71] By this time Prince Salm, Rousseau's former neighbor and visitor,[72] and an intimate friend of Fernán Nuñez and of George Keith, was in the service of Spain. Nor should it be forgotten that it was Luis Pignatelli and his wife Alphonsine, the son and the daughter-in-law of the Count of Fuentes, Spanish ambassador in Paris until 1772, to whom Rousseau read his *Confessions*. The third reading was at the château of the Count of Egmont, her father.[73] As late as 1775 Rousseau was kept in touch with Spain and his friends who had lived there by Dupeyrou, who passed through Paris on his return from a trip through

---

[70]July 21, 1772, *ibid.*, 554.
[71]*Mercurio histórico y político*, August, 1764, p. 381.
[72]Rousseau to D. Rougin, September 17, 1764, in *Correspondance*, XI, 287–289; Morel-Fatio, *Études sur l'Espagne*, 27–29.
[73]*Ibid.*, 141; Josephson, Matthew, *Jean-Jacques Rousseau* (New York, 1931), 493, 495, 502; Courtois, Louis J., *Chronologie critique de la vie et des œuvres de Jean-Jacques Rousseau*, in *Annales*, XV, 217.

Spain. Especially did the author of the *Confessions* take pleasure in hearing the tales of the Valencians who had known Keith during his long residence there.[74]

Another link between Rousseau and the Spanish court was Count Cabarrús, a Frenchman by birth but a naturalized Spaniard, who was so deeply impressed with Rousseau's ideas that, for the Spain of his day, he was a violent radical. Using as a basis of argument the *Social Contract*, widely known after the establishment of professorships of natural and international law in the Spanish universities in 1776,[75] Cabarrús railed openly against conditions in Spain, and pleaded earnestly for the abolition of arbitrary rule, hereditary nobility, and the outworn system of education. Establishment of free, public, secular education and the creation of a representative lawmaking body he regarded as fundamental to progress. He further advocated the adoption of a simple political catechism and the study of constitutional rights; by such a policy he believed that the errors of twenty centuries could be obliterated in twenty years. A few excerpts from letters he wrote much later to Jovellanos will reveal at once something of his indebtedness to Rousseau.

Tal es aún, tal fué, y será siempre el pacto social; se dirige á proteger la seguridad y la propiedad individual, y por consiguiente la sociedad nada puede contra estos derechos, que la son anteriores; ellos fueron el objeto, la sociedad no fué más que el medio, y ésta cesa con el mero hecho de quebrantarse aquéllos.

Son muy efímeras . . . todas las instituciones que no se fundan en la razón y en la utilidad común; ya todos los hombres saben que Dios no formó ni las monarquías ni las repúblicas; que desaparecen a sus ojos las diferencias accidentales de familias, de individuos, de gobiernos, y que sólo exige de todos la justicia. . . .

El único medio de perpetuar y asegurar las monarquías es el reconciliarlas con el interés y la voluntad general, o con el objeto del pacto social. . . .

Todo hombre en una sociedad nace ciudadano; bajo del primer respecto ningún óbice debe tener la curiosidad de que le dotó la naturaleza para conocer su verdadero bien; y antes bajo del segundo

[74]Dupeyrou to Madame de la Tour, Neuchâtel, May 9, 1779, in Macdonald, Frederika, *Jean-Jacques Rousseau* (New York, 1906), I, 355.

[75]Menéndez y Pelayo, *Historia de los Heterodoxos*, VI, 274 ff.

debe encontrar siempre prontas las luces de que esta sociedad fué depositaria ... se le debe criar como hombre y como ciudadano.[76]

That Cabarrús dared to voice such views even in private letters is ample evidence of the infiltration of liberalism at the Spanish court. That some of his demands were granted by the Constitution of 1812 suggests that ideas of Rousseau were germinating in Spanish soil. Much later we shall hear vigorous refutations of the arguments advanced in these letters.

Further evidence concerning the wide dissemination of Rousseau's ideas in court circles was given by Felipe Samaniego, "arcediano de Pamplona, caballero de Santiago y Consejero," who was so thoroughly frightened by being present at Olavide's condemnation by the Inquisition that he presented himself the following day before that body and confessed that he, too, had been an assiduous reader of prohibited books, including those of Rousseau. To secure absolution, he was required to give a list of all those who had furnished him with such works, discussed them with him, or seemed inclined to agree with such views. In the long list which he furnished appear such names as Aranda, Campomanes, Floridablanca, Ricardos, Masones de Lima, Montalvo, O'Reilly, Lacy, Ricla, and Almodóvar. While none of these was found guilty, thanks to their position and influence, Samaniego was undoubtedly telling the truth about their literary interests and liberal tendencies.[77] Godoy, in writing many years afterward, said that the ideas of Olavide were the same as those of his friends Aranda, Campomanes, O'Reilly, Ricardos, Roda, Ricla, Almodóvar and other scholars and writers of the same period. "La Inquisición quiso hacer un escarmiento y escogió a Olavide, que fué el cabrón emisario sobre el cual el Santo Oficio echó los pecados de los filósofos espa-

---

[76]"Cartas sobre los obstáculos que la naturaleza, la opinión y las leyes oponen a la felicidad pública," in *B.A.E.*, LXII, 552, 554, 568. According to the introductory letter, dated 1795, p. 551, these were written in 1792, and, according to the editor's note, not published until 1808. The *B.A.E.* version is based on an 1820 edition.
[77]Llorente, *Historia de la Inquisición*, V, 316–318; Menéndez y Pelayo, *Historia de los Heterodoxos*, VI, 261–262.

ñoles."[78] In this instance Godoy probably stated the facts correctly—something he seldom did.

The lesson the Inquisition hoped to teach by making an example of Olavide had small effect. Knowledge of Rousseau even before his death was so general in cultured circles that there was no longer even a pretense of ignorance. Only two years after Olavide was sentenced, a work appeared at Madrid which discussed freely the life and writings of the Genevan, compared his ideas with those of Voltaire and other philosophers, and openly praised many of the views he advanced. This *Década epistolar* was written by the Duke of Almodóvar, who had been the diplomatic representative of Spain at various courts, had spent much time in Paris, and was intimate with many of the writers he discussed.[79] In order to be free to give a good sketch of Rousseau's life, he stated that he was translating a chapter from Sabatier's *Tres siglos de la literatura francesa* (Paris, 1779) ; to this he added his own rather frank impressions. In the translated portion, Rousseau is termed "El escritor más entero, más profundo y más sublime de este siglo," and is credited with "la más viva y fecunda imaginación; un espíritu fléxible para tomar todas formas, intrépido en todas sus ideas; un corazón endurecido en la libertad republicana, y excesivamente sensible; una memoria enriquecida de quanto ofrece de más reflexivo . . . en fin una fuerza de pensamientos, una viveza de coloridos, una profundidad de moral, una riqueza de expresiones, una abundancia, una rapidez de estilo, y sobre todo una misantropía. . . ."[80] To these glowing words of a Frenchman, Almodóvar added his own rather mild comments. After speaking lightly of Voltaire's accomplishments, he compares the two writers, whom he terms the greatest of that age:

---

[78]*Cuenta dada de su vida política* (Madrid, 1856), II, Chapter XLI.
[79]*Década epistolar sobre el estado de las letras en Francia.* Su fecha en Paris Año de 1780. Por D. Francisco María de Silva. Madrid, Sancha, 1781. Morel-Fatio [*Études sur l'Espagne*, 210] comments that this work, although lacking the merit of Luzán's *Mémoires littéraires de Paris* of 1751, was very successful in Spain.
[80]*Ibid.*, 51–52.

Mejor opinión tengo respectivamente del ginebrino Juan Jacobo Rousseau. Este nació calvinista; aquel católico, y profesó serlo. Véanse las obras de uno y otro en el punto de Religión, de que tanto han hablado ambos, y obsérvese la vida y la muerte de ellos. Los dos fueron ambiciosos de gloria: pero hay mucha diferencia entre la moderación de Rousseau, y la soberbia de Voltaire enemigo suyo; y en quanto a Filosofía no tiene comparación la Lógica del uno con la del otro.[81]

Later in the work he carries the comparison even further.

Los desbarros de Rousseau merecen compasión: como Calvinista giraba su creencia por un círculo muy distante del centro de la verdad; no debe estrañarse que como filósofo a las orillas del precipicio haya caído en él, suelta la rienda de su fogosa imaginación. Las contradicciones que nacen de semejante desorden, dexan de serlo respecto a este mismo principio, en cuyo supuesto puede asegurarse que Rousseau fué muy consecuente en sus escritos, y acciones, y no tuvo la variación y contrariedades que a cada paso se notan en Voltaire.

Uniforme en su conducta, en su modo de pensar, y en su modestia, o quizás orgullo (pero orgullo por aquel término tan particularmente suyo y muy singular en estos tiempos) nunca mudó sistema, jamás alteró su método, siempre siguió la marcha que había tomado, y hasta su muerte misma en la buena edad de 52 [sic] años, mantuvo las mismas huellas.

Mucho es la diferencia que hallo entre el filósofo de *Hermenonville*, y el de *Farney* [sic]: la pluma de aquel abrasa quanto corre, pareciéndose a la encendida *laba* en las irrupciones del Vesubio: no tiene el mismo fuego la pluma de éste. Por eso al mismo tiempo que considero más disculpable a Rousseau, le juzgo más peligroso, mayormente para las personas de talento cultivado. Voltaire lo es más para las superficiales, aquél seduce sin sentirse; en éste se dexa percibir la seducción. . . .[82]

Mention is also made of Beaurieu, author of *L'Élève de la nature*, "que publicó bajo el nombre del célebre Juan Jacobo Rousseau. Algunos, y por poco tiempo lo creyeron, o la confundieron con el *Emilio* de dicho Rousseau: equivocación muy pasagera, como que la diferencia es extralímites de toda comparación."[83] In his discussion of the French theater, Almodóvar states that in 1775 a play called *Pigmaleon* [sic] was given, "a la que su autor Juan Jacobo Rousseau puso el nombre de *Escena Lírica*."[84]

[81]*Ibid.*, 5.
[82]*Ibid.*, 65–66.
[83]*Ibid.*, 99–100.
[84]*Ibid.*, 246.

With these comments, in addition to fourteen pages devoted entirely to Rousseau's life and works, in circulation in Spain, there was little reason why an educated Spaniard should pretend never to have heard of him.

From other sources we know that Spanish writers had taken up the cry of Rousseau in regard to the duty of mothers to nurse their children. One of the many works which has this idea as its basis is Colomer's *Oír, ver y callar, y el mayor monstruo del mundo,* of which the latter part of the title has reference to the woman who refuses to suckle her child, and the general theme is opposition to wet nurses.[85] From court circles also comes confirmation, for Fernán Núñez, who served as Spanish ambassador at the leading courts of Europe, in a letter written to his sons in 1786, called attention to the hold the idea had taken in Spain.

> Aujourd'hui c'est devenu une mode et même une vanité que de nourrir ses enfants, et j'ai vu des mères exposer leurs jours pour soutenir cette espèce de gageure. Tout extrême est également mauvais. Le raisonnable est que ces mères-là seules allaitent leurs enfants que nous choisirions pour leurs nourrices et que les autres, qui n'ont pas les qualités requises s'abstiennent de ce soin.[86]

It was the court group, headed by the ministers Campomanes and Floridablanca, that was especially active in promoting the societies modeled on that which originated in the land of Altuna. Seventy of these came into existence before the close of the reign of Charles III, and all turned their attention to the promotion of education and industry, especially agriculture and the trades.[87] To such an extent were the useful arts encouraged that even the Prince of Asturias and the other royal children occupied themselves, as Rousseau advocated, many hours of the day in all kinds of manual arts, thus setting an example

---

[85]Colomer, Juan Estevan, *Oír, ver y callar, y el mayor monstruo del mundo* (Madrid, 1781), 96 ff.

[86]"Carta de Dn. Carlos de los Ríos XXII señor y VI conde de Fernán Núñez a sus hijos," in Morel-Fatio, *Études sur l'Espagne,* 324–325. First published in Paris in 1791.

[87]"Memorial presentado al Rey," October 10, 1788, in *Obras originales del Conde de Floridablanca,* in *B.A.E.,* LIX, 322.

to the lower classes.[88] In literary circles we have the interesting case of Moratín who, as a result of reading *Émile*, apprenticed his son to a jeweler. From Leandro's own diarial jottings, we can see the future author of *El sí de las niñas* advancing from three to eighteen *pesetas* a day in the workshop of the royal jeweler.[89] Among those eager to promote the advancement of Spain through the encouragement of scientific and industrial pursuits, Floridablanca, who advocated a plan of general education for the whole country, was easily a leader.

A su voz empezó a desterrarse la envejecida barbarie de las universidades del reino, y a introducirse en el estudio de las ciencias el método y lenguaje que les es propio. Las academias, los cuerpos científicos, los establecimientos literarios, que antes presentaban un aspecto cadavérico, recibieron, bajo su protección, movimiento y vida. . . . Pero entre todas las instituciones sabias, ninguna le mereció más afecto y protección que las sociedades patrióticas. Estos . . . fueron entonces los más protegidos. . . ."[90]

Some of the diplomatic documents directed to Floridablanca contain curious allusions to Rousseau and his teachings. For instance, Aranda, in demanding in no measured terms his prompt recall from the post of Spanish ambassador at Paris, suggests the echoes of Rousseau's posthumous publication of 1782 by opening his letter thus: "Exmo. Vaya de confesión, sin ser de Sn. Agustín, ni de Jean Jacques Rousseau; si sólo de un hombre de bien a otro. . . ."[91]

Another document throws light upon the general circulation of Rousseau's ideas in the court group. Among those interested in encouraging the colonization of Louisiana, then under the government of Spain, by settlers from Kentucky was a certain Pedro Wouves d'Arges, who was

---

[88]"Instrucción reservada," July 8, 1778, *ibid.*, 221.
[89]See *Obras póstumas de D. Leandro Fernández de Moratín* (Madrid, 1867), III, 394, 415.
[90]Lista, A., "Elogio del conde de Floridablanca," in *B.A.E.*, LIX, 519. Almodóvar's *Década epistolar* was published for the benefit of the Madrid *Sociedad económica* of which Floridablanca was a sponsor.
[91]Aranda to Floridablanca, Paris, December 8, 1786, in Archivo histórico nacional [hereafter referred to as A.H.N.], Estado, Legajo 2850, No. 27.

authorized by Floridablanca to promote that movement. In the course of this singular correspondence, the desirability of a key or cipher by which confidential correspondence might be carried on was considered. The promoter forwarded a cipher based on the use of books in any language, and in the course of his explanation of the key he offered the following *Exemplo* to illustrate its operation:

> Bien que un Filósofo moderno haya grangeado no poca fama y crédito, en atribuyendo una superioridad al estado primitivo, al estado de naturaleza, en fin al estado del Indio, sobre el estado de sociabilidad; no obstante con algún fundamento se puede decir, que si aquel mismo Filósofo hubiera establecido sus razonamientos, menos en la theórica y la especulación, y más en la experiencia y la prática, no sería, imposible, que al contrario, hubiese entonces considerado al hombre de la naturaleza, al hombre sylvestre, como al animal el más cruel y el más feroz, de todos los que se hallan esparcidos en la inmensidad de las selvas y desiertos. . . .[92]

Certainly in the Spanish court circle Rousseau had both friends and admirers, some of whom did not hesitate to avow, both before and after the Inquisition had set the stamp of its disapproval on his works, their sincere appreciation of his genius and their personal loyalty. They were the first to read his works and to defend his views; they were the leaders in disseminating them; and they were the pioneers in applying them to Spanish conditions. That Rousseau's works continued to circulate in the peninsula after their prohibition there is abundant evidence; and some of the attempts of the counselors of Charles III to improve conditions in the peninsula may be traced to his teachings. In literary, economic, and industrial life the ideas of Rousseau wère active agents in fomenting progress long before the French Revolution.

---

[92]Pedro Wouves d'Arges to Floridablanca, August 16, 1787, in A.H.N., Legajo 3889.

CHAPTER III

THE JESUITS AND ROUSSEAU

While Aranda and the court circle were disseminating the doctrines of Rousseau in the Spanish world through various channels, especially under cover of the patriotic societies, members of the Jesuit order which was banished from Spain in 1767 were unwittingly also active in introducing his ideas to Spanish readers. Far from their homes and friends, and deprived of their regular work, these educated men now had leisure, which some used in acquainting themselves with current literature, while others went further and voiced their reactions to the ideas advanced. Hence it is not strange that among them were translators, critics, and imitators of Rousseau, or that from Italy there flowed back into Spain a steady stream of literature, some of which carried to the limits of the Spanish dominions many of the Genevan's ideas.

Among these Jesuits there were wide differences of opinion in regard to Rousseau and his ideas, but for that very reason their views reached a wider circle of readers. Some were broad-minded scholars ready to recognize both good and bad features of the works they discussed; others were narrow and sectarian in their views; a few accepted Rousseau as a model worthy of imitation; while many merely maligned him and declaimed against his deism. The circulation of all these conflicting views helped to make Rousseau a familiar name in Spain.

Scarcely had the Jesuits been a decade in Italy before publications and letters in Latin, French, Italian, Spanish, or in Spanish translations, broached his views. In his *Curso de filosofía ecléctica* (1777), Ignacio Monteiro showed himself thoroughly familiar with the thought of his day; he praised Shaftesbury, Rousseau, and Helvetius, and from them deduced certain ethical doctrines.[1] Only a

---

[1]*Ars critica rationis dirigendae*, Vol. I, Pt. I (Venice, 1778), 2nd edition. Cf. Menéndez y Pelayo, *Historia de los heterodoxos*, VI, 284–285.

few months later José Isla, who had railed at Altuna and his "triunvirato," was lamenting at Bologna the dissemination in Spain of the ideas of the French philosophers. Only during the preceding year had he become aware that "la peste de la gran moda—los libros de los filósofos a la *dernière*—había cundido hasta la ciudad santa," as he termed Santiago, the city of St. James. At last, however, he was only too bitterly aware that the "pestilentes libros y apestados filósofos de la última moda" had invaded even that sacred section of Spain, "porque los Voltaires, los Rousseaus . . . y otros corifeos de la moderna impiedad" were everywhere. "Sólo sé que el partido de los volteristas y de los rusistas es muy numeroso; no lo es tanto, ni con mucho, pero lo es bastante para no ser despreciado. . . ."[2]

The infiltration of Rousseau's ideas among the orthodox can scarcely be wondered at when it is realized that *L'École des Mœurs* by Blanchard, a French Jesuit, in which many of the ideas advanced in *Émile* were adapted to a more Christian type of education, had a wide circulation in Spain both in the original language and in the Spanish translation made by Ignacio García Malo.[3] Blanchard did not hesitate to mention Rousseau by name, but his comments on him and his ideas were not uniformly eulogistic. In his first reference to *Émile*, Blanchard says that the work has been justly stigmatized by both ecclesiastical and secular authorities, but that its most absurd paradoxes have been effectively refuted by *Lettres d'une mère à son fils*. Yet this Jesuit took the watchword of Rousseau—temperance and work—as his own, and approved the Genevan's teachings in regard to the position, influence, and duties of a wife and mother in the home.

---

[2]Isla to Archbishop of Santiago, Bologna, January 25, 1778, in *Obras escogidas del Padre José Francisco de Isla*, in *B.A.E.*, XV, 610–611.

[3]Blanchard, Jean-Baptiste, *L'École des Mœurs* (Lyon, 1782). The Spanish version, *Escuela de costumbres ó reflexiones morales é históricas sobre las máximas de la sabiduría*, was published in Madrid in 1786, 1797, 1824, and 1844. A translation with notes was issued by Vicente Valor, 1852 and 1856. Several translations or editions were issued in Mexico, one in 1822.

He cites specifically Rousseau's eulogy of the Bible, his insistence on the need of religious faith, and his words concerning charity to beggars and others more deserving; shares his views concerning the theater as a form of amusement; and praises the *Lettre à d'Alembert*. Nevertheless, he recommends limiting the reading of Rousseau to those capable of distinguishing the true from the false.[4]

No such restriction was imposed by the first of the Spanish Jesuits to call Rousseau openly and favorably to the attention of his countrymen; instead, Juan Andrés justified the consideration of Rousseau as a writer, regardless of his religious views.

> Pero considerando la religión y las letras como dos cosas distintas en un todo, veo que puede un filósofo estar abandonado de Dios según los deseos de su corazón, y tener sin embargo sutil ingenio y fino discernimiento, y pensar justa y verdaderamente en las materias literarias. Si no pueden adquirirse tales prendas sin menoscabo de la religión, prefiriré ciertamente una pía ignorancia al más exquisito saber; pero si la erudición y el ingenio pueden separarse del libertinage e irreligión, y unirse con la piedad, como efectivamente vemos que sucede con frecuencia, no comprendo por qué no se pueda, y por mejor decir, no se deba desear el fino gusto de Voltaire, la elocuencia de Rousseau y la erudición de Freret, antes que los talentos medianos de gran parte de sus contrarios.[5]

Although Andrés was composing this work at the same time Isla was bewailing the invasion of Spain by the "corifeos de la moderna impiedad," the former calmly states as a fact that Rousseau and Voltaire are known and respected by all classes of the people—"no sólo de las doctas y cultas personas, sino hasta de la más baja e ínfima plebe." Then he continues:

> Si la elocuencia no es otra cosa que el arte de hacer pasar con rapidez, e imprimir con fuerza en el ánimo de los lectores el profundo sentimiento de que está penetrado el escritor, ¿quién podrá alegar tanto derecho a la gloria de elocuente, como el que manifiesta Rousseau en sus escritos? El asienta proposiciones nuevas y extrañas, que

---

[4]Vol. I (Paris, 1830), 256 and 365; II, 83–84, 142; and III, 209–211, 241, and 305.
[5]*Origen, progresos y estado de toda la literatura* (Madrid, 1784), II, 353–354. Translated by his brother from the original Italian and published by Sancha in Madrid from 1784 to 1806.

chocan al principio; pero acumula luego tanta multitud de razones, y las profiere con tal ímpetu y fuerza, que es preciso ceder a la violencia de su irresistible facundia, y sentir la fuerza de la persuasión de aquellas cosas mismas que no se creen, y que no consiente la razón. Tanta novedad y vigor de pensamientos, tanta vivacidad de imágenes, tanta gallardía de expresiones, tanta copia y riqueza de palabras y de sentencias, tanta fuerza, energía y rapidez en todo el discurso, arrastra y arrebata con violencia la mente de los lectores, donde su extraño ingenio gusta de conducirla. De su ardiente pluma salen rayos y relámpagos en vez de frases y palabras. No, no puede ponerse la vista en sus escritos sin que luego se sienta inflamar el pecho, herir el corazón, arrebatar el ánimo, y experimentar una universal conmoción de todos los sentidos.[6]

No less just to Rousseau did Andrés show himself in his penetrating criticism of *La nouvelle Héloïse:*

La *Julia* es un romance lleno de tantas luces de discusiones filosóficas y de toda clase de noticias, y está animado de un tan viva elocuencia, que no sólo merece un lugar distinguido entre los escritos de este género, sino que con razón debe ser tenido por una obra original, y respetado de los filósofos no menos que de los poetas, y de los lógicos igualmente que de los oradores. . . . No es . . . una obra de sólo imaginación y afecto, sino que es un libro lleno de conocimientos útiles e importantes, es un libro de filosofía. El modo de leer los libros, las preocupaciones sobre la desigualdad de las condiciones, el debido respeto a la voluntad paterna en la elección del matrimonio, el duelo, el suicidio, el adulterio y otros muchos puntos semejantes están tratados con una sutileza, y con una fuerza de raciocinio, que nadie lo hubiera esperado en un romance. . . . Esto no es decir que yo quiera alabar todas las opiniones del autor sobre estos puntos importantes, ni que piense aprobar su doctrina económica, moral y teológica cuando antes bien conozco los inexcusables delirios en que le ha hecho caer el amor a la novedad; tampoco creo que sean siempre oportunas y traídas a tiempo sus disertaciones, que muchas veces me parece que vienen fuera de propósito, y que sirven para resfriar el afecto, el cual interesa más a los lectores sensibles, que las discusiones.filosóficas. . . . El estilo está tan lleno de entusiasmo, que a veces parece elevarse demasiado, y exceder los términos de una oportuna sublimidad dando en enfático e hinchado, sirviéndose de metáforas y de alusiones demasiado remotas, y haciendo uso de conceptos muy refinados y forzados, y de pensamientos sobrado elevados y sutiles. Pero el autor introduce desde el principio un ardor tal en el afecto, que parece necesario el desahogo en aquel enfático estilo; el vapor de la pasión sube al cerebro, y causa el delirio, que prorrumpe naturalmente en

[6]*Ibid.*, V (Madrid, 1789), 251-252.

aquellas exageradas y fantásticas expresiones, y sigue sin detenerse ideas, imágenes, conceptos y pensamientos como se le presenten, sin poderlos moderar con el regulado juicio: el ánimo del lector participa de aquel fuego, y él mismo desea aquel ardor de sentimientos, aquella rapidez de pensamientos, aquella audacia de expresiones, y se enoja con el autor si alguna vez desciende a un estilo más llano, y toma el tono más bajo y natural. . . . Un amor tan furioso no sufre las frías cuestiones filosóficas, ni las circunstanciadas y amenas descripciones de países, sino sólo las expresiones de su ardor; . . . pocas reflexiones fuertes y vigorosas son toda la lógica de las pasiones: las razones examinadas con sosiego, los argumentos balanceados, las sutiles y exactas discusiones manifiestan más el deseo de filosofar del autor, que la pasión de las personas que escriben aquellas cartas; y esto es un defecto del romance de Rousseau, que disminuye mucho su mérito. La ilusion no puede durar por mucho tiempo. . . .[7]

Aside from their admirable literary qualities, this critic found that the works of Rousseau abounded in errors; to these, Andrés attributed the increasing desire for independence and the general decline in religious convictions.

Considerando sólo su moral tanto en el *Emilio*, y en la *nueva Heloísa*, como en las otras obras suyas ¡qué mezcla no encontramos en ellas de ideas singulares, de paradojas, de errores, de sentimientos exagerados, de virtudes frenéticas, de rasgos sublimes, de sutiles raciocinios y de superiores gracias! Merece lugar en los fastos literarios de nuestro siglo, y tal vez en la historia de nuestras costumbres, su famoso discurso inconsideradamente premiado por la academia de Dijón, en el cual quiere probar que la cultura de las ciencias sea perjudicial a la pureza de las costumbres, y que haya contribuido siempre a su corrupción. El afortunado suceso de éste su primer arrojo sirvió tal vez más que todo para animarle a la producción de las otras fatigas literarias, las cuales ciertamente han causado gran daño a las costumbres, a la religión, y a la humanidad. ¡Quién ha movido a los pueblos a las anárquicas revoluciones, que ponen en combustión a toda Europa, más que el *Discurso sobre la desigualdad entre los hombres,* y el *Contrato social* de Rousseau!(8)

Another Jesuit admirer of the literary excellence of Rousseau's work was Manuel Lassala, who made an Italian translation of *Pygmalion,* first published in 1783 in a volume entitled *Ormesinda,*[9] and later translated into

---

[7]*Ibid.,* IV (Madrid, 1787), 510–516.
[8]*Ibid.,* X (Madrid, 1806), 328–329.
[9]*Ormesinda. Tragedia. Con alcune scene liriche.* In Bologna, A. S. Tomasso d'Aquino, 1783. Cf. Fuster, Justo Pastor, *Biblioteca valenciana* (Valencia, 1827–1830), II, 330.

Spanish. Of all of Rousseau's works, *Pygmalion* was the most popular in Italy; six editions of it appeared before Rousseau's death, and thirteen others were issued by 1809, we are told by a careful bibliographer.[10] And yet Lassala's version had escaped him. The history of this dramatic monologue in Spain is told in Chapter VI.

Just and far-seeing as were both Andrés and Lassala in recognizing the genius of Rousseau, their works reached only certain circles of Spanish readers; from the pen of another Jesuit came the first Spanish work which openly espoused Rousseau's general views on education and unmistakably disseminated them to a large part of the Spanish-speaking world. This was *Eusebio*,[11] a pedagogical novel based on *Émile*, which was written by Pedro Montengón. The central figure of the novel is Eusebio, a vigorous Spanish orphan of noble birth who, after being shipwrecked when six years old on the Maryland coast, is rescued by a family of well-to-do Quakers. His protectors secure for him as a teacher George Hardyl, an unmarried, well educated basket-maker, whose principal recommendation is his character. This counterpart of Émile's teacher, like him, receives no salary, but takes the boy to live with him, teaching him from the first

¡Cuan grandes son los disgustos y daños que acarrea al hombre su propia presunción . . . aquella estima y concepto que concibe o de su nacimiento o de su riqueza, o de su talento y prendas exteriores.[12]

Eusebio, like Émile, was taught to live frugally, to be moderate, to be generous with the needy, to work with his hands, to overcome fears that proceed from superstitions, and to dominate such passions as anger and pride.

---

[10]Schiff, Mario, "Editions et traductions italiennes des œuvres de Jean-Jacques Rousseau," in *Revue des Bibliothèques*, 1907, pp. 183–216, and 1908, pp. 9–39; and Sommervogel, Charles, *Bibliothèque de la Compagnie de Jésus* (Paris, 1893), IV, col. 1544.

[11]*Eusebio. Parte primera, sacada de las memorias que dexó él mismo*, Madrid, 1786; segunda parte, 1787. Republished "corregido," according to the demands of the Inquisition, Madrid, 1807–1808, and frequently thereafter both at Paris and at Barcelona as late as 1840–1841.

[12]*Ibid.*, I, 33.

All this his teacher effects indirectly through ingeniously created situations. Nor is Eusebio brought into social contact with a young girl until he reaches a marriageable age. The parallel between the two boys at this point may be seen from the following excerpt from the Spanish *Émile:*

> Si Hardyl no recabó destruir en el ánimo de Eusebio la afición que había cobrado a la graciosa hija de Smith, obtuvo por lo menos sosegar su pasión e infundirle temor para no abandonarse a ella ciegamente, divirtiéndosela también en parte el estudio de la historia que continuaba, como tambien el exercicio del estilo con que la interrumpía, sin perdonarle Hardyl el trabajo del oficio por las tardes, o el exercicio de sus fuerzas en el huerto, siendo ya Eusebio tan crecido que le faltaba poco tiempo para salir de su minoridad. Para este tiempo había tratado Hardyl con Henrique Myden enviarlo a España para que tomase posesión personalmente de sus haciendas, y con este motivo hacerle viajar condescendiendo Hardyl en acompañarlo en su viaje.[13]

After a European trip, during which Eusebio saw London, Paris, and his ancestral home, he married. The latter part of the work is devoted to the rearing of his son, thereby giving the author an opportunity to bring out Rousseau's ideas concerning the early life of the infant, which could not be applied to Eusebio himself, as he is six years old when the story opens. Freedom, fresh air, and country life entailing manual labor are all stressed; while frequently the author declaims against the corruption of the cities and the evils of artificial politeness. Among the general topics introduced which seem to be further echoes of Rousseau are dueling and slavery—practices the Genevan bitterly opposed.[14]

As a novel *Eusebio* is poor; as an educational treatise it is of decided interest, for it disseminated widely Rousseau's conception of the purpose of the process and the means he advocated. The whole work voices a reaction against the underlying ideal of eighteenth-century education—the formation of subtle men and women of the

---

[13]*Ibid.*, I, 284.
[14]*Ibid.*, II, 328 ff., and IV, 206.

world. But Montengón went one step too far—he committed the unpardonable error of omitting, in the first two volumes, any instruction in religion—to the horror of all churchmen. The author rectified this error to some extent in the later volumes, and the work continued in circulation. Novels were scarce in Spain, and *Eusebio* responded to a popular demand to such an extent that sales were heavy. But its success, coupled with the well known fact that it was based on the prohibited *Émile,* brought the work repeatedly to the attention of the Inquisition. In 1790, 1794, and 1796 denunciations were lodged with that body; finally in 1799, after *Eusebio* was well known, even in the colonies, it was prohibited.[15] Not until 1807–08, after its author had patiently corrected over and over the many passages criticised by the various censors appointed, was a new but much pruned edition issued. Other editions, especially that of Oliva in 1840–41, attest its continued popularity in Spain;[16] it was also translated into Italian.[17] The 1807–08 edition, since it least represents what Montengón originally wrote, is of slight interest; but the later versions, based on the prohibited, were not only widely read but seriously discussed in Spain, where Julio Nombela, who was born in 1836, tells us that in his youth parents compared, in heated arguments, the relative merits of the work of the Jesuit and of Rousseau.[18] Copies of the original edition which were sent to the New World served to interest thinkers there in educational problems, for both *El Periquillo* and *La Quijotita* of Fernández de Lizardi reveal the author's indebtedness to Montengón and Blanchard as disseminators of the ideas of Rousseau.

With his next novel, *Eudoxia, hija de Belisario,* which was sent to Madrid for publication in 1789 but did not appear until 1793, Montengón won the approval of the

[15]*Suplemento al índice,* 37.
[16]González Palencia, A., "Pedro Montengón y su novela *El Eusebio,*" in *Revista de la biblioteca, archivo y museo,* III (1926), 343–365.
[17]Fuster, *Biblioteca valenciana,* II, 383.
[18]*Impresiones y recuerdos* (Madrid, 1914), I, 92.

censor, who described the purpose of the work as the intention to show "la necesidad que tienen las damas ilustres del estudio de la filosofía moral, para que con las sólidas máximas que aprendan, destierren aquellas preocupaciones que las inspira el mundo, y abracen constantemente la virtud, y se hallen prevenidas para sufrir con fortaleza los reveses de la fortuna."[19]

The story, laid in Constantinople in the sixth century, furnished Montengón the opportunity to express his views in regard to the education of women. Belisario, a successful general, is married to a haughty woman of the world, whose pride leads to the downfall of the whole family. To his one daughter, the general is devotedly attached; he teaches her himself when at home, and when absent, entrusts her to a wise woman, in order that she may learn the essentials of virtue. She is taught that poverty is no disgrace, and that the basic qualities of a husband are more important than his wealth or position.

The general scheme of a woman's education is outlined. Arithmetic, which presupposes reading and writing, should be studied; then the sciences; above all, every type of household art should be mastered. Moderation in all things, and contempt for the trappings of wealth are stressed, while rural life and the peaceful joys of the tiller of the soil are exalted. In this respect Montengón echoes Rousseau frequently.[20]

Eudoxia is given opportunity to apply all these ideas, for her father loses favor at court and is blinded at the monarch's command; the mother and daughter are deposited in a hut in the country. Here the mother dies, regreting her folly; but the father and daughter are able to find joy even in the midst of their misfortunes. An humble suitor who follows Eudoxia into exile and assists in making life tolerable is rewarded with her love. Eventually

[19]González Palencia, op. cit., 346–347.
[20]"Desde que se apartaron los hombres del sencillo estado de la naturaleza, corrompieron su verdadera felicidad, fomentándose otra ideal y engañosa, delineada en su fantasía por la codicia y ambición."—Cf. pp. 80–81; 234 ff.; 256.

the father is pardoned; life at court again beckons; but they have learned to appreciate rural contentment and gladly renounce idle pleasures and allurements. The whole work voices in general those ideas that Rousseau set forth in the teachings of the Savoyard vicar.[21]

In his other works, too, Montengón gives evidence of absorption of the philosophic spirit. The earlier odes, in which he extols Clavijo, Aranda, and Campomanes, and sings the praise of industry and labor, further suggest Rousseau. There are romantic strains in his translation of Ossian, but his poetry in general lacks inspiration. That he possessed and helped to circulate copies of other works of Rousseau is evidenced by a letter to his publisher Sancha, in which he expresses regret at not having received news of the receipt of the copy of the *Desigualdad social* he had sent to Madrid through José Pizarro, a diplomatic secretary.[22]

The difficulties placed in the way of Montengón by the Spanish ecclesiastical censors were shared by another Jesuit, Lorenzo Hervás y Panduro, in publishing his *Historia de la vida del hombre,* which treats of the development of man from the moment of conception until death. The first volume, issued in 1789, was prefaced by a dedicatory letter to Floridablanca and an introduction of twenty-four pages. Scarcely was the second volume off the press in 1793 before the circulation of the work was prohibited on the ground that in the introduction to the first volume the author had stated that "todos nacemos iguales y que son espurias las denominaciones de noble y plebeyo." To the censor who voiced this objection, Hervás replied heatedly that Nature made no such distinctions.

La naturaleza, al morir los nobles o ricos y los plebeyos o pobres, no envía a estos encarcelados o esclavos a las oscuras concavidades

---

[21]"Il n'y a point de vrai bonheur sans sagesse. . . . L'enthousiasme des vertus sublimes étoit peu d'usage dans la société; . . . la continuité des petits devoirs toujours bien remplis ne demandoit pas moins de force que les actions héroïques. . . ."—*Confessions,* Pt. I, Bk. III, in *Oeuvres complètes,* VIII, 63.

[22]González Palencia, *op. cit.,* 349. The letter is dated at Venice, December 5, 1795.

en que reina Plutón, ni embarca a aquellos para llevarlos a gozar de las fingidas delicias de los Campos Elíseos. Ella, a todos los hombres que entran o salen de la vida mortal presenta dos puertas igualmente anchas y altas, que son la del nacimiento y la de la muerte. En el umbral de la puerta del nacimiento están los honores, las riquezas, la pobreza y la miseria, que no son producciones de la naturaleza, sino parte de la industria o del descuido de los hombres y reliquias o efectos de los primeros castigos, fortuna o desgracia de los antepasados. En el umbral de la eternidad, en el que se entra al haber pasado por la puerta de la muerte, está la eterna justicia, con los irrevocables decretos o sentencias de los premios o castigos, que nunca acabarán. En este sentido claro y sano, que la malicia no podrá jamás oscurecer ni viciar con siniestras y falsas interpretaciones, el autor, afirmando que todos los hombres nacen iguales, dijo en esta expresión y en su sentido claro una verdad o un dogma filosófico, civil o cristiano, que desde que hay hombres no se ha contrastado ni interpretado siniestramente sino solamente por el censor.[23]

After a long controversy, it was agreed that publication might proceed providing the entire introduction were eliminated from all copies. This was done; volume one still circulates without these twelve leaves. In each of the later volumes Hervás was forced to make so many changes, in order to secure censorial approval, that the seventh volume was not published until 1805.

The relation of this *Historia de la vida del hombre* to the thought of Rousseau has brought forth conflicting opinions from modern critics. Altamira and Farinelli regard Hervás as a follower of the Genevan;[24] Menéndez y Pelayo sees in him a stern refuter of the teachings of *Émile.*[25] It is certainly true that Hervás does not speak of the Genevan in complimentary terms; neither does he attribute to him a single idea that he advances. Nevertheless, the plan of the work is borrowed from Rousseau,

----

[23]"Respuesta apologética." Ms. in Archivo Histórico Nacional. Excerpts have been published by Angel González Palencia, in "Nuevas noticias bibliográficas del abate Hervás y Panduro," in *Revista de la biblioteca, archivo, y museo,* V (1928), 345–359.

[24]Altamira y Crevea, Rafael, *Cosas del día* (Valencia, 1908); Farinelli, Arturo, *Il romanticismo nel mondo latino* (Turin, 1927), I, 114.

[25]Menéndez y Pelayo, *Historia de los heterodoxos,* VI, 277.

and in the fundamental principles advanced both writers are in accord; in details only do they differ. As his authorities, Hervás cites Locke and the other writers from whom Rousseau drew his ideas; among the sources he mentions is Ballexerd, whose *Crianza física* followed shortly after the publication of *Émile*.

A comparison of some of the ideas expressed by these two writers will suggest the debt of the Jesuit to the educational treatise of Rousseau, to which Hervás states that he does not refer "porque todo lo que propone de nuevo, es efecto de una mente delirante. Rousseau en una nota de su primer tomo llama sueños sus meditaciones, que entre los filósofos más libres pasan por verdaderos delirios."[26] A few excerpts will suggest that Hervás availed himself, nevertheless, of some of Rousseau's ideas. The following comparison of statements in regard to the selection of a wet-nurse will suggest the closeness of the resemblance:

Conviene informarse bien del natural del ama de leche. . . . Hay estrecha relación entre las pasiones y los humores del hombre. . . . La mujer más sana y de mejor leche, con un acto de cólera grande es capaz de viciar toda su leche. El ama de leche debe tener buena organización y disposición corporal.[27]	Il faudroit une nourrice aussi saine de cœur que de corps; l'intempérie des passions peut, comme celle des humeurs, altérer son lait; de plus, s'en tenir uniquement au physique, c'est ne voir que la moitié de l'objet. Le lait peut être bon et la nourrice mauvaise; un bon caractère est aussi essentiel qu'un bon tempérament.[28]

Both Hervás and Rousseau oppose the practice of binding the limbs of infants. The former makes an effort to follow Nature; in declaiming against the current practice, he asks:

¿Este bárbaro modo de obrar, conviene con el suave y discreto de la naturaleza? El Filósofo que observa a ésta y en ella descubre y ve de bulto la sabia y adorable Providencia que la gobierna, con-

---

[26]Vol. I, 343–344.
[27]*Ibid.*, 215–216.
[28]*Émile*, Bk. I, in *Oeuvres complètes*, II, 25.

virtiéndose despues a contemplar el modo con que a la naturaleza corresponde la industria de los hombres se admira de la ceguedad y obstinación de ellos. La Naturaleza con su dulce y suave obrar nos presenta a los niños sanos y robustos; y el duro y violento obrar de los hombres con faxas, . . . destruye en los infantes la sanidad y robustez . . . disforma los cuerpos bien formados.[29]

In regard to the process of birth, Hervás advises that Nature be allowed to rule whenever possible; that a new-born child be washed with a rag dipped in wine; and that the hair of children should be clipped until the age of ten[30]—all practices advocated by Rousseau. The Jesuit gives credit for them, however, to Ballexerd,[31] whose *Éducation physique des enfants* "fué premiada el 21 de mayo de 1762 por la Sociedad Holandesa de las Ciencias." Like Rousseau, Hervás advises that children be given no meat, that they be bathed in cold water, that they exercise in the open air, be reared in the country, and not be permitted to acquire ridiculous fears and superstitions.[32]

In general, Hervás declaims against the education advocated by the philosophers.

Uno de ellos (Rousseau) que se ha metido a formar un plan de educación, propone que su prosélito hasta la edad de veinte años no oiga que hay Dios; que tenemos alma; y que hay otra vida. Este es el pensar de este Filósofo, que ha hecho justicia a la santidad de la moral cristiana, y ha casi reconocido por divino a su Autor. Se saben los funestos efectos, que han experimentado los imprudentes que han querido poner en práctica este método de educación.[33]

Yet, like Rousseau, Hervás believes that man possesses the inherent faculty of determining for himself what is right and what wrong. Bad education might warp this faculty, but not entirely destroy it. At this point he explains certain respects in which he considers Rousseau wrong.

[La educación] podrá influir a obrar el mal por hábito; pero jamás hará que la razón y conciencia juzguen bien moral el mal moral. He aquí los efectos ciertos y constantes de la educación, que

---

[29]Hervás y Panduro, *Historia de la vida del hombre,* I, 229–230.
[30]*Ibid.,* 113, where Hervás adds "como nota bien Ballexerd"; 198, 273.
[31]*Ibid.,* 322–323.
[32]*Ibid.,* 269–277; 330–331; 356–359.
[33]*Ibid.,* II, 46.

Rousseau en su *Emilio* confunde con ignorancia verdadera o afectada; por lo que aplica a la educación los delirios que Montesquieu pretendió verificar en el clima.[34]

Since education is such an important process, it should be entrusted primarily to the parents; for the first three years the mother should have charge; after that time the sons should be in the immediate care of the father.[35]

Aside from such agreement of ideas in regard to the rearing and education of children, the volumes of Hervás reveal similarities of thought along more general lines. In more than one instance Hervás shows himself a defender of social equality; he declaims against luxury as vehemently as does Rousseau; and both were opposed to the theater.[36] But of far more importance than these specific similarities of thought is the fact that Rousseau first called attention to man as a subject worthy of study, and that Hervás was the first Spaniard to devote himself seriously to the problem of human development. In this respect his indebtedness to Rousseau is great, although unacknowledged.

During the years in which the treatise of Hervás was issuing from the press, other works by Jesuits whose object was primarily to refute the teachings of the Genevan, especially those advanced in *Émile,* were being written, translated and published. One of these was a two-volume work entitled *Del único principio que despierta y forma la razón, el buen gusto y la virtud en la educación literaria,*[37] by Joaquín Millas, a native of Saragossa, a missionary in Paraguay and at Tucumán, and after the banishment of the Jesuits a professor of metaphysics at the royal college of San Pedro at Placencia, who was an ardent psychologist. The second part of this work is

---

[34]*Ibid.,* V, 209.
[35]*Ibid.,* 57.
[36]*Ibid.,* 261–279; and 302 ff.
[37]The first part was printed at Mantua, 1786, in two sections; the second in Bologna, 1788. See Latassa, *Biblioteca nueva de escritores aragoneses.*

largely devoted to diverting into more orthodox channels the ideas Rousseau had broadcast in regard to education.[38] Among the many other works directed against Rousseau which issued from Jesuit pens in Italy were *Gian Jacopo Rousseau, accusatore de'novi Filosofi* (Assisi, 1798),[39] and *L'Emilio disingannato*, in the first part of which Alfonso Muzzarelli utilized the arguments of the *Diccionario antifilosófico, Los errores de Voltaire*, and the works of Bergier in refuting the teachings of *Émile;* in the second part, he argued against the *Contrat Social*.[40] After being reprinted three times in the original Italian, it was translated into Spanish by Francesco Traversí, who sent it to Madrid for publication.[41] A refutation of "la famosa paradoja" of Rousseau was published at Verona in 1792 by Antonio Pinazo under the title of *Sull'influenza delle lettere e delle scienze nelle stato civile e politico delle nazioni*.[42]

Rousseau's theories concerning music, poetry, and gesture were also discussed by Spanish Jesuits, some of whom agreed with him in certain respects. Both Antonio Eximeno[43] and Estevan de Arteaga emphasized the importance of melody, while the latter maintained that an opera is a vast complex poem in which poetry, music, decorative arts, declamation, dance and pantomime should function jointly,[44] much as Rousseau had in mind in sketching *Pygmalion*.

Through a Portuguese Jesuit, Teodoro de Almeida, an imitation of *Héloïsa* circulated widely in Spain. *El hombre*

---

[38]Menéndez y Pelayo, *Ideas estéticas en España*, V, 110.
[39]Reprinted under the title of *Memorie del Giacobinismo estratti dall'opere de Gian Jacopo Rousseau*, Ferrara, 1800.
[40]Siena, 1783. *Continuazione dell'Emilio disingannato, o sia confutazione del Contratto sociale di Gian Jacopo Rousseau*, Foligno, 1792.
[41]Hervás y Panduro, *op. cit.*, III, 138. Cf. also Sommervogel, *op. cit.*, V, Pt. I, col. 1489.
[42]Menéndez y Pelayo, *Ideas estéticas en España*, VI, 49.
[43]*Del origen y regla de la música*, translated by Francisco A. Gutiérrez, Madrid, 1796. On other points, Eximeno disagreed with Rousseau.
[44]*La Rivoluzione del teatro musicale italiano . . .*, Bologna, 1783. *Investigaciones filosóficas sobre la belleza ideal*, Madrid, 1789. Cf. Menéndez y Pelayo, *Ideas estéticas en España*, VI, 410.

82ROUSSEAU IN THE SPANISH WORLD BEFORE 1833

feliz,[45] which passed through several editions in the Spanish translation, had as its fundamental concept that true happiness is found only in virtue whose fullest development and greatest rewards are experienced in the country, while court life brings only pain and misery. In tracing the development of the passions, Almeida follows Rousseau still further, for he asserts that self-love, which is in its origin good, is their basis. That the Spanish translator also was familiar with Rousseau's works is attested by several of the notes he added. In one instance he refers to Rousseau's praise of the Bible; in another, he cites the Genevan's statement concerning the necessity of recourse either to authority or reason.[46] Today Almeida's work appears most insipid, but its popularity through several generations was so great that it was more widely read than Cervantes.[47] In another work,[48] Almeida discusses truth and error in *Émile* and quotes Rousseau's eulogy of the Bible.

Following these echoes of Rousseau from the Jesuit chorus in Italy came reverberations of his political theories that were directed squarely at the Spanish government. Among the members of this order were some Spanish Americans who had become open enemies of the country that had driven them from their native land—a fact that was well known. In 1786 when a South American, Francisco Miranda, of whom we shall hear more later, visited Italy, he secured several lists of Jesuits who had been expelled from the Spanish Indies. At the end of one was the name of a Peruvian, Juan Vizcardo y Guzmán, who, by 1797 was in London, like Miranda, presenting plans to the English government for the liberation of the Spanish colonies. After his death in 1798, the papers of the Jesuit

---

[45]*El hombre feliz, independiente del mundo, y de la fortuna; o Arte de vivir contento en qualesquier trabajos de la vida.* Obra escrita en portugués . . . traducida y exornada . . . por el Dr. D. Benito Ertaun de Riol, Madrid, 1790. A Spanish translation by Joseph F. Monserrate y Urbino was published in 1784.

[46]Vol. I, 25, 126.

[47]Menéndez y Pelayo, *Historia de los heterodoxos*, VI, 412.

[48]*Armonía de la razón o teología natural . . . contra las absurdas opiniones de los filósofos del día* (Madrid, 1798), 80–84.

passed through the hands of the American minister Rufus King into the possession of Miranda, who published in Philadelphia in 1799 and later in London, Vizcardo's appeal to his countrymen to throw off the Spanish yoke.[49] The directness and extent of this Jesuit's indebtedness to Rousseau will be revealed later when we shall trace the circulation and influence of his ideas, especially in Spanish America.

From these various sources it can be seen that the Jesuits were busy during several decades disseminating various and conflicting opinions concerning Rousseau and his ideas, or making practical application of them. Lassala's translation of *Pygmalion* proved one avenue for its entry into Spain; the criticism of Andrés called attention to the *Nouvelle Héloïse;* the novel by Montengón became the best known of the fictional works in Spanish inspired by *Émile;* and Vizcardo's *Lettre aux Espagnols-Américains* spread abroad some of the teachings of the *Social Contract.* Before they were permitted to return to Spain in 1798,[50] the members of the order that Rousseau hated and that Aranda banished had contributed materially to the Rousseau literature of the period, and thereby served as a channel through which there penetrated into the Spanish intellectual world many of the Genevan's ideas.

[49]*Lettre aux Espagnols—Américains . . .;* Robertson, W. S., *A Life of Miranda,* I, 69, 195; Vargas Ugarte, Rubén, "Juan Pablo Vizcardo y Guzmán, 1747–1798," in *Boletín del museo bolivariano,* Año I, No. 4 (December, 1928), 74–93.
[50]Those who returned to Spain were much more cultured and more versed in the world's affairs than those who left in 1767.—Gil de Zárate, Antonio, *De la instrucción pública en España,* I, 89.

CHAPTER IV

EARLY REFUTATIONS OF ROUSSEAU
IN SPAIN

It must not, however, be supposed for a moment that while the Basques, the court group, and many of the Jesuits were giving favorable voice to the ideas of Rousseau, no opposition to them was being expressed in other quarters. Refutations began in Spain with Feijóo, but they did not end with Coriche in Puebla in 1763, or with the prohibition of Rousseau's works in the following year. It is true that they were not attacked as violently as were those of Voltaire, with whom he was closely associated in the public mind; but almost every reference to the prophet of Ferney brought in some warning words with regard to the Genevan. It is of interest, though, that even those most opposed to his teachings in general could not fail to recognize certain admirable traits both in the man and his works.

The refutations of Rousseau which circulated in Spain before 1793 were written by four types of men: (1) foreigners, whose works were translated into Spanish; (2) those connected with institutions of learning; (3) church officials; and (4) literary men. All were directed primarily to the defense of the church: some of the translations were made by ecclesiastics; the professors in the universities who preached against Rousseau were, in many cases, friars defending their own religious convictions; and even the attacks upon Rousseau's exaltation of the primitive state and the arguments against his theory of the origin of social inequality had for their main purpose the protection of Catholicism. Not until after the fall of the Bastille was the need of defending the state widely felt. The literary value of all these refutations is negligible; but they reached many readers of varying types and exerted some influence, especially among those of limited education or narrow range of reading; the comments and arguments cited are of interest only as evidence of the zealous efforts to stem the flood of foreign ideas and to divert to more orthodox channels those which had already penetrated into Spanish consciousness. Often, however, these very refutations must have served to introduce Rousseau to people who had never before heard his name.

Of the foreign refutations which circulated in Spain, the French were the most numerous; among these were the works of Beaumont, Guyon, André, Beaumelle, Nonnotte, and Caraccioli. The *Mandement* of the famous Archbishop is too well known to require discussion.[1] In Guyon's *El oráculo de los nuevos philósofos* published in Spanish translation in 1769[2] are two works directed specifically at Rousseau—André's *Réfutation* of *Émile* and a *Carta dirigida a Rousseau*.[3] In the preface of the translator, Pedro Rodríguez Morzo, is an explanation of the necessity of such works in Spain. After stating that both the Parlement of Paris and the Inquisition had prohibited Rousseau's works, he adds:

> Sin embargo de estas precauciones tan saludables, y eficaces, no son invisibles las Obras prohibidas de que hablamos. Por más cuidado que haya en mantener el Cordón para el resguardo del contrabando, se hacen introducciones clandestinas de algunos libros, capaces de pervertir, y corromper, no solamente a la incauta, y fogosa juventud, sino también a los que en la madura edad . . . pasan . . . a la subida prevaricación.[4]

Since the poison is in circulation, he wishes to administer an antidote. And the most poisonous of the sophists, Morzo considers "el aclamado Viejo de la Montaña, Juan Jacobo Rousseau."

---

[1]Beaumont, Christóval de, *Instrucción pastoral. Traducida del francés.* Valencia, n.d.

[2]*El oráculo de los nuevos philósofos, M. Voltaire, impugnado y descubierto en sus errores por sus mismas obras.* En dos tomos. Escritos en francés por un anónymo y traducidos al español por el R. P. Mro. Fr. Pedro Rodríguez Morzo. En Madrid, Imp. de Gabriel Ramírez, 1769–1770.

[3]*Ibid.*, II, 279–320; 321–416.

[4]"Prólogo del traductor," *ibid.*, I, iv–v.

No contento este Autor con haber denigrado la Profesión Literaria, atribuyendo casi todos los excesos de los hombres al estudio de
las Ciencias, ha querido despojarnos de lo más sagrado del Santuario de nuestra Religión, que es la Divina Revelación, y los Milagros, que la acreditan. . . . Exime a todos de la obligación de seguir
la Religión Revelada, y promueve la tolerancia universal de todas
Sectas, siendo Patrono, y Caudillo de la actual incredulidad. Con
el especioso pretexto de Conservador de la razón natural, quiere des-
terrar cuanto no se sujeta a las leyes del discurso humano. . . . Un
desprecio alto del Evangelio, de los Milagros de Jesu-Cristo, de la
Historia de Moisés, qué pueden abortar sino un monstruo como
Rousseau! . . . No le disputemos su talento, ni erudición. En esto
le culpamos más que a sus Colegas. . . . Norabuena sea Rousseau
talento del primer orden; pero con el abuso que hace de él, se
extravía más, entumecido con su saber, y engañado con su artifi-
ciosa locución. Todo Impío lleva consigo el discurrir mal; pero el
Impío, que finge que no lo es, obra, y piensa lo peor. Sólo puede
prender Rousseau en algún rústico, o en algunos, que forman una
gran parte del Reino; esto es, en el Vulgo; pero no lo conseguirá
en los instruídos, y mediamente iniciados en los Misterios de nuestra
Religión.[5]

Especially was this work intended to discredit the Savoyard
Vicar, who loomed as such a terrible figure before both
French and Spanish dogmatic thinkers.

Nonnotte's works, while directed specifically at Voltaire,
also contain passages concerning Rousseau. In *Los errores
de Voltaire* these are of slight importance, but in the
Diccionario antifilosófico[6] are numerous articles concerning the Genevan and his work. Under "espíritus fuertes,"
he discusses this "hombre de un espíritu original, y de
una conducta y de un modo de vivir aun más original y
más singular," whom he accuses of writing solely for his
own glorification. In a footnote he inserts an extract
from Sabatier's estimate of Rousseau, which had been

---

[5]"Prólogo del traductor," *ibid.*, II, iv–v.

[6]*Diccionario antifilosófico, o comentario y correctivo del Diccionario Filosófico de Voltaire, y de otros libros que han salido a luz
en estos últimos tiempos contra el cristianismo.* Por el abate Claudio
Adriano Nonote, y traducido al español por D. A. O. D. Z. B.
[Madrid], Imp. de Benito Cano, 1793.

published in its entirety in Almodóvar's *Década epistolar* in 1781.[7]

Under the heading "Querellas filosóficas," Nonnotte recounts Rousseau's relations with Voltaire and Hume, and cites some of the epithets applied to him after he had broken entirely with the philosophers:[8] he quotes four extracts from Rousseau concerning the beauties of religion;[9] deplores the fury of unbelievers for proselyting, referred to in the "Carta a M. de Alembert";[10] and finally gives a general estimate of the character of the Genevan's work; to this is appended, as a footnote, Rousseau's eulogy of the Bible.[11]

Another French work, *La religion de l'honnête homme* (Paris, 1766) by Louis-Antoine Caraccioli, which had for its main purpose persuading people that Rousseau should not be read, was soon made available to Spanish readers by Francisco Nipho. In *Religión del hombre de bien,* which passed through four editions by 1779, the author explains how a simple pamphlet may make, in a

---

[7]In this Sabatier represents Rousseau as saying to himself:

" 'Tengo erudición y ingenio; mi alma se inflama prontamente, y mi entendimiento se acomoda a todo sin dificultad; mi imaginación es fecunda en recursos; y los argumentos se me presentan en tropel para apoyar cuanto concibo; puedo pues desviarme de los caminos comunes. En probar lo que es verdadero se alcanza poca gloria: dejemos pues obrar a la naturaleza: cedamos a las impresiones aunque momentáneas, y seamos singulares para ser célebres.' En virtud de este principio (continúa Sabatier) entablado por sistema, o seguido por instinto, todo se hizo problemático en pluma de Rousseau. Así se ve que razona en favor y contra el duelo; que hace la apología del suicidio, y condena este frenesí; que excusa o palía la fornicación y el adulterio, y demuestra su error con las razones más fuertes. No tienen otro origen sus declamaciones contra el hombre social, y sus enagenaciones en amor de la humanidad; sus ímpetus violentos contra los Filósofos, y la manía de favorecer sus modos de pensar. Por la misma causa impugna con sofismas la existencia de Dios, y confunde con argumentos invencibles a los Ateístas: combate la Religión cristiana con objecciones capciosas, y la ensalza con sublimes elogios. Sería cosa de nunca acabar." *Ibid.*, I, 240.

[8]*Ibid.*, III, 22–24.

[9]*Ibid.*, III, 38–41.

[10]*Ibid.*, 31.

[11]*Ibid.*, 77–82. Another work of this writer which discussed Rousseau was *Defensa de los puntos más interesantes a la religión acometidos por los incrédulos; sacada de las célebres obras que escribió en francés el Sr. Abate Nonnete*, of which the Spanish translation was made by Josef de Palacio y Viana.

day, a thousand unbelievers. If the author is "de moda y escriba originalmente, nadie mira ni la verdad de las citas, ni la exactitud del raciocinio. De aquí nace que la *Carta* de Juan Santiago Rousseau al Arzobispo de París, es aplaudida como un fenómeno filosófico, aunque real, y verdaderamente no contiene más que sofismos, y argumentos llenos de polvo, y polilla por envejecidos; y de que el mandamiento de este ilustre Prelado no ha logrado todos los aplausos que merece, aunque es del todo admirable."[12] Later on in the work he comments on the folly of the public fascinated by impious works. Generally those who read least are most fascinated; they exclaim that the author is "un hombre asombroso, admirable, y digno de ser universalmente citado y admirado." But what the writer really said, they do not realize: that he advocated educating a youth until twenty without religious instruction, claimed we were born to walk on four feet, and still believed us immortal.[13] "¡El estilo es tan nervioso; las comparaciones son tan naturales, y tan ricas, lo sublime y lo trivial se contrarrestan tan singularmente, las ideas son tan originales!" that the readers are fascinated. The strange thing, the French writer observed, is that people who pass for virtuous and consecrated to God read such things as *Emilio* and *El Contrato o Pacto Social,* which should scarcely be named by a good Christian! In his discussion of *Émile,* Caraccioli stressed the fact that its author, while wishing to refute the Bible, established its truth more effectively than any other writer; in the lengthy discussion of the *Social Contract,*[14] he pointed out that therein Rousseau, in opposition to his other writings against state and church, defended a state religion and advocated in its behalf measures more drastic than those of the Inquisition.[15] In conclusion the writer stated his belief that those

[12]*Religión del hombre de bien* (Madrid, 1779), 171.
[13]*Ibid.,* 204.
[14]*Ibid.,* 210–227.
[15]In this connection Caraccioli quoted the death penalty clause—a quotation we find repeated over a quarter of a century later in Mexico by Fernández de Lizardi, who cites this author as his source. —*El Pensador mexicano,* No. 16 (December 16, 1813).

who read the *Social Contract* understood neither it nor its real purpose. This work of Caraccioli is typical of many which were circulated widely with the hope of refutating the ideas inspired especially by *Émile* and the *Social Contract.*

Spain had not long to wait for original treatises directed to the protection of society against the teachings of the Genevan. In 1774 Fernando de Ceballos y Mier, professor at San Isidro in Madrid, began publication of one of the most extensive of these, *La falsa filosofía, crimen de estado,*[16] which gained wide circulation and won considerable fame for its author. In it, he considered and refuted the many errors of thought then current, and tried to show that the end of human power was not to be found in reason, in the elements of law, or in returning, either by way of force or the softer chains of the social pact, to the state of Nature from which man had departed. In the sixth volume, Ceballos ventured too far in his defense of the church and its rights; he had already attacked two works then highly regarded by the leading cabinet members—*Esprit des lois* and *Dei Delitti e delle Pene*—and he stated he was prepared to go further. Instead, he was refused authorization for a seventh volume, and the rest of his work still remains in manuscript. So far as Rousseau is concerned, *La falsa filosofía* served much as did Feijóo's *Carta*—it made his ideas better known; for in the Spanish work many extracts are quoted, and a few accorded praise, but with reservations. Ceballos was a zealous refuter of Rousseau, for among his other unpublished works are an *Análisis del Emilio* . . . and *Causas de la desigualdad entre los hombres.*[17]

An outstanding example of the florid oratory directed against Rousseau in the universities is to be found in a sermon delivered by Joseph Marín, a Franciscan professor

---

[16]*La falsa filosofía, o el Ateísmo, Deísmo, Materialismo, y demás nuevas sectas, convencidas de crimen de estado* . . . Segunda impresión. Madrid, Imp. de Sancha, 1775–1776.

[17]Menéndez y Pelayo, *Historia de los heterodoxos*, VI, 374–375; Vidart, Luis, *La filosofía española* (Madrid, 1866), 102–103.

at the University of Salamanca, who seized the occasion of honoring a deceased colleague to preach against the philosophers and their teachings.[18] Taking as his text, "Porque yo no he conocido literatura, entraré en las Potencias del Señor," he delivered himself of a typical tirade against "la literatura infernal, que introduce el desorden, y un sempiterno horror en las costumbres, en el Estado, y en la Religión." Some of these writers, he proceeds, want to prescribe educational tenets; they tell us not to mention religion until a child is twenty years old. The subject of this eulogy never knew so exotic a doctrine. His parents reared him in ignorance of that liberty prescribed by the philosophers as a preliminary to education. He never was subjected to "conversaciones que corrompan, diversiones que disipen, juguetes y enredos que distraigan." He knew little of that favorite science of the age—philosophy. Marín admits and deplores the progress of all these ideas.

¿Quien ignora los insultos que por su causa padece la Fe en nuestros tiempos? ¿Hubo jamás una plaga tan grande de libelos impíos. . . .? Ni los Diques de la Potestad Real, ni el muro fuerte de la Santa Inquisición bastan para contener el ímpetu de esta grande avenida, que agitada horriblemente por los pujantes vientos del Aquilón, quiere inundar desgraciadamente mucha parte de nuestra Península. . . . Libros, que corren clandestinamente, que se buscan a todo precio, se leen con ansia, y con anhelo: y sin la menor licencia gustan hasta las damiselas, y jovenes su doctrina con aquella hambre, que excita en un apetito desreglado la misma novedad y prohibición. . . . Libros que constituyen el Estado natural del hombre en una abstracción de toda Religión, como si el hombre no fuese más que un Bruto, y un Ente del todo material criado para lo sensible, y no para conocer y venerar al Criador. . . . Libros que afirman que la Justicia es la que nace de la voluntad de los hombres, y de los pactos con que se juntaron, cuando inventaron vivir en sociedad. . . . Libros, que no dan otro principio a la Potestad Real, que cierta porción, o partícula de libertad que cada uno libremente ha transferido en un Depositorio común, y que pueden reasumir de acuerdo cuando se les antoje,

---

[18]Marín, Joseph, *La Sabiduría del siglo convencida de necedad, o Elogio de un sabio en lo mismo que ignoró.* Díxolo en la . . . Universidad de Salamanca el día 15 de Julio de 1777 en honra del difunto Doctor D. Francisco Lorenzo Agudo de Pedraza . . . Barcelona, [1777].

quedándose el Monarca . . . como uno de tantos en la calle; y en caso de no convenirse, qualquiera vasallo es árbitro a declinar de su dominio, tomándose del Depósito la porción de su libertad, y retirándose con ella a los montes para obrar solo, y a su riesgo impunemente en la piratería, en el robo, en el homicidio, y en aquella guerra de todos contra todos, que se dice natural al hombre antes de aquella asamblea general de los Pactos Sociales. . . . Libros que . . . numeran con mucha gracia el Dogma y Professión de la Religión Católica; y eso que el Autor se dice un Incomparable Publicista, y célebre Expositor de la Escritura. . . . Las ideas son todas de irreligión, de independencia, de desorden, y libertad. . . . 'El deleite, dicen, y el interés personal son las fuentes de la justicia humana, y de todas las virtudes. El placer sensible, y el amor propio, son los dos polos y ejes sobre que rueda todo el universo moral. El deleite, siguen, es el único motor de los hombres, y es nada menos que extravagancia, y locura el guardarse de sus atractivos, cuando Dios mismo gusta que nos dejemos llevar por él. . . .' Pueden leerse entre Católicos máximas tan sucias, y tan impías, sin que se les hiele la sangre de las venas? . . . Afuera de estos patios ciencia tan animal, que se dedignara profesar un discípulo de Mahoma. Váyanse a vivir a los despoblados, y entre las piaras de los animales, unos filósofos que en nada se diferencian de los más inmundos. . . . En hablando de los Derechos de la sociedad: qué dulzura de estilo! qué almíbar! qué humanidad! qué igualdad persuaden entre los hombres! qué libertad absoluta les conceden, hasta borrarles la idea del primer ser, de su Providencia, y de su Justicia. . . . Lo mejor es no leerlos, despreciarlos, ignorarlos; pero si os hallaseis con las licencias que se requieren para su lectura: si tuvieseis . . . aquella perspicacia y fondo de doctrina para poder con utilidad, y sin peligro manejarlos, hacedlo en buen hora. . . .

Los profesores Salmantinos detestan en sus aulas doctrinas nuevas promotoras de la libertad, y destruidoras de la quietud pública y de la sumisión debida a las potestades.

In conclusion he exhorts his hearers to flee these temptations; they should say to themselves:

Esta Doctrina no se enseña en Salamanca; luego es falsa, tumultuaria, e indigna de que yo deba contestarla. . . . A un lado pues novedades . . . impiedad abominable . . . pestilencial Ateísmo, libertad execrable, nada tendréis jamás que ver conmigo.

Instead, many students, after hearing such a tirade, probably hastened to read at the first opportunity the prohibited books cited.

A further outcry against the philosophers was raised in educational circles in Spain as the result of a publication by Cesareo Pozzi,[19] an Italian Benedictine, who dared to point out the ignorance of the Spanish monks and to outline a program of educational reforms. He was promptly answered by Juan Bautista Muñoz,[20] who showed that the Italian's work was nothing more than a rehash of various writers, including Rousseau, Helvetius, and Locke—all of whom were wrong. Pozzi was forced to flee from Spain, and the Inquisition prohibited the book.

From the University of Seville came another attempt to administer an antidote against the new philosophy that Spain was too rapidly absorbing. One of its professors, Pérez López, struck out along new lines: he tried to establish an underlying principle which would justify the "eternal truths" of religion.[21] He considered a knowledge of natural law, profession of true religion, and "la sana política" as the three essentials to human happiness. Man has no natural or inner gifts that will enable him to know his obligations.

Rousseau por el contrario hace el hombre manso por su naturaleza; pero tan estúpido que era incapaz de discernir la hermosura de una mujer a otra, y tan insociable que ni con la misma mujer, que por casualidad desfrutaba, ni con sus hijos, tendría sociedad alguna; mas no obstante le llama feliz por la quietud de espíritu, semejante a la de las piedras y troncos, y sin otro testimonio que su palabra, dice: que todos los males vienen de la sociedad, y que tal estado (el cual es más salvage que el de los osos) es natural al hombre. Estos y otros principios de igual clase son la basa de los famosos sistemas que se celebran en el día. . . . ¡Qué efectos tan sediciosos puede causar la sentencia de Rousseau! Lo cierto es que en sus escritos y en otra inundación de libros luchan entre sí la naturaleza, la religión, y la política: y unas veces los tiranos subyugan la tierra: y otras los súbditos se revelan contra las Potestades legítimas. . . .[22]

[19]*Saggio di educazione claustrale* . . ., Madrid, 1778.
[20]*Juicio del Tratado de educación*, Madrid, 1778.
[21]Pérez y López, Antonio Xavier, *Principios del orden esencial de la naturaleza* . . ., Madrid, 1785.
[22]Ibid., x–xi, xxii.

In reply to Rousseau's ideas concerning the happiness of man in the natural state, Pérez y López replies:

¡Buena felicidad por cierto! Por esa regla serán los perros y gatos más felices que el hombre. ¿Mas de dónde habrá sacado Roseau semejante idea? La historia no la ofrece; y la naturaleza humana está tan lejos de sugerirla, como de persuadirse que las palomas fueron árboles en sus principios, y que con el tiempo se hicieron aves, y aprendieron a volar.

Fuera de esto, semejante quietud de espíritu es más bien insensibilidad que felicidad positiva, para cuyo goce se requiere conocimiento, como todos los hombres lo reconocen no teniendo por felices a los brutos por falta de él.

Y sobre todo, el hombre por su naturaleza, facultades y relaciones se dirige al conocimiento de la verdad, y también es sociable, y por lo mismo sin el goce de estos fines no puede ser feliz, como se ha mostrado: de manera, que se ha hecho evidente que esos y otros sistemas filosóficos semejantes son meros sueños de hombres despiertos.[23]

From the church, itself, came a flood of literature directed against the philosophers. In western Spain, Archbishop Bocanegra issued a pastoral letter[24] in 1777 designed to warn his flock of the dangers attendant upon the reading of the works of Rousseau and Voltaire; it may have been as ineffective as that issued in 1769 by the bishop of Coimbra, but burned by order of the royal censors who disapproved the prohibition of certain books as prejudicial to morals; for, they contended, "si los habitantes de aquel Obispado oyesen los nombres de Voltaire, y de Rousseau, ignorían enteramente si eran nombres de piedras o de plantas, si eran cuadrúpedos, o si eran anfibios."[25]

A decade later the dean of the Cathedral of Palencia, Vicente Fernández Valcarce, issued a four-volume work,

---

[23]*Ibid.*, 173.

[24]*Declamación oportuna contra el libertinaje del tiempo que en forma de carta pastoral dirigió a su rebaña el Ill. sñr. D. Francisco Alejandro Bocanegra, arzobispo y señor de Santiago.* Madrid, 1794.

[25]*Mercurio histórico y político*, March, 1769, p. 252; May, 1769, pp. 64–65. Sentencia de la Real Mesa Censoria contra la Pastoral manuscrita que el Obispo de Coimbra Don Miguel de la Anunciación esparció clandestinamente entre los Párrocos de su Diócesis proferida en Lisboa el 23 de Diciembre de 1768, p. 87.

Desengaños filosóficos,[26] which also pointed out the errors of various thinkers, among them, Rousseau, and warned his flock against them.

Muchos se llaman Filósofos, sin embargo de que no aman la verdadera sabiduría. . . . Nuestros críticos saben muy bien que se llaman Filósofos, y se precian de tales Espinosa, Rousseau, Voltaire, . . . y otros innumerables, los cuales no amaban la verdadera sabiduría, antes bien hacían cuantos esfuerzos podían para obscurecerla, y cuanto fué de su parte la viciaron y corrompieron.[27]

Under the circumstances, Fernández Valcarce observes, it is very difficult to distinguish false from true philosophers, and no less so to discover and destroy their errors. Especially is he disturbed by Rousseau's reference[28] to modern science as a source of explanations of purported resurrections.[29] To these statements Fernández Valcarce replies that miracles do not take place in the presence of Pharisees, Gentile magistrates, princes, or in the company of Rousseau and Voltaire.

Allied with the conservative element against the French philosophic group were a few men of literary ability; among these, Juan Pablo Forner easily holds the place of distinction—not that his ability was so outstanding, but because most of the leading writers and thinkers were converts to the French influence. Forner, although given little encouragement in literary circles, battled manfully against foreign ideas, which he regarded as disturbing to Spanish well-being. Among the many lines he penned with this end in view are the following—an introduction to an unfinished satirical poem:

> Allá en la edad que recibió del oro
> El título halagüeno en tiempo cuando
> Fué más escudriñado su tesoro;
>   En aquel bello siglo, en que matando
> Los hombres a los hombres que podían
> Con libre imperio y voluntario mando,
>   Sus leyes naturales mantenían

---

[26]Madrid, Blas Román, 1787–1788.
[27]*Desengaños filosóficos*, I, 27.
[28]*Lettres écrites de la montagne*, III, 156.
[29]*Desengaños filosóficos*, I, 42; II, 202. Cf. also *Émile*, II, 273.

> (Según Hobbes lo vió), y en robo y muertes,
> Estado entonces natural, vivían.
> Cuando privilegiaba a los más fuertes
> La corrupta después naturaleza,
> Y en la rapiña colocó sus suertes;
> O cuando manteniendo la entereza
> Que a un racional compete, conservaba
> De bruto la ignorancia y la fiereza;
> Y siendo racional no razonaba
> Y con entendimiento no entendía
> Que así su ser el hombre ejercitaba.
> (Rousseau lo afirma, que lo vió, a fe mía,
> Y trató a dos salvajes que le hablaron,
> Aunque él dice que nadie hablar sabía).[30]

Not content with this attack on the current philosophy of the eighteenth century, Forner wrote, in answer to the question "Qué se debe a España?" an *Oración apologética por la España y su mérito literario* in which he drew a comparison between the intellectual contributions of Spain and those of thinkers in other countries and incidentally showed his contempt for Rousseau and the French philosophers.

> Vivimos en el siglo de los oráculos. La audaz y vana verbosidad de uno tropa de sofistas ultramontanos, que han introducido el nuevo y cómodo arte de hablar de todo por su capricho; de tal suerte ha ganado la inclinación del servil rebaño de los escritores comunes, que apenas se ven ya sino infelices remedadores de aquella despótica revolución con que, poco doctos en lo íntimo de las ciencias, hablaron de todas antojadizamente los Rousseaus, los Voltaires y los Helvecios. . . . Tal es lo que hoy se llama Filosofía: imperios, leyes, estatutos, religiones, ritos, dogmas, doctrinas . . . son atropellados inícuamente en las sofísticas declamaciones de una turba, a quien, con descrédito de lo respetable del nombre, se aplica el de Filósofos.[31]

Especially was Forner hostile to the theories Rousseau advanced in the two discourses. In commenting on the terrible state of the savages on the Orinoco, he added: "Y que se nos vengan después los admiradores de Juan

---

[30]*Poetas líricos del siglo XVIII*, in *B.A.E.*, LXIII, 341.
[31]*Oración apologética por la España y su mérito literario* (Madrid, 1786), 7–9.

Jacobo a celebrar con él la felicidad envidiable de los sal-
vajes."³² Of the happiness of man in the primitive state
and his development of reason and rule through law, he
drew a satiric picture:

Fué un tiempo (dicen) cuando el hombre, falto
de entendimiento y locución, vivía
dichosamente en cavernosos montes,
cual viven ora los rapaces lobos.
. . . .
No entre los hombres amistad, no el lazo
de saludables leyes. Vagabundos,
huéspedes rudos de confusos bosques,
al sol, al aire, a la inclemencia expuestos,
sin más razón que el natural instinto,
y con fuerza robusta, siendo fieras,
al ser de racionales no aspiraban.
. . . .
Cansóse, empero, el hombre de su dicha,
y empalagóse (como en todo suele)
de su estado feliz. . . .
                    . . . A las crines
y ensortijada barba, neciamente
trocar quiso el abrigo y la decencia.
Substituyó a las rústicas moradas
o el techo de azulados horizontes
. . . .
y ciegamente en su infortunio diestro,
cuanto más, inventando nuevas artes,
la majestad del hombre descubría,
tanto más se apartaba (según dicen)
del estado a que el hombre fué creado.
Halló el discurso los sagrados medios
de hacer seguras del insulto inicuo
la posesion y la salud. . . .
                    . . . ¡Triste tiempo,
tiempo infeliz, cuando los hombres mismos,
estableciendo leyes, se obligaron
a ser forzosamente virtuosos!
Entonces fué cuando arrojaron lejos
la pureza de sí: su esencia entonces
debió al desvelo de querer con ansia
perfeccionar de su Razón los dones,
la vil depravación que en sí percibe.
Vino el hombre a ser hombre finalmente,

---

³²*Preservativo contra el ateísmo* (Sevilla, 1795), 133–134.

y salió del estado que le toca,
si no miente el gran genio de Ginebra.
De la razón que en su vigor se fía,
tales son las groseras invenciones.
Hacernos brutos para hacernos buenos,
y reducir el hombre a que posea
sin uso la que engendra sus virtudes,
dueño de un alma inútil; ¿con qué labio
osa dar la impudencia a los delirios
título de sagaz filosofía?[33]

How carefully the works of Rousseau were studied by those whose views differed from his is well illustrated by a note which Forner added to the text of his *Preservativo contra el ateísmo*. In stressing the divine element in government and the small right of the people to interfere with its established order, he calls to his support even the argument of the despised philosopher.

Tenemos aquí en nuestro favor el celebérrimo Juan Jacobo Rousseau y precisamente en una de las obras donde más se esforzó para sostener la causa de la independencia—a saber, *El Discurso sobre el origen de la desigualdad entre los hombres.* Examinando en su segunda parte el derecho recíproco de los miembros de la sociedad civil, condena abiertamente la arbitrariedad en el pueblo para alterrar la constitución recibida; y hace esta saladísima reflexión "Las horrendas disensiones y desordenes infinitos que acarrearía necesariamente esta peligrosa arbitrariedad, prueba, más que otra cosa, la necesidad que tienen los gobiernos humanos de apoyarse en un cimiento más sólido que la sola y simple razón."[34]

In other connections he declared that Rousseau taught that civil institutions had caused the degeneration of man; that sovereigns were a pack of wolves introduced to establish universal slavery; and that the Christian religion was opposed to the constitution of the state.[35]

Joined with the efforts of all these writers to belittle the teachings of Rousseau and to prevent his works from gaining circulation were those of the Inquisition, which

---

[33]*Discursos filosóficos sobre el hombre* (Madrid, 1787), 110–113. In the notes to this text, pp. 283–292, he discusses at length Rousseau's arguments against the arts and sciences. Reprinted in *B.A.E.*, LXIII, 366–367, but without the notes.
[34]*Preservativo contra el ateísmo*, 154–155, note.
[35]*Discursos filosóficos*, 3.

was by no means inactive during their period. Most of the cabinet ministers of the liberal group were denounced once or more; Samaniego and the Marqués de Narro, as well as Iriarte, Clavijo, Cañuelo, and Nipho, were warned or punished for their reading of prohibited works and their defense of doctrines not sanctioned by the Catholic Church or the Spanish state. Prohibition of books continued, by order both of cabinet ministers and of the Inquisition. *Les confessions,* published first in 1782 and the second part in 1789, was prohibited the latter year, as were also the first eight numbers of *Discursos literarios, políticos, y morales* (Madrid, 1789), which were found to reproduce "el fatal sistema de Hobbes, Espinosa y Helvecio . . . Volter, Ruso y otros semejantes monstruos de impiedad y de irreligión."[36]

---

[36]*Indice último de libros prohibidos.* See also *Annales,* I, 139–140, describing a catalogue of books prohibited in 1789, two of which referred to Rousseau.

CHAPTER V

ECHOES OF ROUSSEAU IN PERIODICAL LITERATURE

Periodical literature during the reign of Charles III was an important channel for the dissemination of liberal ideas, as many of the editors were protected by one or more influential cabinet ministers. While some of the early promoters of this type of literature used considerable caution and did not state the sources of the ideas presented, later editors ventured to discuss subjects and to express opinions far different from those usually ascribed to Spanish writers of the period. Although nearly all of these editors were summoned before the Inquisition at one time or another, few became its victims; and while some periodicals were suppressed after only a brief existence, others were protected to such an extent that the opinions voiced are surprisingly fearless.

Of the periodicals that flourished during this period, the pioneer was *El Pensador* of Clavijo; attention has already been called to some of his articles voicing Rousseau's ideas. *El Censor* (1781–1786), edited by Luis Cañuelo, was even more a disseminator, especially of the views expressed in the first and second *Discourses* and the *Social Contract*. In the "Oración apologética por el Africa y su mérito literario," which is evidently a reply to Forner's defense of Spain, the writer admits the first *Discourse* as one of his sources; in line with its arguments, he sarcastically claims highest honors for Africa as it has neither a horde of writers on politics nor any philosophers; it does not even think.[1] In the subsequent number, Rousseau's theories are referred to indirectly.

¿Por qué clamar con tanta energía contra todas las artes que no son de primera necesidad? ¿Por qué quererlas proscribir como las más crueles enemigas del género humano? ¿Por qué tanto echar

---

[1] Discurso CLXV.

menos la comunión de los bienes, tanto acriminar las voces *tuyo* y *mío*, tanto empeño en persuadir que es necesaria para nuestra felicidad una absoluta igualdad de fortunas. . . . Este modo de pensar es el que me propuse combatir en mis Discursos.

In a discussion of the evil effects of the regulation of everything by too many laws, and also in an article directed against torture as a form of punishment, there are clearly echoes of the *Social Contract*. In the first case, the writer argues that if men sacrificed a part of their liberty, it was certainly to secure other rights; that if they bow to others, it is to secure protection against such as might endanger their happiness; but that they will certainly neither subscribe to nor obey laws which benefit solely others.[2] In decrying torture, as permitted by Spanish law, he echoes Rousseau directly:

Los derechos de la suprema Potestad en cualquiera Sociedad que sea, no son más que el agregado de los que cada uno de sus individuos, viviendo en el estado natural con todos los demás que la componen, tendría sobre ellos. Sea que las potestades civiles vengan inmediatamente de Dios, sea que vengan del Pueblo mediante los pactos de sociedad; en cualquiera de las dos hipótesis me parece una verdad incontestable. . . . Es constante que Dios no ha concedido a las supremas Potestades otros derechos sobre sus súbditos que los necesarios para el fin de la Sociedad; este fin no es otro que la felicidad temporal de todos sus individuos. . . .

He then proceeds to show that in any institution destined to produce the happiness of the individual there is no place for torture.[3] The natural abridgment of parental authority after the child has attained maturity[4]—a theme Vizcardo was to sing to the Spanish Americans later—also suggests the *Social Contract*.

---

[2]Discurso CLVI.
[3]Discurso LXIV.
[4]"El fundamento de la potestad, que la naturaleza concede a los padres sobre sus hijos, y del derecho que tienen de dirigir sus acciones, no es otro que la incapacidad en que están éstos en los primeros años de conducirse a sí mismos, y de proveer a sus necesidades. . . . De manera, que en llegando al perfecto y cabal uso de la razón, venga a quedar reducido a un mero derecho de consejo en los padres, y a una obligación de respeto . . . en los hijos."—Discurso XXXV.

An echo of Rousseau's attack on superstition in the *Letters from the Mountain* is to be heard in the forty-sixth Discourse, which calls attention to the marked change which had taken place in the subject matter of sermons; criticisms of the theater and the adornments of ladies have given way to protests against atheism and incredulity. Now no sermon is preached which does not voice "una invectiva contra las máximas del siglo ilustrado, contra la erudición de la moda, contra los filósofos del tiempo"; but none has a word against superstition, which the writer claims is much more general in Spain and much worse. As the result of his merciless attacks on political and religious bigotry, Cañuelo was tried by the Inquisition and found guilty of deism and naturalism,[5] and his periodical was forced to suspend publication.

Its place was partially filled by the *Memorial literario*,[6] whose bibliographical section informed Spanish readers of the existence and content of local and foreign publications. In its pages appeared an address of Jovellanos favoring the admission of women to learned societies and the objections Cabarrús voiced to such procedure. The progress of university reforms is traced in one article. Almodóvar's version of Raynal is reviewed, as is the collection of Foronda's articles, including those published under the pseudonym of "Mr. de Fer." *Las Helvianas* translated by Vial is described as epistolary correspondence with a lady concerning modern metaphysics, with J. J. Rousseau cited as one of the principal writers under discussion.[7] Of special interest for this study is the announcement of the presentation of *Pygmalion* in French at Madrid on January 25, 1788, and the inclusion of a Spanish translation of the whole work, the details of which will be discussed in the next chapter.

---

[5] Llorente, *Historia de la Inquisición*, V, 170–171. Robert E. Pellissier, in *The Neo-Classic Movement in Spain during the XVIII Century* (Stanford University, 1918), sees the influence of Rousseau in *Discursos* III, IX, and X.

[6] *El Memorial literario, instructivo y curioso de la corte de Madrid*, Madrid, 1784–1791; 1793–1797; 1801–1808.

[7] Vol. XI (August, 1787), 464.

Another periodical containing articles concerning Rousseau was *El Correo de los Ciegos,* published after 1787 under the title of *El Correo de Madrid.* Its editors, Manuel Casal, Cayetano Cano, and Manuel de Aguirre, entertained extremely liberal views and showed no hesitation in referring to such a writer as Rousseau by name or in quoting extracts from his works. In addition to various incidental references to him in the first volume, the passage in *Émile* in praise of the Bible is translated in full.[8]

Citations from Rousseau appear in the second volume in the language of the original. For example, the following passage serves as an epigraph for a speech delivered before the Economic Society of Madrid:

"Malgré tous les travaux des plus sages législateurs, l'état Politique demeura toujours imparfait, parce qu'il étoit l'ouvrage du hasard, et que mal commencé, le temps, en découvrant des défauts et suggérant des remèdes, ne put jamais réparer les vices de la constitution: on racommodoit sans cesse, au lieu qu'il eût fallu commencer par nettoyer l'air et écarter tous les vieux matériaux, comme fit Licurgue à Sparte, pour élever ensuite un bon édifice. J J.R. Orig. de l'inég. parmi les hom."[9]

Such injudicious utterances were curbed on September 6, 1788, by the Supreme Council, which decreed that the name of the author of either translations or speeches must be given. Hence, from the third volume on, not all is laudatory of Rousseau. The general attitude toward him is, nevertheless, expressed in a letter which states that an excellent thought may be couched in uncouth terms, but that the greatest absurdities may be set forth in the purest diction.

Tristes testigos de esta verdad son v.gr. las de Voltaire y Rousseau—pocos escritores se han producido con más dulzura, pero también con más extravagancia e ignominia.[10]

A curious discussion of Rousseau's contention that "la ignorancia es acaso preferible a la ciencia en una nación"

---

[8]No. 37, p. 145.
[9]No. 102, October 13, 1787.
[10]No. 205.

appears in the issue of January 24, 1789,[11] in which the writer takes the stand that only he who believes that education modifies but little the natural inheritance should defend ignorance. By citations from *Héloïse* it is shown that Rousseau regarded knowledge derived from books as of slight value; the writer of the article, on the contrary, thinks there is none other. The wish of Héloïse that her son be prudent and good, but not learned, serves as the basis for a discussion of the characteristics of ignorant peoples, whom the writer does not consider happy. Why should Rousseau, who in *Émile* foresees the total depopulation of Europe and the corruption of morals as a result of the arts and sciences, take the part of ignorance, the Spaniard asks. Probably because he thought he could make himself the leader of all the idle and lazy and thus become immortal; but such fame will not last. "¿Qué tormento no sería pues para este autor, si llegase a ver los desprecios que merecerán en lo futuro, y merecen al presente los panegíricos que ha hecho de la ignorancia?" No one will believe that science and letters are injurious to the human race; only a man who wishes to appear singular or to make a show of his eloquence would affirm such an error.

There is further evidence in this periodical that even such little known works of Rousseau as the *Projet de paix perpétuelle* were read and analyzed in Spain. In the issue for July 1, 1789,[12] appears a translation, submitted to the editor, of a *Rescrito del Emperador de la China con motivo de la obra Paz perpetua de la Europa de J. J. R.* In this the Chinese ruler suggests, as the kings of Persia and Turkey as well as himself have been omitted from consideration in Rousseau's work, that a glass house be constructed on the banks of the Seine in which all controversies between church and state, nobles and commons, sword and toga, masters and servants, husbands and wives, and even between authors and readers shall be ironed out. He suggests Rousseau as the first president,

---

[11] No. 227.
[12] No. 272.

since he has taken upon himself the solution of all the problems of rulers. This proclamation, which ends with the benediction "Que tenga en su santa guardia al dicho J. J. R. como también el señor Wolmar y la Madama Julia con su falso botón," is dated at Pekin, "el primer día del mes Hihan del año 1898436500 de la fundación de nuestra Monarquía."

In an article concerning the influence of religion on public welfare,[13] the fact is brought out that men indifferent or even hostile to the Catholic faith have been obliged to confess the necessity of religion. As an example, Rousseau is quoted as saying in his *Lettres écrites de la Montagne:* "Creemos que Jesu-Cristo estuvo dotado de una autoridad divina: en su conducta conocemos una virtud más que humana, y en sus lecciones una sabiduría más que de hombre."

Most surprising to those who believe that Rousseau was referred to only covertly in Spanish periodicals of the eighteenth century is a biography of the Genevan, over 3,000 words in length,[14] in which his career is outlined and his various works reviewed. Of the first *Discourse,* it is stated:

Jamás una paradoja ha sido sostenida con tanta elocuencia. No era el pensamiento nuevo, pero el autor supo darle todas las gracias de la novedad y empleó en él todos los recursos de su saber y de su ingenio. Varios adversarios se opusieron a su opinión. Rousseau se defendió, y de una en otra disputa se halló involuntariamente alistado en la carrera de las letras.

The second *Discourse* is described as full of daring and extravagant ideas, such as that men are equal and were born to live in isolation; yet the work is credited with "hermosos y brillantes coloridos" and an eloquence comparable only to that of the ancients. *"La carta escrita a d'Alembert* comprende entre algunas paradojas las más importantes y palpables verdades"; but in spite of his hostile attitude toward the theater, Rousseau has written

---

[13]No. 313, November 24, 1789.
[14]No. 317, December 9, 1789.

a *pastorela, el Adivino de la Aldea* "cuya música y poesía están llenas de sales y gracia; . . . respira sencillez e inocencia campestre: todo es agradable, todo interesante y muy superior a los fútiles e insípidos dramas del día, puestos en moda entre nuestros modernos." His dictionary of music is described as one of the best of its kind; the articles connected with literature are especially touched with strokes of beauty.

La nueva Heloísa, "publicada en 1761 dividida en 6 partes, en tomos de 12.," is described as a novel whose plot shows little skill,

. . . pero le sucede lo que a todas las producciones del ingenio que se encuentran al lado de ciertas bellezas muchas defectos.

Si hubiese más viveza en los caracteres y más precisión en las narraciones lo juzgaríamos más digno de precio: los personajes que hablan en él son monótonos, y su lenguage es violento y exagerado. Algunas de sus cartas son admirables por la vehemencia y fuerza de la expresión, por el calor de sus sentimientos y por el cúmulo de desordenadas ideas que caracterizan una pas¡ón conducida a su último término ¿pero por qué una carta llena de afectos penetrantes ha de estar las más veces mezclada de unas digresiones frías, de una crítica insípida o de una paradoja enfadosa? ¿por qué se siente uno helado después de haber conocido todo el fuego de unos sentimientos vivos? seguramente no puede consistir sino en que ninguno de los personages son verdaderamente interesantes. El de *Saint-Preux* es débil, y a veces forzado y violento: *Julia* es un conjunto de ternura y de piedad, de grandeza de alma y de coquetería, de naturalidad y de pedantismo. *Volmar* es un hombre violento y cuyo carácter está fuera del natural. En fin en vano ha querido el autor variar su tono y tomar el de sus personajes; se trasluce el esfuerzo que hace para sostenerse; todo esfuerzo oprime a un autor y enfría el espíritu del lector.

The writer of the article was apparently not so familiar with the work on education, for it is called "La Emilia" and the comments on it are more general.

Los preceptos del autor están expresados con la fuerza y nobleza de un corazón poseído de las grandes verdades de la moral. . . . Su estilo es único: no obstante parece afectado y áspero, y procura acercarse al de Montaña [Montaigne], de quien es grande panegirista, y del cual ha renovado varias opiniones y expres¡ones. Lo lastimoso es que deseando educar un joven cristiano, ha llenado el tercer tomo de mil objecciones contra el cristianismo; con efecto hace un elogio (bien que debido y justo) del Evangelio, y una pintura maravillosa de su Divino Autor, pero ataca impiamente y sin consideración alguna los milagros y profecías. Como el autor no admite religión alguna, y que sólo se gobierna siguiendo los sentimientos de la Naturaleza quiere sujetarlo todo a su engañosa razón; así lo separa ésta tanto de lo justo que lo pone en la funesta inquietud con que siempre vivió.

Las cartas de Montaña is characterized, the reviewer states, by less eloquence and more insipid digressions; in the letter [to Beaumont] the errors of the author "resplandecían con el adorno de la más viva e insidiosa elocuencia." The critic concludes his article with the following general estimate of Rousseau:

Su carácter y sus opiniones eran verdaderamente raras; la naturaleza produjo en él cierto germen de singularidad; pero el arte contribuyó infinito a aumentar su extravagancia: se separó en cuanto pudo de todo cuanto hacían los demás, sin duda por no querer encontrar un hombre semejante a él; este extraordinario modo de pensar y de vivir le grangeó algún nombre, y tal vez por esto quizás ostentó demasiada singularidad, ya sea por su conducta, como por sus escritos. Semejante al antiguo Filósofo *Diógenes*, unía la sencillez y pureza de sus costumbres con el orgullo y variedad de su genio. Procuró siempre atraerse la atención de las gentes por las vivas pinturas que hacía de su desgracia y pobreza, aunque a la verdad sus infortunios fuesen menores de lo que él pensaba y decía; pudiendo asegurarse y ponerse al abrigo de su indigencia con los recursos que le prestaba su gran talento. Era caritativo, bienhechor, sobrio, justo; se contentaba con lo puramente necesario, y despreciaba los medios que podían haberle proporcionado riquezas y altos puestos. Jamás habló de la virtud con aquel énfasis estudiado de muchos sofistas, siempre inspiró por ésta los sentimientos más puros y más conformes a la buena razón que cabe en la buena moral: cuando ha hablado de las obligaciones del hombre, de los principios esenciales de nuestra felicidad, del respecto que nos debemos a nosotros mismos, y de los deberes para con nuestro semejante, ha sido siempre con un entusiasmo, con un exceso y una fuerza que sólo puede dictarlo el del corazón. Se cebó desde muy temprano con la lectura de los autores griegos y romanos; y las virtudes republicanas que en éstos se hallan también pintadas, le traspusieron más allá de los límites prescritos por las leyes del patriotismo. Dominado por su imaginación, admiraba todo en los antiguos; y no veía en sus contemporaneos sino espíritus débiles y cuerpos degenerados y corrompidos. Sus ideas sobre la política han sido tan extraordinarias como sus paradojas sobre la religión. Su *Contrato social* que Voltaire llamaba *Contrato insocial* está llena de contradicciones, de errores, y de ciertos rasgos dignos de un pincel cínico; a más de esto es obscuro, mal rumeado y nada digno de su brillante pluma. . . . Dícese que Rousseau tenía entre sus papeles varios escritos, y que entre éstos estaban las *Memorias de su vida;* presúmese con fundamento que habrá en éstas rasgos singulares y extravagantes, y el público prevenido a favor de todas las producciones de este autor, no podrá dejar de recibirla con la mayor satisfacción.[15]

The most liberal of the Spanish periodicals of the era was *El Espíritu de los Mejores Diarios,* established under the editorship of Christóval Cladera and the protection of Floridablanca. As its ostensible purpose was to give a review of world thought for the benefit of Spanish readers, it was possible through extracts and summaries of foreign articles to present views and to utter opinions that might otherwise not have been sanctioned in Spain. In each number there were reviews of works on religion, science, and art; but historical and literary publications were given major attention. In this miscellaneous collection there are many references to Rousseau, both complimentary and otherwise, more often openly in the latter vein. But it is quite possible to get a rather clear notion of his principal teachings from a careful perusal of these eleven volumes, as may be seen from a few of the references to articles concerning him.

In Spedalieri's refutation[16] of the chapters of Gibbon which undertake an examination of the influence of Christianity,[17] Rousseau shares in the general condemnation expressed toward Bayle, Diderot, and Voltaire, all of whose doctrines are said to contradict each other constantly.[18] A Dutch reviewer of Raynal's *Philosophical History*[19] compares the reception of this work at Geneva with that accorded *Émile,* both books having been burnt and their authors proscribed. Many of Raynal's passages are termed eloquent; in these the author is said to show "la fecundidad

---

[15]This statement suggests that the review was written after 1778 but before 1782, when *Les Confessions* appeared.
[16]Abstracted from the *Diario eclesiástico* of Pisa.
[17]*Decline and Fall of the Roman Empire,* Vol. I.
[18]No. 137, July 4, 1788.
[19]Nos. 162–164.

de Rousseau y su vehemencia, pero más naturalidad y rapidez, pues domina su asunto, su lengua, piensa con rectitud y se exprime con calor y felicidad."

More favorably disposed toward Rousseau is Madame Levacher de Valincourt, who replied to Cabarrús' objections to the admission of women to learned societies.

> Juan Santiago para mí es un ente que no he podido definir; le he creído hombre de bien por principios; y filósofo por ostentación; dijo y quiso decir grandes cosas; pero aun ignoro si se entendió a sí mismo; muchas de sus *cartas de la Montaña* y su *Contrato social* me han presentado este problema.[20]

On other reviewers, too, the Genevan had evidently made a good impression, for one of his statements serves as the basis for a comparison in connection with Volney's *Voyage en Egypte et en Syrie*.[21]

There is considerable space given to discussions of the arguments presented in the first *Discourse*. Formey's answer to the question "Has knowledge corrupted morals?" which was read before the royal academy of Berlin, is reprinted. [22] In another defense of letters, Jacobo Antillana Nuero lists Rousseau among those who have abused them. But this abuse, the Spanard says, only proves an established fact—that in literature, as in every other human work, there are many defects.

> Pero por esto, ¿abandonaremos el estudio de las ciencias? ¿condenaremos las tareas de aquellos hombres estimables, que trabajan por hacerse útiles a sus semejantes; o querremos emboscarnos entre las fieras, sumergiéndonos en la más profunda ignorancia, como quiso el célebre maniático Ginebrino?[23]

The review of Carli's continuation of Ulloa's *Cartas americanas* offered another opportunity.

> Todas estas especulaciones *filosóficas* sobre el estado de la naturaleza y sobre el hombre silvestre . . . han venido a parar en sistemas absurdos y en paradojas tan extravagantes como peligrosas pues no han faltado hombres extraordinarios que con toda la energía

---

[20]No. 77, December 29, 1787.
[21]No. 9, July 21, 1787.
[22]Nos. 244–245, August 2–9, 1790.
[23]No. 156, November 24, 1788.

y aparato de la elocuencia han sostenido que el hombre enteramente salvaje, sin ningún uso de la razón, sin comunicación alguna con sus semejantes, se hallaba en el estado de perfección que conviene a su naturaleza, y por consiguiente mucho mejor y más feliz que el hombre que vive en sociedad.[24]

The return to nature is also discussed in a review of Boulanger's posthumous works; in this "Un Solitario" considers various views concerning the causes of evil and the means of attaining happiness.

Juan Santiago había visto estas causas de nuestros males en la falta que cometieron los hombres de civilizarse, de unirse en Sociedad, de establecerse leyes, y de haber abandonado los bosques en que habían nacido, y a los que nos enviaba segunda vez para que fuésemos felices.[25]

A refuter of Manuel de Aguirre's article on behalf of civil and religious tolerance, which had appeared in *El Correo*, refers often and at length to Rousseau, cites, in French, passages, with chapter and section numbers, largely from the *Social Contract* and the *Discourse on Inequality*, but claims that his knowledge of those works was derived indirectly through Bergier's *Deísmo refutado*. The Spaniard defends the governmental policy which attempted to protect its citizens from the false ideas of the philosophers, especially Voltaire and Rousseau, and claims that it is the duty of the state as well as the church to guard all against such perverse ideas. Especially are the political teachings of Rousseau satirized, but nevertheless clearly stated. After reviewing the fundamental teachings of the *Social Contract,* he says:

Estas horibles máximas bastan para trastornar el mundo y hacer una anarquía universal, pero ciñéndonos ahora sólo al orden de la religión y costumbres, vea el filósofo sin preocupación las monstruosas consecuencias que infaliblemente se deducen de su doctrina, y si habría sociedad más extravagante que una compuesta de individuos que pensasen de este modo. Consulte al citado Rousseau, y á pesar de su irreligión le dirá que *parece ser cierto que si el hombre nació para la sociedad, la religión más verdadera es también*

24No. 182, May 25, 1789.
25Nos. 209–210, November 30, December 7, 1790.

la más social y la más humana. Verdad que no puedan dejar de confesar hasta los impíos. . . .

Ideas of political reforms were clearly abroad in Spain by this time, for the writer continues:

Nadie había puesto en duda la Soberana autoridad para castigar todo género de delitos hasta que inventado por Rousseau el famoso pacto social se fué propagando una doctrina capaz de trastornar las monarquías si no se atajan en tiempo sus efectos; apenas sale hoy alguno de tantos librejos como inundan a la Europa, que no nos canse con sus declamaciones a favor *de la humanidad, el bien de las sociedades, la natural libertad del hombre, la igualdad con sus semejantes, la tiranía de la dominación* sobre los entes de su misma especie, con otras mil expresiones vagas que sólo conspiran a romper toda subordinación y fomentar con la impunidad de los delitos el desenfreno de las pasiones. . . .

Further on in the discussion, the writer remarks:

La filosofía de los libertinos enseña a los hombres a resistir el yugo de la sociedad, les pinta como tiránico el dominio de los Señores temporales, y les hace creer que a su natural libertad repugna la obediencia a sus iguales. Con tales máximas sólo puede establecerse una república imaginaria y arruinarse las que se fundaron sobre los principios más sólidos. Cada individuo podrá burlarse de las disposiciones que no le sean agradables, y alegando el pequeño código del pacto social, reclamará su antigua libertad, *haciendo ver que sólo se unió en sociedad con las condiciones precisas para afirmar la seguridad y quietud que buscaba, y que cediendo una corta parte de aquella no quiso obligarse a la observancia de las leyes que no giren al preciso fin que se propuso.*

The writer had evidently searched the works of Rousseau for arguments to support his own contentions, for he stated that Rousseau did not argue for religious tolerance, but, in drafting a constitution, had demanded that a nation have a single religious faith, prohibited the practice of any other without permission of the sovereign, and insisted that dissenters be punished by death.[26]

The teachings of the *Social Contract* were further discussed before the Academy of Santa Bárbara at Madrid by Cladera, the editor of the periodical. He stated that some moderns thought that the people had selected their

_____

[26]Nos. 175–177, April 6–20, 1789.

leaders, and for that reason claimed the power and rights which those in power exercised.

> *Las sociedades comenzaron eligiendo los pueblos a los soberanos, y formando aqu(e)llos ciertas convenciones con éstos para su mutua seguridad;* así se explica un filósofo, cuyo orgullo le hizo despreciar lo que más debía respetar. Habiéndose erigido maestro de los hombres quiso enseñarles los primeros fundamentos de su existencia en cuerpos de naciones. Pero si la opinión [de Hobbes] que acabo de combatir es quimérica, no lo es menos la del autor del *Contrato Social;* ¡con cuánta imprudencia se han atrevido ciertos oráculos a proferir sentencias las más absurdas!

Cladera then shows that since history records no such contract among any people, none was ever made.[27]

One of the most direct in voicing with approval the political views of Rousseau was Valentín de Foronda, a Basque, for a time a member of the economic society, a teacher in its seminary at Vergara, later in charge of the Spanish embassy in the United States,[28] and closely associated with the liberal group in Spain from 1809 to 1814. In his *Cartas económico-políticas*, first published serially in *El Espíritu*,[29] he asserts that the rights of man embrace "el derecho de propiedad, libertad, y seguridad." The meaning of these terms he explains thus:

> Por derecho de propiedad entiendo aquella prerogativa concedida al hombre por el autor de la naturaleza de ser dueño de su persona, de su industria, de sus talentos y de los frutos que logre por sus trabajos. Por el derecho de libertad entiendo la facultad de usar como uno quiera de los bienes adquiridos, y de hacer todo aquello que no vulnere la propiedad, la libertad y seguridad de los demás hombres, y por el derecho de seguridad entiendo que no puede haber fuerza ninguna que me oprima por ningún tipo, y que jamás puedo ser víctima del capricho o del rencor del que manda. En estos principios está cifrado el acierto de los gobiernos; ellos son los elementos de las leyes; el Monarca de la naturaleza los ha escrito sobre el hombre, sobre sus órganos, y sobre su entendimiento, y no sobre débiles pergaminos que pueden ser despedazados por el furor de la superstición o de la tiranía.[30]

---

[27]No. 132, June 9, 1788.

[28]Spell, J. R., "An Illustrious Spaniard in Philadelphia—Valentín de Foronda," in *Hispanic Review*, IV (1936), 136–140.

[29]Nos. 154–164, November 10, 1788–January 19, 1789.

[30]No. 155, November 17, 1788.

In discussing the problem of emigration, he urged that it be prevented by increasing the contentment and happiness of the people at home.

El hombre nace libre, y sólo está sujeto mientras su debilidad no le permite entrar a gozar de los derechos de su independencia: al punto que llega a hacer uso de su razón es dueño de elegir el país y el gobierno que se combina mejor con sus ideas. Si los hombres se han reunido en sociedad, si se han sometido a un jefe, si han sacrificado una parte de su libertad, ha sido por mejorar su suerte. . . .[31]

His articles continued to be published in the periodical for some months; they were then, on the advice of a friend high in authority, judiciously discontinued, but were reprinted with additions in 1793 by permission of Godoy.

If a Spaniard, after reading all these comments on Rousseau's ideas, still had any curiosity about his literary style, it would have been satisfied by an article comparing him and Buffon as writers.

Rousseau tiene la elocuencia del genio . . . analiza cada idea . . . desenvuelve y reune todas las sensaciones que produce un objeto . . . El Ginebrino escribió para oyentes. . . . En las bellas amplificaciones se deleita . . . y casi se enagena en sus pensamientos, se complace en ellos, y les da mil vueltas hasta haberlos agotado enteramente, parecido a un círculo que en el agua más pura y tranquila se ensancha hasta desaparecer de un todo. . . . Rousseau por un efecto de su carácter siempre se hace el centro de sus ideas; éstas le son más personales que propias a su asunta, y la obra sólo presenta su autor. . . . Rousseau, en fin comunicó el movimiento a todos los sentidos que da a la naturaleza. . . .[32]

Of the many comments on Rousseau published in this periodical, the most stinging for the devout Catholic was probably that embodied in a letter of Brissot de Warville to Pedro de Castro, a canon of the cathedral at Seville, who had boldly proclaimed that the University of Paris had never produced such a saint as Thomas Aquinas. To this Brissot assented, but with this comment:

[31]No. 155, November 17, 1788.
[32]No. 82, January 10, 1788.

Confieso que ni *el espíritu de las leyes* ni el *contrato social* valen nada al lado de la *Suma;* ¿pero qué haré yo si el gusto está corrumpido, y si se lee a Rousseau, ignorando la existencia de la *Suma?*[33]

The *Diario de Madrid,* a contemporary of *El Correo* and *El Espíritu,* contributed many references to *Pygmalion* which will be discussed in the following chapter. In an article concerning music in the theater, a reference to the orchestra of the king of Poland, as pictured in Rousseau's *Dictionary of Music,* reveals that that work must have been familiar to the writer.[34]

The days of freedom of expression through the press were meanwhile rapidly drawing to a close. The royal decree of February 24, 1791, and the order of the Council on April 12 brought both the *Espíritu de los Mejores Diarios* and *El Correo de Madrid* to an end. Only the *Diario de Madrid*[35] was permitted to continue, and its issues were closely censored. Almost twenty years were to elapse before Spanish writers, under a constitution which granted freedom of the press, were to find periodicals generally available for the discussion of such controversial subjects.

---

[33]No. 37, September 27, 1787.
[34]*Diario de Madrid,* XV (February 9, 1790), 159.
[35]Altamira, *Historia de España,* IV, 332, but Godoy says *La Gaceta de Madrid.*

CHAPTER VI

PYGMALION AND THE SPANISH STAGE

Rousseau was not only read and discussed in Spain; at least one work of his was seen and heard in the theaters there soon after the work became known in other parts of Europe. As early as 1762 he had written what was described by a friend as "an admirable piece—a drama in one act for one actor . . . Pygmalion";[1] but it was not until the spring of 1770, while the Genevan was passing a short but happy period with friends in Lyons, after his return from England, that music was set to it, or the play acted.[2] News of the event traveled quickly to Paris, and soon comments upon the novelty were circulated through some of the private journals.[3] The text itself was printed in the *Mercure de France,* at Vienna, and at Geneva, in 1771; at Vienna and Brussels the following year; but not until 1775 did a version authorized by Rousseau issue from a Paris press. Another Paris edition appeared in 1781, and one in Brussels in 1786.[4]

In the meantime the vogue of *Pygmalion* had swept over Europe; and translations were general. Ten versions appeared in Italian in the '70's; seven in the '80's; and two as late as 1809.[5] Seven German translations were published between 1771 and 1788.[6] These printed versions were only an index to its popularity on the stage. First

---

[1]Julie de Bondeli to Dr. Zimmerman, January 21, 1763. In Ed. Bodeman, *Julie de Bondeli . . .,* Hanover, 1874, 249. Quoted by Edgar Estel, "La Partition originale du Pygmalion de J. J. Rousseau," *Annales de la Société Jean Jacques Rousseau,* I, Geneva, 1905, 141.

[2]Istel, *op. cit.,* 142.

[3]Fr. M. Grimm, *Correspondance littéraire . . .,* IX, Paris, 1879, 22–23; [Bachaumont, etc.], *Mémoires secrets,* London, 1780, V, 136.

[4]Th. Dufour, *Recherches bibliographiques,* Paris, 1925, I, 219–222.

[5]Mario Schiff, "Éditions et Traductions italiennes des Oeuvres de Jean-Jacques Rousseau," in *Revue des Bibliothèques,* 1908, 18–29.

[6]Edgar Istel, *Die Entstehung des deutschen Melodramas,* Berlin and Leipzig, 1906, 4; Dufour, *op. cit.,* I, 223; O. G. Sonneck, *Catalogue of Opera Librettos Published Before 1800,* Washington, 1904, I, 874.

presented in Paris in 1775, the work was already well known in Germany, for it had been given several times at Weimar in 1772 with the music of Schweitzer, and in Vienna with that of Aspelmeier. It was performed at Gotha in 1779, and many times later with the music of Benda; at Mannheim 14 times before 1803; at Berlin 35 times between 1797 and 1835; and at Weimar again in 1798, 1811, and 1816.[7] In Italy it was at the height of its popularity in the last decade of the century, the favorite setting being that of Cimador.[8]

The secret of the popularity of this *scène lyrique* lay in the novel use of orchestral music and gesture as a means of intensifying the emotional effect of declamation. Rousseau, himself, did not employ music as an accompaniment to the spoken words, but introduced it in the pauses, during which the actor suggested his feelings through gesture. The music consisted of an overture and interludes; but instead of these being, as formerly, unrelated compositions, which suggested, at the most, some exterior action, Rousseau intended that the music should express the emotions of the character. In conception *Pygmalion* was a synthetic work, in which declamation, recitative, gesture, and music all functioned equally. Drama and music were to alternate; the orchestra was to prepare for the spoken word and to interpret the mimicry of the actor. In *Pygmalion* Rousseau sought the union of word, gesture and music, in an advance toward dramatic perfection. The German composers, in their settings of *Pygmalion* and other texts modeled on it, advanced much further musically toward the goal Rousseau sought than he himself did; for they not only added an instrumental accompaniment to the spoken words but, by introducing and using repeatedly the *leitmotif* as a means of intensifying the impression of the emotions portrayed, they employed the very device which Wagner later utilized in accomplishing that unification of the arts, to which Rousseau, in *Pygmalion*, pointed the way.

---

[7] Istel, *Entstehung*, 4–5; 61.
[8] Schiff, *op. cit.*, 25–29.

Interest in the new form was immediate among both literati and musicians; as a result imitations quickly found their way to the French and the German stage. Among these was *Ariadne at Naxos* (Gotha, 1775), with music by Benda, which was given at Paris in 1781, and held a high place in leading theaters, such as that at Mannheim and Weimar, until 1814.[9] This melodrama and *Medea,* with music by the same composer, aroused the enthusiasm of Mozart, who at once planned a similar work.[10] Goethe was lured by the charms of *Pygmalion* to the creation of that most perfect flower in the whole field of melodrama— *Proserpina* (Weimar, 1778). The music consisted of accompanied and unaccompanied declamation and accompanied song, connected by orchestral passages.[11] In the many melodramas produced in Central Europe between 1775 and 1800 the main character was generally a woman of classical lore—Dido, Andromeda, or Cleopatra—who revealed her pain in endless monologues. The male actors, when present, played a minor rôle.

After such a cordial reception in other parts of Europe, not to mention the many imitations, adaptations, and parodies that followed, it is not surprising that *Pygmalion* should have found its way into the Spanish theater, even though Rousseau's works were all prohibited in Spain. Spanish leanings towards French drama were so pronounced in court circles that translations of works on the *Index* were sometimes permitted publication provided the writer's name did not appear on the title page; and prohibited French plays were performed with little protest, so long as the name of the author was not blazed abroad. How early this *scène lyrique* was produced in Spain in its original language the writer does not know; it was probably given in the French theaters of the *sitios reales,* established by Aranda. There is some evidence that it was performed in the French theater in Cadiz which, in spite

---

[9]Istel, *Entstehung,* 21; F. Gaiffe, *Le Drame en France au XVIII*[e] *Siècle,* Paris, 1910, 237.
[10]L. Nohl, *Mozarts Briefe,* Salzburg, 1865, 220.
[11]Istel, *Entstehung,* 88–93.

of the efforts of the French ambassador, was finally closed, on account of the opposition to French plays there.[12]

Yet the French theaters were not the only channel through which *Pygmalion* entered Spain, for it came in by another little suspected—by way of the Spanish Jesuits in Italy. Only a few years after the work was performed in Paris, Manuel Lassala, one of the exiled members of that order, was busy in Bologna, making an Italian translation, which was published in 1783 in a volume entitled *Ormasinda. Tragedia. Con alcune scene liriche*, one of which was "Pimmalione del Sig. Giangiacomo Rousseau, tradotto del francese."[13] When this reached Valencia, Eusebio de Canas made a Spanish translation which was used in the theaters but apparently remained unpublished.[14] Other evidence that the work was known to Spanish playwrights before 1785 is to be found in the notation of Ramón de la Cruz, in granting permission for the publication of a tragedy *Pigmaleón* submitted in that year by Joseph María de Meras, that the work contained "muchas imitaciones de otra extranjera."[15]

That the Madrid public had the opportunity of knowing this work of Rousseau in 1788 we have ample proof. On January 25, at the Coliseo de los Caños del Peral, at that time the center of Italian opera, *Pygmalion* was given in French by Mr. d'Ainville with Rosa Peligrini taking the part of Galatea. Indisposition of the prima donna of the Italian company was given as the reason for this presentation. A prose translation was made available on

---

[12]A member of the French legation wrote: "They reckoned no less than sixteen heretical assertions in the single piece of *Pygmalion*."— Chevalier de Burgoanne, *Travels in Spain*. Translated from the French of the 3rd edition (Paris, 1803), in John Pinkerton, *A General Collection of the Best and Most Interesting Voyages and Travels . . .*, V, London, 1809, 532.

[13]Carlos Sommervogel, *Bibliothèque de la Compagnie de Jésus*, Paris, 1893, col. 1544. This translation is not mentioned by Schiff.

[14]Justo Pastor Fuster, *Biblioteca valenciana*, Valencia, 1827–1830, 330.

[15]A.H.N. Matrículas de imprenta, 5551, No. 2. Dated August 3, 1788.

February 1 for the use of the audience;[16] from that Francisco Durán made a version in verse which was published in the *Memorial literario* for January of that year. Since this is the first Spanish translation of any complete work of Rousseau published openly, it is reprinted in full in the appendix.[17] In the issue of January 27 of the *Diario de Madrid* the story of Pygmalion, as told by Ovid, is summarized. Rousseau is referred to merely as "un ingenio extrangero" who has written a modern version. On February 2, a poem, *Pygmalion*, signed F. G. S., appeared in the same publication.

Other translations quickly followed. In that same year a version by the *sainete* writer González del Castillo was printed in Cadiz and performed in the theater there.[18] A translation made by Juan Diego Roxo was printed in Madrid,[19] and another, of which the translator was probably the indefatigable Francisco Mariano Nipho, was issued in 1790 with both civil and ecclesiastical approval.[20] By the time the 1790 edition of the *Index* was issued—this prohibited all of Rousseau's works to all classes of

---

[16]Cf. *Diario de Madrid*, January 25–27, February 1, 1788.

[17]*Memorial literario*, XIII (January, 1788), 163–174.

[18]Juan Ignacio González del Castillo, *Pigmaleón. Versión parafrástica, en metro castellano endecasílabo, escena lírica original francés, representada en 1788. Cádiz, en la imprenta de D. Juan Jiménez Carreño.* (Listed, but not printed, in *Sainetes de D. Juan Ignacio de González del Castillo*, Cadiz, 1846, IV, p. lx. Also listed, but not printed, by Leopoldo Cano in *Obras completas de Don Juan Ignacio de González del Castillo*, Madrid, 1914.)

[19]"*Pigmalión*. Escena lírica, traducida del francés al castellano por D. Juan Diego Roxo. Papel en 4° de 12 p. Madrid, por Antonio Fernández, 1788."—This bibliographical note, followed by a brief summary of the text, appeared in *Memorial literario*, XIII (February, 1788, 294. The text is probably the same as that advertised in the *Diario de Madrid*, January 30, 1788, as follows:

"Pigmalion. Scena lírica; traducida del Francés al Castellano. Se vende en las librerías de Esparza puerta del Sol y de Francés calle de las Cartetas. Su precio un real. Puede ir en carta. Este Poemita es el que se ha representado en francès en el coliseo de los Caños del Peral en estos días, mereciendo de los inteligentes el mismo aplauso que en otros teatros de Europa, por la valentía de sus afectos y viveza de sus expresiones, que se han procurado conservar en la traducción."

[20]*Pigmalión. Monólogo patético traducido de* [sic] *francés libremente, y aumentado en verso castellano por* D. F. M. N. There is a copy in the Biblioteca Nacional, and also in the Biblioteca Municipal.

readers—there were at least five and probably six Spanish translations of *Pygmalion* in general circulation.

Even before it was thus generally known, the work had caught the attention of a Spanish writer, Tomás de Iriarte, who was also a practical musician and much interested in orchestral music.[21] In 1789 he wrote an imitation of *Pygmalion,* which became the model for many Spanish *monólogos,* or *unipersonales* as they came to be called. This was *Guzmán el Bueno,*[22] which was given its *première* at Cadiz that same year, and was then presented in Madrid at the Príncipe from February 26 until March 8, 1791, when the annual theatrical season closed. Three editions of the play quickly followed; and both the form and subject matter became topics for much discussion. The special interest of Iriarte's work, from a literary standpoint, is due to the adaptation of Spanish subject matter to this new form; while the score, also the work of Iriarte, is noteworthy, for it not only echoes Haydn, the father of chamber music, in thought-content but also reveals points of remarkable similiarity with the score that Rousseau is believed to have written for *Pygmalion* after realizing how far short of his conception the original setting of Coignet fell.[23] Clearly Iriarte, in his music, scored for strings, flute, oboe, clarinet, and trumpet, followed Rousseau rather than any of the German composers of melodramatic music, who added accompaniments to the spoken text, or any of the Italians, who insisted upon having the words sung; for the Spaniard added music only

---

[21]In Iriarte's *Poema de la Música* (Madrid, 1779), which passed through many editions and was translated into English, French, and Italian, the influence of Rousseau's treatises on music are visible. Cf. Menéndez y Pelayo, *Ideas estéticas,* VI, 403.

[22]*Guzmán el Bueno: soliloquio ú escena trágica unipersonal con música en sus intervalos. Por Dn. Tomás de Iriarte.* "Un cuaderno en 8°" announced in the *Gaceta* of February 25, 1791. (Cf. E. Cotarelo y Mori, *Iriarte y su época,* Madrid, 1897, 403.) A Cadiz edition had been issued in 1790, according to José Subirá, "Los 'Melólogos' de Rousseau, Iriarte y otros autores," in *Revista de la biblioteca, archivo y museo,* V, 1928, 146.

[23]Subirá, *op. cit.,* 142–146, who follows E. Istel, *Jean Jacques Rousseau als Komponist seiner lyrischen Scene "Pygmalion,"* Leipzig, 1901.

"in the intervals." That Iriarte's model for this *escena trágica unipersonal* was generally known in Spain at that time is shown by some of the lines of the "Introducción" which Comella wrote to precede its performance.

> "¿Pues por qué ha de pareceros
> extraño que un español
> haga el Guzmán? Dime, ¿el cielo
> hizo distinción de climas
> cuando repartió el talento?
> Además, este Guzmán
> también en Cádiz se ha hecho,
> en donde igualó el aplauso
> a su gran merecimiento.
> ¿El Pigmaleón en Madrid
> no mereció un gran concepto?
> ¿Conque el pueblo de esta corte
> no habrá de gustar de ello
> porque lo hace un español,
> porque es español su ingenio?"[24]

So enthusiastic was the reception accorded the work of Iriarte that imitations soon followed. Its earliest rival for popularity was *El Hijo de Guzmán,* or *El joven Pedro de Guzmán,* an *escena unipersonal* presented in 1793. The music consisted of an overture and eight single numbers; the language was exceedingly high-flown; but the value of the whole was slight, and the work soon disappeared from the stage. Of much greater interest from the standpoint of literary history was a parody written by Félix Samaniego. This Basque had little love to waste on Iriarte, because of the rivalry which had developed over their fables, but he was interested in the theater and in Rousseau, with whose works he was thoroughly familiar.[25] After reading Iriarte's *monólogo,* Samaniego wrote to his uncle, Mariano Urquijo:

Apenas leí el *Soliloquio de Guzmán el Bueno,* exclamé: ¡perdidos somos! El maldito ejemplo de Pigmaleón, perdóneme su mérito, nos va a inundar la escena de una nueva casta de locos. La pereza de

---

[24]Quoted by Subirá, *op. cit.,* 146–147.
[25]See Samaniego's "Carta sobre el teatro," published anonymously in *El Censor,* January, 1786. It is reprinted in *Obras críticas de D. Félix María de Samaniego,* Bilboa, 1898, 81–102.

nuestros ingenios encontrará un recurso cómodo para lucirlo en el teatro, sin el trabajo de pelear con las dificultades que ofrece el diálogo. Cualquiera poetastro elegirá un hecho histórico, o un pasage fabuloso, o inventará un argumento; extenderá su razonamiento, lo sembrará de contrastes, declamaciones, apóstrofes y sentencias, hará hablar a su héroe una o dos horas con el cielo ó con la tierra, con las paredes o con los muebles de su cuarto; procurará hacernos soportable tal delirio con la distracción de *allegro, adagio, largo, presto,* con *sordinas* o sin ellas; y se saldrá nuestro hombre con ser autor de un soliloquio, monólogo o escena trágico-cómico-lírica unipersonal.

"Esta idea me hizo tomar la pluma al momento y poniendo delante a *Guzmán el Bueno,* sin más que seguir su soliloquio, y variar o quitar o añadir lo conveniente a mi objeto, hice mi parodia: leíla, y me pareció una bagatela que podía bastar á cortar los progresos de la monologuimanía, que iba a dominar á nuestros autorcillos."[26]

Samaniego's work was never performed, for while it was in the publisher's hands Iriarte died; and its author felt impelled to recall the manuscript."[27] His prophecy— "nos va a inundar la escena de una nueva casta de locos"— was, however, fulfilled. *Melólogos,* serious and comic, in translations from other languages and in original Spanish, appeared both in the public theaters and in private performances. By 1793 *Ariadna abandonada en Naxos, Hero y Leandro* (translated from French prose to Spanish verse), and *Dido abandonada* were on sale in printed form in Madrid, according to the *Gacetas* of that year; and all appeared on the stage.[28] *Policena,* "escena trágica," was given in 1794.[29] The similarity of the subject matter of these *melólogos* with those produced in Germany and France is striking. *Ariadna* had traveled from Gotha in 1775 to Mannheim, Weimar, and Paris.[30] *Dido,* with text by Goué, given at Munich in 1779, was included in Lassala's volume of 1783; in the translation of Eusebio de

---

[26]"La respuesta de mi tío sobre lo que verá el curioso lector, publicado contra la voluntad de su merced, con licencia, año 1792," in *Obras inéditas o poco conocidas del insigne fabulista Don Félix María de Samaniego,* Victoria, 1866, 218–219.

[27]*Ibid.,* 101–102.

[28]Cotarelo y Mori, *Iriarte,* 403.

[29]José Subirá, "La escena trágica 'Policena,'" in *Revista de la biblioteca, archivo y museo,* V, 1928, 360–364.

[30]Istel, *Entstehung,* 21.

Canas, it became popular in Spain.[31] Other titles of "melólogos," produced in Madrid that same year, indicate that Spanish writers were following Iriarte in adapting the form to a Spanish content, for among the productions were *Los amantes de Teruel, El Arnesto, Florinda,* and *El poeta escribiendo un monólogo.* Comella, the most popular writer of plays of that day, turned his attention also to the new *genre;* in 1793 his *La función casera* was presented and two years later *Juan de la Enreda.* Among the comic works of this type were *Don Antón el holgazán, El famoso Rompegalas,* and *El mercader aburrido.*

Something of the evolution of this dramatic *genre* in Spain is sketched in a review of a "melodrama en un acto," *El amor dichoso,* published in *El memorial literario* in September, 1793:

"De algún tiempo a esta parte dieron los poetas en escribir escenas unipersonales, o de una sola persona, que llamaron monólogos. Como para evitar el cansancio ó el fastidio de una representación larga se dividió en intervalos de música, que acompañaba en los discursos las armonías propias de los afectos, llegó a agradar este género de espectáculo, bien que sólo hacía una parte de una función de teatro, mezclando al mismo tiempo otros dramas cortos de un acto o dos ya de música ya sin ella. Pero bien pronto cansaron los monólogos. Sustituyeron a estos algunas representaciones mudas y de vistosas perspectivas, a manera de mal formadas pantomimas, que gustaron poco. De resulta de esto hicieron una especie nueva de piezas que saliesen de monólogos, y ya había diálogos, y trílogos, acompañando siempre los descansos la música instrumental. Todavía salió una cuarta especie, compuesto de canto representado e intervalos de música, queriendo parecerse en la mayor parte a las zarzuelas, aunque las han intitulado óperas y melodramas. Tales son algunas piezas de que ya hemos dadó razón . . . y tal es ésta."

In a review three months later in the same periodical of *Ariadna en Naxos,* a "melodrama en un acto con períodos de música," there is further reference to the confusion of terms descriptive of the new form:

"A este trílogo se da el nombre de melodrama; ¡otra confusión! Melodrama quiere decir verso suave, verso cantado, canto, y aquí no se canta nada; también a la ópera se llamó melodrama. El segundo título, 'con períodos de música,' no explica más ni menos. Ello es

---

[31] *Ibid.,* 96; Fuster, *op. cit.,* II, 330.

una escena tripersonal para hablar mucho sin sustancia entre los espacios músicos."

The enthusiasm for *melólogos* continued in Spain over a quarter of a century, and parallels the period in which similar works were popular in Germany, France, and Italy. The survival of the type even after the French invasion is attested by *Napoleón desesperado* (1808), *El domingo* by Rodríguez de Arellano (1810), and the performance of *Guzmán el Bueno* as late as 1812. The texts assumed various forms; at first the *unipersonales* held the entire attention; slowly a second actor was introduced; and finally melodramas in which any number of characters figured became popular. By 1794 the Italian influence had so far prevailed that in *Policena* one of the characters sings some of her lines as a recitative and others as an aria, both accompanied by the orchestra. The vogue spread to the colonies; *unipersonales* were produced from Buenos Aires to Mexico City.[32] From the literary standpoint, none of the Spanish productions bear comparison with the work of Roùsseau, as was realized by Quintana when he said that *Pygmalion* should have been the only one of its kind ever written;[33] from the musical, only that of Iriarte shows any genuine feeling for the part which the orchestra, according to Rousseau's conception, was to play.

Pygmalion itself did not disappear from the Spanish stage. Although the González del Castillo version was prohibited in 1793,[34] permission was given that same year for the presentation in Madrid of the version printed in 1790.[35] There Rousseau's *scène lyrique* was again presented in 1796 by the Italian opera company playing at Los Caños; for this the music of Cimador, already extremely popular

---

[32]Fernández de Lizardi's *El unipersonal de Agustín de Iturbide* (Mexico, 1823) is an evidence of its popularity in the colonies, even after the vogue had passed in Spain.
[33]"Sobre la poesía castellana del siglo XVIII," in *B.A.E.*, XIX, 151.
[34]*Suplemento al índice expurgatorio del año de 1790*, Madrid, 1805. The edict is dated February 1, 1793.
[35]See note 20.

in Italy, furnished the background.[36] Ferrer de Orga published in 1813 at Valencia a new edition of the translation by "D. F. M. N."[37] Another version of the text by F. Durán, widely used in the theaters, went through three editions by 1816,[38] by which time the melodrama, as conceived by Rousseau, had fairly well run its course both in Spain and in central Europe.

---

[36]Luis Carmena y Millan, *Crónica de la ópera italiana en Madrid*, Madrid, 1878, 37.

[37]Copy in the Biblioteca Nacional at Buenos Aires.

[38]*Pigmalión, escena lírica puesta libremente en verso castellano por Don F. Durán. Tercera edición corregida*, Madrid, 1816. Copy in the British Museum.

CHAPTER VII

EARLY TRACES OF ROUSSEAU IN SPANISH AMERICA

It was not only in Europe that Spanish subjects were coming into contact with Rousseau; his ideas were penetrating at the same time to the colonial world. While Aranda and his group were liberalizing the intellectual circles in Spain, they had as coadjutors in Spanish America various groups: colonists who had come into touch with liberal ideas through travel or reading; foreigners who, either by commission or subterfuge, traveled in or became residents of those regions; administrators who took with them to the western world liberal views; and contrabandists who found, especially in northern South America and Mexico, an easy market for prohibited books. Rousseau's works, their imitations, and refutations filtered into the western colonies from the time Feijóo and the *Mercurios* first called them to the attention of Spaniards. That educated men were reading of Rousseau in Mexico before his works were put on the *Index*, we have already seen; and that the prohibition of 1764 was no more effective abroad than in Spain is indicated by evidence at hand. In all the capitals there were liberal groups; in many of them *sociedades económicas* were organized as early as in parts of Spain. There was one in Santa Fé by 1784, for extracts from its minutes were published in that year.[1] Many wealthy men, such as Maziel in Santa Fé, Funes in Cordoba, and Terrazas in La Plata, had Rousseau's works in their libraries and placed them freely in the hands of those they deemed intellectually superior.

Although state and church conspired in subjecting Spanish America to the regulations laid down by the Council

---

[1] Medina, J. T., *La Imprenta en Bogotá* (Santiago, 1904), 32.

of the Indies for the government of the colonies, the liberal spirit which had penetrated Spanish ministerial circles was also prevalent abroad. There were viceroys of the type of archbishop Caballero in Santa Fé, active in promoting agriculture, commerce, and public instruction; he went so far as to attempt compulsory school attendance. José de Ezpeleta, who succeeded him, followed a similarly liberal program. In Mexico, the Marquis of Croix, himself a Frenchman, had as successors the Gálvez brothers and Revillagigedo; at the far extreme of the colonial world, Argentina had such progressive governors as Bucareli, Cevallos, and Vértiz. Frequently liberals held high posts in ecclesiastical circles, but these were more often the exception than the rule. Among the people, there were naturally many of both high and low rank who regarded any work of Rousseau as an anathema and rushed to the inquisitors with any breath of suspicion; against these, the worldly-wise were judiciously on their guard. The story told by Ségur,[2] the French diplomat who visited Venezeula just after the American Revolution, of the physician in Caracas who kept his greatest treasures, the works of Rousseau and Raynal, hidden in a hollow beam, well out of reach of official investigators, illustrates the conditions that prevailed where the Inquisition gave evidences of a disposition to be active.

By far the most important group of disseminators of the ideas of Rousseau were the young Spanish Americans who traveled or studied in Europe and were there greatly stimulated by personal contacts, the current freedom of speech, and the prevailing spirit of inquiry. Many made the acquaintance of the Genevan's works first under such conditions; unconsciously they were drawn to the French social philosophy; and some returned to their native land completely converted to the theory of revolution. Rousseau and Raynal became the idols of a host of young enthusiasts; among these mention must be made of Francisco

---

[2]Ségur, Comte de, *Mémoires ou souvenirs et anecdotes* (Paris, 1825), I, 455.

Miranda and Simón Rodríguez of Venezuela, Antonio Rojas of Chile, Antonio Nariño of Colombia, Manuel Belgrano of Argentina, and José Baquijano of Peru. By tracing the early contact of these men with the thought of Rousseau, we gain some notion of its general dissemination among cultured Spanish Americans; as in a bird's-eye view, we see the scattering of the seeds that were to ripen later.

Of the many who came into touch with the ideas of Rousseau through various channels, the most effective disseminator was probably Francisco Miranda, the herald of Spanish-American independence. After receiving a good general education at Caracas, Miranda was sent to Spain in 1771; there he obtained a commission in the army. He soon showed himself a devotee of knowledge; among the first books he acquired was Raynal's *Philosophical History*,[3] which portrayed the Spanish government in no pleasing colors. That the South American made the acquaintance of Rousseau early is shown by a list of his books, dated at Madrid, March 6, 1780, in which appear the *Dictionnaire de Musique* and the *Oeuvres de R . . .* in twelve volumes.[4] After being assigned to duty in the New World, he participated in the successful revolt of the British colonies by aiding at the capture of Pensacola. Two years later, being charged with illicit trade in the West Indies, he escaped from the Spanish dominions to the United States. That Rousseau was not entirely absent from his mind at this time is shown by an entry in the journal he kept during his stay in the young republic, for in regard to a meal at the home of John Tracy, at Newburyport, Massachusetts, he records: "Tuvimos nuestra buena comida en el estilo americano, con algo de Doctrina Rusoyca en la combersación (Emilio comparesio en la mesa)."[5] In 1785 he proceeded to London, and from that

---

[3]Miranda Archives, Mss., Vol. I, quoted by Robertson, *The Life of Miranda*, I, 13.

[4]Archivo del General Miranda (Caracas, 1929–1933), VII, 146–147. Hereafter referred to as Archivo-Miranda.

[5]Archivo-Mirando, I, 334.

point set out on travels which took him over the whole
of Europe and brought him into contact with many of the
best minds of that period. In Venice he visited with
Estevan de Arteaga, the author of the treatise on music
already mentioned; from him the traveler secured a list
of all the Spanish-American ex-Jesuits then in Bologna;
from Tomás Belón in Rome, a list containing the name of
Vizcardo, the Peruvian whose papers were to pass into
Miranda's hands.[6] In 1788 he bought the *Confessions* at
Amsterdam, and confided to his diary, under date of May
17, that although poorly written the work was "original
and contributed not a little to a knowledge of the human
heart"; he only wondered that he had not read it earlier.[7]

In the diarial jottings of a trip made through Switzerland and southern France in the latter part of 1788 there
is further evidence of the interest aroused in Miranda by
all that pertained to Rouseau.[8] At Neuchâtel the South
American visited Du Peyroux, who told him of the Genevan and his reasons for writing the *Confessions*. Both
Motiers and the island at Bienne proved to be "exactly
as Rousseau described them." At Berne, Wittenbach offered
to send him Rousseau's works to read. In October he
reached Vevey; there he purchased a copy of the *Nouvelle
Héloïse* in order that he might re-read the descriptions on
the ground; the bookseller guided him to a high terrace
from which the various points mentioned could be clearly
seen. As he traveled on, Miranda made note of other
traces of Rousseau. From the terrace at Geneva he saw
his statue; in the public library, a bust. At the home of
Madame de Karn, his attention was attracted to a copy
of *Émile*. After reaching Marseilles, he visited with
Raynal, who confided to him, while sipping chocolate sent
from Spain by Aranda, that a certain Heredia, connected
with the Spanish diplomatic corps, had furnished him
much of the material concerning Spanish America he had
used in his history. One evening at the theater, Miranda

[6]*Ibid.*, II, 12–22, 69.
[7]*Ibid.*, VII, 175; III, 277–278.
[8]*Ibid.*, IV, 54–188.

saw *Le Devin du Village;* "qué sencillez griega, y buen gusto tiene esta pequeña composición," he noted. On another visit to Raynal, he met the Marquis de la Torre of Havana, who commented on the rapid changes in styles in literature. First agriculture was all the rage; then the *Émile* of Rousseau; for a time everybody read it, talked about it, it was everywhere—then the style changed. After another visit to the theater, Miranda noted: "Después dió el Pigmaleón de Rousseau . . . qué bello razgo de música! . . . qué sublimes lacónicas ideas! . . . justa imagen me parese del *modo* en que girava la Composición Lírica griega. . . ." Soon after, Miranda returned to London where, a fugitive from Spanish justice, he began pleading with British ministers for aid in effecting South-American independence.

Traces of Rousseau as a direct inspiration to revolution in the Spanish colonies were seen even earlier in Chile, where a conspiracy reputedly planned by two inconspicuous Frenchmen, Vergne and Gramuset, and a prominent Chilean, José Antonio Rojas, came to light in 1781. Antonio Gramuset had lived in the country illegally for a number of years, but was finally given naturalization papers as a reward for serving against the Araucanians in 1769. His compatriot, Antonio Alejandro Vergne, a Latin teacher who had come to Santiago from Buenos Aires in 1776, is credited with having read Rousseau. Vergne was learned but impractical; Gramuset, comparatively uneducated. Each had made certain clerical enemies who retaliated by bringing about their arrest on a charge of seditious plotting. Rojas was a descendant of Spanish nobles, thirty years old, and rich.

In the evidence introduced was a projected constitution, an idealistic treatise, based largely on the teachings of Rousseau. The preamble is devoted to a general defense of a republic, while its provisions include the recognition of natural rights as a basis for laws; abolition of slavery; elimination of social distinctions; the distribution of land in equal portions; and government by a senate composed of members chosen by the citizens, among whom the Araucanians were to be numbered. After the triumph of the projected revolution, an army was to be formed; free commerce established; and fraternity of races insisted upon. The Spanish officials were to be dismissed with courtesy, and the ports to remain open to Spanish boats.

While Vergne has been credited with its authorship,[9] the manuscript records of the case[10] give ample proof that the author was a member of a monastic order. Nevertheless the Frenchmen were, in due time, convicted of treason and ordered transported to Spain. One died en route; the other shortly after reaching there. Rojas, thanks to his prominence, escaped punishment, and remained apparently undaunted by his experience. He did not hesitate to term Raynal "un hombre divino," and to regard him as a philosopher worthy of the praise of the whole world and especially of America.[11] While visiting Paris in 1787 he purchased Rousseau's works, which, under misleading binder's titles, he had the temerity to ship to Chile.

Another Spanish American who came under liberal influences abroad was Manuel Belgrano, born in Buenos Aires in 1770. At sixteen he was sent to Salamanca, where French books and ideas were then circulating. Before receiving his law degree in 1793 he had become a member of several organizations interested in political science. Armed with papal permission to read prohibited books, he early became familiar with the writings of Montesquieu, Rousseau, and Filangieri; from these he absorbed the ideas which served as a basis for his theories of government. After his return to Buenos Aires, he soon

---

[9]Amunátegui, M. L., *Los precursores de la independencia de Chile* (Santiago, 1909), III, 208–255. The name Vergne is spelled by this writer as Berney.

[10]Chile Archivo nacional. Real Audiencia 1644. Archivo criminal, Legajo 14. Año de 1781. Testimonio de la causa criminal formada contra Dn. Antonio Vergne y Dn. Antonio Gramuset, franceses.

[11]Amunátegui, M. L., *La crónica de 1810* (Santiago, 1876–1899), II, 49.

became a leader, and his theories served to determine to some extent the character of the revolution.[12]

In Santa Fé was Antonio Nariño, a young enthusiast, the center of a circle of cultured and liberal thinkers. Born in 1765 of an aristocratic Spanish family, he was early appointed to an important government post by the viceroy. In his magnificent library, which housed a splendid collection of books and a portrait of Franklin in the place of honor, eager young Granadians gathered. While Rousseau is not specifically mentioned in the list of authors read aloud, the fact that this literary society planned to ornament the library with phrases of Voltaire, Rousseau, and Montesquieu suggests that the works of these men were not unknown; and Nariño's later life reveals that he was early saturated with the doctrines the *Social Contract* advanced.[13] Among the periodicals current in Santa Fé was *El Espíritu de los mejores diarios,* which, as we have seen, was a disseminator of liberal ideas.

An even more ardent admirer of Rousseau was Simón Rodríguez, born in Venezuela in 1771, who left his native land at the age of fourteen to live successively in Spain, Germany, and France. After reading *Émile,* he became convinced that pedagogy was his vocation; and upon his return to Caracas he set about writing educational treatises and seeking private students or a post as tutor. His wish was granted; he became the guardian and teacher of Simón Bolívar, who was to play the leading rôle in the struggle of South America for independence. Their joint career will be traced in a later chapter.

In Peru, too, traces of Rousseau and the independent spirit were to be found in José Baquíjano, later the Count of Vistaflorida, who while visiting in Spain in 1773, had become acquainted with Olavide and Jovellanos in Seville.

[12]Mitre, Bartolomé, *Historia de Belgrano y de la independencia argentina* (Buenos Aires, 1913), I, 57–61. In 1796 Belgrano published a translation from the French entitled *Principios de la ciencia política.* Cf. Gutiérrez, Juan María, *Origen y desarrollo de la enseñanza pública superior en Buenos Aires* (Buenos Aires, 1915), 389.

[13]Mancini, Jules, *Bolívar y la emancipación de las colonias españolas* (Paris-México, 1914), 83. Cf. also Posada, Eduardo, and Ibañez, Pedro M., *El Precursor* (Bogotá, 1903), 147–179. In the inventory of his library are works by Voltaire and Montesquieu, but none of Rousseau.

The address of welcome with which he greeted the newly-appointed viceroy of Peru in 1781 left his auditors gasping with amazement, for he not only attacked the Spanish court and its rule but set forth views then regarded as utterly subversive of good government. "El bien mismo deja de serlo si se establece y funda contra el voto y opinión del público. . . . Mejorar al hombre contra su voluntad ha sido siempre el engañoso pretexto de la tiranía,"[14] he dared to state.

Although Baquijano, in spite of his wealth and position, was denounced to the Inquisition in 1789, he continued to circulate French works among his friends. Bayle, Voltaire, "las elocuentes declamaciones de Rousseau," and the *Encyclopédie* passed from hand to hand and were devoured by the cultured *criollos* even in "las tranquilas celdas de los graves religiosos." Among the worthy accomplishments of Baquijano was that of founding the *sociedad económica* in Lima in 1790 and of publishing there *El mercurio peruano*.

Nor were traces of Rousseau entirely lacking in Spanish-American letters before the days of the French Revolution. The introductory *loa*, *La Inclusa*, presented with a drama, *Siripo*, on the stage in Buenos Aires in 1789, showed clearly the influence of *Émile*, according to the censor, who noted that it contained "mucho de la impiedad y libertinaje de los filósofos de esta era, entregada a su capricho y corrupción. Se ve derramado, además, el espíritu de 'Rusó,' sin que se ataquen las máximas de Acracia [personaje de la *Loa*], con todo el nervio correspondiente, para extinguir y aniquilar el veneno que difunden."[15] Clearly Rousseau's works must have been known by this Argentinian censor who thought he could detect such resemblances.

---

[14]*Elogio del excelentísimo Sr. D. Agustín de Jáuregui y Aldecoa . . . pronunciado en el recibimiento que como a su Vice-Patrón, le hizo la real Universidad de S. Marcos el diá XXVII de agosto del año de 1781. 82 pp. See also Riva Agüero, José de, "Don José Baquijano de Beascoa y Carrillo de Córdoba, tercer Conde de Vista-florida en el Perú," in *Revista de archivos, bibliotecas y museos*, XLVI, 465–483.

[15]"El tufillo a Juan Jacobo . . . perturbaba grandemente al buen oidor."—García Velloso, Enrique, *Historia de la literatura argentina*, 4th ed. (Buenos Aires, n.d.), 72–73.

CHAPTER VIII

THE SPIRIT OF THE TIMES

In the half century ending in 1793, Spain, in common with the countries of western Europe, was experiencing an awakening. Many of the leading thinkers and administrators became converts to liberal ideas, and began both to circulate and to apply them. Dissemination and application alike aroused a storm of controversy; boldly did supporters of church and state take up the battle in defense of the time-honored institutions whose existence they thought they saw threatened.

In this awakening the works of Rousseau undoubtedly played a part. Although his interests lay with the common people, he nevertheless attracted the attention of Spain's leading thinkers. Through news items, reviews, and discussions by both advocates and opponents, some of his ideas quickly circulated throughout the peninsula and the colonies. In the fifties the substance of his two discourses, as well as that of Grosley, became known through reviews and periodical articles; during the next decade his educational and political treatises entered Spain; and *Pygmalion* followed in the seventies. Both Alba and Miranda had his complete works in their libraries, we know; and that there were other copies of many of the single works is certainly suggested by the numerous articles and refutations directed against them. *Les Confessions* was known in Spain almost as soon as the first part was printed in 1782; while the general facts of Rousseau's life and the basic ideas he advanced were readily available to the reading public through the pages of various periodicals and the *Década epistolar*. Imitations both of *Émile* and *La nouvelle Héloïse* provided a popular form of fiction.

In this period there are ample evidences of the growing realization of the need of greater liberty. For the first time, the Spaniards seem to have become aware that the king was not an instrument of God but of the people—a view then regarded as subversive of good government. Freedom of speech was advocated and even freedom of the press. Social equality was openly urged and as stoutly opposed. We hear echoes of Rousseau's pleas for equality; the abolition of the nobility is suggested; and the education of the masses urged as one means of equalizing opportunities. The whole educational scheme of Spain was subjected to criticism, and various reforms were instituted, especially in the higher institutions of learning. At the same time, more attention was directed to the importance of the natural development of the young child, and parental responsibilities were impressed both on father and mother. Manual labor was, for the first time, regarded as educative, honorable, and compatible with intelligence.

Even more than the state or the school did the church during this period feel itself an object of direct attack, as is evidenced by the array of forensic talent marshaled in its defense, and by the stream of apologetic literature produced by its supporters. Slowly such institutions as the Inquisition were being undermined by insidious means, which were at once sensed and resented.

The battle for freedom was first launched by those of the upper classes who resented the autocratic rule of the church; they were followed by younger intellectuals who dared to flaunt the evils of absolutism in government. In the distance ominous rumblings of independence were heard from the colonies. A generation of freer thinkers was arriving at manhood. But the combined attacks of these groups were skillfully parried by the entrenched majority; their voices were almost drowned by the mighty defensive chorus. Spain was a confirmed conservative; her radicals constituted only a small minority. Changes in education, government or religious conceptions were not to come over night; each was to require a long period of incubation in which to develop the vigor essential for survival. Yet we have seen that Rousseau's attacks on both state and church, on social distinctions, on the prevailing educational ideals and methods, and his pleas in behalf of the common man had penetrated into the intellectual life of Spain before the full blaze of the French Revolution in 1793 had lighted the sky of all of Western Europe.

BOOK II

THE GERMINATION, 1793-1833

CHAPTER IX

ECHOES OF THE FRENCH REVOLUTION
IN SPAIN

While the Catholic Church in Spain before 1791 was almost alone in its efforts to punish those whose curiosity led them to the consumption of such doctrines as those of the *Social Contract*, the *Essay on Inequality*, and *Émile*, its frantic endeavors after that time were vigorously supported for some years by the government. The French Revolution served as a warning to the rest of the world; clearly any monarch and his ministers, as well as the clergy, might meet the same unexpected fate if the pernicious teachings of Rousseau and other philosophers were once absorbed by the masses—a fact to which even the Spanish liberals were rudely awakened. Floridablanca, their guiding spirit, when finally aroused by the excesses of the extreme faction in France, exerted his best efforts to protect Spain from a similar experience; but in his fear he, too, became extreme and despotic. Edict after edict, both civil and ecclesiastical, was issued in an attempt to stem the tide. First, a census of all foreigners in the Spanish domains was ordered; a succession of decrees against revolutionary literature followed; new censors were stationed on the northern frontier to examine all books and papers; orders were sent to the authorities in the most remote colonies to exert every precaution against the introduction of seditious ideas; and foreigners were even forbidden to receive letters from relatives in France. Denunciations of suspected persons were given careful attention; trials became a daily instead of an infrequent occurrence; suspects were traced from place to place and from continent to continent; in fact, every order that the mind of Floridablanca and his associates could devise to offset French influence was issued, and many were faithfully executed. The periodicals in Spain, some of which, as has been shown, had become very liberal in their expressions, were one after another suppressed; even the *Espíritu de los mejores diarios*, sponsored by Floridablanca himself, came to an end early in 1791. Only the *Gaceta* remained, and that was rigidly censored. At last the church had, for a time at least, secured the coöperation of the state in its attempts to dam the steady stream of literature flowing from France into Spain.

But Floridablanca was serving a weak ruler and a fickle master, for Charles IV showed little appreciation of his minister's efforts to protect Spain from the general contagion. Early in 1792 the leader of the *golillas* was dismissed and the cabinet post given to Aranda. Great was the rejoicing in France. The hope and confidence the Revolutionists placed in him were triumphantly voiced by Condorcet thus:

La filosofía va a reinar sobre España. . . . La libertad francesa . . . encontrará en vuestra persona uno de sus defensores contra la superstición y el despotismo. El destructor de los jesuitas será el enemigo de todas las tiranías. Me parece ver a Hércules limpiando el establo de Augías, y destruyendo esa vil canalla que bajo el nombre de *Sacerdotes* y de *nobles* son la plaga del Estado. Sois el ejecutor testamentario de los filósofos con quienes habéis vivido: la sombra de d'Alembert os protege. Vais a demonstrar a la Europa que el mayor servicio que se puede hacer a los reyes es romper el cetro del despotismo y convertirlos en los primeros siervos del pueblo.[1]

In the face of such favor with the enemy, his well known pro-French attitude, and his liberal and even radical connections at home and abroad, Aranda could not hope to survive long as chief minister to the Spanish monarch; before the end of the year, the old diplomat was forced to retire. Shorn of his power, the aged statesman was even threatened by the Inquisition, but he passed on before becoming one of its victims. His successor, the notorious Godoy, proved to be merely a toy in the hands of the queen. This man, who steered the wavering course

---

[1]Vélez, Rafael. *Apología del altar y del trono*, II (Madrid, 1818), xi–xii, quoting from *El Procurador*, October 30, 1814.

of Spain until 1808, has left us his impressions of the state of affairs at the time he became the ranking cabinet officer.

. . . Puertas y ventanas y respiraderos los encontré murados por el miedo de las luces a quien se atribuyeron los sucesos espantosos de la Francia. El ministro Moñino, que ayudado de muchos, trabajó en favor de ellas en los días serenos, las trató como enemigo cuando llegó a juzgarlas peligrosas y culpables. La carrera de las reformas, emprendida, medio siglo había, con próspera fortuna, hizo larga parada, y aun retrocedió muchos pasos. Se cohibió la imprenta con rigor extremado, el gobierno adoptó un silencio temeroso, y este mismo silencio fué impuesto a todo el reino. Todos los diarios, aun aquellos que se ocupaban solamente en asuntos de letras o de artes, desde el año de 1791 fueron suprimidos en la corte y en todas las provincias. La Gaceta hablaba menos de los sucesos de la Francia que podría haberse hablado de la China.[2]

In spite of all these precautions, French royalists and ecclesiastics, seeking refuge on Spanish soil, poured over the border. In its efforts to protect Spain from dangerous ideas, the Inquisition redoubled its prohibitions, including among them such innocent works as Cadalso's *Militar a la violeta* in 1791; González de Castillo's version of *Pygmalion* in 1793; and novels that merely breathed the spirit of *La nouvelle Héloïse*.[3] In an attempt to stamp out the Revolution, Spain declared war on France that same year; and to prevent the discussion of all governmental matters, the study of political economy in the universities was ordered discontinued in 1794.[4] As Estala wrote to Forner:

No conocerás este mundillo. Pasó el siglo de la literatura. . . . Todo es hablar de noticias, de reformas, de arbitrios, etc. . . . Hasta los mozos de esquina compran la *Gaceta*. . . . No se oye más que batallas, revolución, convención, representación nacional, libertad, igualdad.[5]

The general atmosphere was dark with fear and dread; and dire warnings filled the air of the Spanish peninsula.

---

[2]Godoy, *Cuenta dada de su vida política*, II, 168–169.
[3]*Indice*, Suplemento, 1805.
[4]Gil y Zárate, *La instrucción pública en España*, III, 51.
[5]Pedro Estala to Juan Pablo Forner, 1795, in Papeles de Forner. Quoted by Cueto, L. A., in *Poetas líricos del siglo XVIII*, in *B.A.E.*, LXI, ccii.

But through all this gloom, light somehow flickered. Liberal ideas could not be swept out like cobwebs. At the universities the spirit of inquiry had been aroused; strange happenings in another country could not crush it over night. Blanco White, a student in this period of upheaval, has well described the feelings of the typical young Spaniard upon coming into contact with forbidden books, although he frankly admitted that he did not possess "the cynical habits of mind" which would permit him "like Rousseau" to expose his heart naked to the rest of the world.

[My] first taste of mental liberty was more delicious than any feeling I ever experienced; but it was succeeded by a burning thirst for every thing that, by destroying my old mental habits, could strengthen and confirm my unbelief. I gave an exorbitant price for any French irreligious books, which the love of gain induced some Spanish booksellers to import at their peril. The intuitive knowledge of one another, which persecuted principles impart to such as cherish them in common, made me soon acquainted with several members of my own profession, deeply versed in the philosophical school of France. They possessed, and made no difficulty to lend me, all the Anti-Christian works, which teemed from the French press. Where there is no liberty, there can be no discrimination. . . .

Pretending studious retirement, I have fitted up a small room, to which none but my confidential friends find admittance. There lie my *prohibited books*, in perfect concealment, in a well-contrived nook under a staircase. The *Breviary* alone . . . is kept on the table, to check the doubts of any chance intruder.[6]

Opportunities to secure prohibited works were not lacking. Booksellers, lured by large profits, risked their possession and sale; Alegría and Clemente in Salamanca dealt exclusively in French works. Censors that were appointed were lax, or like the Abate Juan Antonio Melón, a "volteriano refinado," at heart in sympahthy with liberal thought. What actually happened is well described as follows:

Los dos revisores que por Real orden de 15 de octubre de 1792, habían de presidir en las Aduanas al reconocimiento de los libros, lo dejaban correr todo, por malicia o por ignorancia, a título de obras

---

[6]*Letters from Spain* (London, 1822), 133–134.

desconocidas o que no constaban *nominatim* en los índices, siendo imposible que éstos abarcasen todos los infinitos papeles clandestinos que abortaban sin cesar las prensas francesas, ni mucho más contuvieran los dobles y triples títulos con que una misma obra se disimulaba. Además era frecuente poner en los tejuelos un rótulo muy diverso del verdadero contenido del libro, y no era caso raro que las cubiertas de un San Basilio o de un San Augustín sirviesen para amparar volúmenes de la *Enciclopedia*. No exagero si digo que hoy mismo están inundadas las bibliotecas particulares de España de ejemplares de Voltaire, Rousseau, Volney, Dupuis, etc., la mayor parte de los cuales proceden de entonces.[7]

Even the suppression of the chairs of political economy had small effect.

Las obras de Rousseau, Mably, Helvecio y demás utopistas franceses que tan adelante llevaron sus teorías políticas, penetraban por todas partes en España; y ya que no en la enseñanza pública, sus ideas se apoderaban de los ánimos en la lectura particular y secreta, de tal suerte, que al estallar la guerra de la independencia . . . se vió que habían cundido mucho más de lo que se pensaba.[8]

Clearly "las luces," including Rousseau, continued to shine in Spain and to attract the more intelligent.

With the passing of the climax of the French Revolution, a mellowing change in the attitude of the clericals both in France and in Spain toward Rousseau became apparent; selected passages, instead of being belittled, were frequently cited in their own support. There seems to have become general, too, a distinction between Rousseau and the Encyclopedists headed by Voltaire, against whom, as menacers of all religion, the church still declaimed. In Spanish translations of French works, Rousseau's belief in God and immortality, the superiority of man to beast, the indebtedness of civilization to Christianity, his denunciation of atheists, and advice to flee from the seductions of the philosophers are quoted at length.[9] There is no longer any hesitation, in such a translation, about using his name openly or in citing him as a source, so long as his statements could be made to serve orthodox purposes.

[7]Menéndez y Pelayo, *Historia de los heterodoxos*, VI, 305.
[8]Gil y Zárate, *op. cit.*, III, 51.
[9]*Colección de las particularidades de la vida y muerte de un pretendido filósofo moderno*. Escrito en francés, por un autor anónimo . . . traducido al castellano por el Dr. D. M. M. Madrid, Imp. de Villapando, 1796. Cf. pp. 91, 93, 97–98, 109–110, 115, 141–142.

In other circles in Spain the works of Rousseau were being given thoughtful consideration, for it was realized that he was the source of many of the ideas then current. After the study of political economy was eliminated from the universities, one of the professors of that branch, Ramón Campos, devoted himself to a detailed study of Rousseau and later wrote a drastic reply to the 1755 *Discourse*.[10] In this he refuted Rousseau's theory of the natural state of man as that of the solitary beast in the forests; denied that society arose through any contract expressed or tacit;[11] and conceded only the "derecho de trato."[12] But while he pointed out many fallacies in Rousseau's logic, he admitted that the Genevan's style was peerless.[13] Later, in another connection, he returned to the subject of Rousseau with the comment: "El trueno de su elocuencia aturde cada día más el mundo."[14]

Political uneasiness in Spain was largely relieved by the return of France to monarchial government, and the sale of Louisiana to the United States in 1803 proved a temporary solution of one of her colonial frontier problems. But the seizure of Buenos Aires in 1806 by the British and the conspiracies in England and the United States to promote the independence of the colonies, gave new cause for alarm. Before adequate steps to meet the situation could be taken, the ambitions of Napoleon to add Spain to his realm gave occasion for stubborn resistance. With representative government, Spain entered upon an era of liberalism unprecedented in her history.

---

[10]*De la desigualdad personal en la sociedad civil*. Although finished in 1799, the work remained unpublished until brought out in Paris in 1823 by Rodríguez Burón, a friend and admirer of the author, who was killed early in 1808 in fighting against the French. It was republished at Barcelona by Sauri in 1838. A modern criticism of it was written by P. E. Coll. Cf. *La escondida senda*, Madrid, 1927.

[11]*Ibid.*, 20–21.

[12]*Ibid.*, 25.

[13]"El vacía con decoro toda la intensidad con que le hería el pensamiento; y a pesar de su poca invención y no mucho juicio, nadie ha tenido una elocuencia tan suelta, sencilla, fina y penetrante como la suya. De la expresión de J. J. a la de los otros escritores hay una diferencia por el estilo de la de Píndaro a Horacio."—*Ibid.*, 36.

[14]*Ibid.*, 47.

CHAPTER X

THE PRE-ROMANTICISTS

In another realm quite remote from politics—that of lyric poetry—Rousseau's ideas also made an indelible impression in Spain. We have noted many references to *Émile* and the *Contrat Social*, but comparatively few as yet to *La nouvelle Héloïse*, in which its author poured out his feelings so unrestrainedly. Its most direct echo was the voice of Cadalso in *Noches lúgubres*, although Almeida early popularized its underlying theories and epistolary form in his insipid *Hombre Feliz*. Both of these works were in prose; it remained for a Spaniard whose whole career has generally been regarded by his conservative and Catholic countrymen as one continual scandal to head the list of those frequently classed as forerunners of the Romantic poets.

The first Spaniard to give free expression in verse to his passionate admiration for Rousseau, and to live his life in open pursuance of the Genevan's principles as he understood them, was José Marchena, frequently referred to as the "Abate Marchena." Born in 1768 in Utrera, he embarked in Seville upon studies leading to an ecclesiastical career. His unusual linguistic ability showed itself at first in his mastery of Latin and later in his command of French, which enabled him to read the great number of works of the Encyclopedists then circulating among the students. Part of his reading was undoubtedly done at Salamanca where he studied from 1785 to 1788.

Cuantos intelectuales bullían por entonces en esta ciudad leían con avidez aquellos libros que venían a infiltrar en la mente de los mejores españoles una nueva ideología. Unos, como Marchena y Picornell, . . . se identificaron con aquellas doctrinas y las llevaron hasta sus últimos límites; otros, como . . . Meléndez, Cienfuegos, y Quintana . . . fueron más prudentes.[1]

---

[1]Alarcos, Emilio, "El abate Marchena en Salamanca," in *Homenaje ofrecido a Menéndez Pidal* (Madrid, 1925), II, 464.

"He leído," wrote Marchena in 1791, "todos los argumentos de los irreligiosos; he meditado, y creo que me ha tocado en suerte una razonable dosis de espírtu filosófico."[2]

The influence of this reading was evident in his first literary production, in which he boldly argued against the celibacy of the clergy. During his stay at Vergara, where he came to know Vicente María Santibáñez and other partisans of French thought, he organized a literary society as a means of propagating liberal ideas; in the poem read at the opening session of that organization, praise of Rousseau is unconcealed. After the initial lines,

> ¡Mísera humanidad! Las sombras sigue,
> Y afana por labrarse sus cadenas. . . .

the poet proceeds to invoke the shades of the virtuous Socrates and the inflexible Cato

> Y el que siguió sus huellas dignamente,
> Rousseau, de la edad nuestra eterna gloria,
> Y modelo a los siglos venideros. . . .

In the same poem, he launches a fiery attack upon despotism and intolerance, and proclaims that the principal object of the meetings of the group would be the study of the rights of man

> que ignorados
> Del hombre mismo fueran tantos siglos. . . .[3]

With great enthusiasm did Marchena greet the outbreak of the French Revolution, in which he saw Rousseau as a guiding spirit.

> El pueblo su voz santa
> Alza, que libertad al aire suena. . . .
> ¿Quién podrá dignamente
> Cantar los manes de Rousseau, clamando
> Libertad a la gente,
> Del tirano el alcázar derrocando,

---

[2]Bono y Serrano, in *Miscelánea religiosa, política, y literaria* (Madrid, 1870), cited by Menéndez y Pelayo, "El abate Marchena," in *Estudios de crítica literaria*, Tercera Serie (Madrid, 1920), III, 191.

[3]*Obras literarias de D. José Marchena . . .*, I (Sevilla, 1892), 44.

> La soberbia humillada,
> Y la santa virtud al trono alzada?
>
> .   .   .   .
>
> Dulce filosofía,
> Tú los monstruos infames alanzaste;
> Tu clara luz fué guía
> Del divino Rousseau: tú amaestraste
> Al ingenio eminente
> Por quien es libre la francesa gente.[4]

These verses, generally regarded as the first of the revolutionary propaganda type in Spain, were written before and during 1791. Such utterances were naturally not appreciated in Catholic Spain, and that Marchena had even less respect for the intolerance and conservatism of the average Spaniard is indicated by a letter written at Bayonne in 1792, in which he speaks of six years of persecution "dans le pays le plus esclave de la terre" and of the Inquisition which had sought to get him in its clutches.[5] After reaching Paris, Marchena was soon an ardent member of the Girondists, at whose downfall he shared their imprisonment. His poem of vengeance, written when Marat fell victim to the dagger of Charlotte Corday, reveals the spirit of Rousseau both in the love of liberty therein voiced and the unrestrained style of expression which characterizes the whole.

> Salve, deidad sagrada;
> Tú del monstruo sangriento libertaste
> La patria; tú vengaste a los humanos;
> Tú a la Francia enseñaste
> Cuál usa el alma libre de la espada,
> Y cuál sabe inmolar a sus tiranos.
>
> .   .   .   .
>
> La libertad perdida
> ¡Ay! mal se cobra; en pos de la anarquía
> El despotismo sigue en trono de oro;
> Su carro triunfal guía
> La soberbia opresión; la frente erguida

---

[4]"La Revolución francesa," *ibid.*, 16.
[5]Original in Archives du Ministère des affaires étrangères, first published by Morel Fatio in the *Revue Historique*, September–October, 1890. Cited by Menéndez y Pelayo in "El abate Marchena," *Estudios de crítica literaria*, 205.

Va la desigualdad, y con desdoro
El pueblo envilecido
Tira de su señor al yugo uncido.

The views of Marchena in regard to the backwardness of Spain and his dreams for her awakening are forcefully set forth in his *Aviso al Pueblo Español* written in 1793 in an attempt to induce the Spaniards to join with France.

El tiempo llegó ya de ofreceros la verdad; en vano vuestro tirano querría sofocarla; el pays de la libertad, el pueblo soverano os ofrece un asilo en Francia en el seno de los defensores de la humanidad representada en los derechos imprescriptibles del hombre, cuyas semillas fecundas producirán un día la felicidad de todas naciones, derrivando de los sumptuosos tronos la superstición y la tiranía para colocar sobre él la igualdad y la razón; puesto que la naturaleza no destinó el hombre a ser esclavo del hombre; la superstición y la ignorancia sólo pudieron esclavizar los hombres; pero, ahora que la razón se manifiesta, guerra a los hipócritas y opresores.

. . . .

Las otras naciones han adelantado a pasos de gigante en la carrera de las ciencias, y tú . . . ¿dónde está, ay! tu antigua gloria? El ingenio se preparaba a tomar el vuelo, y el tizón de la inquisición ha quemado sus alas; un padre Gumilla, un Masdeu, un Forner, esto es lo que oponen los Españoles a nuestro sublime Rousseau. . . .

No es ya tiempo de que la nación sacuda el intolerable yugo de la opresión del pensamiento? no es tiempo de que el gobierno suprima un tribunal de tinieblas que deshonra hasta el despotismo . . . en España donde el monarca es todopoderoso, donde las luces no obstante todas las precauciones se han difundido harto más de lo que se piensa! . . .

Igualdad, humanidad, fraternidad, tolerancia, Españoles, éste es en cuatro palabras el sistema de los filósofos que algunos perversos os hacen mirar como unos monstruos. . . .

Un solo medio os queda, Españoles, para destruir el despotismo religioso; *éste es la convocación de vuestras Cortes.* No perdáis un momento, sea *Cortes, Cortes* el clamor universal.[6]

It is not strange that Marchena, entertaining such views, should have attempted to arouse his countrymen from their lethargy, nor that he tried in vain—for the time. There was no response from Spain in 1793, but in reality this young Spaniard had scattered seeds that were destined to germinate shortly, both in the peninsula and in the colonies.

---

[6]Reprinted in Menéndez y Pelayo, "El abate Marchena," *Estudios de crítica literaria*, 226–230.

The year 1795, which saw the signing of a peace treaty between France and Spain, arranged by Godoy whose reward therefor was the title of the Prince of Peace, brought to light the first evidence of political disaffection in Spain. With liberal views penetrating more and more from France, and tyranny and despotism characterizing the ruling agencies in Spain, it is not surprising that young and impetuous thinkers found themselves adrift on an uncharted sea of conflicting ideas. Particularly was this true in educational circles, as was revealed by the discovery that year of an insurrectionary plot, known as the *cerrillo de San Blas,* of which the leaders were all prominent teachers. Among them were Juan Picornell, a Majorcan, who had been a fellow student of Marchena at Salamanca, and was later the author of several pedagogical textbooks[7] and the father of a child prodigy; José Lax, an Aragonese professor of humanities; Sebastián Andrés, professor of mathematics at San Isidro; Manuel Cortés, of the College of Pages; and Juan Ponz Izquierdo, teacher of French and translator of the volume *Derechos y deberes del ciudadano.* Although the plot was quickly frustrated, the first four of these well-known men were convicted of treason and condemned to death; but the sentence was commuted to imprisonment in various fortresses in America,[8] where we shall hear of them again four years later. In the meantime, both Marchena and Francisco Miranda, who had been too active in French revolutionary circles, were ordered deported to Switzerland; Miranda managed to remain in Paris, but Marchena went, to become for a time the unwelcome guest of Madame de Stael.[9]

Marchena, a romantic in spirit, but not gifted with poetic feeling of a high order, reveals some of his inclinations and interests in his poems. The "Himno al Sol," included in the fragments of his translation of Ossian

[7]Blanco y Sánchez, R., *Bibliografía pedagógica* (Madrid, 1907).
[8]Menéndez y Pelayo, "El abate Marchena," *Estudios de crítica literaria,* 201–203.
[9]Robertson, *The Life of Miranda,* I, 157.

published at this time, which, according to Menéndez y Pelayo,[10] was to serve later as a model for Espronceda's famous apostrophe,[11] has historic value, if only as an evidence of the growing romantic interest in Spain.

> ¡Oh tú, que luminoso vas rodando
> Por la celeste esfera,
> Como de mis abuelos el bruñido
> Redondo escudo! ¡Oh Sol! ¿De dó manando
> En tu inmortal carrera
> Va, di, tu eterno resplandor lucido?
> Radiante en tu belleza
> Majestuoso te muestras, y corridas
> Las estrellas esconden su cabeza
> En las nubes: las ondas de Occidente
> Las luces de la luna obscurecidas
> Sepultan en su seno; reluciente
> Tú en tanto vas midiendo el amplio cielo.[12]

Nor was Marchena lacking in other romantic qualities—doubt and melancholy appear between the lines. He never did things by halves—he went the whole length. No sooner had he begun to reflect upon himself than the whole question of life and death was before him.

> Dulce esperanza, ¡oh! ven a consolarme.
> ¿Quién sabe si es la muerte mejor vida?
> Quien me dió el sér ¿no puede conservarme
> Más allá de la tumba? ¿Está ceñida
> A este bajo planeta su potencia?
> ¿El inmenso poder hay quien lo mida?
> ¿Qué es el alma? ¿Conozco yo su esencia?
> Yo existo. ¿Dónde iré? ¿De dó he venido?
> ¿Por qué el crimen repugna a mi conciencia?[13]

Closely associated with Marchena, both during the stay of that young firebrand in Salamanca and later during the period of the French invasion of Spain, was Juan Meléndez Valdés, the leader, in a sense, of the group of poets which

[10] "El abate Marchena," in *Estudios de crítica literaria*, 291.
[11] Churchman says it was not, but that Espronceda knew the original English version.—Churchman, M., "Espronceda, Byron and Ossian," in *Modern Language Notes*, XXIII (1908), 13–16.
[12] *Obras literarias*, I, 157–158.
[13] "Epístola a don José Lanz," in Marchena, José, *Lecciones de filosofía moral y elocuencia* . . ., II (Burdeos, 1820), 560–562.

included among others Cadalso, Marchena, Cienfuegos, Jovellanos, and Quintana. In 1781 Meléndez, who had been a student at the University of Salamanca, was appointed to a professorship of humanities there; later he was a judge at Saragossa and at Valladolid. Won over to the French by persuasion, he was induced to accept in 1808 the post of minister of public instruction under Joseph Bonaparte, for which weakness he paid the price. Six years later, with the retreating French, he left Spain, which he realized then he would never see again; and died, an exile, in France.

It was during his student days at Salamanca that he was advised by Jovellanos, with whom he was on very intimate terms, to desist from the creation of amorous poetry and to turn his attention to more serious types— advice which Meléndez was not slow to follow. He began to write essays, epistles, and philosophical odes in imitation of Pope, Young, and Milton; and he read and absorbed at that time many of the ideas of Rousseau, as presented in *Émile, La nouvelle Héloïse,* and the *Contrat Social.*[14] The influence of this reading soon showed itself in his poetry. Meléndez never became an ardent advocate of specific political reforms as did Marchena, but he responded to the sentimental side of Rousseau—the ideas of universal love, the excellence of the savage state, and the superiority of the primitive nature of man—and was also saturated with the melancholy of the romanticist. Rigidly trained to classic forms, he was always timid about departing from them, but in the expression of new ideas he was much more daring.

It is in the *epístolas* that the influence of Rousseau first makes itself clearly felt. Here is the same strong sympathy for the lower classes and the direct attack on wealth.

---

[14]Letter from Meléndez to Jovellanos, Salamanca, April 27, 1779, in *Poetas líricos del siglo XVIII,* in *B.A.E.,* LXIII, 84–85; Menéndez y Pelayo, *Historia de los heterodoxos,* VI, 320; Quintana, Manuel José, "Meléndez Valdés," in *B.A.E.,* XIX, 110.

¡Qué mal al pobre el cortesano juzga!
¡Qué mal en torno a la opulenta mesa,
. . . .
Del infeliz se escuchan los clamores!
. . . .
Insensibles nos hace la opulencia,
Insensibles nos hace. . . .
. . . .
Este incesante hablar de oro y grandezas
          . . . nos fascinan,
Nos embebecen, y olvidar nos hacen
Nuestro común origen y miserias.[15]

And in the same strain he continues in "La despedida del anciano."

El ciego interés completa
La desunión; él consagra
A Dios la virgen, o al necio
Vicioso y rico la enlaza.
Llore la infelice, llore,
Y, víctima desdichada,
El cuello al yugo someta,
Que cual dogal ha de ahogarla
. . . .
¿Por qué el remedio nos tardas?
¿Por qué estos bárbaros usos,
Que a naturaleza ultrajan
Y a los que ella iguales hizo,
Tus leyes no los igualan?
¡Oh interés! tú solo eres
Tú, de tantos males causa,
. . . .
Tú forjaste las cadenas
Del hombre.[16]

In his "Epístola a Llaguno" is further évidence of the extent to which he had been influenced. He portrays existing conditions in Spain in mournful colors, and begs his friend—the translator twenty years before of Ballexerd's treatise—to give special attention to certain fields, particularly education and philanthropy.

---

[15]"El filósofo en el campo," in *Poetas líricos del siglo XVIII*, in *B.A.E.*, LXIII, 205.
[16]*Ibid.*, 256.

Las casas del saber, tristes reliquias
De la gótica edad, mal sustentadas
En la inconstancia de las nuevas leyes
Con que en vano apoyadas titubean,
Piden alta atención. Crea de nuevo
Sus veneradas aulas; nada, nada
Harás sólido en ellas, si mantienes
Una columna, un pedestal, un arco
De esa su antigua gótica rudeza.
. . . .
Ve . . . gemir al mísero colono,
Y al común padre demandar rendido
El pan, querido amigo, que tú puedes
Darle, de Dios imagen en el suelo.
Ve su pálida faz; llorar en torno
Ve a sus hijuelos y a su casta esposa.
La carga ve conque espirando anhela;
Mísera carga, que la suerte inicua
Echó sobre sus hombros infelices,
Mientras el magnate con desdén soberbio
Ríe, insensible a su indigencia, y nada
En lujo escandaloso y feos vicios.[17]

This was radical poetry in Spain in 1795 and its publication demanded moral courage on the part of the author.

Rousseau's views on fanaticism, which he regarded as more pernicious than atheism,[18] probably furnished the inspiration for Meléndez' ode, in which he portrayed the Inquisition as implacable, cruel, and bloody.

El monstruo cae, y llama
Al celo y al error, sopla en su seno,
Y a ambos al punto en bárbaros furores
Su torpe aliento inflama.
La tierra, ardiendo en ira,
Se agita a sus clamores;
Iluso el hombre, y de su peste lleno,
Guerra y sangre respira,
Y envuelta en una nube tenebrosa,
O no habla la razón, o habla medrosa.
. . . .
Entonces fuera cuando
Aquí a un iluso extático se vía,

---

[17]*Ibid.*, 202.
[18]*Oeuvres complètes*, II, 285, note.

> Vuelta la inmóvil faz al rubio oriente,
> Su tardo dios llamando;
> En sangre allí teñido
> Al bonzo penitente;
> Sumido a aquél en una gruta umbría,
> Y el rostro enfurecido,
> Señalar otro al vulgo fascinado
> Lo futuro, en la trípode sentado.
>
> . . . .
>
> De puñales sangrientos
> Armó de sus ministros, y lucientes
> Hachas, la diestra fiel; ellos clamaron,
> Y los pueblos atentos
> A sus horribles voces
> Corriendo van: temblaron
> Los infelices reyes, impotentes
> A sus furias atroces
> Y ¡ay! en nombre de Dios, gimió la tierra
> En odio infando y execrable guerra.[19]

Small wonder that in 1796 he was denounced to the Inquisition as a reader and lover of prohibited books, among them the works of Rousseau.[20]

Meléndez' influence in introducing and disseminating the ideas of Rousseau in Spain was considerable. As a poet he lacked the passionate sweep of either Marchena or Quintana; but he sang, even if in a more temperate tone, the interests of humanity. Of him, his pupil Quintana justly says:

> Los principios de su filosofía eran la humanidad, la beneficencia, la tolerancia; él pertenecía a esa clase de hombres respetables que esperan del adelantamiento de la razón la mejora de la especie humana. . . . Sus versos filosóficos lo manifiestan, y con sus talentos y trabajos procuró ayudar por su parte cuanto pudo a esta grande obra.[21]

While his interest in Nature and his admiration for rural life, derived probably from the forerunners of English romanticism, such as Young and Thompson, as well as from the French, served to direct the attention of other

---

[19] "El fanatismo," *Poetas líricos del siglo XVIII*, in *B.A.E.*, LXIII, 235.
[20] Llorente, *Historia crítica de la Inquisición*, V, 200–201.
[21] *Ibid.*, 120.

Spanish writers to an appreciation of Nature, Meléndez was especially a contributor toward the awakening of the romantic spirit in Spain through his melancholy individualism. In this spirit so reminiscent of Rousseau, Meléndez Valdés was steeped.

> Así huyendo de todos, sin destino,
> Perdido, extraviado, con pie incierto,
> Sin seso corro estos medrosos valles.[22]

In his breast was "una honda llaga que va sangre vertiendo noche y día." Wandering at night, he called upon the moon for comfort:

> ¡Luna! ¡piadosa luna! ¡cuánto peno!
> No, jamás otro en tu carrera viste,
> A otro infeliz cual yo de angustias lleno.[23]

The whole world was colored by this gloom.

> Todo, todo,
> Se trocó a un infeliz: mi triste musa
> No sabe ya sino lanzar suspiros,
> Ni saben ya sino llorar sus ojos,
> Ni más que padecer mi tierno pecho.
> En él su hórrido trono alzó la oscura
> Melancolía. . . .

Already he was suffering from that dread which marked the romanticist later—fear and doubt drove him "un desdichado . . . al abismo." He suffered as the romanticists suffer, saturated with melancholy:

> . . . en las tinieblas
> Con fugaz planta discurrir perdido,
> Bañado en sudor frío, de mí propio
> Huyendo, y de fantasmas mil cercado![24]

Rousseau himself might have written such lines, and poets later were to echo them.

A student and later a friend of Meléndez was Nicasio Álvarez de Cienfuegos, whose work was so strongly tinged with the sentimentalism of Rousseau as to justify his

---

[22]"El melancólico, a Jovino," in *B.A.E.*, LXIII, 250.
[23]"De las miserias humanas," *ibid.*, 251.
[24]"El melancólico," *ibid.*, 250.

inclusion among the precursors of romanticism in Spain. Menéndez y Pelayo has described him as a caricature of the bad features of Meléndez and a Quintana in embryo, romantic to a certain extent, and suggestive of the sentimental, descriptive, hazy, and philosophic.[25]

The general indebtedness of Cienfuegos to Rousseau may be seen in such lines as the following from "La Primavera" in which he exalts the advantages of primitive life, equality of opportunity, and admiration of Nature.

> ¡Oh Helvecia, oh región donde natura,
> Para todos igual, ríe gozosa
> Con sus hijos tranquilos y contentos!
> . . . .
> ¡Bienhadado país! ¡Oh! ¿quién me diera
> A tus cumbres volar? Rustiquecido
> Con mano indiestra, de robustas ramas
> Una humilde cabaña entretejiera,
> Y ante el vecino labrador rendido
> Le dijera: . . .
> "Oye a un hombre de bien, que las ciudades
> Huyendo, cual abrigo de maldades,
> Busca en esta aspereza montañosa
> La paz y la ventura. . . ."[26]

As Cienfuegos was a court official and for years the editor of the *Gaceta* and *Mercurio,* both official organs, he was forced to use caution in his public expressions. It would be interesting to know what he might have written under different conditions, but one poem, "En alabanza de un carpintero llamado Alfonso," unpublished during his life, suggests the lengths to which he might have gone. In this, as has been pointed out by many writers, appear tendencies which may be termed almost socialistic.

> ¿Del palacio en la mole ponderosa
> Que, anhelantes, dos mundos levantaron
> Sobre la destrucción de un siglo entero,
> Morará la virtud? ¡Oh congojosa
> Choza del infeliz! a ti volaron

---

[25]*Historia de los heterodoxos,* VI, 324.
[26]*Poetas líricos del siglo XVIII,* in *B.A.E.,* LXVII, 17.

La justicia y razón, desde que fiero,
Ayugando al humano,
De la igualdad triunfó el primer tirano.
. . . .
¿Pueden honrar el apolíneo canto
Cetro, toisón y espada matadora,
Insignias viles de opresión impía?
. . . .
Disipad, destruid, oh colosales
Monstruos de la fortuna, las riquezas
En la perversidad y torpe olvido
De la santa razón; criad brutales
En nueva iniquidad nuevas grandezas
Y nueva destrucción; y el duro oído
A la piedad negando,
Que Alfonso espire, en hambre desmayando.[27]

The exaltation of the individual, regardless of his social station, here too, finds voice:

Es el hombre de bien: oscurecido
En miseria fatal, nubes espesas
Su virtud anublaron, despremiada
Su difícil virtud. Si, enardecido
De la fama al clarín, arduas empresas
Obra el héroe, su alma es sustentada
Con gloriosa esperanza:
Mas la oscura virtud, ¿qué premio alcanza?[28]

Traces of melancholy and deep feeling, such as are evident in *La nouvelle Héloïse*, are also to be found in such poems of Cienfuegos as "La escuela del sepulcro" and in "A un amigo en la muerte." "La mort est douce aux malheureux,"[29] said Rousseau. Cienfuegos echoes:

Nada penetra los oídos sordos
De la muerte insensible. Nuestros ayes
A los umbrales de la tumba llegan,
Y escuchados no son; que los sentidos
Allí cesaron, la razón es muda,
Helóse el corazón, y las pasiones
Y los deseos para siempre yacen.
Yacen, sí, yacen, el dolor, empero,

---

[27]*Ibid.*, 28–29.
[28]*Ibid.*, 28.
[29]Lettre à M. de Saint Germain, 1770, in *Correspondance*, XII, 198.

> También con ellos para siempre yace,
> Y la vida es dolor.[30]

And in "La escuela del sepulcro" he sees the uselessness of all the vanity of men.

> . . . Caiste
> Y ya otro rastro de tu sér no queda
> Que las memorias que de tí conserven
> Los que te amaron. Pasarán los días,
> Y las memorias pasarán con ellos;
> Y entonces, ¿qué serás? El nombre vano,
> El nombre sólo en tu sepulcro escrito,
> Con que han querido eternizar tu nada.
> Tirano el tiempo, insultará tu tumba,
> Con diente agudo röerá sus letras,
> Borrará la inscripción, y nada, nada
> Serás por fin. ¡Oh muerte, muerte impía![31]

The influence of Cienfuegos in molding the ideals which were later embodied in the Constitution of 1812 was not inconsiderable. As an echo of Raynal arousing the Americans, he first stirred the fire of Quintana, who answered even more passionately.

> Virgen del mundo, América inocente!
> . . . .
> Con sangre están escritos
> En el eterno libro de la vida
> Esos dolientos gritos
> Que tu labio afligido al cielo envía.
> . . . No son bastantes
> Tres siglos infelices. . . .

But Cienfuegos has little hope for better conditions in his life:

> Tal vez un día la amistad augusta
> Por la ancha tierra estrechará las almas
> Con lazo fraternal. ¡Ay! no; mis ojos,
> Adormecidos en la eterna noche,
> No verán tanto bien. . . .[32]

His direct influence on Quintana is frankly acknowledged by the latter in the following lines:

---

[30]"A un amigo en la muerte de un hermano," in *B.A.E.*, LXVII, 23.
[31]*Ibid.*, 30.
[32]"Mi paseo solitario de primavera," *ibid.*, 19.

De tí aprendí a no hacer de la literatura un instrumento de
opresión y de servidumbre, a no envilecer jamás ni con la adulación
ni con la sátira la noble profesión de escribir, a manejar y respetar
la poesía como un don que el cielo dispensa a los hombres, para que
se perfeccionen y se amen, y no para que se destrocen y corrompan. . . .

A la vista y casi en las garras del despotismo insolente y bárbaro
que nos oprimía, cantabas tú la alabanza de la libertad; y en medio
de la corrupción más estragada y del desaliento más pusilánime que
hubo nunca, tu voz vehemente y severa nos llama poderosamente a la
energía de los sentimientos patrióticas y a la sencillez y dulzura de
las costumbres inocentes.

.   .   .   .

Otras contarán después el triunfo. . . . Entonces tus vigorosos versos,
dignos precursores de libertad y de virtudes, serán aplaudidos con
igual gratitud.[33]

Closely associated with the literary men just mentioned
was Gaspar Melchor de Jovellanos, who early came into
contact with liberal ideas through Olavide in Seville.
After holding a judicial position there, he was called by
Charles III in 1778 to Madrid where he was thrown with
such men as Floridablanca and Cabarrús, both of whom
were later, under Charles IV, to pay the price of liberalism. Cabarrús was the first to go, in 1789; Jovellanos, as
his friend, next. After five years of exile from court, the
latter was recalled by Godoy to become the successor of
Llaguno in the ministry of *Gracia y Justicia*, only to be
removed in less than a year and again banished to Gijón.

How early Jovellanos came into direct contact with the
writings of Rousseau we do not know, but during his stay
in Seville, he was a member of the "Amigos del País" and
interested in the promotion of agriculture, industry, and
education. There he established a school for thread-mak-
ing, and disseminated instruction in improved methods of
dealing with the olive and other agricultural products.
During his first exile, he established the Real Instituto
Asturiano in Gijón, planned for it a curriculum including
science and modern languages, and introduced modern
methods of teaching.

---

[33]"A Cienfuegos," in *Obras completas de Quintana,"* in *B.A.E.,*
XIX, 1–2.

Until this period of his life we have no direct evidence concerning his reading, but his diary, in which there are entries at intervals from 1790 to 1801,[34] throws light upon the sources of some of his ideas and reveals his private views on many issues. By this time Rousseau's influence along certain lines was being reinforced by the works of Saint-Pierre, which were also circulating in Spain. The *Études de la Nature* had been published in 1784 and *Paul et Virginie* three years later. In 1794 we find Jovellanos reading the *Estudios de la Naturaleza*,[35] a prohibited work generally admitted to be the direct influence of Rousseau on a very intimate friend, and soon afterward the exiled minister determined to make a Spanish translation of *Paul et Virginie* with the intention of printing it for the benefit of the Institute.[36] In February he received Meléndez' "Epístola a Llaguno," in which the author had been unable to refrain from comment on the unjust treatment Jovellanos had received at the hands of Charles IV. "No apruebo que la haya publicado," noted Jovellanos in the diary,[37] and he at once wrote reproving the author for so doing. In April he was still working on the translation of Saint-Pierre.[38] In May he wrote to Hardings, the English consul at Oviedo: "Prevenciones sobre nuestra correspondencia; que no se puede tratar de todo; que sólo privada y confidencial se deben exponer libremente las ideas."[39] In August and September of that year the statesman was reading *Las Confesiones de J. J.*, volumes which were supplied by Hardings.[40] After reading the fourth "promenade," he comments:

El cuarto paseo, en que refiere su doctrina sobre la mentira, está lleno de sofismas. Si la verdad es absolutamente buena, habrá una razón constante para que lo sea; la mentira es una operación con

[34]*Diarios (Memorias íntimas)*, 1790–1801. Publícalos el Instituto de Jovellanos de Gijón. Madrid, 1915.
[35]*Ibid.*, January 11, 1794, p. 120; *Suplemento al índice* (Madrid, 1805).
[36]*Ibid.*, April 6, 8, 10, 13, 18, 1794.
[37]*Diarios*, February 18, 1794, p. 128.
[38]April 13, 1794, p. 140.
[39]May 24, 1794, p. 147.
[40]Pp. 166–169.

esta razón; el hombre no deberá respetarla solamente en favor de su prójimo, sino también con respecto a sí mismo, que reconoce esta razón, y con respecto a Dios, a quien debe reconocer por su autor. Hasta aquí no he hallado en esta obra sino impertinencias bien escritas, muchas contradicciones y mucho orgullo.[41]

Further light is thrown upon the circulation of prohibited books by entries in this diary. In October of 1794 Jovellanos notes: "Llegó una remesa de libros de Salamanca, carísimos sobremanera; no se encargará otra a Alegría." Alegría was the French bookseller in Salamanca who supplied the student body with prohibited books at extravagant prices; now here in Gijón, the disgraced minister of Charles IV is purchasing from him. After finishing Rousseau's *Lettres*, perhaps supplied through the same convenient source or through Hardings, he noted: "Apenas hay cuatro dignas del autor del *Emilio*. Pueden ser justas sus quejas, pero muestra un espíritu suspicaz y quejumbroso y vano; el fondo bueno."[42] Apparently he had long been familiar with *Émile*. From an entry on October 13, 1794, we learn that he returned the five volumes of the *Confessions* to Hardings, with a corrected manuscript copy of his own *Ley Agraria*, through a trusted messenger.[43]

Here, then, is indisputable evidence that Jovellanos knew the works of Rousseau privately; unfortunately for the Spaniard, their names were destined to be associated publicly. In March, 1800, there arrived in Gijón a stranger who stated that a Spanish translation of the *Social Contract* had just been printed in France, and that in it Jovellanos and Urquijo had been eulogized while the Spanish government was severely censured. Jovellanos at once advised Urquijo, then Minister of State, of the report, and received from him two replies, one confidential, the other official. In the latter, he was informed that both Urquijo and the king already knew of the existence of

[41]*Ibid.*, 169. Refers to "Rêveries du promeneur solitaire. Quatrième promenade," in *Oeuvres complètes*, IX, 352 ff. This was included in the 1782 edition of *Les Confessions*.
[42]*Ibid.*, 176.
[43]*Ibid.*, 178.

the translation, and curtly ordered him to report from whom the information came and from what port the stranger had sailed; in the former, Urquijo assured his friend that there was no cause for worry.[44] When Jovellanos was ordered shortly afterward to collect all the copies in circulation, he was unable to locate a single one. After a miserable year of uncertainty and forebodings, in March, 1801, the blow fell. He was arrested and taken under escort to Majorca, where he spent seven years in prison.

It was from France, according to the information given Jovellanos by the stranger, that the first Spanish translation of the *Social Contract* came. But the title page of this rare volume reads as follows: *"El Contrato Social, o Principios del derecho político.* Segunda edición. Londres, Año de 1799."[45] At once the question arises as to who the probable translator was; to this, only the "Advertencia del Traductor" and his notes offer a clue. The "Advertencia" opens with the statement that "el principál merito del Autor de esta obra es el haber demóstrado en ella *á prióri* una verdad fundamental de economía Social, es á saber que *toda potencia que no dimana de la Nación, es tyranica é ilegitima"*; and that to Rousseau must also be ascribed the credit of destroying "el absurdo mas funesto y contrario al órden social, el que mas envilece la dignidad de hombre, el que mas retarda los progresos de la razón, y el que mas deseca y agota los manantiales de la riqueza publica . . . *la institución de la nobleza y de las clases privilegiadas."* The translator states as his object—

. . . que las ideas liberales se extiendan y propaguen, y que la Patria de los *Lucanos* y *Padíllas,* en el día agoviada baxo la ferula del *despotismo civil y religioso,* conozca sus derechos y se exfuerze a vindicarlos. A la verdad ninguna nación de la Europa está hoy día tan sojuzgada como la Española. La ignorancia, los privilegios, la pobreza y la fuerza, todo concurre á su mayor abatimiento.

---

[44]These documents, dated March 26, April 2 and 3, 1800, and a secret denunciation against Jovellanos (undated) are published as Documents IX–X of the Appendix of Somoza de Montsoriú, Julio, *Las Amarguras de Jovellanos* (Gijón, 1889).

[45]For further bibliographical details, see Bibliography, No. 29. Typographical errors of the original are retained in the quotations.

At this point the translator opens a fiery attack upon the clergy, the Inquisition, and the nobles, but expresses sympathy for the Spanish masses, oppressed by taxation and unjust laws. His attitude toward the government, as contrasted with his regard for Jovellanos and Urquijo, is emphatically shown by the note appended (Bk. III, Chap. VI) to Rousseau's statement that a man of real merit is seldom found as a monarchial minister.[46]

Por nuestra desgracia hémos visto ultimamente harto verificada esta verdad en nuestra Peninsula donde una chusma de Ministros uno trás otro no han hecho sino mirar por sus intereses particulares y enriquecerse soberbiamente à expensas del pobre Puéblo. Decretos para abolir el estudio del derecho natural, reformas inutiles dirigidas a aumentar el poder del Monárca y propias para obstruir los canales del Comercio de las Provincias, en fin inmensas sobrecargas que hán empobrecido la Nación mas opulenta, hé aqui todo el vasto talento de nuestros Visires. ¡O *Jovino! Jovino!* Tu solo meréces el homenage de todo buen Español, Oxála que *Urquijo* siguiendo tus pasos, despliegue todo su genio emprehendedor y haga conocer al Monárca sus verdaderos intereses que son los del mismo Puéblo. De otro modo la ruina parece inévitable y todo concurre a acelerarla: en otro tiempo sería temible; pero atendida nuestra dura y laméntable situación, se dexa naturalmente desear con vivas ansias. [Nota del Traductor.][47]

From the tone of these remarks, it can easily be seen that the translator was deeply imbued with the principles of the French Revolution, and from the reference to Urquijo, it may be assumed that the translation was made after he succeeded Jovellanos as minister of *Gracia y Justicia* on August 15, 1798. Various Spaniards have been suggested as the translator. Alonso Arango Sierra is mentioned by Jovellanos' friend, Carlos González Posada.[48] In the catalogue of the manuscripts at the Menéndez y Pelayo Library in Santander,[49] Vicente María Santibáñez is named as the probable translator, but he had been dead four years when Urquijo became a minister. Menéndez y

---

[46]*Le Contrat Social, in Oeuvres complètes,* III, 347.
[47]Pp. 161–162.
[48]*Memorias históricas del Principado de Asturias* (Tarragona, 1794), [*sic*], I. Cited by Somoza de Montsoriú, *Inventario,* 198.
[49]Núñez de Arenas, M., "Don Vicente María Santibáñez. Un madrileño en la revolución francesa," in *Revista de la biblioteca, archivo y museo,* II (1925), 375.

Pelayo, who made a careful study of the life and works of Marchena, thinks there is small probability of his having done the work, because all the translations made by him that the Spanish savant had seen bore the translator's name on the title page; but he adds that "con ningún fundamento le han atribuido otras, por ejemplo, la rarísima de *El Contrato Social* (Londres, 1799)."[50] But the fact that the translation was apparently made shortly after Jovellanos served as minister (1797–1798), at which time Marchena was gaining a living by making translations for various Paris booksellers,[51] and evidence that Marchena both knew and admired Jovellanos,[52] added to the sentiments, language, and general tone of the prefatory note, suggest strongly the possibility that he was indeed the translator.

Not only the life of Jovellanos, affected so tragically by the first Spanish translation of Rousseau's celebrated political treatise, but also the works of the Spanish statesman, which suggest the extent to which he had absorbed Rousseau's ideas, reveal contacts between Rousseau and Spain.

---

[50]"El abate Marchena," in *Estudios de crítica literaria*, III, 314.
[51]*Ibid.*, 281–283.
[52]In the *Discurso* written for the opening of a Sociedad literaria, Marchena draws the line clearly between the able and the insipid writers of the day:

"Ni negará Terpsícore sus sales
Alguna vez, cuando burlar queramos
Los fríos Iriartes, los Trigueros
Insulsos y pesados, la insufrible
Charla de Vaca, y el graznar contino
De la caterva estúpida, que infecta
De dramas nuestro bárbaro teatro.
Apolo templará su acorde lira
Cuando de Jovellanos y Batilo,
Del dulce Moratín y Santibáñez
Los loores cantemos, por quien alzan
Su voz las patrias Musas, que yacieran
En sueño profundísimo sumidas."
—*Obras literarias*, I, 45.

Even in *El Delincuente honrado,* written about 1770, against the code of honor which supported dueling, Jovellanos is using a theme frequently treated by Rousseau. One of the characters also comments on the extent of French influence in Spain at that time:

Todo se reduce a libritos en octavo, y no contentos con hacernos comer y vestir como la gente de extranjía, quieren también que estudiemos y sepamos a la francesa.[53]

In this same play, written before the death of Rousseau, he concludes one scene with the words: "Todos estos modernos gritan: la razón, la humanidad, la naturaleza. Bueno andará el mundo cuando se haga caso de estas cosas."[54]

In 1788, in his "Elogio de Carlos III," there is an echo of the principle of the *Social Contract:*

Si los hombres se han asociado, si han reconocido una soberanía, si le han sacrificado sus derechos más preciosos, lo han hecho sin duda para asegurar aquellos bienes a cuya posesión los arrastraba el voto general de la naturaleza. ¡Oh príncipes! Vosotros fuisteis colocados . . . en medio de las naciones para atraer a ellas la abundancia y la prosperidad. Ved aquí vuestra primera obligación.[55]

But there was another side of Jovellanos, seldom emphasized, which links him still more closely in spirit with Rousseau. Beneath the austere exterior of the statesman was only another melancholy soul, who complained alike of his fate and of the world, who wandered aimlessly over vales and hills, who recoiled with fear and horror from a monastery in which he well knew there dwelt neither demons nor spirits.

> De una escasa
> Luz el distante y pálido reflejo
> Guía por ellos mis inciertos pasos,
> Y en medio del horror y del silencio,
> ¡Oh fuerza del ejemplo portentosa!
> Mi corazón palpita, en mi cabeza
> Se erizan los cabellos, se estremecen
> Mis carnes, y discurre por mis nervios
> Un súbito rigor que los embarga.
> Parece que oigo que del centro oscuro

---

[53] Act I, scene v.
[54] Act II, scene ix.
[55] *Obras de Jovellanos,* in *B.A.E.,* XLVI, 312.

> Sale una voz tremenda, que rompiendo
> El eterno silencio . . . me dice
> "Huye de aquí."[56]

But in vain. Not only was he oppressed with melancholy but he had lost interest in the world and his earlier dream of hope in death, which for him had become merely the "único puerto a los extremos males."

> ¿Ay ¡cuándo cuándo deseado día
> Vendrá a acabar con mi perenne llanto![57]

"Románticos, descabellados románticos, desapoderados románticos; románticos antes, mucho antes del estreno de *Hernani* en París," says Azorín of Cadalso, Meléndez, and Jovellanos.[58]

While Jovellanos was unquestionably influenced to some extent by Rousseau, he exhibited none of the unbridled enthusiasm of Marchena for doctrines of the Swiss philosopher. Unlike Marchena, he never accepted Rousseau's theories without carefully digesting them. With many he agreed; with others he differed after having subjected them to careful analysis. Rousseau served to point out to him the defects of existing conditions; he adapted the Genevan's remedies only in so far as he considered them practicable. With the French Revolution as a step to progress he had small sympathy; he saw the dangers of such an application of the *Contrat Social*.

De la perversión de los principios de la moral natural nació el más monstruoso de estos errores; so pretexto de amor al género humano y de conservar a sus individuos la integridad de sus derechos naturales, una secta feroz y tenebrosa ha pretendido en nuestros días restituir los hombres a su barbarie primitiva, soltar las riendas a todas sus pasiones, privarlos de la protección y del auxilio de todos los bienes y consuelos que pueden hallar en su reunión, disolver como ilegítimos los vínculos de toda sociedad y . . . envolver en un caos de absurdos y blasfemias todos los principios de la moral natural, civil y religiosa.[59]

---

[56]"Fabio a Anfriso," *ibid.*, 42.
[57]"Jovino a sus amigos de Sevilla," *ibid.*, 41.
[58]*Obras completas*, XVIII, 14.
[59]"Memoria sobre educación pública," in *B.A.E.*, XLVI, 254.

It was his hope that Spain might avoid the terrible upheaval through which he had seen the neighboring country pass in the process of readjustment; and he believed that time and gradual changes would bring about the desired ends. Due to the atmosphere in which he lived while at court, Jovellanos had learned caution; we never find him blazing forth as Marchena did; still he had the courage to express views which he well knew could win for him little approval from the powerful church party. In his *Ley Agraria*, he discussed the question of church property and advised the clergy that a generous concession of their rights would be better than "aquiescencia a un despojo que se envilecerá"[60]—advice that later destined the work to the *Index*.

Greater than Jovellanos from a literary standpoint, but also a disciple of Rousseau in Spain was Manuel José Quintana, a pupil of Meléndez Valdés and a friend of Cienfuegos. Subjected to many of the influences which left an impress on all of these, Quintana voiced, in his early life, more directly the spirit of Marchena. Like him, he dared to think and dared to write in terms too forceful and too passionate to be misunderstood. Liberty was for him, as with Marchena, a passion.

La libertad es para mí un objeto de acción y de instinto, y no de argumento y de doctrina; y cuando la veo poner en el alambique de la metafísica me temo al instante que va a convertirse en humo.[61]

Like Rousseau, Quintana saw that progress must come through the destruction of intolerant thought and selfish policy, such as had actuated Spain through centuries. As early as 1797 he boldly addressed his mother country:

¡Ah! vanamente
Discurre mi deseo
Por tus fastos sangrientos, y el contino
Revolver de los tiempos; vanamente
Busco honor y virtud: fué tu destino

---

[60]*Obras de Jovellanos*, in *B.A.E.*, L, 103.
[61]"Prólogo" a "Cartas a Lord Holland," in *Obras*, *B.A.E.*, XIX, 532.

Dar nacimiento un día
A un odioso tropel de hombres feroces,
Colosos para el mal;

.   .   .   .   .   .

"Y aquella fuerza indómita, impaciente,
En tan estrechos términos no pudo
Contenerse, y rompió: como torrente
Llevó tras sí la agitación, la guerra,
Y fatigó con crímenes la tierra.
Indignamente hollada
Gimió la dulce Italia, arder el Sena
En discordias se vió, la África esclava,
El Bátavo industrioso
Al hierro dado y devorante fuego.
¿De vuestro orgullo, en su insolencia ciego,
Quién salvarse logró? Ni al indio pudo
Guardar un ponto inmenso, borrascoso,

.   .   .   .   .   .

Y es la inocente América un desierto."

.   .   .   .   .   .

Viles esclavos, . . .
Sois la risa y baldón del universo.[62]

In the cause of the Americas, Quintana was one of the first Spaniards to put into verse and later into prose Rousseau's indictment, put into the mouth of Saint-Preux, that "les Européens . . . ont fait un désert pour s'en assurer l'empire."

J'ai vu sur les rives du Mexique et du Pérou le même spectacle que dans le Brésil: j'en ai vu les rares et infortunés habitans, tristes restes de deux puissans peuples, accablés de fers, d'opprobre et de misères, au milieu de leurs riches métaux, reprocher au ciel en pleurant les trésors qu'il leur a prodigués. J'ai vu l'incendie affreux d'une ville entière sans résistance et sans défenseurs. Tel est le droit de la guerre parmi les peuples savans, humains et polis de l'Europe; on ne se borne pas à faire à son ennemi tout le mal dont on peut tirer du profit, mais on compte pour un profit tout le mal qu'on peut lui faire à pure perte. J'ai côtoyé presque toute la partie occidentale de l'Amérique, non sans être frappé d'admiration en voyant quinze cents lieues de côte et la plus grande mer du monde sous l'empire d'une seule puissance qui tient pour ainsi dire en sa main les clefs d'un hémisphère du globe.[63]

---

[62]"A Juan de Padilla," *ibid.*, 3–4.
[63]Rousseau, *Oeuvres complètes*, IV, 287.

With no less vigor did Quintana call the Spanish discoverers "bárbaros y malvados," and fling to the world the following fiery verses:

> . . . ¿No son bastantes
> Tres siglos infelices
> De amarga expiación? Ya en estos días
> No somos, no, los que a la faz del mundo
> Las alas de la audacia se vistieron,
> Y por el ponto Atlántico volaron:
> Aquellos que al silencio en que yacías,
> Sangrienta, encadenada, te arrancaron.[64]

In his poem "A una negrita," Quintana expresses himself strongly in opposition to slavery, which was still tolerated in the Spanish colonies, although Rousseau's attack upon the institution in his *Contrat Social* had already set on foot a strong movement for its suppression.

> . . . los hombres
> Lo agitan todo en la tierra:
> Ellos a la tuya un día
> La esclavitud y la guerra
> Llevaron, la sed del oro,
> Peste fatal; su violencia
> Hace que los padres viles
> Sus míseros hijos vendan.
> ¡Bárbara Europa![65]

Almost as a refutation of Rousseau's denunciation of the printing press and the evils brought upon humanity by it, Quintana expresses himself strongly in favor of the press as a means of enlightenment through the destruction of the Inquisition.

> Dijo, y la imprenta fué; y en un momento
> Vieras la Europa atónita, agitada
> Con el estruendo sordo y formidable
> Que hace sañudo el viento
> Soplando el fuego asolador que encierra
> En sus cavernas lóbregas la tierra.
> ¡Ay! del alcázar que al error fundaron
> La estúpida ignorancia y tiranía!
> El volcán reventó, y a su porfía

---

[64]"A la expedición Española," in *Obras, B.A.E.*, XIX, 5.
[65]*Ibid.*, 14.

> Los soberbios cimientos vacilaron.
> ¿Qué es del monstruo, decid, immundo y feo
> Que abortó el dios del mal, y que insolente
> Sobre el despedazado Capitolio
> A devorar el mundo impunemente
> Osó fundar su abominable solio?
>
> . . . .
>
> Llegó pues el gran día
> En que un mortal divino, sacudiendo
> De entre la mengua universal la frente,
> Con voz omnipotente
> Dijo a la faz del mundo: "El hombre es libre."
> Y esta sagrada aclamación saliendo,
> No en los estrechos límites hundida
> Se vió de una región; el eco grande
> Que inventó Guttemberg la alza en sus alas;
> Y en ellas conducida,
> Se mira en un momento
> Salvar los montes, recorrer los mares,
> Ocupar la extensión del vago viento:
> Y sin que el trono o su furor la asombre,
> Por todas partes el valiente grito
> Sonar de la razón: "Libre es el hombre."[66]

Although Quintana seems unmoved by religion, love, or admiration of Nature, he also voices Rousseau's advice to flee the crowded haunts of men.

> Busca la soledad, ella en sus brazos
> Dió siempre al triste favorable asilo;
> Y dulce y melancólica, en su seno,
> Renovando memorias deleitosas,
>   Templará tu amargura. Huye la vista
> De esos hombres de mármol, que crueles,
> A los suspiros del dolor se cansan
> O con mofa sacrílega le siguen:
> Huye de ellos. . . .[67]

There are romantic traces in Quintana, although he was still primarily the philosophic poet of the eighteenth century. In his youth he was moved by the aspirations of the romanticists—the spirit of rebellion against existing conditions; he was the master of a superb lyric style; and he possessed the fire and vigor of a real poet. His

[66]"A la invención de la imprenta," ibid., 33–34.
[67]"A Fileno," in Obras completas, in B.A.E., XIX, 17.

interests were leading him to the medieval field. His gaze was clearly directed to horizons which beckoned to romantic fields when he began the collection of old ballads issued in the *Cancionero* of 1796 and in his first *Parnaso*. But the French invasion turned his steps in other directions; and six years of struggle for liberty, followed by six of imprisonment, served largely to disillusion him and to rob him of faith and hope, but not his impassioned style. The brief interval of liberalism which brought him freedom only accentuated the return to the old conditions in 1823. While he lived on until the fervor of romanticism had largely spent itself, Quintana was never again moved by its spirit, but remained the eighteenth-century advocate of civilization and progress, whose heroes were Gutenberg, Copernicus, Galileo, Jenner, Franklin, and Rousseau.[68] His faith in the possibilities of fervid youth in the face of century-old intolerance and despotism had been so deeply shaken that never again did he compose verses equaling those of the early odes, in which he was directly inspired by the teachings of Rousseau.

---

[68]Menéndez y Pelayo, *Estudios de crítica literaria*, V, 335.

CHAPTER XI

ROUSSEAU AS INSPIRATION TO EDUCATIONAL PROGRESS BEFORE 1808

Rousseau's influence in Spain was not limited to the political and literary fields; his ideas on education, in which are to be found, despite their extravagance, the truths upon which most of the educational progress of the nineteenth century is based, had slowly, unostentatiously, and often by a most circuitous route, filtered into the currents of Spanish thought. "A prophet denouncing the evil of the old; foretelling, yet seeing vaguely and in distorted outline, the vision of the new," Rousseau became the inspiration of all the educational reformers of the half century after him, a few of whom reduced his vagaries to practicable procedure. The three lines of progress he indicated—the psychological, the scientific, and the sociological—pointed the general directions which educational development in Spain was to take, slowly and haltingly, during the next century and a half.

The first application of the psychological and the scientific method we have seen in the school at Vergara, founded by Altuna's friends, and directed by the Basque society; Samaniego's fables were a response to the appeal for materials that would make the learning process more attractive to its students. Among its teachers were Marchena, Santibáñez, and Foronda, all clear and far-seeing thinkers. But in Spain, as in France, the old régime was so thoroughly intrenched in the whole social organization that change could come only as the result of violent revolution. The teachings of *Émile* were generally regarded as direct attacks upon the aristocracy and the church, which indeed they were, and the vested interests and authority were constantly invoked against its teachings, as we have seen. Nevertheless, an increased interest in elementary education, which showed itself in various ways, can be traced. In the plans drawn up in 1767 for the education of the children of the colonists in the Sierra Morena, there were certain features—compulsory secular primary schools with emphasis upon vocational training— which the old régime could not countenance; and after Olavide's disgrace, the outlook for educational reformers who gave evidence of French influence was not encouraging. But while the direct channels by which they would normally have reached Spain were being blocked, Rousseau's educational ideas penetrated by other slow, devious, but nevertheless effective channels. Even outside of Spain attempts to popularize his teachings and to apply them in a practical manner were no more warmly welcomed. Basedow's *Elementarwerk* (1774), a direct echo, which urged improvement in textbooks and radical revision of the subject matter presented, was at once prohibited in Germany;[1] and the prohibition was naturally republished in Spain. The same reformer's *Metodenbuch für Väter und Mütter* and his *Neues Metodenbuch*, translated into French by Huber, both reached Spain, but were promptly prohibited when discovered.[2] Basedow as a teacher was not much more practical than Rousseau as a thinker, but after the Philanthropium at Dessau proved a failure, the theories of the one as adapted by the other, were given a more practical application at Hamburg by Heinrich Campe, who not only conducted a successful school but issued a series of texts, which were the pioneers of juvenile educational literature.[3] Among his pupils in the Hamburg school was a nephew, Johann Nikolaus Böhl von Faber, who appears as Juanito in Campe's adaptation of Defoe's *Robinson Crusoe (Robinson der jüngere)*,[4] which was published in 1779. Böhl, the father of Fernán Caballero, established himself in Spain about 1790, and later

[1]Cf. Hahn, G. P. R., *Basedow und sein Verhältniss zu Rousseau*, Leipzig, 1885.

[2]Edict dated March 18, 1801. See *Suplemento al Indice* (1805), 5.

[3]Cf. Hartmann, Ernst, *Jean-Jacques Rousseaus Einfluss auf Joachim Heinrich Campe*, Neuenburg, W. pr., 1904.

[4]Fernando de Gabriel y Ruiz de Apodaca, *Fernán Caballero, Noticias biográficas*, in *Cosa cumplida . . .*, in *Obras completas de Fernán Caballero* (Madrid, 1909), IX, 342.

became prominent in Spanish literary history. But before Böhl could personally serve as a connecting link between Campe and Spain, Iriarte had published a Spanish translation of Campe's version.[5] He did not follow directly the German text, of which he knew only a French translation, but so altered it as to give more smoothness and movement to the narrative. His excellent language won for *El nuevo Robinson* many admirers among scholars, while the transformation of the hero into a Spaniard and the shifting of the action to a Spanish island gave added interest to the story for the Spanish and Spanish-American child, for whom this has proved, until the present day, an entertaining and instructive reading book.

Here, for the first time in Spain, we find an outstanding writer of the period translating and hispanizing a juvenile text—in this case a version of the one work Rousseau recommended for Émile. It was, no doubt, the preparation of this work that suggested to Iriarte another embodying other ideas of Rousseau—his *Lecciones instructivas sobre la historia y la geografía* (Madrid, 1791)—which passed through many editions. In its day, this educational contribution of Iriarte played an important rôle both in Spain and her colonies and was, with justice, highly regarded by educators.[6]

That the work of Basedow and Campe, which represents the first positive formulation in practice of those revolutionary ideas given only in negative form by Rousseau, aroused even in Spain a general interest in the problems of elementary education is shown by the publication and wide sale of such works as the juvenile texts of Iriarte just mentioned, Barro's *Los dos Robinsones . . . Carlos y Fanny* (Madrid, 1792), Olivier's *Petit Pierre* (Hamburg,

---

[5]*El nuevo Robinson, historia moral, reducida a diálogos para instrucción y entretenimiento de niños y jóvenes de ambos sexos . . . traducida . . . al castellano por D. Tomás de Iriarte. Madrid, Imp. de Cano, 1789.*

[6]Cotarelo y Mori, *Iriarte y su época*, 383.

1786), *Colección de ideas elementales,*[7] and Campe's *Treatise on Education,* translated, according to Godoy, by Clemente y Miro.[8] But that any trend toward an educational system based on teachings other than those of the Catholic Church was not to be tolerated is clearly shown by the fact that every one of the works mentioned, except those of Iriarte, was prohibited by the Inquisition at some time before 1804, and also by the disfavor which the clerical element showed toward the school Jovellanos established in Gijón.

Beyond all other subjects—government, economics, or philanthropy—this statesman was interested in education, for in it he saw a means of enlightening the people of Spain—"remover estorbos a la circulación de ideas," as he said.[9] He worked on plans for all types of schools—elementary, secondary, technical, and professional—and on courses of study and methods of teaching, but he realized that changes must come slowly.

> No somos muy sabios en política, que sin escritores, sin imprentas, sin compradores de libros, la luz que nos puede venir por este medio es escasa y tardía.[10]

He recognized the extent to which Spain had been retarded by the many obstacles placed in the way of freedom of both thought and expression. Probably because he saw the crying need for unbiased thought he interested himself especially in establishing a good library in his Institute; in it there were prohibited books—a fact that officials of the Inquisition suspected.[11] In his regulations for the College of Calatrava at Salamanca is a complete outline of studies in which he went so far as to recomment textbooks almost Jansenistic in their teachings. But most extensive and detailed of his educational contributions is his *Memoria sobre educación pública,* drawn up

---

[7]*Colección de ideas elementales de educación para el uso de una academia de maestros de primeras letras y padres de familias,* Sevilla, 17[82]–1784.

[8]*Cuenta dada de su vida política,* IV.

[9]*Diario,* 131.

[10]Letter to Lord Holland, in *B.A.E.,* L, 320.

[11]Somoza de Montsoriú, *Las amarguras de Jovellanos.*

while he was a prisoner at Bellver.[12] In the clutches of the Church and entirely at the mercy of the Inquisition, it was only natural that he laid stress upon religious instruction; whether he really advocated all he wrote under such circumstances may be doubted. As fundamental principles he set down the following: the object of instruction is a knowledge of God, man, and Nature; education must be general and public, for the prosperity of the state depends upon the education of its people. Like Rousseau, he opposed the use of Latin in teaching such subjects as law and theology; deprecated the prevalent over-emphasis on grammar; urged the study of science and of modern languages; and emphasized the need of physical education.

The impress of Rousseau's thought can also be seen in ideas advanced by clericals in Spain with the opening of the new century, for in the *Tratado metódico para la educación física e intelectual de los niños*,[13] the author, the Bishop of Saragossa, found that man in society, as compared with the savage, was physically inferior; luxury had brought him only ill health and an untimely death. Arteta advised that children be reared in the country; be nursed and cared for by their own mothers; be permitted to exercise freely; and be fed simple food. To the fundamental belief that "la naturaleza es recta, . . . el hombre nace inclinado a la virtud"—a conviction not original with Rousseau but one eloquently and widely disseminated by *Émile* and its imitations—Arteta subscribes, although it was a belief at variance with that generally accepted by the Catholic Church in his day. No less is he echoing Rousseau in the following appeal to teachers and parents:

Dejad pues jugar al niño y mezclad la instrucción con el juego, procurando que la ciencia no se le muestre sino por intervalos, y con un semblante risueño: guardaos de fatigarlo por una exactitud indiscreta: una de las cosas más importantes es dejar fortificar los órganos, no aprisando anticipadamente la instrucción.[14]

[12]*B.A.E.*, LXVI, 230–267.
[13]Arteta, Antonio, *Tratado metódico para la educación física e intelectual de los niños*, Valencia, n.d. [c. 1800].
[14]*Ibid.*, Pt. III, 14.

In spite of these similarities of thought, Arteta acknowledges not Rousseau but Locke, Buffon, Betzski, Ballexerd, and Hervás as his sources.

The only one of the new educational methods to receive official sanction in Spain was that of Pestalozzi; by it Rousseau's ideas were applied not to the individual but to the masses. Although reports of the successful work of the Swiss reformer had drifted into Spain by various channels before 1800, and direct contacts between him and Spain—looking toward the official introduction of his methods—were established in 1803 by Juan Andúxar—a Murcian ecclesiastic, tutor to the sons of the Duke of Frías, and also the editor of the *Gaceta de Madrid*—his ideas were already being applied by that time at Tarragona in instructing the children of soldiers of a Swiss regiment.[15] The promoter of this school was Francisco Voitel, who, while in Switzerland in 1801, saw the possibility of adapting the method in teaching the children of poor soldiers in his regiment; he was assisted by José Döbely, a Swiss Catholic chaplain, who had become acquainted with Pestalozzi and his methods during a leave in 1802. News of the Tarragona school soon reached Madrid and attracted the interest of the Cantabrian economic society, presided over by the Duke of Frías, in whose home Andúxar served.

Through the enthusiasm of the Murcian, the organization was persuaded to invite Voitel to Madrid; but he declined until the government would sponsor the proposed institution. Instead, he placed his assistant at the disposition of the society; and under its auspices the chaplain conducted such a successful school that the members decided to send him to revise the methods of their school in Santander, where he opened a normal class in 1805.

In order to secure the help of Godoy, who had shown an interest in public secular education, Andúxar enlisted the aid of his private secretary, Francisco Amarós, who,

---

[15]Morf, H., "Pestalozzi en España," in *Boletín de la institución libre de enseñanza*, XI (1887), 20–22, 52–54, 86–89, 115–123. See also Blanco y Sánchez, *Bibliografía pedagógica*, III, 197–250.

seeing the scheme as a possible step to his own advancement, soon had a commission dispatched to Tarragona to
report on Voitel's school, and, through the *Gaceta,* circulated widely news concerning the method and its success
elsewhere.

The combined efforts were successful. By a decree,
dated February 23, 1805, a Pestalozzian school was ordered
established at Madrid and, in the same year, Andúxar was
authorized to print Pestalozzi's works. Articles on the
new method appeared in various periodicals, and were
reprinted in cities as far distant as Havana.[16] Funds
were provided by the municipality, Voitel was appointed
director, and teachers were invited to observe the new
methods. On November 4, 1806, the school opened; its
success was so great that larger quarters soon became
necessary. Unfortunately for the welfare of the institution, the ambitions of Amorós led to his being named as
director, while Voitel was relegated to the humble rôle of
instructor. In spite of the resulting friction, which con-
tinually increased, the name of Pestalozzi became every
day more popular in Spain and the *Real instituto pestaloz-
ziano militar* was a center of much interest. Goya painted
the coat of arms over its door; the royal press printed
its publications; two more teachers were brought from
Switzerland in 1807 to supplement the staff; and observ-
ers—even friars—came from all the provinces, while the
Bishop of Havana sent a youth to observe the work done
and bring back details. The Duke of Frías insisted that
his daughter be instructed by its methods, and the education of Prince Francisco was entrusted to Amorós. When
examinations were held in November, 1807, the results
were pronounced eminently successful; and wide publicity
was given the achievements of the institution.

---

[16]*Suplemento a la Gaceta de Madrid del viernes 29 de agosto de
1806. Exposición sumaria del nuevo método de instrucción elemental
de Enrique Pestalozzi* . . . Havana, Imp. Esteban J. Boloña, 1807.
At the end is a notice that the Sociedad Económica de Havana,
February 22, 1807, sent Juan Bernardo O–Gaván to Madrid to
study the method. See Blanco y Sánchez, *Bibliografía pedagógica,*
IV, 356.

But with the approach of the French troops, Godoy, assigning as his reason that various parents objected to the instruction, on January 13, 1808, signed an order which closed the school; the printing of Pestalozzi's works was suspended; the seminary at Santander ceased to function; and the attempt of Eugenio Luque to establish a Pestalozzian school at Cadiz, for whose support it was planned to tax theater tickets, came to an abrupt end. Among those mentioned by Godoy as having especially distinguished themselves during this trial of Pestalozzi's method were Juan Andújar and various "literatos de la Comisión"—Miguel Alea, Melchor Andario, José María Blanco,[17] and Isidoro Antillón. Literary traces, in the form of a poem to Pestalozzi by the Duke of Frías and an ode by Arjona, celebrating the opening of the Madrid institution, were the only tangible remains of the undertaking.[18]

This was not the only attempt to reform primary education. Various suggestions before 1790 had pointed to a national plan of education, which Floridablanca himself favored, but not until after the French Revolution laid the basis for the institutional organization of education did the demand in Spain for a national plan become general.

Los pedagogos de entonces [1780–1808] instruídos en las doctrinas de Rousseau principalmente, dieron muestras de iniciativas importantes, de que son ejemplo los planes presentados al Consejo por Romero del Barrio, Torio de la Riva (1798), González Cañaveras (1801), Palet (1808), Cabarrús y otros, en todos los que se advierte una marcada intención educativa . . . y en alguno la aspiración a que se enseñase el idioma francés (Palet), o las ciencias naturales y los ejercicios físicos (Cabarrús).[19]

From merely the mention of these various plans it can be seen that in Spain, as in France, much was projected, but little was actually carried out, and only in certain phases of these plans can the influence of Rousseau be detected,

---

[17]The Blanco White referred to in earlier and subsequent chapters.
[18]Blanco y Sánchez, *Bibliografía pedagógica*, III, 197–250.
[19]Altamira y Crevea, R., *Historia de España* . . ., Barcelona, 1914, 3a. ed. corregida y aumentada por el autor. IV, 320–321.

although leading thinkers all reveal their acquaintance with his ideas and approval of certain fundamental principles he had emphasized.

Before the Pestalozzian experiment was abandoned, a new plan of education was promulgated, which is of interest if only for the conflicting opinions it brought forth.

> Por las materias que añadía a la enseñanza, como el derecho público y la economía política; por la mayor importancia que concedió a las ciencias físicas y naturales; por el orden que estableció en el estudio de las facultades; por su regularidad, y por muchas disposiciones que contenía sobre grados y otros puntos interesantes, era muy superior a cuantos hasta entonces se habían publicado, teniendo también la ventaja de ser general para todo el reino, y de acabar con la anarquía que . . . era uno de los principales vicios de nuestros antiguos sistemas.[20]

Such is the judgment of an impartial observer writing almost a half century later; but its principal ideas were regarded at the time as far from progressive by Narganes de Posada, who knew thoroughly both Rousseau's educational ideals and Spanish educational conditions.

> El plan es lo que debe ser, siendo la obra de un Gobierno que cree que toda su autoridad depende de la estupidez de los gobernados: es el plan que conviene a una nación donde hay tantos que viven a expensas de la ignorancia de los otros, y tantos cuya autoridad y usurpaciones caerían por tierra el día que el pueblo abriese los ojos: en una palabra, es el plan más propio para mantener la nación en la barbarie, y para hacer que las pocas luces que empezaban a brillar se apaguen enteramente.[21]

Posada describes the teachers of the elementary schools, especially in the smaller towns, as ignorant beggars; and the schools as places in which children of all classes, ages and sexes, read aloud all the time at the top of their voices as strenuously as their tender lungs permit—an ingenious method devised by the teachers as a means of knowing who was at work.[22] Moral education consisted

---

[20]Gil y Zárate, *De la instrucción pública en España*, I, 83.
[21]Narganes de Posada, Manuel Josef, *Tres cartas sobre los vicios de la instrucción pública en España, y proyecto de un plan para su reforma.* Madrid, en la Imprenta Real, 1809, pp. 8–9.
[22]*Ibid.*, 14–15.

solely of memorizing a catechism, of learning four prayers, going to mass, and staying on one's knees at the risk of stripes. After discussing the horrible punishments inflicted upon innocent children, he continued:

¿Qué hubiera dicho el preceptor de Emilio: y qué dirías tú, ¡oh buen Pestalozzi! si visitaras las escuelas de España, y vieras la niñez, la preciosa niñez, objeto de tus estudios y de tu celo, tratada de un modo tan bárbaro y tan atroz; y si oyeras dar a esta carnicería el sagrado nombre de educación? ¡Qué agüeros tan funestos formarías para la patria que ha de tener algún día semejantes ciudadanos! ... no hay educación primaria en España; la que hay no merece tan sagrado nombre.[23]

In reviewing the Spanish educational system, he added:

Hemos visto un tiempo en que el buen gusto empezaba a difundirse por toda nuestra nación. Veíase la juventud atormentada del deseo de saber, y agitada de aquella inquietud que es siempre precursora de todas las revoluciones. Vimos la ignorancia refugiarse amedrentada al asilo de los claustros, y aun de allí esperábamos lanzarla. El Gobierno mismo protegía al parecer este movimiento general, y como que quería despertar del letargo en que había yacido por tanto tiempo. Pero pronto conocimos que nuestras esperanzas habían sido vanas: que un gobierno como el nuestro ni podía ni debía proteger las luces; y nos convencimos que lo que habíamos mirado como una protección de su parte, no era más que un efecto necesario del impulso general que arrastra, aun a pesar suyo, a los que gobiernan. Entonces fué cuando se aprobaron para algunas universidades y colegios planes de enseñanza mejores que los que habían regido anteriormente; y entonces fué cuando se crearon las sociedades patrióticas.[24]

In regard to a plan for reform, he says:

La [reforma] que exige la educación pública en España debe ser muy radical, puesto que se trata de curar males muy envejecidos, y de remediar abusos que tienen a su favor la veneración de muchos siglos. . . . una reforma a medias, lejos de curar los males, suele empeorarlos.[25]

He proposed that education should be adapted to the needs of the children according to their station and the demands of their future occupation: general primary schools for the manual laborer; secondary institutions for

[23]*Ibid.*, 24–25.
[24]*Ibid.*, 55–57.
[25]*Ibid.*, 89–90.

those who would exert a wider influence on the general welfare; and higher schools for those whose future occupation demanded specialized knowledge and training.[26] For the primary schools he urged the system of Pestalozzi, which seemed to him excellent:

> Lo tengo por el más filosófico, por el más conforme a la naturaleza, y por el más propio para formar la razón; y aun desearía que el Gobierno no perdiese de vista un descubrimiento que puede ser tan útil, y que tanto honor hace a la inteligencia humana; pero tratar de adoptarlo para toda la nación, es pedir una cosa que . . . en el día ofrece mil dificultades insuperables.[27]

He referred with regret to the Pestalozzian school, in favor for a day, and then abandoned. The sole hope, as he saw the situation, lay in reforming such schools as existed, finding teachers unwilling to be mere machines, separating the sexes, and selecting texts from which children would learn some elements of history and morals as well as how to read.[28]

But even while his lines were being penned, the French troops were marching south to Spain. With their arrival at Madrid, a new era in the intellectual life of the peninsula began.

---

[26]*Ibid.*, 92.
[27]*Ibid.*, 97.
[28]*Ibid.*, 101.

CHAPTER XII

THE GROWTH OF LIBERALISM IN SPAIN, 1808–1814

The year 1808 wrought amazing changes in Spain. With the French army, Marchena came marching back protected against the Inquisition by Murat, whom he served as secretary; the prison doors opened for Jovellanos; and to him, as to Quintana, the French offered governmental posts. If the part Rousseau played in the French Revolution requires a volume for its discussion, a detailed study of the influence he exercised in Spain from 1808 until 1814 would require several. Here were the French themselves, bringing in their ideas derived not only from the reading of Rousseau but from the application of his principles during the Revolution; here were the *afrancesados*, the Spaniards who knew and admired the teachings of the Encyclopedists. From both of these groups direct action toward the attainment of liberty for all, equality for all, and fraternity for all was to be expected, especially as in the latter group were Urquijo, Ceballos, Cabarrús, Piñuela, Azanza, Meléndez Valdés, and Marchena—practically all of whom had suffered from the intolerance of the government of Spain and the despotic hold of the Catholic Church. Yet the only definite step taken by this group to the attainment of the ideals set forth by Rousseau was the abolition of the Inquisition.

In the group which formed to defend the country against the invaders were two other parties: the conservatives and churchmen, "los serviles," who would have none of Rousseau or his teachings—resistance meant to them the survival of the old order; and the liberal party which came into existence with the assembling of the Cortes, and was composed, again, of two distinct groups—the radicals, who wanted reforms at once at any price, and the more conservative, who believed in progress but realized that it would not come overnight. In these two groups were Spaniards thoroughly familiar with Rousseau and most eager to realize his ideals; in the latter group were men famous in governmental circles in former days, such as Floridablanca and Jovellanos, who had long been struggling for reforms and who now, already old men, became the leaders of the Junta Central. In the radical group in the Cortes of 1810 were younger men—Calvo de Rozas, Ruiz Padrón, Argüelles, Mejía, and later Toreno— few of whom brought experience in political life to their assistance; but all had ideas, and that most of these had French roots cannot be denied by any intelligent student of the period. Even Menéndez y Pelayo deplores while he admits this:

> ¿Qué educación habían recibido aquellos prohombres sino la educación del siglo XVIII? ¿Qué doctrina social habían mamado en la leche sin la del *Contrato social* de Rousseau? . . . Las ideas dominantes en el nuevo Congreso tenían que ser . . . las ideas del siglo XVIII, que allí encontraron su última expresión y se tradujeron en leyes.[1]

While the Spanish patriots rallied and struck back at the French in an unorganized fashion, the English furnished the backbone necessary to repel the invaders. Spain had the spirit, but lacked organization, finances, and other resources to carry on such a struggle alone. The sole authority for governmental action was vested in the juntas—first the local groups and then the Junta Central, whose task it was to steer the helm through those perilous times. Small wonder that little progress politically was made. Danger beset on all sides; the place of meetings was shifted to the south for safety. On the one hand were complaints that nothing was accomplished; on the other, problems which the outside world could little understand.

Sixteen months did the Junta Central continue its labors. Floridablanca, its president, died in office; its meeting place was finally shifted to Cadiz. One of the best defenses of the work of this group is that of Jovellanos,

---

[1] *Historia de los heterodoxos*, VII, 41.

who struggled resolutely in an attempt to solve the many problems which had to be faced.

El plazo de diez y seis meses, en que yo concurrí al desempeño de sus funciones, fué a la verdad breve en el tiempo pero largo en el trabajo, penoso por las contradicciones y peligros, y angustiado por el continuo y amargo sentimiento, de que ni la intención más pura, ni la aplicación más asidua, ni el celo más constante bastaban para librar a la patria de las desgracias que la afligieron en este período.[2]

A thankless task it was, indeed, both for Jovellanos, who died before the Junta completed its labors, and for Quintana, who, after refusing Napoleon's appointment, was made its secretary. To him fell the writing of its proclamations and manifestos, and ably did he respond to the opportunity. In his prose as in his poetry he raised an impassioned voice in defense of the downtrodden.

Of the accomplishments of the Junta Central, there is little to note. Without its authority the free press came into existence. An announcement in the *Semanario patrió-tico* (No. X, November 3, 1808) states that Quintana's *Oda a la Invención de la Imprenta* was then available "con las variantes que no pudieron darse a luz cuando el autor la publicó con otras poesías suyas en 1802." On May 22, 1809, Rousseau and Raynal gained a victory with the announcement that the Americans were to be given representation. The proclamation, written by Quintana as secretary of the Junta, suggests much of the tone of his earlier philosophic odes.

No sois ya los mismos que antes, encorvados bajo el yugo, mirados con indiferencia, vejados por la codicia, destruidos por la ignorancia. . . . Vuestros destinos ya no dependen, ni de los ministros, ni de los vi-reyes, ni de los gobernadores, están en vuestras manos. . . .

One definite step was taken—the Cortes was to be assembled. The sovereignty of the people, proclaimed without controversy while the people were in fact sovereign, was now an accepted principle, at least for the time, and was vigorously supported in the various issues of the *Sema-nario patriótico*, edited by Quintana and his collaborators,

---

[2]"Memoria en defensa de la Junta Central," in *B.A.E.*, XLVI, 560.

among them Lista and Blanco White. Many articles in this paper are almost translations of selections of Rousseau.

Es verdad que así como para vivir los hombres en sociedades han tenido que sacrificar parte de su libertad natural, igual sacrificio han hecho de la igualdad en que se consideraran los individuos si pudieran vivir aislados. Para la tranquilidad y el orden es preciso que haya una subordinación que haga de todo el estado un solo cuerpo. Pero igual regla debe dirigir las dos limitaciones de libertad é igualdad. En tanto se puede privar a los hombres de estos naturales derechos en cuanto sea necesario para el bien de todos. La sociedad que desnivele la suerte de sus individuos más allá de lo que exige la consecución de este objeto, quebranta las obligaciones más sagradas y se prepara su exterminio.[3]

With the convening of the Cortes at Leon on September 24, 1810, the liberals were in strong evidence. Among them during the next year was the Conde de Toreno, to whom, while still a mere youth, the Abad of Monserrate had furnished copies of *Émile* and the *Contrat Social;* and at the feet of Rousseau is laid all the credit for his liberalism. The current idea as late as the forties of the influence of Rousseau on individuals who came into contact with his works is clearly voiced in the following words by Toreno's biographer:

A ser posible, ¡qué estudio ideológico tan interesante hubiera sido el de las impresiones producidas en un alma nueva y ardiente por tan seductora lectura! Cuánto debieron conmoverla la inspiración apasionada y la elevación espiritualista del *Emilio,* y cuánto agitarla el tono imperioso, los axiomas decisivos, la novedad de las reflexiones, la lógica impetuosa de los argumentos y hasta las abstracciones del *contrato social!* ¡Qué vasto é inesperado campo debía éste abrir a una imaginación inesperta, presentando la reforma política al lado de la renovación social! No comprendía seguramente entonces el joven que así alimentaba sus naturales instintos de libertad, que las meditaciones de Rousseau, formadas en un tiempo en que no se tenía idea de las violencias demagógicas, consagraban sin la experiencia necesaria la infalibilidad de la muchedumbre; que no limitándose a establecer la preponderancia legal de las clases populares, dejaban sin fuerza ni protección al pueblo contra las demasías del pueblo mismo; y que no poniendo coto alguno a la independencia individual, y fijando desatentadamente la mira en ejemplos de la

---

[3]*Semanario patriótico de España*, No. 4, 1809, p. 69.

antigüedad inaplicables cuando la situación y las costumbres eran tan diferentes, no hacían sino corregir un despotismo con otro aun más odioso.[4]

Echoes of Rousseau are to be found, indeed, in the seventy volumes which record the debates and decrees of that Cortes, but not alone from the voice of Toreno. On October 15, 1810, the Americans were given representation, and at intervals during the next year the rights of the colonists were paraded with much oratory.[5]

Freedom of the press was another measure contested bitterly with more high-flown oratory but finally passed on November 5, 1810, after Argüelles had opened the debate by comparing the prosperity of England with that of Spain, "oscurecida por la ignorancia y encadenada por el despotismo."[6] In the discussion of *señoríos y derechos jurisdiccionales,* Toreno raised his voice in a peroration clearly inspired by the *Contrat Social:* "los hombres se constituyen en sociedad para su felicidad, no para darse grillos"; "las naciones no son manadas que se dan y toman a gusto de su dueño"; and "los reyes jamás pudieron ni debieron hacer regalos con los pueblos como si fueran joyas." He objected to any indemnity to the purchasers of rights over certain districts because "tales compras eran ilegítimas, porque nadie había tenido derecho para vender los pueblos."[7]

The crowning act of the Cortes was the promulgation on March 18, 1812, of a constitution, democratic in theory, by which the influence of the church was considerably reduced and the sovereignty of the people substituted for the divine right of kings. The monarchy remained, but was limited; the religion of Spain was still Catholic; the legislature consisted of only one chamber; the *ayuntamientos* were to be chosen by the people; and the press

---

[4]Cueto, Leopoldo A. de, "Don José María Queypo de Llano, Conde de Toreno," in *Galería de españoles célebres contemporáneos* (Madrid, 1843), III, 5–6.
[5]See *Diario de las discusiones y actes de las cortes* (Cádiz, 1811), I–III.
[6]*Ibid.*, I, 43–76.
[7]*Ibid.*, VI, 208 ff.

was declared free by this new declaration of the rights of the people of Spain.[8] But the spirit of Rousseau, strongly in evidence during the debates, was not yet to be stilled.

On the 22nd of April, 1812, the question of disposing of the Inquisition came before the Cortes, and was brought up again and again during the rest of the year. One of the fiery voices raised against it was that of Toreno, who declared:

El objeto de la religión, dirigido a proporcionar a los hombres su felicidad eterna, es del todo diverso del que se proponen las leyes políticas formadas por hombres. . . . El evangelio en su letra y en su substancia inculca a cada paso esta doctrina, y su divino autor contestaba a aquellos que creían que su reino era de este mundo: *Regnum meum non est de hoc mundo.* . . . Sus armas son la predicación y la persuasión. . . . Hasta el nombre de Inquisición es anticonstitucional. Nació la Inquisición y murieron los fueros de Aragón y Castilla. . . . Consiguió por fin la Inquisición acabar en España con la ilustración. . . .[9]

Ruiz Padrón, a priest who had traveled extensively in America and had known Franklin at Philadelphia, declared that such an institution was entirely useless in the church of God, that it was contrary to the constitution, and opposed to the spirit of the Bible. In the time of the apostles there were no inquisitors. The Inquisition had driven from Spain all useful sciences, agriculture, arts, industry, and commerce. He referred to the trial of Galileo and wondered whether future nations could ever believe that such a court could have existed. On the 13th of February, 1813, the Inquisition was decreed abolished, and in a manifesto ordered issued to the nation it was declared that

. . . la ignorancia . . . el atraso de las ciencias, la decadencia de las artes, del comercio, y de la agricultura, y la despoblación y pobreza de España procedían en gran parte del sistema de la Inquisición.[10]

---

[8]*Ibid.*, X, 109–410; XI, 210–391.
[9]*Discusión del proyecto de decreto sobre el Tribunal de la Inquisición* (Cádiz, 1813), 219–232.
[10]*Ibid.* See also Villaba Hervás, Miguel, *Ruiz de Padrón y su tiempo* (Madrid), 1897).

To go into further details concerning the views expressed in this Cortes would exceed the limits of this study, but much of the blame heaped upon its accomplishments, by Spanish conservatives and monarchists, even of a much later period, has been laid at the door of Rousseau.

. . . "Aquellos filosofastros y leguleyos *sensibles* y declamadores, a la Juan Jacobo, privados de sentido histórico," de que nos habla Capmany refiriéndose a los Diputados de la Asamblea de la Revolución francesa, fueron el modelo a los Diputados de la Asamblea de los revolucionarios españoles. Todo el tecnicismo rousseauniano, todo la cursilería de aquel zorro de Ginebra que disfrazado de armenio, había sido el fundador del sistema abominable del reclamo, todo el sentimentalismo falso, todo el ridículo humanitarismo de *La Cabaña* y de *Pablo y Virginia*, el optimismo pueril y bufo a la vez, toda la gárrula palabrería manida del antipático repertorio francés de aquel tiempo, será adoptado por nuestros Jacobinos. . . . No será, pues, de extrañar que la ridiculez espiritual del Emilio y del pobre Chactas cristalice en aquellos artículos de la Constitución gaditana que decretan que todos los españoles han de ser justos y benéficos. . . .[11]

It was with the hope of establishing some degree of religious and intellectual freedom that the Cortes did not overlook the importance of education. The Junta Central had entrusted the formulation of plans for a system of public education to Jovellanos; in these, he followed Rousseau to the extent of putting first emphasis upon physical education and introducing into the curriculum science and modern languages.[12] As the Genevan had urged, corporal punishment was prohibited. It was ordered that the constitution be taught in the universities and primary schools, and even read at mass. So eager were the lawmakers to instill political wisdom that various political catechisms were ordered to be included in the course of study.[13]

Quintana was named head of a commission to supervise the creation of public schools. Some idea of his attitude toward education may be gleaned from a few excerpts from the report he wrote as member of that group. In

[11]Antón del Olmet, Fernando de, *El cuerpo diplómatico español en la guerra de la independencia* (Madrid, n.d.), V, 253–254.

[12]*B.A.E.*, XLVI, 268–276.

[13]Gil y Zárate, *De la instrucción pública*, III, 51.

speaking of the difficulties which had served as obstacles
to the establishment of any system of education, he asked
in his usual vigorous style:

¿Cómo . . . proponer ni esperar mejora alguna en la instrucción
pública de un país sugeto al influjo de la Inquisición, y en donde él
que se atrevía a hablar de imprenta libre era tenido por delirante,
cuando no por delincuente? Sin romper este doble yugo que tenía
oprimido y aniquilado el entendimiento entre nosotros, en vano era
tratar de abrirle caminos para que explayase sus alas en las regiones
del saber. Y como en el diccionario de la razón *ignorante* y *esclavo*
son sinónimos, si el español no podia dejar de ser esclavo, ¿a qué
empeñarse inútilmente en que no fuese ignorante?[14]

Otro . . . de los atributos generales que deben acompañar a la
instrucción es el de la libertad, porque no basta que el Estado pro-
porcione a los ciudadanos escuelas en que adquieran los conocimientos que los han de habilitar para llenar las atenciones de la profesión a que se dediquen, es preciso que tenga cada uno el arbitrio
de buscarlos en donde, como y con quien le sea más fácil y agradable
su adquisición. No hay cosa más libre que el pensamiento; el camino
y los medios de formarlo y perfeccionarlo deben participar de la
misma franquía; y si la instrucción es un beneficio común a cuya
utilidad todos tienen un derecho, todos deben tenerle también de
concurrir a comunicarla.[15]

Yet even the fiery Quintana refrained from quoting
Rousseau as a source or giving him credit for ideas, even
under a free press in 1813, as may be seen from a few
lines of a section of this *Informe* devoted to a consideration of the rules of grammar.

. . . Porque estas reglas, según ha dicho un filósofo, resultados
demostrados para él que sabe y ha meditado las lenguas, no pueden
de modo alguno ser medios de aprenderlas para el que las ignora.[16]

The authorization of freedom of the press by this Cortes
in 1812 was a long step toward progress, but one not fully
understood by many who shared its privileges. Within two
years more publications were issued in Spain than in any
two previous decades. This avalanche of pamphlets and
periodicals gave evidence of the eagerness of the people

---

[14]*Informe de la Junta* . . .(September 9, 1813), in *B.A.E.*, XIX,
176.
[15]*Ibid.*, 178.
[16]*Ibid.*, 179. Cf. Rousseau, *Émile*, in *Oeuvres complètes*, II, 315–
316.

to avail themselves of their opportunity, but, like repressed children, they showed little discretion in the exercise of unaccustomed liberty. Despite the censorial board set up to restrain writers who expressed themselves too violently with regard to individuals, the presses poured forth a continuous stream, colored in part by liberal, in part by conservative views. Rousseau furnished subject matter for both groups, being exalted by the former, and blamed by the latter for all the troubles Spain had experienced in over half a century.

Among the first works issued at Valencia after the decree became effective were a new edition of *Pigmaleon*[17] and a so-called "nueva traducción" of the whole of the *Social Contract,* the first Spanish translation of Rousseau's political treatise published openly in Spain. In reality, it was little more than a variation of the 1799 edition with different notes, only two by the original translator—one of these the eulogy of Jovellanos—being retained. The 1799 translator's "advertencia" was omitted. While this edition circulated widely, and furnished the basis for much of the discussion in the Cortes, its translator and editor preserved his anonymity. A reprint of this edition was issued at Havana in 1813.

Another Spanish version of the *Social Contract,* published in La Coruña in 1814, was the work of Valentín Foronda,[18] one of the pioneers in disseminating liberal ideas in Spain through his "Cartas económico-políticas" and other articles on economic subjects. In 1798 while at Victoria, where he founded a branch of the Sociedad Vascongada, he was closely associated with the Marquis of Narros and the fabulist Samaniego, on whose intimate acquaintance with the works of Rousseau we have already commented. In 1801 Foronda was appointed consul-general in the United States, a post he held for eight years, becoming during that time a close friend of Jefferson. Some of the ideas of government he absorbed are reflected in his *Apuntamientos sobre la nueva constitución* (Philadelphia, 1809).

[17]See Bibliography for further details of all editions mentioned.
[18]Cf. pp. 113–114.

Back in Spain during the stormy years from 1810 to 1814, he used his pen vigorously in defense of liberal ideas. During 1812–1813 while a member of the censorial board in La Coruña, he prepared for publication his simplified version of Rousseau's political treatise.[19] In this adaptation, all numbering of chapters, articles and sections has disappeared; some portions, especially the first book, are much condensed; at times the translation is literal, at others, very free. In the matter of religion, Foronda bowed to the judgment of Spanish theologians who pronounced Roman Catholicism the best; but he deplored the fact that Rousseau, a man of such talent, had not reached the same conclusion. For his remarkable talent, Foronda expressed great personal admiration, and called attention to the fact that even those who condemned most bitterly Rousseau's religious views conceded his eloquence. As many of Rousseau's Spanish critics had never actually read a page of his writings, Foronda included in his introduction, dated February 15, 1814, some of the Genevan's statements concerning religion, God and the Bible. After quoting Rousseau's description of a Christian republic, the editor commented that any nation, composed of such real, not so-called, Christians would be fortunate. In summarizing Rousseau's views, Foronda now frankly added to the rights he listed in 1788—security, liberty, and property—that of equality, but he modified the term by showing the distinction between physical and civil equality, and emphasized, as he did not do before, that men are born free.

When all the copies of the 1812 edition of the *Social Contract* were exhausted in 1814, the Valencian publisher Ferrer de Orga issued another; but discretion, at this time, led to its disguise under the title of *Principios del derecho político* and the omission of the name of the author. The text was unchanged, but the chapter on

---

[19]*Cartas sobre la obra de Rousseau titulada: Contrato Social* en las que se vacía todo lo interesante de ella y se suprime lo que puede herir la religión católica apostólica romana. Por el ciudadano Valentín de Foronda. Coruña, en la oficina de Antonio Rodríguez, 1814.

"Civil Religion" and all of the 1799 notes were omitted. Rousseau's notes were shifted to the bottom of the pages, instead of being placed, as formerly, at the end of the work.

The periodical articles, pamphlets, and books issued between 1810 and 1814 which discuss or refer to Rousseau are too numerous for detailed consideration. Only a few replies of those who spoke out boldly in the face of the liberals can be mentioned here.[20] One declaimer against Rousseau and his teachings was Luis Cerezo y Matres, an Augustinian who attempted to prevent the adoption of the constitution when it was under consideration in 1811 by publishing in Valencia *El Ateísmo bajo el nombre de Pacto social, propuesto como idea para la constitución española.*[21] Needless to say, his voice was lost in the general chorus of "El pueblo es el manantial de toda autoridad." Another zealous protector of the Spanish people against liberty, equality, enlightenment, and reforms—watchwords which he believed had devastated Europe—was Rafael de Vélez, later Bishop of Ceuta, who issued in 1812 an earnest and eloquent appeal[22] to the nation not to allow itself to be misled. As leaders of the enemy, he named Frederick of Prussia, d'Alembert, Voltaire, and Rousseau; among the writings that he believed had wrought greatest havoc, he cited the *Social Contract.* Regretfully he admitted that French works which attacked the Church both directly and indirectly not only circulated in Spain but were echoed everywhere, even in the theaters, in spite of the vigilance of the Inquisition, whose powers had been shorn until the institution existed in name only. In concluding his exhortation, Vélez quoted from *Émile*[23] Rousseau's denunciation

---

[20]Some of the proponents will be considered later, as they drew fire from the conservative press between 1815 and 1820.

[21]Cejador y Frauca, *Historia de la lengua . . .,* VI, 353.

[22]*Preservativo contra la irreligión, o los planes de la filosofía contra la religión y el estado realizados por la Francia para subyugar la Europa, seguidos por Napoleón en la conquista de España, y dados a luz por algunos de nuestros sabios en perjuicio de nuestra patria.* Cádiz, Imp. de la junta de provincia, 1812.

[23]*Ibid.,* 133.

of fanaticism and from the *Social Contract*[24] a passage
attacking the Catholic Church. Especially did this theo-
logian raise his voice against the *Semanario económico,
El Conciso,* and other periodicals of the Spanish liberals;
and earnestly did he plead with his flock to resist these
seductive voices luring them from their duty to God
and men.

Another voice that was raised with persistence if not with
eloquence was that of "el filósofo rancio," Francisco Alvarado (1756–1814), who issued innumerable pamphlets,
many of which were directed to refuting the teachings of
Rousseau, although in his letters he sometimes called the
Genevan's views to the support of his own arguments.
For instance, in 1810, in writing against the theater, he
cited Rousseau's condemnation of that institution,[25] and in
a later letter[26] added that Rousseau had shown the impos-
sibility of effecting its reform; during the next year he
confided to a correspondent that Spanish philosophers had
deduced freedom of the press and of conscience from "el
Pacto Social del impío Jacobo Rousseau . . . y su *Emilio.*"
Alvarado also published a long series of letters in which
he refuted the teachings of the *Social Contract,*[27] but his
logic was weak, except to the orthodox who regarded him
as an infallible oracle.[28] In spite of the fact that these
attacks on Rousseau revealed that the writer was familiar
with all the current theories of law, Alvarado claimed[29]
that he had never read a single one of the Genevan's
works. Certainly Catholic refuters of Rousseau in Spain,
from Feijóo on, felt themselves endowed with some special
ability to divine rather than to digest ideas!

---

[24]*Ibid.,* 151.
[25]*Cartas inéditas del filósofo rancio* . . . (Madrid, 1846), 64.
[26]*Ibid.,* 97.
[27]*Carta crítica del filósofo rancio en que continuó la impugnación del dictamen del Sr. Gordillo . . . que establece los bases del
pacto social al gusto de los filósofos de moda.* Cádiz, Imp. de la
Junta superior, 1811.
[28]As late as 1912 new editions of selections from his works were
being issued.
[29]Letter 7, p. 29.

CHAPTER XIII

TRACES OF ROUSSEAU IN SPAIN, 1814–1833

With the return of Ferdinand VII and the restoration of his despotic government, sweeping changes were made overnight. The liberals, their dreams shattered, either fled or were imprisoned; the old court favorites came again into power; and but few of the *afrancesados* dared to return. The Inquisition was restored; the press was again brought under subjection; and liberty of thought, speech, or press became only a dream. Literary production of the liberals was almost completely stifled by the autocratic rule of a short-sighted monarch. Back to France went Marchena, penniless and more disillusioned than ever; into jail went Quintana, Foronda, and a host of other liberals not fortunate enough to escape.

No sooner had the reactionaries swept into power than their voices were raised en masse in defending the old social and political system and in denouncing Rousseau and the philosophers. Among the works issued at this time whose primary purpose was the refutation of the *Social Contract* and the *Discourse on Inequality* were *La voz de la Naturaleza*[1] and *Cartas sobre la nobleza o El Emilio desengañado.*[2] In the former, misleading arguments were advanced against the theory of equal rights and the sovereignty of the people. The importance attributed to Rousseau as their exponent is clearly shown in the following passage:

Todo el mundo conoce el contrato social de J. J. Rousseau y sus discursos sobre el origen de la igualdad y la economía política. . . . De todos los autores que han escrito en favor de las convenciones,

---

[1]*La voz de la Naturaleza sobre el origen de los gobiernos.* . . . Traducida del francés al castellano de la segunda edición que se publicó en Londres en 1809. Impreso en Santiago, 1813. Reimpreso en Tarragona, Oficina de Brusi, 1814.

[2]*Cartas sobre la nobleza o El Emilio desengañado.* . . . Traducidas del francés al castellano, de la edición que se publicó en Londres en 1812. Santiago, Montero, 1814.

este hombre célebre es el que ha sentado mejor el problema y desen-vuelto todas las condiciones del pacto social. . . . Por esto me he fijado a este autor, como el que ha entendido mejor el sistema. . . . Los absurdos que se ve obligado a devorar, debemos devorarlos con él; las sutilezas y las abstracciones en que se ve obligado a caer, deben hacernos caer también con él. El sistema es el mismo para todos los partidarios. Hablando a J. J. Rousseau, hablo a todos: refutándole, los refuto a todos; y la refutación de su contrato social es la refutación de todos los que pretenden que son los pueblos los que se han dado gobiernos y arreglado su forma. Uno y otro es igualmente imposible.[3]

In the *Cartas* the rights and importance of the nobility are set forth ingeniously by a priest who, representing the Savoyard vicar, discourses on a high cliff, command-ing a magnificent view of the sea, to another Émile. In turn, the pupil adds his reflections as he recounts the arguments advanced by this chaplain. Today they seem trivial and foolish in the extreme; but when written they were eagerly seized upon by those whose ancient privileges were being threatened or destroyed.

Another voice promptly raised against the followers of Rousseau was that of "El Amigo de la Verdad," an exile in Malta during the liberal régime, who, upon hearing of a Valencian edition of a Spanish translation of the *Social Contract,* disguised in title and without the name of the author, on sale at the capital of Majorca, published as an antidote his *Folleto,*[4] in which he described the revolution-ary character of the "Russoianos" and gave clues by which the "malos filosofistas Russoianos españoles" who pretended to be friends of the king might be identified. He declaimed especially against *El Redactor, El Conciso, El Tribuno,* and *La Abeja* as circulatory agencies of per-nicious ideas, and warned that even in the comparative silence after 1814 there was still danger. He claimed that the *Social Contract* was only a satire of Rousseau on the

[3]*La voz de la Naturaleza,* I (Tarragona, 1814), 66.
[4]*Folleto contra los filosofistas españoles, amigos de Rousseau,* formados por ellos mismos y por su maestro, escrito por El Amigo de la Verdad. Madrid, Imprenta de Ibarra, 1815. This title and the summary were furnished me by Professor E. H. Hespelt, who consulted the copy owned by the Hispanic Society.

philosophers; that he, like Cervantes, was merely laughing at the follies of his contemporaries; nevertheless, its extravagances and contradictions needed to be pointed out to the unwary. The favorite weapons of the followers of Rousseau in deceiving and enslaving the people were adulation and bad faith; as examples, articles in the *Aurora patriótica mallorquina* by Isidoro Antillón and Lucio Veranio were cited. In a concluding note, the author announced his two-volume work, *El Burlador de los hombres Rousseau,* as ready for publication.

Miserable in quality as are most of the apologetic works published between 1814 and 1820, through all runs the realization of the extent of the influence that Rousseau had exerted in Spanish thought. Only four examples of the refutations of the *Social Contract* need be mentioned here. Noteworthy merely because it first called attention to the false tradition of the political oath of the kings of Aragon was the weak work of José Bassa.[5] Making use of well-worn arguments, Félix Torres Amat attacked Rousseau's political treatise indirectly through a refutation of Spedalieri's *Los derechos del hombre,*[6] which he regarded as a softened exposition of the doctrine of the French work. With more plausible logic, the Benedictine Atilano de Ajo Solórzano attempted to show[7] that the primitive state of man was not the savage one Hobbes and Rousseau conjectured, but that tradition, history, and psychological observation testified that man was born for conjugal, family, and civil society. Incidentally he set forth the advantages of monarchial government, explained what he considered the only true and fundamental concept of liberty, and defended the indissolubility of matrimony. Another verbose answer to the teachings of the *Social*

---

[5] *Soberanía del pueblo, cartas con honores de discurso. . . .* Lérida, 1815.

[6] *Seis cartas a Irénico, en que se dan claras y distintas ideas de los derechos del hombre y de la sociedad civil,* y se desvanecen las del contrato que se finge como origen o fundamento necesario de toda soberanía. . . . Por D. Macario Padua. Barcelona, 1817.

[7] *El hombre en su estado natural.* Cartas filosófico–políticas. . . . Valladolid, 1819.

Contract, reprinted in this era, was that of Hernández Morejón,[8] prepared as early as 1764 as an antidote against the poisonous philosophy then coming into vogue.

The most vigorous of the funeral sermons preached over the remains of the liberals was that of Rafael Vélez, whose allegiance in 1812 had in the meanwhile brought as a reward a bishopric. In his *Apología del altar y del trono* (Madrid, 1818), he traced the development of liberalism in Spain from the middle of the eighteenth century, when the evil, as he termed it, began with the introduction of French books. In the lengthy list of contaminating works, the *Social Contract* is included, but Vélez came closer home in placing the direct blame for the liberal ideas which had caused such an upheaval in nineteenth-century Spain. Of the Spanish works which had attacked directly both state and church, he considered the letters of Cabarrús[9] the most damaging; their source he found in Rousseau.

"Las ideas que este filósofo esparció . . . están vaciadas en este pequeño *Emilio* de sólo cuatro cartas. Los errores de Rousseau sobre educación, y sobre la fé de los cristianos, y el modo de hacer la regeneración del hombre están aquí reunidos."

Vélez was convinced that Cabarrús drew directly from Rousseau his conception of man; his ideas regarding religion from the third volume of *Émile;* and the notion that religion should not be taught the youth until some powers of reflexion have been attained, from the *Letters from the Mountain.*

Las ideas que de los hombres, de los gobiernos, de los príncipes, de las leyes dió Rousseau en su *Pacto Social,* en su *Emilio,* y en su *Origen de la desigualdad,* son las mismas que repitió entre nosotros el señor C. Las cartas ponen a los hombres en sociedad por *pactos;* la autoridad de la ley la hacen recibir del *pueblo.* Los reyes no son . . . más que unos *caudillos en tiempo de guerra.* La *igualdad y libertad* de todos los hombres . . . son dos bases en que apoya todo su plan.[10]

---

[8]*El triunfo de la razón.* . . . Madrid, 1814.

[9]Cf. Chapter II, pp. 60–61. Intelligent men rated them highly at the time they were written. Jovellanos termed the third "la más sublime de todas, sabia y elocuente" [*Diarios (Memorias íntimas), 1790–1801,* September 13–24, 1795].

[10]*Apología del trono,* II, 13.

Vélez also awarded Cabarrús the honor of having been the first in Spain to suggest such wide-sweeping reforms. "Cuanto se ha hecho después por las cortes todo estaba detallado en su plan de regeneracion."

After having shown conclusively that Cabarrús was one of the greatest enemies Spain had known, Vélez next turned his attention to Quintana, whose articles in various papers, especially the *Semanario patriótico*, he regarded as highly prejudicial to religion. He charged that Quintana, after he had reached the masses through his poetry, had taken from Cabarrús the cry of calling the rulers tyrants; through *manifiestos*, projected constitutions, pamphlets, and periodicals, had popularized the notion of the sovereignty of the people; and had turned them against the authority of the king and the church. Also influenced by Cabarrús, in the opinion of the good bishop, was Flores Estrada, who drafted the first projected constitution providing for religious toleration. The constitution adopted in 1812 was nothing more than the French constitution of 1791, a comparison Vélez made in great detail. Even with that abolished, papers clamoring for a constitution continued to invade Spain.

> Estos pactos, estas reuniones para hacerse los hombres de una cabeza, y darse una ley al gusto de todos, ya he manifestado que es el plan de Rousseau, que jamás ha existido, ni que pudo existir en algún tiempo.

While all this breath was being spent in belittling Rousseau's views, his ideas were being brought directly to the Spanish-reading public. In 1814 *La nouvelle Héloïse* was issued at Bayonne in a Spanish translation marked by the omission of many words, phrases, and chapters of the original; the notes are largely a defense of the Church and criticisms of Rousseau's comments on religious matters. The general tone is so clearly in keeping with Catholic doctrine as to bar the possibility that Marchena was the translator, unless he was trying to secure the publication of the work in Spain, which seems improbable.

In 1817 a Spanish translation of *Émile*, which bore on the title page the name of Marchena as translator, was published at Bordeaux, in three volumes; this was promptly prohibited by the restored Inquisition.[11] Two years later a four-volume edition, as yet unseen by the writer, was published at Paris by Alexis Eymery. In that same year a translation of the *Social Contract* was issued at Lyons, where it was on sale at the store of Corman and Blanc; this text corresponds exactly with that of 1799, except that some typographical and linguistic errors have been corrected. In 1820 a second edition of the 1814 version of *Julia o la nueva Heloísa* was issued by Beaume at Bordeaux in four duodecimo volumes. The initials given on the title page, A.B.D.V.B., have so far not served to identify the translator. This edition is "corregida y aumentada con las dos cartas, y todo lo demás que se había suprimido en la primera edición." As there would have been little demand for Spanish versions in France, these were undoubtedly the output of publishers who must have had reasonable assurance of a Spanish market. During this period more than one Spaniard tried to eke out an existence by translating prohibited French works; these passed the frontier as contraband, and were eagerly seized upon, especially by students.

The events of January 1, 1820, leveled all barriers at once. The constitution of 1812 was accepted by the king who, for the moment, appeared paralyzed. Freedom of the press, abolition of the Inquisition, and the reëstablishment of the Cortes gave ground for hope that Spain was entering upon a new and peaceful era. At last the liberals who had languished in fortresses for years regained their liberty; and the *emigrados* were free to return. The steady stream of literature which poured from the press in the first period of constitutional government became, in the second, a veritable torrent.

—— ——

[11]Paz y Melia, A., *Catálogo de los papeles de Inquisición* (Madrid, 1914), No. 1353.

Of great importance in any study of Rousseau in Spain must be the translations of his various works which were now published there openly. Of the *Discourse on Inequality,* one edition, the work of Marchena, was issued at Madrid in 1820; another, that same year at Gerona; a third, at Valencia in 1821; and a fourth, at Madrid in 1822. The first Spanish edition of *La nouvelle Héloïse* was a reprint of that of Bordeaux with "Madrid, 1820," on the title page, but without the name of the publisher. During 1821 a translation which bore the name of Marchena and is distinctly different in tone and language from that made by A.B.D.V.B. was published at Toulouse by Bellagarigue and reprinted the following year by Benito Cano at Madrid. Both include "Los amores de milord Eduardo Bomston," which did not appear in the earlier edition.

No sooner was the revolt of Riego recognized as successful than José Collado issued at Madrid a translation of the *Social Contract,* described on the title page as "Nueva edición, revista y corregida." This was no other than the 1799 and 1819 edition, but more errors had been corrected. The similarity of these editions, and the fact that Marchena translated all the other important works of Rousseau, gives support to the possibility that this version was in reality his work, although his name never appeared on its title page. Another Madrid edition, that of Ramos, 1821, which bore on the verso of the fly-leaf the notation "Se hallará en Lyon, Librería de B. Corman y Blanc," serves to connect it by the same thread. The Collado edition served the Philadelphia firm of Carey and Lea as the basis of its reprints of 1821 and 1822. Another version, based on Ferrer de Orga's 1812 translation, was published in Madrid in 1820 by Repullés. This, which included the chapter on civil religion and the notes borrowed from the 1799 edition, served in 1822 as the basis for a Mexican edition, to be discussed in the following chapter.

Nor was the Spanish public left without ample copies of *Émile* in its own tongue. A Bordeaux edition (three volumes) of 1821 which bore the name of Marchena as translator led the vanguard; a "nueva edición" in two volumes of Albán at Madrid followed the same year; a third was issued at Bordeaux in 1822; and Collado furnished the fourth—four editions within two years. During 1822 and 1823 *Los Pensamientos* was published in two volumes at Madrid and also at Bordeaux. In all, eighteen editions of Rousseau's most important works were supplied to an eager Spanish public during these three years of constitutionalism. Besides, the *Supplément* to the *Contrat Social* which Gudin had published at Paris in 1791 was added in 1821 to the long list of related works available to the Spanish public.

By this time most of the early champions of Rousseau in Spain had died—Aranda in 1795; Almodóvar in 1799; Floridablanca in 1808; Cabarrús in 1810; and Jovellanos in 1811; but some of the pioneer advocates of free thought and speech remained to exult in the triumph of popular sovereignty. With the success of the Revolution of 1820 Spain opened her doors to the *afrancesados* once more; among them returned Marchena, expecting, no doubt, recognition and appreciation from the liberals whose cause he had always championed. But he was doomed to further disappointment. The people of Seville received him with doubt, some remembering his association with the French invaders, while others, willing to forget this episode, were scandalized by his freedom of speech. His disrespect for the church, contempt for Spanish conservatism, apparent indifference to tyranny, and lack of resentment against the king aroused alike their fear and dislike. One difficulty followed another until, in a letter written at Osuna on December 6, 1820, Marchena blazed forth for the last time:

¿Quién se ha de persuadir de que soy yo un enemigo de la libertad? . . .

Cuando en España pocos esforzados varones escondían en lo más recóndito de sus pechos el sacrosanto fuego de la libertad; cuando ascendían los viles a condecoraciones y empleos . . . alzaba yo un grito en defensa de la humanidad ultrajada por los desenfrenos de la más loca democracia. Mas nunca los excesos del populacho me harán olvidar los imprescriptibles derechos del pueblo; siempre sabré arrastrar la prepotencia de los magnates, lidiando por la libertad de mi patria.[12]

In this same letter Marchena drew a comparison between himself and Rousseau, and between this letter of his and that of the Swiss philosopher to the authorities of Geneva, a parallel which brought down upon his head a derisive attack from a fellow member of the Reunión Patriótica of Seville.

¿Qué obras pueden igualar a este nuevo autor con aquel célebre filósofo, si ya no es el desenfreno de sus pensamientos e ideas en materias de religión? Sepa el Sr. Marchena que la comparación hubiera sido más propia si se hubiese acordado de Esopo y de sus fábulas, ya que (aun olvidada la semejanza de su persona) a este género pertenecen todos los hechos y particularidades que refiere? . . . ¿Quién ha escrito entre nosotros contra las obras de este autor, cuando no se conocen ni pueden conocerse? . . .

El es un extranjero en su propio país, por los muchos años de ausencia y sus relaciones y enlaces íntimos con alguno de los personajes de la revolución francesa, que nada tiene de común con la nuestra, a excepción de los principios generales del derecho de la naturaleza y de las gentes. . . .[13]

Shortly after, Marchena, one of the most direct links between Rousseau and Spain, passed from the scene. Like Rousseau, he was a propagandist with all the zeal of a missionary; he lacked neither vision nor audacity in spreading his gospel of liberty. It required courage of no mean order, in Spain of his day, to preach the rights of man and the interest of the downtrodden. Yet in his poetry, prose, and speech he carried Rousseau to the upper classes in Spain; through his translations he made the works of Rousseau speak for themselves to the common people. Mistaken in his judgment he may at times have

---

[12]Cited by Menéndez y Pelayo, "El abate Marchena," in *Estudios de crítica literaria*, III, 352–353.

[13]*Impugnación de la carta del abate Marchena al . . . D. Juan Odonojú* (inserta en el *Diario de Cádiz*), Sevilla, 1821. Quoted in part by Menéndez y Pelayo, "El abate Marchena," in *Estudios de crítica literaria*, III, 355-356.

been; but his sincerity and real love for Spain cannot be questioned. Violent and extreme as Rousseau himself, ablaze with enthusiasm, he passed like a brilliant meteor across the literary sky of Spain leaving behind him, as evidence of his passing, the teachings of Rousseau and the recollection of his novel-like life.

Back from prison in Pamplona came Quintana in 1820, but it was not the Quintana of the ode "A la imprenta." Yet with Vargas Ponce, Clemencín, Tapia, Navas, and Gil de la Cuadra he took up again the task of planning and establishing an educational system which should be national, liberal, and free to all. On June 29, 1820, the *Bases generales de la enseñanza pública*—substantially the plan Quintana had earlier submitted—went into effect. It provided for a wide extension of the educational system: elementary schools in every town of one hundred inhabitants; secondary schools similar to those of today; an increased number of institutions of higher learning; and special schools of medicine, pharmacy, commerce, navigation, agriculture, music, and art, as well as a polytechnic school and a National Academy of Science. It abolished the last trace of the old autonomous system of government of the universities; that of Alcalá de Henares was moved to Madrid, and there opened in 1822 with an inaugural address by Quintana. The plan was in operation too brief a time to have received a fair trial, for with the many other changes, it was swept out in the absolutist reaction of 1824. In spite of its defects—too great centralization of control and the omission of machinery providing the requisite funds—it remains as a worthy monument to its formulators, who therein expressed many of Rousseau's fundamental ideas of education.

From the fortress of Pamplona came also Foronda, now a man almost seventy, but in whom the fighting spirit still lingered. At once he issued a third edition of his *Cartas*, using now as an epigraph "La verdad se descubre con mucha lentitud; pero se acelera su inquisición dejando a las opiniones que luchen entre sí." In the prologue, Foronda called attention to his own daring in publishing these forty years earlier.

Cuando escribía en 1780 sobre la libertad de la imprenta y que presenté mi disertación a la sociedad de Valladolid en el año 1786, qué distante no estaba de esperar la verificación de mis deseos; pero yo sembraba, y puse a mi campo un custodio en un paréntesis que se puede quitar dando más rapidez al período en vez de enervárselo; pero me cubría entonces en algún modo de los tiros de la inquisición y del gobierno: pues decía, que iba a probar que si no había libertad de escribir, y de decir cada uno su parecer en todos los asuntos (a reserva de los dogmas de la religión católica. y determinaciones del gobierno) todos nuestros conocimientos yacerian en un eterno olvido.

He añadido en mi primera carta el derecho de igualdad a los 3 de propiedad, seguridad, y libertad, y le he definido como lo hice en las cartas sobre el contrato social de Rousseau.[14]

In reviewing conditions, Foronda pointed out that all that he had written on criminal law thirty-three years before could now be read in the works of Montesquieu, Brissot de Warville, Mably, Beccaria and Filangieri, from whom he had drawn "en el tiempo que la feroz inquisición y la estupidez del Gobierno prohibían la entrada de las luces." He cited Rousseau among the philosophers of first rank who claimed that society had the right to impose punishments, and advanced his arguments with the further exhortation:

Oiga Vd. al sublime Rousseau, y aunque ya ha leído lo que voy a decir en la página 45 y siguientes de mis cartas sobre el contrato social me prometo no les disgustará una segunda lectura.[15]

In recounting his own experiences with freedom of the press, he added:

Ya sabe Umd. lo que ha pasado en varios reinos de la Europa, cuando los gobiernos bajo del pretesto del orden y del interés público persiguieron a los escritores, que en la actualidad son el objeto de nuestra admiración, y a quienes tributamos nuestros respetos en orden a los derechos del hombre, tales fueron Montesquieu, Voltaire, Mabli, Beccaria, Filangieri, Rousseau, &c. &c., cuyos escritos declaraban los tribunales subversivos del orden público, y trastornadores de las leyes

---

[14]Foronda, Valentín de, *Cartas sobre los asuntos más exquisitos de la economía–política, y sobre las leyes criminales. . .*, Tercera edición (Pamplona, 1821), "Prólogo," xx–xxi.

[15]*Ibid.*, II, 253–254.

fundamentales. Yo también tuve la honra de ser perseguido en el año 14, por este delito, según el idioma de aquella triste época, en la que se me hizo un cargo furibundo y muy amplificado por uno de los jueces, que me tomaron declaraciones: ¿de cómo había osado traducir y publicar el contrato social, cuando las potencias de Europa le tenían proscrito?

Si, amigo, así calificaba mi Juez la obra que ha contribuído más a conocer los derechos de las Sociedades.

Despite his praise of Rousseau, Foronda rejoiced that the Spaniards had shown the fallacy of his statement that "los pueblos podían pasar de la esclavitud a la libertad, pero que si la perdían no podían recobrarla jamás." He dared to prophesy further:

Si es de fé divina, que la santa Religión Católica prevalecerá contra las puertas del infierno, es de fé humana que nuestra Constitución prevalecerá contra todos los ataques del servilismo, del despotismo, y del fanatismo.[16]

During this interval of the free press many works hitherto prohibited were issued in Spanish translations. Volney, Dupuis, Destutt-Tracy, and Bentham were read by those interested in philosophical and governmental problems, while Voltaire was read by all. So general was political discussion that Moratín, writing to a friend, begged:

. . . por los clavos de Dios, que no hable de política, ni de los derechos del hombre, ni del equilibrio de los poderes, ni de la libertad legal, ni de la soberanía del pueblo, ni de ningún otro artículo de la moderna jerigonza. . . .[17]

Refuters of the works issued in the preceding period by the conservatives now had their turn in defending the social contract theory.

El contrato social ha sido mirado por algunos como un pensamiento ingenioso; y nada hay a mi parecer más sencillo y natural que suponer dicho contrato tácito en todas las asociaciones: no es moderna esta opinión.[18]

---

[16]Ibid., "Prólogo," xxiii–xxiv.
[17]Obras póstumas de Moratín (Madrid, 1867), II, 460.
[18]Refutación de la obra titulada: "Voz de la naturaleza sobre el origen de los gobiernos" (Madrid, 1821), 13.

In some cases the arguments paralleled closely those of the *Second Discourse*.

La conservación del individuo es la primera ley de la naturaleza; y para cumplirla hay en todos los seres una voluntad y una fuerza: la primera adopta los medios, la segunda los ejecuta: de manera que la mobilidad nerviosa, y la resistencia muscular componen el principio conservador.

En el estado de la naturaleza no tiene el hombre otra propiedad que la de su fuerza, por cuyo medio realiza sus deseos para satisfacer su primera necesidad.

Pero el más fuerte extiende los medios de ejecutar su voluntad en razón de lo que el débil los limita: la necesidad es igual en uno y en otro: la conservación del mismo modo exigente en ambos; mas los recursos diferentes, porque lo es la fuerza.

A esta uniformidad de necesidades, y desigualdad de recursos, seguían las violencias y opresiones. El débil inquieto por su existencia, y contínuamente molestado, busca un arbitrio para usar con tranquilidad de su derecho,[19] y le encuentra en otro igualmente ofendido e incomodado.[20]

Scarcely had many of the *emigrados* found courage to return to Spain before they were again forced to scatter to the four winds. Backed by France, Ferdinand reasserted himself in 1823; again he became an absolute monarch. Gone was the constitution and all the freedom for which it provided; gone in all directions were the liberals who devised and supported it. Regulations of the most drastic type were clamped on overnight. Quintana was returned to prison; Foronda died; and many liberals fled to England. The teachings of Rousseau which had come to be considered as a matter of course during the constitutional period, so generally were they accepted, were once more open to a strenuous attack in which the king himself led. Far from respecting the few national rights of the people, he now abolished even the municipal elective system. The purpose of the decree he issued on October 17, 1824, is clearly an attack on the Genevan's

---

[19][Editor's note:] "Por derecho, entiendo, la facultad que tiene cada hombre de usar libremente de su fuerza para su conservación y bien estar, siempre que no perjudique a la de otro."

[20]*Reflexiones políticas sobre la legalidad y legitimidad del Congreso nacional, o Cortes extraordinarias establecidas en la isla de León en 1810* (Madrid, 1820), 4–5.

teachings: "Con el fin de que desparezca del suelo español hasta la más remota idea de que la soberanía reside en otro que en mi real persona. . . ." The only despotic agency of the past that was not resurrected was the Inquisition, but ignorance and fanaticism carried on its work, as is forcefully shown by the case of Cayetano Ripoll, a poor schoolmaster of Valencia. While serving in the Spanish army during the struggle for independence, he had been taken as a prisoner to France, and there came into contact with the ideas of Rousseau. Later, as a teacher, he used his own judgment concerning the religious instruction of the children under his care—to the consternation of members of the community. Into the clutches of a semi-Inquisition, set up in Valencia under the title of "Junta de Fe," fell the poor schoolmaster. Menéndez y Pelayo tells the tragic story:

> Puéstole en ocasión de escuchar malas conversaciones y leer peores libros, de donde resultó perder la fe, cayendo en el deísmo *rusoyano* . . . por ser hombre de sentimientos humanitarios y filantrópicos, tanto que en la misma cárcel repartía su vestido y su alimento con los demás presos. A los niños de su escuela no les inculcaba más doctrina religiosa que la existencia de Dios, ni más doctrina moral que el Decálogo, única parte del Catecismo que explicaba. Se hicieron esfuerzos increíbles para convertirle, pero nada venció el indomable aunque mal aprovechado tesón de su alma, y murió impenitente en la horca el 31 de Julio de 1826.[21]

And so passed from this life one who was so deeply imbued with the spirit of Rousseau that he died for it—the last man hanged in Spain for refusing to accept a prescribed religious belief.

Few and poor, comparatively speaking, were the books issued in Spain during the ominous decade which followed the reëstablishment of absolutism. With the intellectual leaders—the liberals—silenced, political discussion was ended, except by the daring few who managed to conceal the truth in the trappings. But the works of Rousseau in Spanish translations continued to be issued both in and outside of Spain. The Marchena translation of *La nouvelle*

---

[21]*Historia de los heterodoxos*, VII, 143.

Héloïse was reprinted at Versailles; *Émile,* with the addition of "Los solitarios," was revised by Rodríguez Burón and published at Paris. The *Pensamientos,* which somehow escaped the censor, came out at Madrid in 1824 in two volumes and in the same form at Marseilles in 1826. The *Social Contract* was republished in Spanish at Paris in 1827 and at London in 1832. Of his important works, only the *Discourse on Inequality* failed to be reissued during this period; but the four editions published between 1820 and 1822 may have supplied the demand.

At last, in 1833, Ferdinand VII passed from the scene; and with his death a new and more hopeful era in the history of Spanish thought began.

CHAPTER XIV

ROUSSEAU IN SPANISH AMERICA

It was not alone the security of Spain that was set at stake by the French Revolution; it was her hold on the colonies that was being menaced. Even before the fall of the Bastille, Aranda had written to Floridablanca: "Mientras la tengamos [the American colonies] hagamos uso de lo que nos pueda ayudar para que tomemos sustancia, pues en llegándola a perder, nos faltaría ese pedazo de tocino para el caldo gordo."[1] After Charles IV had called Aranda to the governmental helm, that statesman, foreseeing the loss Spain was to suffer unless drastic steps were taken, wrote warningly to the king:

> No se piense que nuestra America está tan inocente como en los siglos pasados, ni tan despoblada, ni se crea que faltan gentes instruídas que ven que aquellos habitantes están olvidados en su propio suelo, que son tratados con rigor, y que les chupan la sustancia los nacidos en la matriz. . . . No se les oculta nada de lo que por aquí pasa; tienen libros que los instruyan de las nuevas máximas de libertad; y no faltarán propagandistas que irán a persuadirles. . . .[2]

Aranda was right; America was both reading and thinking. The hunger for books among the more intelligent was general; and in response to that demand the works of Rousseau as well as those of other French and English thinkers were finding their way into the colonies through various channels, not the least important of which were the Frenchmen who traveled and settled there.

In Mexico the introduction of French colonists, books, and ideas had been augmented by the cession of Louisiana and by the appointment as viceroy in 1766 of a Frenchman, the Marquis of Croix, to whom the position was ten-

---

[1] Aranda to Floridablanca, July 21, 1785. Archivo Histórico Nacional, Estado. Quoted by Amunátegui, *Los precursores de la independencia de Chile*, III, 261.
[2] Aranda, Representación al rey, February 23, 1793. Quoted by Amunátegui, *Los precursores*, III, 273–274.

dered in recognition of his services to the king of Spain; it was only natural that under such rule the enforcement of Spanish prohibitions against foreigners should have relaxed in vigor. Many of his suite and retainers were French; some of these remained in New Spain after the viceroy returned to his native land in 1771. Gálvez and Revillagigedo, among the viceroys who succeeded, were also liberals; under the latter, especially, many French of varying interests and professions entered Mexico.[3] None of these men made serious efforts to stem the inroads of foreigners or of foreign literature. The liberalism of viceroys and minor governmental officials in various parts of South America had permitted French influence to attain considerable weight there, too, before cause arose for investigation of conditions.

Following the outbreak of the French Revolution, drastic orders were issued against the admission of foreigners and of French literature into the colonies; when the first of these was received in Mexico, Revillagigedo replied calmly that all was serene in his territory and that there was no cause for alarm. The church officials, however, felt differently. Scarcely had news of the constitutional assembly and the Declaration of the Rights of Man, "or the *Social Contract* of Rousseau," as it was termed, reached Mexico, before a Dominican, Servando Teresa de Mier, was refuting it in a sermon preached on January 1, 1791, in which he exploded such ideas "hasta agotar la materia con todo género de razones y autoridades."[4]

Tactics radically different from those of Revillagigedo were adopted in 1794 by his successor, the Marquis of Branciforte, a brother-in-law of Godoy. As a result of an investigation of those suspected of French sympathy, he unearthed what he believed were wholesale attempts to

------

[3]México, Archivo general, "La Masonería en México. Siglo XVIII," published as Vol. II of *Precursores ideológicos de la guerra de independencia* (México, 1932), xxviii.

[4]"Declaración" of Dr. Mier to the Inquisition of Mexico, September 5, 1817. In Hernández y Dávalos, J. E., *Colección de documentos para la historia de la guerra de independencia de México* (Mexico, 1877–1882), VI, 794 and 873.

overthrow the viceregal government. Some of the men caught in the net were laborers of small intellectual attainments, as was one Armando Mexanes, a cook, who, when accused by the Inquisition of French sympathy and possessing prohibited books, testified that he had a "Parnaso de Vulter [sic] and Monsieur Ruso [sic]"; when told that they were prohibited, he guilelessly replied that he "could not understand that; that he was French and in France, they were allowed."[5] Another victim of the anti-French campaign was Juan Laussel, who had come to Mexico as the cook of Revillagigedo. Soon after his arrival he became closely associated with Juan Estevan Laroche, whose store served as a gathering place for the French. There they read and discussed the gazettes from Holland, French publications, and prohibited books of the Encyclopedists. At the death of Laroche, his executor burned his books, among which he found a copy of "Cartas de Rouseau en la Montaña."[6] Laussel, not as fortunate as Laroche in dying at a propitious moment, was summoned before the Inquisition on September 18, 1794, on a charge of being a Mason and of having committed many suspicious acts. In the inventory of his possessions made several weeks later, the following books appear: "Memoria interesante para la historia de la especie humana, con una disertación sobre la América y los Americanos," works of Destouches, Marivaux, Racine, *Cuentos* of Marmontel, "Diversas obras de Mr. J. J. Rousseau de Genebe [sic]," and *El Paseador solitario.*[7] As punishment, Laussel was exiled from the courts of Madrid and Mexico and from all parts of America; in addition, he was sentenced to imprisonment in an African fortress for three years.[8]

Others accused of fomenting French ideas in Mexico were highly educated. A conspicuous example of this type was Manuel Enderica, who, in his testimony, betrayed an astonishing acquaintance with contemporary events in

[5] *Precursores ideológicos de la guerra de independencia*, I (Mexico, 1929), 214.
[6] *Ibid.*, II, xxxi.
[7] *Ibid.*, 315.
[8] *Ibid.*, 412.

Europe and admitted the ownership of works by Raynal, Robertson, Voltaire, Pope, Locke, Montesquieu, the *Sistema de la Naturaleza* attributed to Mirabeau, and the *Historia de Carlos V*. He added that another defendant, Alles, had lent him the *Cartas de Eloísa* of Rousseau and two volumes of the *Encyclopedia*. *Fray Gerundio* he had bought in Bayonne, Raynal and Robertson he had secured from New Orleans; a naval officer, Fr. Maurelle, had lent him the *Social Contract*. A possible explanation of Enderica's acquaintance with current works is offered by the list of subscribers printed at the end of Volume VII of the *Espíritu de los mejores diarios*, for there his name appears. Clearly in Mexico as in South America the organ sponsored by Floridablanca had brought contact with works which were frankly liberal. As punishment for such reading, Enderica was condemned to ten years' exile from the courts of Madrid and Mexico.[9]

An interesting illustration of the exhaustive efforts of Spanish governmental officials to prevent Spanish Americans from reading books not approved by them is furnished by a volume, *Desengaño del hombre* (Philadelphia, 1794), in which the author, Santiago Felipe Puglia, attacked the Spanish government, church, and nobility, openly and violently. Although Rousseau's name is not mentioned in the text, the teachings of the *Social Contract* are openly advocated, except that Puglia favored a democracy. Before the end of 1794, a confiscated copy had been forwarded to the viceroy of Mexico by the governor of Florida, who advised that plans were on foot to introduce the work into Mexico by way of New Orleans. To prevent this, the viceroy sent warnings to Vera Cruz and New Santander (now the Mexican state of Tamaulipas), and, as he feared ingress through Texas, also advised its governor to be on the watch.[10] Five days earlier the

---

[9]*Ibid.*, I, xlvii–lv.

[10]Prohibition of the Inquisition, October 24th, and letter of viceroy to Pedro de Nava, October 29, 1794, in *Precursores ideológicos de la guerra de la independencia*, I, 302–305.

Inquisition of Mexico had prohibited the work as "pernicious, destructive of morals, and designed to undermine the authority of his Majesty." The matter did not rest there. Upon receipt of this information from Mexico, Godoy ordered the Spanish representative in Philadelphia to make vigorous protests to the United States government, and to demand that the printer be punished. The only satisfaction received was a reply from the Secretary of State, Edmund Randolph, stating that he was totally ignorant of the publication except from newspaper notices, and could only repeat what Jefferson had written on a previous occasion—that the government had no authority to prevent such publications, as freedom of the press was guaranteed.[11] In spite of the attempts to prevent its circulation in Spanish America, Puglia's work became widely known, and as late as 1822 a new edition was issued.[12]

Such treatment as Spain would have meted out to Puglia had he been in her power, and that accorded intelligent men such as Enderica, did not help to create a friendly feeling for her government, against which some self-appointed representatives of Spanish America were already conspiring. The most active and persistent of these was Francisco Miranda, who, after participating in the French Revolution, settled in London for the purpose of enlisting English aid as a step toward independence. His earlier acquaintance with the ideas of Rousseau had been strengthened by his experiences as an officer in the French army: he had heard the ideals of the Genevan exalted on every hand; after his capture of Antwerp, he ordered the name of Rousseau and of Helvetius, as emblems of liberty, substituted on conspicuous columns for those of Spanish despots.[13] After 1798 he devoted himself ceaselessly to the accomplishment of South-American independence.

---

[11]Archivo Histórico Nacional, Madrid. Estado, Legajo 3896. Jaudennes and Viar to Alcudia, Philadelphia, July 29, 1795.
[12]Colombia, Biblioteca nacional. Catálogo de las obras existentes en la Biblioteca Nacional. Bogotá, 1897. There is also a copy in the National Library of Mexico.
[13]Robertson, Life of Miranda, I, 131.

Through many years traces of Rousseau swirled through his mind. When he moved into the Grafton Street house in 1803, he had Rousseau's works among his possessions,[14] and references and citations scattered throughout his papers show that he had not only read but absorbed his teachings, along with those of such writers as Jovellanos, Vattel, Montesquieu, and Locke. Especially was the Venezuelan influenced by the philosophy of the *Social Contract*, for, according to his biographer, that work served as the basis of much of Miranda's reasoning about political rights.[15] Through the proclamations, constitutions, and revolutionary plans he formulated, and through his correspondence and contacts with minds from many lands, he served as an active disseminator for the ideas of Rousseau which he and others adopted as their own.

Especially was this true in the case of Viscardo, the embittered Peruvian, who, after enjoying a pension from the English government, to which he had furnished plans for the liberation of Spanish America, died in London in 1798. Shortly afterward, his papers passed into the hands of Miranda, who at once busied himself with their revision; within a year he was distributing copies of Viscardo's *Lettre aux Espagnols-Américains* (Philadelphia, 1799).[16] Translated into Spanish,[17] it circulated widely in Spanish America. In 1801 Miranda was distributing copies;[18] in 1806, when he reached the mainland of South America, he scattered many in Colombia. In 1808, he induced the father of John Stuart Mill to write an article on it, as a means of creating an English attitude sympathetic to South America.[19] Two years later Miranda sent an English translation to Wilberforce, with a note commending the truth, justice, and solid reasoning of Viscardo.[20]

[14]*Ibid.*, II, 218.
[15]*Ibid.*, 235.
[16]*Ibid.*, I, 195–196.
[17]A copy of the Spanish translation, printed by Miranda's order in London, is included among his papers at Caracas.
[18]Robertson, *Life of Miranda*, I, 227.
[19]*Ibid.*, II, 50; *Edinburgh Review*, January, 1809, pp. 277 ff.
[20]Robertson, *Life of Miranda*, II, 64–65.

Since there is in Viscardo's incendiary document much reminiscent of Rousseau, its contents deserve momentary consideration here. At the outset, he called the attention of his countrymen to the fact that their ancestors removed to America seeking a state of natural independence, a quest which was frustrated by Spain. He argued:

Truth informs us that every law which opposes itself to the general good of those for whom it is made, is an act of tyranny; and that to exact observance to [sic] it, is enacting slavery; that a law which would directly tend to undermine the foundation of the national prosperity, would be monstrous beyond expression. . . . Since men began to unite in society for their mutual interest, Spanish America has been the most imposed upon. . . . The claim of . . . Spain to a passive obedience to its arbitrary laws, is founded principally on the ignorance which she has taken care to keep up and encourage, especially with respect to the indefeasible rights of man, and the indispensable duties of every government. She succeeded in persuading the common people, that it is a crime to reason . . . and . . . a duty to extinguish the precious torch which the Creator has put into our hands to enlighten and conduct us.[21]

He cited as an instance of a social contract the oath of the king of Aragon and the rights which the people distinctly retained; and showed that with the usurpation of power by her kings, the decline of Spain had been rapid.

Especially did Viscardo attack Spain for having exiled the Jesuits, thereby robbing 5,000 Spanish citizens of their rights:

The preservation of the natural rights, and especially of the liberty and security of persons and property, is undoubtedly the foundation-stone of every human society . . .; it is therefore the indispensable duty of every society . . . not only to respect, but still further effectually to protect the rights of every individual. . . . Nature has separated us from Spain by immense seas: a son who should find himself at a similar distance from his father, would without doubt be a fool, if in the conduct of his least concerns, he always waited the decision of his father. The son is set free by natural right; and ought a numerous people, who do not depend for anything on another people . . . be subjected to them like the vilest slaves? . . . The moment has arrived to free ourselves. Let us seize it . . . and . . . well-ordered

---

[21] An English version of the letter, written apparently in 1791, is printed in William Walton's *Present State of the Spanish Colonies* . . . (London, 1810), II, 326–349. See pp. 328–329, 336–337.

liberty . . . will commence her reign in the New World, and tyranny will be speedily exterminated. . . . Our cause is so just, so favourable to mankind, that there is but little chance of finding amongst other nations, one who will load itself with the infamy of combatting us; or who . . . will venture to oppose the general wishes in favour of our liberty.

The whole letter is an impassioned plea against the three centuries of Spanish rule in America, marked by what Viscardo termed enslavement of the Americans, ingratitude, and injustice on the part of the Spanish government. Here is a disciple of Raynal crying again against the despotism and misrule of Spain; but this time it is a native voice eloquent with suffering that is heard.

While Miranda lived, no stone within his reach was left unturned. In 1797 he was plotting against Spain with Olavide, then a fugitive from the Inquisition. In London he gathered around him a group of eager South Americans who carried his message to many parts of their continent. After his first expedition to Caracas in 1805, Miranda was forced to return to England for protection; his second, five years later, was, for a time, successful; but the Spaniards reconquered the territory and captured the leader. He was not permitted to witness the realization of his dream. As a prisoner of the Spanish government he was transported to Spain where, in a Cadiz dungeon, the beacon light which blazed the path to Hispanic American independence was snuffed out.

Miranda was not the only subject of Spain to suffer the horrors of her fortresses between 1793 and the attainment of independence by the colonies. Thousands were the victims of the Spanish determination to stamp out French ideas, another name for dreams of independence, in the colonies. One of those long and unjustly persecuted was the patrician Antonio Nariño, whose splendid library of more than 6,000 volumes of well-chosen works, of which we have already spoken, was suggestive of his tastes and ideas. In deference to his position as treasurer of tithes—one of great trust—Nariño was permitted by government

officials to own a private press on which he had authority—a rare privilege—to print anything of less than a
sheet of printing paper in length without governmental
sanction. Naturally the small world of Santa Fé was
aghast when it awoke one morning in 1794 to find that
such a man had been imprisoned on a charge of having
printed *Los Derechos del hombre*, a document pronounced
seditious by the viceroy.

The circumstances at the moment were unfortunate for
Nariño. Warnings of projected conspiracies had just been
received from Spain; the viceroy was much wrought up
over the discovery of some seditious placards; and ecclesiastics, through the confessional, had located some "highly
seditious" works, such as those of Rousseau and Voltaire.[22]
At once the viceroy saw in Nariño a promoter of such
troubles, and promptly ordered all copies of his publication confiscated and him imprisoned.

What had actually happened is briefly told by Nariño
himself in his testimony:

Había hecho imprimir los *Derechos del hombre* que tradujo de un
tomo de la *Historia de la Asamblea constituyente de Francia*. . . . Su
intención no era conmover el reino sino vender aquel impreso, del
que mandó tirar ochenta o cien ejemplares; pero . . . habiendo sabido
que se hacían por el gobierno algunas averiguaciones sobre el ex-
presado papel, recogió todos los impresos sin dejar ninguno y los
había quemado.[23]

He justified his action from three standpoints: that, in
printing under a civil privilege, he had committed no
crime; that the principles enunciated in the pamphlet
already circulated in various Spanish books; that, when
compared with peninsular publications, no new views were
therein expressed; and, as a result, the work, judged in
the light of reason and its real intent, was in nowise
prejudicial.[24] As evidence, he submitted a document of
seventy-three folios in which he showed, by citations to

---

[22]*Documentos para la historia de la vida pública del Libertador
de Columbia, Perú y Bolivia . . .,* José Félix Blanco (ed.), (Caracas, 1875), I, 247.
[23]*Ibid.,* 258.
[24]*Ibid.,* 259.

specific numbers and pages, that every idea embodied in his publication had been discussed openly in *Filangieri,* the *Encyclopedia metódica,* and even the Spanish laws themselves; and that *El Espíritu de los mejores Diarios,* published at Madrid, with the king and principal ministers heading its list of subscribers and popular in Santa Fé even among women and children, voiced not only the principles in question but others of broader import.[25] From the various issues of this periodical Nariño quoted extracts illustrative of passages set forth in the Declaration of Rights—a selection which revealed not only his own intelligence but the importance of the periodical as a disseminator of the teachings of Rousseau.

> Que el hombre nace libre y su sujeción a un jefe es para mejorar de suerte; Que los hombres son iguales, y todos deben gozar las delicias de la libertad. . . . Que ningún hombre recibió de la naturaleza el derecho de mandar a los otros; Que la autoridad de los Reyes dimana de los Pueblos; Que el Príncipe recibe de sus súbditos la autoridad; Que no puede disponer de ella sin el consentimiento de la Nación; Que la Corona, el Gobierno, la pública autoridad son bienes de la nación; Que ésta es la propietaria y los Príncipes son usufructuarios; Que a ninguno se puede inquietar en sus opiniones, aunque sean Religiosas, como su manifestación no turbe el orden público.[26]

Here we have the echoes of Foronda daringly quoting the *Social Contract.*

Nariño further showed that articles in *El Espíritu* had painted the Spanish *conquistadores* in the blackest colors by quoting such passages as:

> La humanidad debía haber llorado las funestas consecuencias de dha. conquista hasta la época preciosa, hasta el tiempo para siempre memorable en que la América llegase a ser el Santuario de la razón, de la libertad y de la tolerancia.

He brought the issue even nearer home by showing that the *Mercurio peruano* of January 6, 1793, had voiced the wrongs of the colonies in language even more drastic than his, and that his judge, Manuel de Blaya, who now showed small sympathy toward one accused of revolutionary

---

[25]*Proceso de Nariño* (Cadiz, 1914), 101.
[26]*Ibid.,* 83–84.

tendencies, was the author of an article in *El Espíritu,* which expressed ideas that might be regarded as more seditious than those in *Los derechos del hombre.* From Blaya's article, "Sobre los medios de promover mayor número de matrimonios,"[27] he quoted paragraphs in which such statements as the following occurred: "Es la causa de la humanidad que da voces clamando sus justos derechos. . . . Que nada o muy poco se la ha concedido de sus sagràdos derechos. . . ." Harshness of the government and celibacy were mainly responsible for the declining population. After stating

> Sería mucha debilidad llegar a persuadirse que sea un delito manifestar los defectos de los gobiernos. Esto sólo cabe allá en el despotismo oriental donde tan afrentosamente se trata a la humanidad,

Blaya pointed out the weak spots in the governments of Europe and thus accused them:

> A sus mismos hijos tiernos servidores del estado les quita el pan de la boca, no pocas veces para pagar a un comisionado o Receptor del fisco que con la autoridad del gobierno parece va anunciando la desolación de los Pueblos.[28]

When forced to acknowledge the authorship of such statements, Blaya, in exasperation, tried to clear himself by claiming that his article was merely a plagiarism from the *Encyclopedia metódica* and *Filangieri,*[29] while the tactics of Nariño in attempting to inculpate his judge were clearly "una refinada malicia."[30]

Nariño was sent as a prisoner to Spain, but escaped and made his way to France and England where he tried to interest those governments in assisting Spanish America. In 1797 he returned to Santa Fé and gave himself up to the court. Imprisoned again for years, he became one of the leaders of the revolutionary movement in 1810, and, after independence was assured, vice-president of Colombia.

Hardly had the excitement over Nariño's imprisonment subsided in Spanish America before there arrived at La

---

[27]No. 141.
[28]*Proceso de Nariño,* 120, 121.
[29]*Ibid.,* 77.
[30]*Ibid.,* 79.

Guayra Picornell and his associates who had been sentenced to life imprisonment. At once they made common cause with those who hated Spain, and soon a conspiracy, generally known by the name of its leaders, Gual and España, was brought to light through the activity of zealous Spanish authorities. España and five of his companions were executed; but Picornell, Cortés, and Andrés became fugitives. Picornell first carried on his activities at Trinidad, later in Santo Domingo, and finally in the United States; from time to time he issued seditious proclamations and various editions of Ponz Izquierdo's *Derechos del hombre*.[31] Cortés and Andrés betook themselves to London. All ultimately became traitors to the colonists who had assisted them to freedom; in return for services to the Spanish government, they were welcomed back by Ferdinand VII, and Picornell, at least, was well rewarded.

The 1793 appeal of Marchena, which had served to incite these men to conspiracy against Spain, also circulated in the colonies. In the case of Antonio Pérez Alamillo, who was denounced to the Inquisition in Mexico for irreligious views and for favoring the French Revolution, a "papeleta" brought from Havana was introduced as evidence.[32] This "papeleta," attributed to Olavide, was a manuscript copy, with slight changes in phraseology, of Marchena's *Aviso*. Evidently his eloquence was not entirely wasted; for in Spanish America ideas of liberty were slowly germinating.

Whatever the influence of Rousseau in general on the youth of South America, certainly on none was it more specifically and singularly exerted than on Simón Rodríguez, whom we left in Caracas in 1790 writing educational treatises and looking for students. His activity in

[31]*Derechos del hombre y del ciudadano, con varias máximas republicanas y un discurso preliminar dirigido a los americanos.* Madrid, En la imprenta de la Verdad, año de 1797. Of this the *Discurso* covers 211 pages and the *Derechos del hombre*, 15. A later reprint was issued at Santa Fé de Bogotá, Impr. del Estado, 1813. Cf. Medina, J. T., *La Imprenta en Bogotá, 1729–1821* (Santiago, 1904), p. 99.

[32]See *Precursores ideológicos de la guerra de independencia*, I, xxiv–xxvii, in which the "papeleta" is reprinted.

popularizing the educational ideas of Rousseau may have been inspired by the hope of himself applying them. At any rate, shortly after presenting to the city council of Caracas a treatise on primary education,[33] which was favorably received, he was made the tutor of a small boy, a member of a rich and influential family in Venezuela. Before turning to their relations, it may be well to consider the influence which Rousseau is credited with having exerted on the tutor.

Las ideas subversivas de Juan Jacobo Rousseau, su sentimentalismo, y, también, la seducción, el énfasis declamatorio y no obstante magnánimo de su estilo, habían, por fuerza, de llegar al corazón mismo de la juventud liberal del Nuevo Mundo, y de arrebatar deliciosamente su imaginación, entusiasta y fogosa como ninguna. A estas cualidades, arraigadas en él como en sus compatriotas y por los mismos motivos, añadía Rodríguez disposiciones particulares que hicieron de él, durante toda su existencia, una especie de caricatura de Juan Jacobo. Las excentricidades, las debilidades, o las manías del angustiado escritor de *Las Confesiones* reviven incorporadas en el *dromomano* impenitente, en el preceptor sistemático, en el sofista, y, en fin, en el visionario hipocondríaco, que, al renunciar, en 1840, a la pedagogía por el comercio de velas en Valparaíso, decía a un visitante: "Yo que desearía hacer de la tierra un paraíso para todos, la convierto en un infierno para mí."[34]

Very different was the effect of Rousseau's ideas on the child who passed into the charge of Rodríguez. Born in Caracas in 1783, Simón Bolívar was deprived of his father at the age of three, and by the time he was seven was so spoiled as to be regarded as incorrigible. Nevertheless, he yielded to the influence of his young teacher, and when both his mother and grandfather died two years later, the full responsibility for the boy and his property fell upon the tutor.

Investido de la suerte de omnímoda autoridad sobre su discípulo predilecto, pensó entonces Rodríguez en realizar un proyecto particularmente grato a su corazón, el de tratar de poner en práctica el sistema por excelencia de educación preconizado por Rousseau. El

---

[33]Amunátegui, M. L., *Ensayos biográficos*, III (Santiago de Chile, 1894), 227, 303.
[34]Mancini, *Bolívar y la emancipación de las colonias españolas*, 116–122.

niño que le había sido confiado era, como debe de ser Emilio, "rico," "de gran linaje," "huérfano," "robusto y sano," y, a su vez, ¿no realizaba Rodríguez el ideal de preceptor deseado por Juan Jacobo? "Joven," "prudente," "célibe e independiente," "una alma sublime," cualidades o atributos a que podía pretender Simón Rodríguez quien por entonces, tenía, veintiún años, gozaba de la reputación de ser el mejor profesor en la ciudad, esposo más que descuidado, y a quien su extremada independencia de aficiones y de carácter permitía trato íntimo con los más amplios pensamientos. . . . Se dedicó, pues, al "difícil estudio de no enseñar nada a su discípulo." A fin de que pudiera éste quedar en el "estado natural" y prepararse a justificar el axioma según el cual "la razón del sabio suele asociarse al vigor del atleta," Rodríguez prolongó la estancia en el campo, y consiguió al menos desarrollar en Bolívar la maravillosa aptitud a los ejercicios corporales, llegando a ser el andador incansable, el notable jinete, el intrépido nadador, con quien, más tarde, no pudo competir ninguno de su compañeros de armas.

Al cumplir los trece años, Simón había llenado, ateniéndose en un todo a las prescripciones del educador, la primera parte del programa trazado por Rousseau. Las caminatas por la selva, las correrías a caballo en la sabana, los ejercicios de remos en el lago de Valencia le habían dado, cumplidamente, fuerza y destreza.[35]

But Rodríguez had been implicated in various revolutionary schemes which came to light between 1794 and 1797; and found it prudent to take his departure from his pupil and his native land.

¡Adiós hermosos proyectos a la Juan Jacobo! Simón tenía catorce años: la sociedad de algunos jóvenes había despertado en él curiosidad por conocer algunas obras literarias. Habló de esto a Rodríguez, enseñándole al mismo tiempo unos cuantos libros. . . . ¡Libros! Tuvo remordimientos el preceptor. De sobra sabía qué libro había de leer Emilio, "el primero, el solo que, durante largo tiempo, había de componer toda su biblioteca," el maravilloso Crusoe, y, seguramente que en loor de Juan Jacobo y movido por un sentimiento de reparación secreta y de pesar, una vez más, cambió de nombre Rodríguez, adoptando, desde aquel día, el de Robinson.[36]

After the departure of his tutor, Simón became a cadet, but when he showed no disposition to study, it was decided to send him to Europe. He embarked in 1799. While in Spain, through his uncle's social contacts, he came into

---

[35]*Ibid.*
[36]*Ibid.*

close touch with the court and cultural circles of Madrid;
he read scientific and literary works; and surprised those
who regarded him as frivolous. Soon the impetuous youth
was wildly in love; obstacles only increased his passion;
in 1802 he sailed for Caracas with his bride, only to have
her die in his arms the following year. At nineteen, he
was a widower. In his despair he remembered that he had
promised Rodríguez to join him in a tour through the Old
World; at once he put the plan into execution. Before
meeting his old teacher he engaged in a serious course of
reading—Montesquieu, Voltaire, Rousseau

. . . sobretodo éste, cuyo sortilegio respiraba nuestro joven. Los
infortunios de los amantes de la *Nueva Heloísa* debieron de arran-
carle lágrimas de aquellas en que tanto se complacía la "sensibili-
dad" de la época, extravagancia que padeció Bolívar como sus demás
contemporáneos, pero que, siquiera en él, tenía por sincera excusa
los ecos despertados en un corazón cuya herida estaba tan reciente.
En las obras filosóficas del "ciudadano de Ginebra" vió de nuevo las
teorías preferidas de su maestro, y hasta pasajes enteras que Rodríguez recitaba. Animábase en su espíritu el entusiasmo de las virtudes públicas. Este sentimiento se precisaba a veces hasta dejarle
entrever, en repetinos fulgores, visiones de porvenir. ¡La libertad!
esta palabra causaba en él hondísimos estremecimientos. ¿No estaba
él destinado a consagrarse a su vez a la religión nueva de la que
había hallado más numerosos adeptos en su reciente visita a Caracas? Tal era, sin duda su pensamiento, y, tan pronto como desem-
barcó en Cádiz, se puso en relaciones con compatriotas desconocidos
acudidos a su encuentro, quienes, pocos días después, le admitían a
los misterios de la "Gran Logia Americana," en la que le hicieron
prestar el solemne juramento: "Nunca reconocerás por gobierno
legítimo de tu patria sino a aquél que sea elegido por la libre y
espontánea voluntad de los pueblos: y siendo el sistema republicano
el más adaptable al gobierno de las Américas, propenderás por
cuantos medios estén a tus alcances, a que los pueblos se decidan
por él."[37]

In Europe he wrote various letters which breathe much
of the air of "los delirios, de los suspiros y de las miradas
al cielo de que están cuajados los escritos de Saint Preux
y de Julia." His letters to the woman whom he called
"Teresa"—the name of his lost wife—"son pues, puro

---

[37]*Ibid.*, 130-131.

romanticismo; pero por eso mismo resultan más características del estado de alma del discípulo de Rodríguez y del apasionado lector de Juan Jacobo Rousseau":

"El presente no existe para mí, es un vacío completo donde no puede nacer un solo deseo que deje alguna huella grabada en mi memoria. ¡Ah, Teresa, esto será el desierto de mi vida! . . . Apenas tengo un ligero capricho lo satisfago al instante, y lo que yo creo un deseo, cuando lo poseo, sólo es un objeto de disgusto. Los continuos cambios que son el fruto de la casualidad, ¿reanimarán acaso mi vida? Lo ignoro; pero, si no sucede esto, volveré a caer en el estado de consunción de que me había sacado Rodríguez al anunciarme mis cuatro millones. . . ."38

To Rome they went together, and there the youth made a vow to free his native land from Spanish rule.

If any one work contributed directly to the accomplishment of Bolívar's life purpose—the independence of Hispanic America—it was the *Social Contract,* but it also exerted a wide influence on others before Bolívar became an active participant in the struggle. In 1802 Camilo Henríquez was denounced in Chile for reading the *Social Contract* in its original language.39 The Spanish edition published in 1799 penetrated to all sections. The consternation of the Spanish officials when the work was circulated in Asturias was shared by those in many parts of the New World. An interesting evidence is the following excerpt from an edict published in *La Gaceta de México,* December 16, 1803:

Asimismo renovamos la prohibición, aun para los que tienen licencia de leer Libros prohibidos, de otro titulado el *Contrato Social o principios del Derecho político,* traducido al Castellano, é impreso en Londres año de 1799. Esta obra es de Juan Jacobo Roseau, prohibida en Roma por decreto de 16 de Junio de 1766, y comprendida en la prohibición general que la Inquisición de España publicó año de 1764 de todas las obras de este filósofo, deísta y revolucionario, y la traducción lo está en la Regla 13 del Expurgatorio; pero merece especial anatema, porque no solamente renueva el sistema pernicioso antisocial e irreligioso de Roseau, sino porque este traductor anima a los fieles vasallos de S. M. a sublevarse y sacudir la suave

---

38Quoted by Mancini, *ibid.,* 134–135.
39Medina, J. T., *Historia del tribunal del santo oficio de la inquisición de Chile,* II (Santiago, 1890), 539–542.

dominación de nuestros Reyes, imputándola el odioso nombre de despotismo, y excitándoles a romper, como él dice, las trabas y grillos del Sacerdocio y de la Inquisición, expresión impía, que nos hace creer que este Traductor del *Contrato Social* es el mismo Autor del de la *Bororquía, o la Víctima de la Inquisición.*

Y aunque hasta ahora no tenemos noticia de que se hayan extendido estos exemplares en nuestro Distrito, conociendo por su contexto, y por el aviso que nos dió el Señor Comandante general de Provincias Internas, la infame temeridad y atrevimiento de este autor, y que es muy posible que auxiliado de los enemigos de la paz se empeñe a toda costa en introducir tan venenosa zizaña en esta piadosa y fiel América; hemos juzgado de nuestra principal obligación publicar cuanto antes este edicto. . . .

Difficult it was, indeed, to prevent the reading of Rousseau. In 1803 there appeared the first Spanish translation of the *Discourse on Inequality,* bearing on its title page Charleston, South Carolina, as its place of printing.[40] This may have been a subterfuge, but the translator was apparently an American; at least he refers to "nuestra América" in more than one instance. In the prologue he praised the philosophers who had laid the foundations for American independence; and showed himself strongly opposed to nobility and titles, especially Spanish, and ecclesiastics. He commented on the miserable state of the Spanish army—humiliated and despised; and begged for justice for those in Spanish prisons. In a note on p. 58 the translator showed unusual familiarity with the animals of Mexico and Nicaragua. These are the only clues to his identity.

There is also some evidence that a Spanish translation of the *Social Contract* circulated with a similar title page. Professor Marden of Princeton University, shortly before his death in 1932, told the writer he had clipped such an item from the catalogue of a dealer in old books and sent it to Professor Christian Gauss, who has since been unable to locate it but recollects the item and thinks the printer's name was Black and the date about 1800. It is his conviction that the edition was antedated and the imprint of

---

[40]For details, see Bibliography.

Charleston merely a blind for a Spanish or Spanish-American publication.[41]

In the same year in which the Charleston item was printed, Antonio de Castro, an employee of the tribunal of commerce of Vera Cruz, was condemned to six years' exile in the Philippines for admitting that he had read *Émile* "with pleasure";[42] and Bolívar was digesting the *Social Contract* at the same time preparatory to rejoining his former tutor in France. In 1808 officials in Mexico felt impelled to issue a circular in which they warned that

aquellas ideas del contrato social de Rousseau, del espíritu de las leyes de Montesquieu, y otros semejantes filósofos, por las cuales en la elección de príncipe concurre cada partícula con la porción de su independencia, que puede cuando quiere recoger, están pros-scritas, porque contribuyen a la libertad e independencia con que solicitan destruir la religión, el estado, el trono y toda propiedad, y establecer la igualdad que es un sistema quimérico impracticable, de lo cual nos da un ejemplo la misma Francia.[43]

So deeply had ecclesiastics in Mexico impressed upon their parishioners the crime of reading such a heretic as Rousseau that José Roxas was denounced by his own mother for having such a volume in his possession, and was confined for several years in the dungeons of the Inquisition. He escaped, but died soon after reaching New Orleans.[44] At Caracas José María Vargas made a translation of the *Social Contract* in 1809,[45] and Juan Germán Roscio was writing to Andrés Bello, then in London, to remind him that it was in that city that the *Social Contract* "obtuvo la mejor apología."[46]

---

[41]Christian Gauss, Princeton, October 28, 1932, to writer.

[42]Medina, J. T., *Historia del tribunal del santo oficio de la inquisición de México* (Santiago, 1905), 451.

[43]"Esposiciones de los fiscales contra las opiniones de los nova-dores," in Hernández y Dávalos, *op. cit.*, I, 756. México, August 9, 1808, doc. 260, pp. 672–680.

[44]Ward, H. G., *Mexico in 1827* (London, 1828), I, 110; Alamán, L., Historia de México (Mexico, 1849–1852), I, 121; Brackenridge, H. M., *Voyage to South America in 1817–1818* (London, 1820), I, 27.

[45]Blanco, J. F., ed., *Documentos para la vida pública del libertador*, I, 236.

[46]Amunátegui, M. L., *Vida de D. Andrés Bello* (Santiago, 1882), 84.

By this time the common people of South America were, in the eyes of an Englishman at least, more enlightened and in possession of more sources of information than those of Spain.

Unshackled, in some degree, by the thraldom of the illiberal bigot in power, works are to be found in the hands of the opulent, which, in Spain, it would have been next to treason to have. . . . The works of Raynal and St. Pierre are not uncommon on the main, besides a variety of other philosophic and learned works, which seem to have been left there by the many French literati, who have, at different periods, travelled in the country.[47]

As Buenos Aires was the first city in Hispanic America to drive the Spaniards completely from the field, so it was the first to publish the *Social Contract* in a Spanish translation. The man inspired to this accomplishment was another of the close students of Rousseau, even under the Spanish régime. Born in 1778 in Buenos Aires, Mariano Moreno studied under Cayetano Rodríguez there, and later took his law degree at Chuquisaca, where Don Matías Terrazas placed at his disposal a splendid library including many prohibited books.[48] Here Moreno absorbed the ideas of Rousseau both directly and through Spanish writers who, like Jovellanos, knew their Rousseau.[49] After engaging in his profession in Buenos Aires, in 1810 he became the secretary of the first local *junta* and editor of *La Gaceta de Buenos Aires,* through whose pages many of Rousseau's ideas were brought directly to the general reading public. In the issue of October 4, 1810, is a discussion of popular sovereignty; in the extra of November 6, he quotes Rousseau by name and appeals to the people to support the authorities and to know their rights; in that of November 13 is a discussion of "Voluntad general" and "Soberanía," borrowed almost literally from the *Social Contract.* In the series "Sobre las Miras del Congreso," first published in fragmentary form in the same organ,[50]

---

[47]Walton, William, *Present State of the Spanish Colonies,* II, 137.
[48]Rojas, R., "Noticia Preliminar" to *Doctrina democrática de Mariano Moreno* (Buenos Aires, 1915), v.
[49]Rojas, R., *La literatura argentina,* I, 45–47.
[50]October 28, November 2, 13, 15, 28, 1810.

he not only sets forth the main tenets of the *Social Contract* but quotes directly from it, citing the author by name.[51] Specific passages scattered through his various works are cited by the caustic critic Groussac[52] as derived from Rousseau.

But Moreno went much further; he published the first Spanish translation of the *Social Contract* issued in Buenos Aires. More definite evidence of this South American's estimate of Rousseau could scarcely be offered than the following excerpt from the prologue Moreno wrote for the edition he issued there in 1810:

> En tan críticas circumstancias, todo ciudadano está obligado a comunicar sus luces y sus conocimientos; y el soldado que opone su pecho a las balas de los enemigos exteriores, no hace mayor servicio que el sabio que abandona su retiro y ataca con frente serena la ambición, la ignorancia, el egoísmo, y demás pasiones, enemigos interiores del Estado, y tanto más terribles, cuanto ejercen una guerra oculta y logran frecuentemente de sus rivales una venganza segura. Me lisonjeo de no haber mirado con indiferencia una obligación tan sagrada, de que ningún ciudadano está exceptuado, y en esta materia creo haber merecido más bien la censura de temerario, que la de insensible o indiferente; pero el fruto de mis tareas es muy pequeño, para que pueda llenar la grandeza de mis deseos; y siendo mis conocimientos muy inferiores a mi celo, no he encontrado otro medio de satisfacer éste, que reimprimir aquellos libros de política que se han mirado siempre como el catecismo de los pueblos libres, y que por su rareza en estos países, son acreedores a igual consideración que los pensamientos nuevos y originales.
>
> Entre varias obras que deben formar este precioso presente, que ofrezco a mis conciudadanos, he dado el primer lugar al *Contrato Social*, escrito por el ciudadano de Ginebra, Juan Jacobo Rousseau. Este hombre inmortal, que formó la admiración de su siglo, y será el asombro de todas las edades, fué, quizá, el primero que disipando

---

[51]*Doctrina democrática de Mariano Moreno* (Buenos Aires, 1915), 250, 267. The editor, Ricardo Rojas, notes that Rousseau and the French encyclopedists furnished the basis for this series ("Noticia preliminar," 22–23); as does also Ricardo Lavene, *La Revolución de mayo y Mariano Moreno* (Buenos Aires, 1926), II, 270.

[52]He refers to pp. 325, 388, 390–391, 398, 412–413, 427–428, etc., of Norberto Piñero's edition of *Escritos de Mariano Moreno* (Buenos Aires, 1896) as examples of this borrowing (*La Biblioteca*, I (1896), 142). His review of this edition is also reprinted in his *Crítica literaria* (Buenos Aires, 1924), 231–278.

completamente las tinieblas con que el despotismo envolvía sus usur-
paciones, puso en clara luz los derechos de los pueblos, y enseñándoles
el verdadero origen de sus obligaciones, demostró las que correlativa-
mente contraían los depositarios del Gobierno.

. . . .

El estudio de esta obra debe producir ventajosos resultados en
toda clase de lectores; en ella se descubre la más viva y fecunda
imaginación; un espíritu flexible para tomar todas formas, intrépido
en todas sus ideas; un corazón endurecido en la libertad republicana
y excesivamente sensible; una memoria enriquecida de cuanto ofrece
de más reflexivo y extendido la lectura de los filósofos griegos y
latinos; en fin, una fuerza de pensamientos, una viveza de coloridos,
una profundidad de moral, una riqueza de expresiones, una abundancia, una rapidez de estilo, y sobre todo una misantropía que se
puede mirar en el autor como el muelle principal que hace jugar
sus sentimientos y sus ideas.

This edition of the *Contrato Social* has given rise to
several bibliographical problems. Gutiérrez[53] and officials
of the Bibliothèque Publique at Geneva describe the work
as having 92 pages; Palau's copy had only 66; yet the
title pages were identical. Inspection of a complete copy
in the National Library of Argentina revealed that the
work was issued in two installments: the first contained
92; the second, 66 pages; but each carried the same title
page.[54] Copies of the first part are more numerous.[55] By
the time the second part was issued, early in January,
1811, the more conservative element had come into control of the *cabildo,* which decided on February 5 that the
work was not desirable for public consumption and ordered
200 copies turned back to the printer.[56]

---

[53]Gutiérrez, J. M., *Origen y desarrollo de la enseñanza pública
superior en Buenos Aires* (Buenos Aires, 1916), 390.
[54]Had Palau examined his copy closely he would have found that
it began with signature "N" and the text with Chapter VIII (of
Book III).
[55]Zinny, Antonio, *Bibliografía histórica de las provincias unidas
del Río de la Plata desde el año 1780 hasta el de 1821* (Buenos
Aires, 1875), p. 50.
[56]Medina, J. T., *Historia y bibliografía de la imprenta en el
antiguo virreinato del Río de la Plata*, La Plata, Buenos Aires, Londres, 1892. See Pt. 3, *La Imprenta en Buenos Aires*, 1780–1810,
xxxvii.

The question of the translator is not so easily solved. There have been various conjectures. Jovellanos was suggested as the translator[57]—a possibility eliminated by facts already presented; the edition was said to be a reprint of that which circulated in the Peninsula[58]—apparently the London, 1799; but a comparison of the texts proves conclusively that it was not. If the edition is, as its title page affirms, a *reimpresión*, it must have been either from the Vargas translation (Caracas, 1809), the purported Charleston edition, or some other, unknown as yet to the writer. The suppression of the chapter and principal passages in which Rousseau discussed religion antedates by four years the first Spanish peninsular edition with these omissions. Two problems that remain are: the identification of the translator and the discovery of the edition from which Moreno reprinted.

The direct influence of Rousseau in the thought of Argentina at this period is generally recognized by all who have analyzed its content,[59] and the Buenos Aires edition of the *Social Contract* circulated widely.[60] The establishment by Moreno in 1810 of the National Library

---

[57]Groussac [*Crítica literaria*, 251] credits this conjecture to Dr. López, but it was repeated by others as late as 1922. See Bibliography, p. 283.

[58]Even Groussac affirms this, but without having seen a copy of the earlier edition.

[59]"La influencia de Rousseau en nuestra revolución está a la vista. . . . En toda la literatura revolucionaria se tropieza con las huellas de esta influencia: el pacto social, la voluntad general, la salud pública, la soberanía inalienable, la reasunción de la soberanía por violación del pacto fundamental, son giros corrientes, que usan hasta los predicadores en el púlpito."—Korn, Alejandro, *Influencias filosóficas en la evolución nacional* (Buenos Aires, [1937]), 88–89.

"Era el [álito] de Juan Jacobo, revolucionando al mundo con enseñanzas que no eran las de antes; teorías liberales que a esa hora ya andaban dando vuelta al mundo, y no podía atajarlas nadie."—Bosch, Mariano G., "Luis Ambrosio Morante . . ." in *Boletín de la Academia argentina de letras*, III (1935), 154–155.

[60]This was noted by a North American in 1817: "[It] is well executed, and seems to have been much relished by the middle class of people. But it is difficult to say whether it was not more injurious than beneficial; it was likely to make raw and visionary politicians, whose notions, not having sound political experience for their basis, would be as wild as various."—Brackenridge, H. M., *Voyage to South America*, II, 133.

of Argentina, the first public library in Buenos Aires, put
into circulation at least one of Rousseau's works, for
among the books bequeathed to that institution by Bishop
Azamor was "un tomo de Rousseau," "probablemente el
Contrato Social" opines the scholar J. T. Medina.[61] In the
original "Libro de donaciones" is an entry[62] recording the
gift of a copy of Rousseau's Dictionary of Music in 1814,
and among the Funes books added later were "Oeuvres
Politiques" de Rousseau—5 tomos."[63]

As early as 1811 members of a patriotic society busied
themselves, according to the historian Rojas, with discussions of the teachings of Rousseau.

Se sostenía el principio de que el pueblo había reasumido la
soberanía, desde que el Emperador de los franceses había cautivado
la de los Reyes; que el pueblo tenía derecho para darse la Constitución . . . que garantía a todos los ciudadanos, sin excepción, sus
derechos de libertad, de igualdad, y de propiedad, invocándose en
apoyo el Contrato Social. . . .[64]

A member of this organization, Bernardo Monteagudo,
editor of one issue per week of the Gaceta from November 1, 1811, to March 25, 1812, had also studied the political theory of Rousseau, and seems in those years to have
accepted the doctrine of a social contract. Especially
through his articles of February 14, 21, and 28 as well as
that of March 6 runs the idea of such a contract as an
assurance of liberty, equality, and security. "Entre el
hombre y la ley, entre la magestad y el ciudadano, entre
la constitución y el pueblo hay un pacto recíproco por el
cual se obligan todos a conservar y sostenerse en los pre-
cisos límites que les designó la necesidad al tiempo de la
convención," he wrote on the latter date. In an inaugural

[61]Tribunal del Santo Oficio de la Inquisición de las provincias del
Plata (Santiago, 1899), 254–255.
[62]Folio 15.
[63]Lista de los libros del Deán Funes. Ms. No. 689 in Biblioteca
Nacional, Buenos Aires, 4 ff.
[64]Rojas, R., La Literatura argentina (Los proscriptos, I,), Vol. V.
322–324.

address delivered before the Sociedad Patriótica on January 13, 1812,[65] he summarized in his opening paragraphs some of the teachings of the *Second Discourse*, and saw as the purpose of the organization—"grabar en el corazón de todos esta sublime verdad que anunció la filosofía desde el trono de la razón—la soberanía reside sólo en el pueblo, y la autoridad en las leyes."[66] In the second section, he declared that ignorance was the basis of all the misfortunes of man, although he admitted that some people have been happy through ignorance.

Tampoco me he propuesto combatir al ciudadano de Ginebra demostrando que el progreso de las ciencias no ha contribuído a corromper las costumbres, sino antes bien a rectificarlas; dejemos a la Academia de Dijon que examine este problema, mientras la experiencia lo decide sin necesidad de ocurrir a razonamientos sutiles.[67]

Years later, in explaining his changed political conceptions, he referred to his earlier views:

. . . las ideas demasiado inexactas que entonces tenía de la naturaleza de los gobiernos, me hicieron abrazar con fanatismo el sistema democrático. El Pacto Social de Rousseau y otros escritos de este género, me parecía que aun eran favorables al despotismo.[68]

In educational as well as in political circles in Argentina the name of Rousseau was early familiar. Juan C. Lafinur did not hesitate to refer to him openly before his class in philosophy at the College of San Carlos in 1819, for, in considering the subject of God, he stated:

Hay dos cosas que la Filosofía debe respetar, decía frecuentemente *Juan Jacobo Rousseau; Dios* y la *espiritualidad del alma.* Estos grandes objetos son los apoyos de toda moral y los fundamentos de la dicha pública y particular.[69]

At the conclusion of the course in August, 1820, Lafinur made an address in which he refuted the *First Discourse.*[70]

---

[65]Pelliza, Mariano A., *Monteagudo, su vida y sus escritos* (Buenos Aires, 1880), I, 243–263.
[66]*Ibid.*, 252.
[67]*Ibid.*, 255.
[68]"Memorias sobre los principios políticos que seguí en la administración del Perú," March 17, 1823, *ibid.*, II, 256.
[69]Curso filosófico dictado . . . en Buenos Aires, 1819. Ms. No. 127, p. 78, in Biblioteca Nacional, Buenos Aires.
[70]*Ibid.*, p. 77.

Among his hearers was Fray Francisco Castañeda who had written:

> Deseo con impaciencia que amanezca el día 31 para tener el placer de oir el discurso de usted contra el extravagante Juan Santiago, de quien el sabio Laharpe dice: *Jean Jacques Rousseau c'est le ne plus ultra de l'orgueil humain.*[71]

In various types of writings of other Argentinians of the era, references to Rousseau abound. Even in such a work as "Memoria sobre la agricultura"[72] by Deán Funes is a reference to "El ciudadano de Ginebra Juan Santiago que deseaba haber nacido en un país donde el gobierno y el público no pudieran tener sino un solo interés, a fin de que todos los movimientos de la máquina no pudiesen dirigirse a otro blanco que a la felicidad común."[73]

No such freedom of thought or speech was tolerated in Mexico, where, at the first signs of actual revolution, late in 1810, the Spanish authorities began a studied attack upon the intellectual sources of the insurrection. In response to an edict of December 1st of that year exhorting ecclesiastics to refute the writings of the French,"[74] many hastened to the pulpit and the press with warnings to New Spain against Napoleon, freemasonry, and, incidentally, Rousseau. One writer declared that the social pact was as nothing compared with the word of God, who had permitted, as a punishment for Spain, that Napoleon should put into practice "todas las artes diabólicas y venenosas de Voltayre, Rousseau, d'Alembert, Diderot, y de toda la caterva de falsos filósofos que excavaron con sus escritos pestilenciales los cimientos de los tronos que los hombres tenían por indestructibles."[75] Another writer, Florencio Pérez y Comoto, brought forward arguments

---

[71]Gutíerrez, *Origen y desarrollo de la enseñanza . . . en Buenos Aires*, 86–87.

[72]Ms. No. 7956, in Biblioteca Nacional, Buenos Aires.

[73]Quoted by Rojas, *La literatura argentina*, V, 140–142.

[74]Hernández y Dávalos, *Colección de documentos . . .*, II (Doc. 222), 448–449.

[75]"Desengaños que a los insurgentes de Nueva España seducidos por los francmasones agentes de Napoleón dirige la verdad de la religión católica y la experiencia," *ibid.*, IV, 589.

against equality of political and social rights,[76] and a Mexican doctor issued a series of letters against the leader of the revolution under the general title of *El Anti-Hidalgo.* In the eighth letter is the following gibe directed at Rousseau:

> Unos dicen que ya, según el sistema de Rusó, has emprendido el estado que él llama *natural,* viviendo en las cuevas de los montes como las bestias, y al modo de las bestias; y que empezabas a andar en cuatro pies, parte por elección *rusoyana,* y parte por necesidad aculqueña.

In the ninth, he says:

> Juan Santiago Rusó en la colección de sus cartas (t. 24) protesta más de una vez, que está creído de que no debería empezar ni acabar la revolución más favorable para los pueblos, si había de costar la sangre de un solo hombre.

In the notes he accuses Hidalgo of planning to "realizar en éste que llamas *vasto continente,* todas las hipótesis de Diderot, Helvecio, Rusó . . . estableciendo el estado *de pura animalidad y ser su régulo.*[77]

With better logic, the liberal bishop of Michoacán, Manuel Abad y Queipo, took up the sin of insurrection against an existing government; in support of his views he utilized statements made by Rousseau in the *Second Discourse* and the *Social Contract.*

> El citado ciudadano de Ginebra, ese hombre singular, ese defensor ardiente de la libertad de los pueblos, que como deísta puro, en nada se detiene, ni admite otra regla que la de su razón o su capricho, tampoco se opone o contradice a esta doctrina católica, aun en su contrato social con que ha hecho tanto ruido y tanto daño en el mundo. En esta célebre producción, que él mismo confiesa haberla abandonado por la insuficiencia de sus fuerzas, que es impracticable, y que sólo la propone como una escala o pitipié para medir la perfección o imperfeccion de los gobiernos establecidos; dice: que una sociedad como sociedad, o un pueblo como soberano, nunca puede ofender directamente a los individuos particulares de que se compone; pero si puede ser leso y ofendido por los mismos particulares: en cuyo caso no pueden éstos separarse de la sociedad, y deben ser

---

[76]Impugnación de algunos errores políticos que fomentan la insurrección de N. España," *ibid.,* 400–408.

[77]Reprinted, *ibid.,* II (Doc. 256), 650, 659, 685.

reprimidos y castigados por la fuerza pública. De que resulta, que toda sublevación contra la sociedad es inicua y punible. Dije advertidamente aun en el contrato social, porque fuera de esta obra y de algunas expresiones inconejas que ha sentado, esforzando el *pro y el contra;* es indubitable que aun el impío Rousseau miró con mucho respeto los gobiernos establecidos, aun los más viciosos, como era el de Polonia, sobre que fué consultado por algunos señores polacos que lo querían reformar y dar la libertad al pueblo, que es allí ascripticio o siervo de la tierra. La contestación que les dió sobre este asunto, le hace mucho honor. En ella brillan la humanidad, la política y sobre todo la más acendrada prudencia preventiva de todos los males que podían resultar de una novedad semejante. Les dice entre otras cosas: guardaos mucho de conceder de pronto la libertad del pueblo. La libertad es muy preciosa, es un manjar muy apreciable; pero requiere estómagos fuertes, hombres virtuosos, hombres ilustrados. Instruid, pues, y preparad al pueblo ante todas cosas; porque de otra suerte, en vez de ciudadanos sólo tendréis gavillas de amotinados, que todo lo pondrán a sangre y fuego. Y en una carta a un paisano sobre el gobierno de Ginebra, modificado por un reglamento que dieron a esta ciudad las potestades vecinas, que se hicieron mediadores para apaciguar una de sus revoluciones, ponderando Rousseau los beneficios que resultaron a los ginebrinos de esta mediación, dice: los mediadores se hicieron garantes de vuestros derechos, dispensándoos de defenderlos por vosotros mismos y con vuestra sangre. ¡Ah! exclama: '¿por ventura en la miseria de las cosas humanas hay algún bien que valga la pena de ser comprado con la sangre de nuestros hermanos? no por cierto. La libertad misma es muy cara a este precio.' Tales son los sentimientos de este hombre extraordinario y singular en sus teorías, cuando trata práctica y determinadamente de los gobiernos establecidos, por imperfectos y defectuosos que sean.

He begged his parishioners to deprecate "los delirios elocuentes del ciudadano de Ginebra que pretende persuadir que el hombre es más feliz errante y solitario en los montes y en las selvas, que constituido en sociedad," and offered them instead his own explanation of the origin of society.[78]

But the Mexicans were not confining their reading to chosen selections whose purpose was to save souls and to maintain peace for the Spanish government; instead they were reading London periodicals advocating independence. In an attempt to curb the circulation of such seditious

---

[78]Abad y Queipo, Manuel, "Carta pastoral del obispo de Michoacán," September 26, 1812, *ibid.*, IV, 441, 445–446.

material, an edict prohibiting *El Español*, published in London by Blanco White, who had fled there from Spain, and *El Colombiano*, published by Miranda and Cortés, who had escaped from chains at La Guayra, was issued in Mexico on November 14, 1810.[79] In September, Roscio wrote from Caracas to Bello in London that he had just read the first two numbers of *El Español* and found them well worthy of subscription.[80] An article devoted to Rousseau, which appeared in that periodical, helped to popularize his ideas in Spanish America.[81] One of its contributors under the pseudonym of "Un Americano" was José Servando de Mier, who had preached the first sermon in Mexico against the *Social Contract* in 1791. Later he had ample opportunity to learn something personally of the workings of the Inquisition and the Spanish government, knowledge which he turned sharply to the advantage of his revolting compatriots. Especially did Mier contribute vitally to the independence movement through the publication in London of his *Historia de la revolución de Nueva España*, in which he supported the colonies and showed the many ways by which the Spanish officials tried to prevent the people from learning of or exercising their rights. He held up to scorn the edict of 1808—"El rey recibe su potestad y autoridad de Dios; y lo debéis creer con fe divina"—which had for its main object the refutation of the theory of the sovereignty of the people. All books or papers which encouraged independence or insubordination to the existing rulers, and especially those that voiced the heresy of the sovereignty of the people, he said, had been sternly prohibited. Many copies of Mier's *Historia* and the periodical *El Español* circulated widely in Spanish America before he himself returned to enter the struggle. Among his possessions when captured as a member of a revolutionary expedition in 1817 was a copy of "Oeuvres de Jean-Jacques Rousseau, tome troisième. A

---

[79]Hernández y Dávalos, *op. cit.*, II, 222.
[80]Amunátegui, *Vida de Bello*, 84.
[81]*El Español*, VI (1813), 421–426. Extract from Villemain's "Tableau de littérature française pendant le dix-huitième siècle."

Amsterdam, 1763"[82]—in other words, Rousseau's letter to Beaumont—and Moreno's works.

That Mier's letters to *El Español* were widely circulated by liberal thinkers is shown by the appearance of several of them in the *Aurora de Chile*, a paper edited by the same Camilo Henríquez who was denounced to the Inquisition in 1802 for reading Rousseau in French. In one case the issues are referred to as "circulating here very secretly."[83] But this editor went even further in echoing Rousseau than Moreno in the *Gaceta* of Buenos Aires; in the first issue, he inserted "Nociones fundamentales sobre los derechos de los pueblos"; in that of February 13, 1812, he began a lengthy discussion of the social pact as the foundation of "la potestad suprema" and the obligations of the people under this "pacto social."[84] On May 14 he was discussing "origen y fundamento de la soberanía"; on the 28th, "De las diversas formas de gobierno democrático, aristocrático." Through the various issues he continued a discussion of freedom of the press. This same Henríquez in 1811 drew up a plan of education for the Instituto Nacional which included a group of studies he termed "ciencias morales," one of whose objects was: "Establece los derechos de la patria; fija el gran principio del pacto social . . . establece las obligaciones i prerogativas del hombre en todos los estados i bajo todos los respetos." Under his tutelage opposing doctrines were advanced:

---

[82]Hernández y Dávalos, *op. cit.*, VI, 687, 843.
[83]October 22, 1812, and February 25, 1813.
[84]Donoso, Ricardo, *Hombres y ideas de antaño y hogaño* (Santiago de Chile, 1936), 117, quotes the following statement of the royalist friar Melchor Martínez in his *Memorias Histórica:* "No padecieron engaño los que eligieron a Camilo Henríquez para redactor porque desde la primera página de su periódico empezó a difundir muchos errores políticos y morales de los que han dejado estampados los impíos filósofos Voltaire y Rousseau, aunque en la doctrina del segundo estaba más iniciado, pues traslada por lo común literalmente los fragmentos de sus tratados. Todo el afán es probar que la soberanía reside en los pueblos, que las leyes reciben la autoridad del pueblo."

"a lado de trozos manifestamente inspirados por Rousseau y Montesquieu se esponen teorías del más añejo escolasticismo."[85]

In Mexico control of the press remained in royalist hands. The rôle liberals were forced to play there while Spanish officials were in control is well illustrated by the case of Francisco Maldonado, editor of the first Mexican revolutionary periodical, *El Telégrafo Americano*, which began publication in Guadalajara on December 10, 1810. His liberal views had already created for him various enemies, one of whom had denounced him to the authorities for possessing copies of "Bolter Roson y Dorod Reynal [*sic*] [y] de otros impíos que era su biblioteca."[86] After the defeat of Hidalgo, the leader of the revolution, discretion whispered to Maldonado that it was wiser to dissemble. So successfully did he do this that in the following year, after being pardoned for having strayed from the paths of political rectitude, he was continued as editor of the same paper, which was henceforth conducted from a viceregal viewpoint.[87] That Maldonado's convictions were in nowise impaired by this desertion from the insurrectionary ranks is shown by the fact that a decade later he was to publish the first Mexican edition of the *Social Contract*.

Other journalists felt the choking clutch of the governmental hand after having expressed themselves too freely. One of these was Fernández de Lizardi, better known as "El Pensador mexicano," a pseudonym derived from the periodical he began to publish as soon as the edict authorizing the free press was promulgated in Mexico in October, 1812. His portrayal of conditions in Mexico, his condemnation of the Spanish colonial system, and finally his appeal to the viceroy to revoke a decree directed at the

---

[85]Amunátegui Soler, Domingo, *Los primeros años del Instituto Nacional, 1813–1835* (Santiago, 1889), 86, 94.

[86]Fragmento de varias advertencias añónimas," published by Juan B. Iguíniz in "Apuntes biográficos del Dr. D. Francisco Severo Maldonado," which appeared in *Anales del museo nacional de arqueología, historia y etnología*, III, 131–154.

[87]Hernández y Dávalos, *op. cit.*, III, 339.

insurgents led to the suppression of the free press in December of the same year, and his own imprisonment. After being granted his liberty some six months later, he continued publication of his paper but desisted from criticising the government; instead, he directed attention to educational and social conditions. In *El Pensador mexicano* (a title borrowed, no doubt, from Clavijo's 1762 *Pensador*) and also in his other works, especially *El Periquillo Sarniento* (1816) and *La Quijotita*, he adapted to his own purposes many of Rousseau's views on government and education. In the first of these novels he urged that mothers nurse their children, that all binding of infants be eliminated, that educational methods and curricula be reorganized, and that boys be taught a trade. Especially did he emphasize in both these works the sad consequences of the failure to provide practical education. In *La Quijotita* he applied many of Rousseau's ideas to the education of women, and drew a sharp contrast between real and superficial education. Lizardi was also familiar with the works of many followers of Rousseau: among these, Ballexerd, Blanchard, and Montengón, all of whom concerned themselves with the problems of physical and mental development. As a direct trace of the romantic spirit, we find Lizardi in 1819 writing a novel entitled *Noches tristes,* modeled closely on Cadalso's *Noches lúgubres;* but the realistic rather than the romantic was Lizardi's field. Especially does he deserve a place in connection with the dissemination of Rousseau's ideas in the New World, for it was under cover of his works that the educational ideas of the Genevan first circulated openly in Mexico.[88]

That copies of the *Social Contract* had penetrated to Havana and that the work was highly regarded there is shown by a Spanish edition published early in 1813 from the press of Antonio José Valdés.[89] This 132-page work, which Trelles describes as "una de las mejores impresiones

[88]Spell, J. R., "The Educational Views of Fernández de Lizardi," in *Hispania*, IX (1926), 259–274.
[89]Bachiller y Morales, Antonio, *Apuntes para la historia de las letras y de la instrucción pública en la Isla de Cuba* (Habana, 1859–1861), II, 71.

de la Isla,"[90] must have enjoyed some circulation during the liberal régime, but was no doubt promptly suppressed with the return of absolutism. The brief period during which Havana knew a free press brought out various other works which touched upon some aspects of Rousseau. The printer Valdés himself included an "Apología del cristianismo de Rousseau" in a typographical display";[91] the *Diario Cívico* (1812–1814) turned to philosophical questions "y hasta se ocupó de las obras de Rousseau";[92] while "El verdadero filósofo" occupied himself, in his first series, with refuting the *Social Contract* "que se imprimió entonces traducido." In this work, the name is always written "Rusó," as in the Charleston imprint dated 1803, and the publisher added a note in which he defended "la escritura por la pronunciación."[93] In the fourth part of a first-year course in philosophy issued in 1816, Félix Varela considered man and society, but termed "delirios" the ideas of a certain philosopher that man's natural state was "fuera de la sociedad." In a note he added: "Nadie hubiera hecho caso del soñador, si sus impugnadores no le hubieran dado el ser que no tenía."[94]

In the meantime revolutionary leaders in Mexico were translating into laws the teachings of Rousseau. In 1813 there was drawn up and printed at Apatzingán the first constitution for the projected Mexican republic. At the opening of the congress which ratified it, José María Morelos, who for more than three years directed the insurgents so skillfully that the royalist army was held at bay, made a speech, apparently drafted if not entirely written by Carlos María Bustamante, in which he asserted:

Que la soberanía reside esencialmente en los pueblos. . . . Que trasmitida a los Monarcos por ausencia, . . . refluye hacia aquellos. . . . Que son libres para reformar sus instituciones políticas siempre

---

[90]Trelles, Carlos M., *Bibliografía cubana del siglo XIX* (Matanzas, 1911), I .[1800–1825], 110–111.
[91]"Ideas de los caracteres con que principia la imprenta de D. Antonio José Valdés, Habana, 1813." See Bachiller, *op. cit.*, II, 71.
[92]*Ibid.*, 121.
[93]"El verdadero filósofo," Havana, 1813–1814. See *ibid.*, 123.
[94]*Ibid.*, III, 73.

que les convenga. . . . Que ningún pueblo tiene derecho para sojuzgar a otro, si no precede una agresión injusta. . . . Among the specific points to be incorporated in the constitution, Morelos included the following:

5a. La soberanía dimana inmediatamente del pueblo, el que solo quiere depositarla en sus representantes dividiendo los poderes de ella en legislativo, ejecutivo y judiciario, elijiendo las provincias sus vocales, y éstos a los demás, que deben ser sujetos sabios y de probidad.[95]

Among the charges brought against him when summarily tried by court-martial after being captured by the royalists were these:

Que este reo induce las sospechas más vehementes, no sólo del tolerantismo, sino de ateísmo y materialismo; por estar imbuído en las máximas fundamentales del herético pacto social de Rousseau . . . y otros filósofos reprobados. . . . No se contentó de leer semejantes libros . . . sino que trascribió, copió, subscribió a sus delirios firmándolos en la Constitución Americana, tales son, decir que la ley es la expresión de la voluntad, que la sociedad de los hombres es de mera voluntad y no de necesidad; y de aquí proviene el considerar al hombre independiente de Dios. . . . Como en el sistema de este libertino no es necesario y natural la sociedad de los hombres, decidió en su abominable Constitución que los racionables no tienen otras obligaciones que aquellas a que se comprometen por el pacto social o por la expresión de la voluntad general, que es el resultado de la representación nacional, . . . y se expresa terminantemente por este infame en el artículo 18 de su perversa y ridícula Constitución.[96]

After the execution of Morelos in 1815, the royalists seemed to be left, for a time, masters of the Mexican field. But brief was their triumph. With the adoption of the constitution in Spain in 1820, Mexican ecclesiastics and conservatives, to prevent encroachments upon their powers, proclaimed the independence of Mexico. How completely these groups reversed their opinions at the moment may be seen from a sermon preached by Bishop Pérez of Puebla, in which he compared America to a captive bird

---

[95]Hernández y Dávalos, op. cit., VI, 212–215.
[96]Medina, Historia del tribunal del santo oficio de la Inquisición en México, 530. Original in Archivo de Simancas, Legajo 28, Inquisición de México.

caught when young by Spain, now full-fledged and struggling for freedom.[97] This is clearly an echo of the same passage that Vizcardo had earlier quoted from the *Social Contract*, which Pérez had undoubtedly read while a deputy of the Cortes, 1810–1814. Even the viceroy, Apodaca, in writing to the King of Spain of conditions in Mexico, ascribed what had happened there principally to "el filosofismo o iluminismo, los libros extranjeros, principalmente franceses."[98]

It must not be supposed that, with independence, the Mexican government had become broad-minded overnight; instead, the liberals had to continue to guard both their speech and writing with great care. In April, 1821, under the rule of Spain, Francisco Maldonado was making most unfavorable comparisons between the Golden Rule and "el principio atroz, inhumano, impío y antisocial de Juan Jacobo Rousseau" as voiced in the *Second Discourse*— "Procura tu bien con el menor posible daño de otro . . . " —in a *Nuevo Pacto Social propuesto a la nación española*, which Maldonado had drawn up for submission to the Spanish congress. A year later, with independence proclaimed, he was writing of "la monstruosa legislación española"; "las leyes bárbaras y absurdas que prohiben la enseñanza del derecho natural y de gentes"; and of the "estolidez y la audacia del tremendo rayo de la excomunión incesantemente lanzado por el santo oficio contra qualquiera estudioso que leyera un Rousseau o un Dupaty." As there had been little cultivation of the moral and political sciences in Mexico, and only a few expensive books published concerning social organization, in order to popularize such works as would give the nation knowledge of its rights, Maldonado planned, like Moreno, a series of ten or twelve books:

---

[97] [Rivera, Agustín], Paralelo entre el *Contrato Social* de Juan Jacobo Rousseau y el Sermón del Illmo. Sr. D. Antonio Joaquín Pérez . . . predicado en el púlpito de su catedral en pro del Plan de Iguala el día 5 de agosto de 1821. . . . Lagos, [1894].

[98] Quoted by Germán Latorre, in "Separación del virreinato de Nueva España," in *Revista de Archivos, Bibliotecas, y Museos*, Año XVIII, Vol. XXXI (1914), 234.

. . . una colección de lo mejor, más raro, exquisito clásico y verdaderamente sublime que hasta hoy se ha publicado en materia de
legislación, política y economía, tanto por los escritores católicos,
como por los heterodoxos y los llamados filósofos, purgándolos de
los errores que los inficionan en sus fuentes.

But that he did not dare to carry out this plan openly, as
Moreno did, is shown by the fact that his publication of
the *Social Contract*, the third of the series, is introduced
without title or author, and appears to the casual reader
to be a continuation of the "Teoría del pacto social" by
Martínez de Marina, which begins on page 162 of a publication entitled *El Fanal del imperio mexicano*.[99] About the
middle of page 164 the translation of paragraph 3, Chapter II, Book I, of the *Social Contract* begins: "La familia
es el primer modelo de las sociedades políticas." From this
point, the text proceeds uninterruptedly, but Chapter V,
"The Right of Life and Death," and Chapter VII, from
the Judaic law on, are omitted from Book II, as is all of
the chapter on Civil Religion. The only direct clue to the
true content of the material is the heading on page 203,
which reads, "Continuación del *Contrato Social* de J. J.
Rousseau." In such form did the first, and, so far as the
present writer knows, the only, Mexican edition of the
Social Contract see the light. In it, the text of the Repullés
edition of 1820 was reprinted. In the second volume of
the same work is a "Pacto social de los mexicanos,"[100]
which is clearly modeled on Rousseau's theories, and a
"Contrato de asociación para la república de los estados
unidos de Anáhuac."

While Buenos Aires was the earliest,[101] it was not the
only city in Spanish America in which prohibited books
were permitted to circulate without restrictions. In Santiago, Chile, such thinkers as Henríquez were fast clear-
ing the French encyclopedists from the clerical stigma.

[99]*El Fanal del imperio mexicano o miscelánea política*, extractada
y redactada de las mejores fuentes por el autor del *Pacto Social*,
para inteligencia de esta obra, es decir, de la única forma de
gobierno digna de los seres inteligentes y libres. México, 1822. 2
vols. The "Teoría del pacto social" is in Vol. I, pp. 162–288.
[100]See pp. 113–217.
[101]Brackenridge, *Voyage to South America*, 141–142.

Not content with impressing upon the people that the sovereignty resided in them, he dwelt at length on its various implications. In *El Mercurio* he wrote:

> Soberanía es el poder superior a todos los demás poderes de la sociedad. . . . Supongamos aceptado y consolidado el pacto representivo ¿qué parte le queda a la nación de su soberanía? . . . La facultad de revisar y modificar tal pacto.

Through the tenth and succeeding issues he continued the discussion of the rôle of the people in representative government. With all this as a prelude, in the twenty-third issue he stated his main theme:

> Voltaire, Rousseau y Montesquieu son los Apóstoles de la razón. Ellos son los que han roto los brazos al despotismo, los que han elevado barreras indestructibles contra el poder invasor, los que . . . han borrado los nombres de señor y esclavos; . . . y los que han lanzado al averno la intolerancia y el fanatismo. Sus escritos en que resplandecía la verdad entre todas las flores de la elocuencia, se acogen, se devoran con un ardor inexplicable. Todas las imaginaciones se incienden, la del joven, la del helado anciano; aun el sexo al cual la naturaleza y la educación alejan de sus asuntos graves, siente latir su corazón al santo nombre de libertad.

Such a public eulogy of prohibited writers could not go unchallenged. The reply came in the form of *Los apóstoles del diablo* (1822), a twenty-two page attack on all three writers, Henríquez, and the authorities who permitted such works to be known in Chile. After showing that Voltaire had done all possible harm to religious convictions, the writer, Fray Tadeo Silva, a Dominican, turned his shafts against Rousseau, who, he claimed, questioned whether adultery should be condoned, whether suicide is justifiable, whether duels should be permitted, whether there is a God, and whether Christianity is divine. Silva believed that to champion a writer who had tried to show the evil effects of the arts and sciences would have the effect of encouraging idleness in the young, once they were shown that learning corrupted society. He summarized, in his own fashion, the teachings of the *Second Discourse*, showed that the *Letters from the Mountain* attacked religion and especially miracles; that "*Émile*" was only "otro conjunto de verdades y de errores perniciosos"; and that, in the *Social Contract*, the Catholic Church was ridiculed and Christians described with gross calumny. The tirade is concluded as follows:

> ¡Infeliz juventud! Cerca estás de perder la Religión de tus padres, si te aplicas a la lectura de tan perversas producciones. Si sigues los consejos del P. Agonizante Camilo, aprenderás a mal vivir, para tener al fin un mal morir. . . . Suiza proscribió a Rousseau, Ginebra lo expelió de su gremio por su Emilio, Francia y casi toda la Europa persiguieron a Voltaire; y Chile sufre indiferente la venta pública de todos sus escritos perniciosos, y el Periodista del Gobierno los recomienda con audacia. Dios sabrá vengar su Religión ultrajada.

As the presses in Spanish America were generally, nevertheless, closely muzzled, the opportunity to supply what the people wanted was open to enterprising printers. Such a publisher was Matthew Carey in Philadelphia, who, foreseeing the importance of the Spanish-American markets, arranged with a representative at Gibraltar to furnish him with one copy of each of the fictional and political works then popular in Spain; from this he could reprint. In 1821 he brought out an edition of the *Social Contract* by reprinting from Collado's 1820 edition; the copy belonging to the Library Company at Philadelphia bears the proof-reader's corrections. The work must have sold well, for the following year another edition, reprinted from the same type, with the exception of the title page, was brought out by H. C. Carey and I. Lea. Copies of both of these issues are still to be found in Mexican and South American libraries.

These are not the only traces of Rousseau in Spanish America before its independence was acknowledged by Spain. Two writers deserve especial attention—José María Heredia, the Cuban poet, and Manuel Vidaurri, the Peruvian Rousseau. The first of these has left us his estimate of the Genevan in an article he published in Mexico;[102]

---

[102]"Ensayo sobre el carácter de J. J. Rousseau, su *Julia y sus Confessiones*," in *Miscelánea, periódico crítico y literario*, II (México, 1830), 33–44.

the influence of Rousseau is evident in many of his most inspired poems. The life of Vidaurri, reminiscent of Rousseau, has been sketched by one of his countrymen.[103] But since both of these writers are linked in characteristics more specifically with the romantic group which dominated the Spanish field after 1830, they will be reserved for a later and more detailed study of Rousseau's influence in that period.

Both the beginning and the end of the revolutionary period of Spanish America were marked by an edition of the *Social Contract*. That of Buenos Aires in 1810 also marks the establishment of the free press in Spanish America; it was the first of prohibited texts to be published openly and to circulate freely. The 1813 Havana edition symbolizes the existence—though brief—of such freedom in Cuba. While the attainment of independence was marked in Mexico by a Mexican edition, the fact that the text had to be concealed beneath another title is in itself evidence that the free press had not been attained. In Chile, where no such publication was attempted, there was, in the person of Camilo Henríquez, an editor who dared to follow the lead of Moreno in bringing to the people, through the pages of the *Aurora* and later the *Mercurio*, the political theories of Rousseau as incitement to action whose purpose was the betterment of the general welfare. And already in this vast area echoes of Rousseau's educational doctrines were heard.

The influence of Rousseau on Spanish America in the colonial period was threefold—political, educational, and literary; and these different threads were sometimes strangely and inextricably interwoven. From the first remote trace of his political influence—in the constitution drawn up for Chile in 1780—until after the middle of the nineteenth century, the *Social Contract* was the inspiration of most Spanish-American leaders. How early the educational influence was felt is not so definite; but in the work of Simón Rodríguez we have a concrete example.

---

[103]Leguía, J. G., *Manuel Lorenzo de Vidaurri*, Lima, 1935.

Not only radical thinkers preached his educational doctrines; even parish priests were his missionaries; Sarmiento tells us that the doctrines enunciated by the priest
in his mother's village suggested that he knew Rousseau
as well as the Bible, while the lessons he preached to
mothers on rearing their children gave reason to suspect
that *Émile* was hidden beneath the clerical robe. The few
evidences of his literary influence in the colonial era are
scarcely a fair index to the actual assimilation of his
thought, for Spanish America was, in the nineteenth century, primarily and persistently romantic. It is probably
no exaggeration to say that Rousseau, for a century after
his death, wielded more influence in shaping the thought
of Spanish America than did any other single writer. The
many-sidedness of his influence is best seen in Bolívar,
who was nurtured in the thought of Rousseau, reared
according to his precepts, and became a most genuine
representative of the romantic school in love, language,
and in the quest of liberty. This influence shows itself in
every phase of his later life. From the *Discourses* came
the basis of Bolívar's vocabulary to such an extent that
in reading Bolívar one is led at times to believe he is reading a translation of Rousseau. When his military successes
were to be celebrated with *fiestas,* Bolívar turned for
advice upon the subject to the *Letter to d'Alembert.* The
Social Contract furnished him a political code throughout
his career; and the Profession of Faith of the Savoyard
Vicar served him for religion. The style and passion of
the *Héloïse* are especially marked in his *Delirios,* written
after ascending Chimborazo in 1824. Probably his career
and accomplishments furnish the best testimonial South
America can ever offer to the efficiency of the educational
system advocated by Rousseau, for he achieved the independence of three countries and called forth a new spirit
in the Spanish-American world.

Nor should it be forgotten that South America can
claim some Rousseau items of bibliographical interest. It
was the copy of the *Social Contract* which had shared the

exile of Napoleon at St. Helena that Bolívar bequeathed, at his death in 1830, to his native city Caracas. There, beside the educational projects of Rodríguez and the journals and papers of Miranda—two Spanish Americans whose vision, guided by that of Rousseau, was far in advance of the day in which they lived—rests this precious volume; and in the National Library at Buenos Aires there are still treasured copies of the first Argentinian edition (1810) of that same work.

They are mute testimonials of a period of deeds and dreams. Men forged onward to a destiny never clearly defined. The attainment of one objective, such as independence from the mother country, brought in its train new problems to be solved, new difficulties to be surmounted. These became in turn the work of another era, in which further traces of Rousseau are also to be found.

CHAPTER XV

LATER TRACES OF ROUSSEAU

The material presented in the preceding pages should be sufficient to disprove the hitherto generally accepted statement that the works of Rousseau were not known in Spain until the Marchena translations became known about 1820.

While it is not the purpose of the present work to trace either the dissemination or the influence of Rousseau further in detail, it should at least be pointed out that neither came to an end either in Spanish America with the attainment of independence or in Spain with the death of Ferdinand VII. Instead, in both cases, the ideas of Rousseau became better known and undertsood by the general public as the years passed, and out of this more intimate acquaintance came literary and political developments strangely conflicting in theories. These will be sketched here only in a general way; future studies will supply the details.

The popularity of Rousseau in the period of Spanish literary history known as "romantic" is shown conclusively by the twelve editions of *La nouvelle Héloïse* published in Spain in 1836 and 1837, five of these being Marchena's translation, while Félix Enciso y Castrillón and José Mor de Fuentes each supplied a new one. No longer was the *Eloísa* a despised work of fiction to be consumed in secrecy; in the preface of the Oliva edition of 1836 it was boldly stated:

No es solamente una novela, sino una obra moral y filosófica, un tratado de costumbres, de educación, un conjunto de profundas y sabias reflexiones sobre las varias situaciones de la vida. . . . Se trata de una obra ya conocida, de una obra inmortal que todo el mundo admira.

The influence of Rousseau may be traced in the works of some of the outstanding Spanish romantic writers, especially Espronceda and Larra. In Espronceda, who was affected both directly and also indirectly through Byron, converge the melancholy of Cadalso, the Ossianic interests of Montengón and Marchena, the doubt and hopelessness of Cienfuegos and Jovellanos, the ideal of a simple life and the innate goodness of man as shown by Meléndez, and the passionate hatred of Byron for restraint—all characteristics developed from the teachings of Rousseau. Espronceda, like Rousseau, was the poet of the people as opposed to aristocracy, and the poet of youth as opposed to the conservatism of age; constant was his sympathy for the downtrodden and his protests against the penalties civilization imposed on the lower classes. He sang the song of country, of liberty, and of love in tones more passionate than any of his predecessors. In the detail with which he traced the emotions as they surge toward fulfillment and end only in disillusionment, he showed the lack of restraint of Rousseau in *La nouvelle Héloïse*. The similarity between the two writers may easily be seen if the following words descriptive of the Spanish poet are in turn applied to the Genevan:

Espronceda fué en su tiempo el tono de la nueva generación; el grito de protesta . . . [y] la emancipación del pensamiento humano. Espronceda no es el poeta de escuela, sino de inspiración. . . .[104]

Larra reveals himself as a reader of Rousseau in many lines. In the early articles of "El pobrecito hablador" are mocking echoes of the *First Discourse;* in his consideration of society, he classes man as an "animal social" and declines to accept the theory "que su verdadera posición es la de los cuatro pies," even though he concedes that society is the worst of the necessities of life. Sarcastically he echoes phrases of the *Second Discourse* in "Yo quiero ser cómico," and clearly he is following Rousseau in his discussion of dueling, for he cites him by name in that connection. He also refers to the letters of *La nueva*

[104]Rodríguez Solís, E., *Espronceda, su tiempo, su vida, y sus obras* (Madrid, 1883), 270.

Eloísa as an element in the making of hasty and ill-considered marriages.

While these details have not hitherto been commented on, the indebtedness of Larra in *El Doncel* to Rousseau has been pointed out by more than one critic. "El Doncel is no fifteenth century troubadour, but rather a modern *désillusionné;* Macías is entirely of the Rousseauesque tradition," says Walton in his discussion of the Spanish novel of the nineteenth century. "Su erotismo refinado, mezcla de impulsos sensuales y de sofismas éticos, viene en linea recta de Juan Jacobo Rousseau, ciudadano de Ginebra" concedes Menéndez y Pelayo. While the character treatment is indeed subjective, Larra could never bare his soul without reticence as did Rousseau; his passion never found free expression in prose. It is in the tragedy of Macías that the exaltation of unrestrained love finds adequate voice.

The attitude toward Rousseau in the romantic era that was to be the heritage of the younger generation is well exemplified by the lectures which Alcalá Galiano delivered at the Ateneo in 1844. Of the twenty-six lectures treating of the literature of the eighteenth century, three were devoted to Rousseau, whom he described as

... un hombre de especie nueva que había de influir tanto como Voltaire en el mundo; que había de dirigirse particularmente a la política; que había de conmover no sólo los tronos, sino la sociedad toda; que había de tener no sólo admiradores ... sino devotos, hombre en quien relucían muchos dotes del verdadero clasicismo, a pesar de que de éste se apartase en otras y no pocas cosas; hombre diferente de los de su siglo; hombre en quien iban hermanados con la filosofía moderna que despreciaba, aunque en parte profesándola, el espiritualismo, la devoción verdadera y los principios religiosos, si bien no los de nuestra religión; hombre en fin en quien había cosas que le constituían en un ente de especie nueva, y al cual, quien quiera que tenga un alma sensible no puede menos de admirar, aunque le admire llorando.

He found, as had Almodóvar in 1780, the impressive lessons of *Julia* even more dangerous than immorality taught by lesser writers, for they were entangled in "un manantial de nobles pensamientos, cierta vena de ideas verdaderamente laudables." *Émile* he regarded as an immortal work, and its burning in 1764 at the hands of the Inquisition as an honor to its writer! He pointed out the extreme to which the *Social Contract* might lead—that the "poder absoluto" might become pure "tiranía." The work itself, in that day, he said, was more cited than read. He urged that Rousseau be digested thoughtfully and with an open mind.

During the romantic period, the germs of a new literary interest began to develop, almost as a contradiction, from seeds Rousseau had scattered. Larra had foreseen the coming of a new form of literature which was to be "toda de verdad; sin más regla que esa verdad misma; sin más maestro que la naturaleza misma," but there is no evidence that he recognized Rousseau as its first master. As early as 1838 an anonymous periodical writer, in an article classifying the novel as historical, supernatural, and *costumbrista*, pointed out that Rousseau's work belonged to the latter group—that *La nueva Eloísa* was "la sencilla pintura de costumbres y pasiones." Eleven years later, from the pen of Fernán Caballero—the woman who wrote despairingly that there was not a man in Spain who could read that had not read Voltaire, Rousseau, and the encyclopedists, and who had herself escaped neither the sentimentalism of Rousseau nor the lacrymosity which distinguish many of the romantic writers—came *La Gaviota*, the first of Spanish novels to present an exact picture of the life and customs of a region. In this, as in her later novels, the narratives are simple and are based on actual events; her descriptions of places are picturesque and animated, and her work has the flavor of the soil. Her pages supply the fundamental characteristics of the realistic novel.

Later critics, including some hostile to many of the specific teachings of Rousseau, do not hesitate to point to him as the fountain head of this new type.

La nueva Eloísa . . . fué una anticipación del romanticismo y a la vez del género realista.
Rousseau era el carro de árgoma y de leña que descargaba en medio de la calle urbana, repulida; era la montaña trayendo sus aromas a la ciudad. Era la Suiza morigerada y casta, la Suiza sobria y de costumbres sencillas, que se oponía a la Francia gastada de tanto placer, a la Francia donde las marquesas perfumadas se entregaban ya a sus lacayos, haciendo gala de fastidio, de cansancio y de genialidad. Parece ser ley de la historia que las pequeñas nacionalidades sirvan siempre como ejemplos de moralidad, de trabajo y de progreso. . . . Rousseau era Suiza que quería moralizar a Francia. La ɾelajación de costumbres de su siglo le traía tan preocupado como la causa de su relajación. . . .
¿Como no había de estar en oposición con su siglo Rousseau, que creía a la mujer de un carbonero más digna de respeto que la querida de un príncipe?

From Fernán Caballero, in whose works the predominance of similar realistic elements was first sensed, came, in turn, the numerous realistic writers of the latter half of the nineteenth century, some of whom, like Galdós, have much in common with the Genevan.

Out of the new educational groundwork begun in Spain about the middle of the century by Giner de los Ríos and his group, came a new interest in *Émile,* which one might think had been entirely forgotten had not such works as *El Emilio o el hombre original* and *Cecilia o la virtud en los trabajos* evidenced its persistence as a model. The work was first to reach the level of the general reading public through its serial publication in *Las Novedades,* a newspaper which came into existence in 1850 under the guidance of Fernández de los Ríos. From the same type, a separate edition was published, which had a wide circulation. Five years later, in a collection called *Eco de los folletines,* another reprinting appeared with twenty-seven engravings. In 1872 and 1879 there were other editions. From the date of its appearance in *Las Novedades,* its teachings were the common property of educated Spaniards, not all of whom subscribed to the theories therein advanced.

The political interest in Rousseau came again into strong evidence with the revolution of 1868. New editions of the *Social Contract* appeared in that year, and five more during the eighties. By that time, the reëstablished monarchy had taken a firm hold, and republican dreams were fast fading. But references to Rousseau are scattered through the pages of some of Spain's greatest statesmen of that era, Cánovas del Castillo and Castelar included.

With the publication of the first Spanish translation of the *Confessions* in 1869 and 1870, and a new edition in 1889, autobiographies and memoirs became the vogue in Spain. The leading writers were to imitate that work, which Castelar termed "the eternal model of the art of confidences." Among the early contributors in this form were Alcalá Galiano, Bretón de los Herreros, Zorrilla, Somoza, Mesonero Romanos, Escosura, and Avellaneda. And the vogue continued—Chávez, Casa Valencia, Fernán Caballero, Nombela, Béquer, Campillo, Valera, and Palacio Valdés were all to follow in the wake of the author of the *Confessions* with some form of an autobiography.

At the close of the century the influence of Rousseau can still be traced without difficulty in the works of Ganivet. Especially was this Spaniard following in his footsteps in *Pygmalion,* a "drama místico" written shortly before his death in 1899. Using the basic thought present in the Rousseau version, Ganivet portrays in highly poetic form the eternal struggle of the human soul toward its own perfection.

While these traces of the Genevan can be followed in Spain, the romantic strains of *La nueva Eloísa* and the political teachings of the *Social Contract* had their repercussions in Spanish America. After Heredia in Mexico and Vidaurre in Peru, both romanticists in life and in their work, came a long line of weaker imitators of Rousseau, few of whose efforts were of permanent literary value. In 1828, Varas y de la Barra expounded Rousseau's teachings in Chile in his *Lecciones de Moral,* and the first Chilean novel, *La Vida de un Amigo,* by Vial Guzmán, published in 1846, adopts the epistolary form and breathes much of the spirit of the *Héloïse,* although the work is crude. In Argentina, Rousseau's teachings were intelligently refuted in 1836 by Gorriti in his *Reflecciones,* but for years they had been brutally assailed there by Castro Barros, a Catholic priest who pleaded for a new inquisition to extirpate them all. It was the blood and thunder attack of this ecclesiastic that first drew Sarmiento's attention to the French writer. In *Recuerdos de Provincia* are many references to Rousseau's life, works, and influence in South America; and in *Facundo* the disastrous effects of the *Social Contract* on people unprepared to digest it are clearly brought out. In the works of Echevarría, a contemporary Argentinian, are also traces of Rousseau; the *Social Contract* reappears in the *Dogma socialista,* a code drawn up for the group that refused to submit to the tyranny of Rosas; in the poem "Avellaneda" are references to Moreno's introduction to the first Argentinian edition; and in "La Cautiva," the descriptions of nature and the sentimental strain of the *Héloïse* are linked for the first time with an Argentinian background. In Uruguay, Pérez Gomar, in his *Idea de la Perfección humana* admits Rousseau as the source of many of his ideas; and Nin Frías, according to the critic Carlos Roxlo, shares in the feeling for nature so characteristic of both Rousseau and Chateaubriand.

Best known of the South American echoes of the *Héloïse* is the romantic idyll *María* (1867) by a Colombian, Jorge Isaacs—the most widely read work of fiction yet written by a Spanish American. In this, we have the introspection, the lacrymosity, the descriptions of nature, the intensity of passion over trifles, the grimness of fate in María's death—all characteristics of that phase of the romantic movement which emanated from Rousseau. In turn this work became a model for later novels of the sentimental type, but, in poetic conception and presentation, all fall far below it. To be convinced that the influence of Rousseau still pervades contemporary fiction, one need only turn the pages of *Un Perdido* by Eduardo Barrios, a work which strongly suggests the *Confessions*.

Further details of the persistence and influence of Rousseau in Spain and Spanish America in the twentieth century, and the part his ideas have played in leading up to the terrible conflict now in progress in the Peninsula, may be found in an article prepared by the writer which is to appear shortly in periodical form.

APPENDIX A

PIGMALION[1]

Poema Lirico

*El Teatro ha de representar un taller de Escultor con los adherentes
necesarios, habrá además en el fondo, cubierta con alguna estofa, una
estatua de Galatéa sentada sobre un pedestal, al que se sube por
graderia de marmol.*

*Pigmalion en ademan de hombre abatido toma el cincél y el martillo,
mira las Estatuas del obrador, las dá de quando en quando alguna
cincelada, y dice:*
> Sin alma están, nada expresan:
> Son de piedra, están sin vida:
> Nada de ellas sacar puedo
> Por mas que intento pulirlas. . . .
> ¿Dónde estás ingenio mio?
> Mi fuego es solo ceniza.
> Ya solo saco del marmol
> Estatuas que á nadie admiran.
> ¡Pigmalion! ya no haces Dioses:
> Solo eres vulgar artista:

Arroja los instrumentos.
> Andad viles instrumentos
> Origen de mis fatigas,
> Ya que no me dais hoy fama,
> No me causeis ignominia.

Pasease como pensativo.
> ¡A que extremo tan funesto
> Llegó ya la suerte mía!
> ¡Qué raro trastorno es este,
> Que tanto á mi alma agita!
> Tiro, ¡Ciudad opulenta!
> De las artes que en ti brillan
> Los eternos monumentos
> La admiracion no me excitan:

[1]"Coliseo de los caños del Peral. El dia 25 de este mes, por
indisposicion de la primera Dama de la Opera Italiana, se repre-
sentó por Mr. d' Ainville el Melodrama francés intitulado *Pigmalion,*
del qual se publicó una traduccion en prosa Castellana, la que ha
puesto en verso D. Francisco Duran, y nosotros la insertamos aqui."
—*Memorial literario,* January, 1788, pp. 163–174.

Los Filosofos me cansan:
Los Poetas no me inclinan:
Y esquivamente rehuyo
El trato de los artistas:
La alabanza ni la gloria
No me mueven ni me animan:
Aborrezco los elogios;
Aun aquellos que podria
La posteridad rendirme:
Perdió ya la amistad fina,
Para mi sus atractivos;
Y la sociedad me irrita.
¡Y vosotras, delicados
Objetos, obras dignas
De la gran naturaleza,
A quienes yo me atrevia
A imitar, quando tan solo
Me complací en vuestra vista!
¡Vosotros, modelos mios,
Que en mi espíritu encendiais
El fuego de amor é ingenio,
No me causais ya harmonia
Desde que excedió mi mano
A vuestra hermosura misma. . . .!

Se sienta, mira un rato el obrador, y dice muy pausadamente.
Un encanto incomprehensible,
En este obrador me liga,
Y ni á trabajar acierto,
Ni es facil de él mi salida.
Vagando de grupo en grupo,
Paso las horas y dias,
Y mi cincel desconoce
Ya la mano que le guia;
Ni estos bosquexos ya sienten
La que darles pudo vida,

Levantase con impetu y agitacion.
Sí, perdido está mi ingenio:
En mi juventud se mira
Mi talento amortiguado:
¡Ah! Cielo ¿qué llama activa
Me consume interiormente?
¿Pueden encontrar cabida,
Donde el ingenio está muerto,
Conmociones tan prolixas?
¿Es posible que se sientan

Pasiones tan combatidas,
Sin que á comprender yo llegue
La causa que las motiva?
Creí que admirando mi obra
Mis tareas distraia:
Con ese pavellon quiso
Cubrir mi mano atrevida
El glorioso monumento
Que en la obscuridad se abisma
Pero desde que la oculto,
Crece mi melancolia
Y no pienso en otra cosa. . . .
¡En quánto aprecio y estima
Tendré obra tan insigne!
Quando ya desvanecida
Mi industria no me produzca
Otra alguna de mí digna,
Mostrando á mi Galatéa
Diré á voces: esto hacia
Pigmalion en otros tiempos. . . .
¡Oh Galatéa divina!
Tú, quando todo me falte,
Consolarás mis fatigas.

Mira la cortina que oculta á Galatéa y suspira.
Mas ¿por qué quiero ocultarla?
¿Qué gano en no descubrirla
Obligado á estar ocioso?
¿Por qué privar á mi vista
Del placer de estar mirando
De mis obras la mas linda?
Quizá tendrá alguna falta,
Y quizá podré añadirla
Algo mas para su adorno;
Produccion tan peregrina
Las gracias todas merece
Que en ella se hallen unidas.
Tal vez mi imaginacion
Revivirá con su vista:
Volvamos á exâminarla;
Pero ¿qué digo? ¿Por dicha
La he exâminado? ¿He hecho
Mas que admirar sus maravillas? . . .

Va á correr la cortina y se suspende con turbacion.
Yó no sé que me sorprende
Al llegar á esta cortina:

Un grande asombro me yela:
Parece que mis indignas
Manos tocan el Santuario
En que una Deidad habita. . . .
¡Insensato, es una piedra
Obra de tus manos mismas! . . .
¿Qué importa? Tambien los Dioses
Que en nuestros templos se fixan
Son de la propria materia
Y hechos por el mismo artista. . . .

*Va titubeando, corre la cortina, se descubre Galatéa y se arrodilla
con grandes extremos de agitacion.*

¡Oh celestial Galatéa!
Culto mi amor te dedica. . . .
Pero ¡qué ilusion! ¡Qué engaño! . . .
Queriendo sacarte ninfa
Te hice Diosa, en gracia excedes
La Venus que rindió á Alcidas[1] . . . .

Levantase.

Vanidad. . . . Flaqueza humana. . . .
Mas cada instante me admira. . . .
Me arrebata el amor propio,
Y parece que me excita
A adorarme en esta obra. . . .
¡Qué bella está! ¡Qué concluida!
No la han hecho igual los Dioses,
Ni naturaleza misma. . . .
¿Posible es que esta hermosura
Salió de las manos mias?
¡Ellas tocarla pudieron! . . .
Mi boca tuvo osadia. . . .
Pigmalion, mira una falta. . . .
La ropa está muy subida,
Aquellas gracias que oculta
Es menester descubrirlas.

*Va ácia la Estatua con cincél y martillo, sube como receloso y
asombrado, va á dar un golpe y se retira.*

¡Qué temblor! ¡Qué turbacion!
¡El cincel se me desliza!
Ni puedo yá, ni me atrebo;
Enmendarla es destruirla.

------

[1]Alcidas fue un joven que se enamoró de una sobresaliente
Estatua de Venus que los Gentiles veneraban en la Ciudad de Gnido.

Da al fin un golpe, dexa caer el cincél y martillo, y dando un grito
queda como atonito.

    ¡Dioses! . . ., ¡Qué nuevo asombro es el que toco
    Viviente carne en el cincel se vibra!

Baxa trémulo.

    ¡Qué temor vano! ¡Qué capricho necio! . . .
    Nó . . . no la tocaré . . . me atemorizan
    Sin duda alguna los Dioses,
    Para divinidad está escogida. . . .
    Mirala, Pigmalion, ¡qué mudar quieres!
    ¿Qué nuevas gracias tienes que añadirla?
    Su misma perfeccion es su defecto:
    Si asi no fuera ¿qué la faltaria?
    El alma sola falta á su belleza
    Solo á su perfeccion falta la vida.

Mirando tiernamente á Galatéa.

    Mas para tanta perfeccion de cuerpo,
    ¡Qué alma tan grande no se necesita! . . .
    ¿Qué deseos impuros son los mios?
    ¿Qué votos insensatos encaminas
    Triste Pigmalion? ¡Sagrados Cielos!
    Quando está mi ilusion desvanecida,
    Si examinar mi corazon quisiera,
    Me causára rubor, me indignaria.

Se entrega á un abatimiento que le obliga á apoyarse en algo.

    ¿Y es esta la pasion que me arrebata?
    ¿Un insensible objeto es quien me obliga
    A no salir de aqui? ¿Un marmol duro
    Que trabajó este hierro me domina?
    Vuelve insensato en ti: atento advierte,
    Que estás en grave error, que ya deliras.

Con ímpetu.

    Mas nó, que sano tengo el juicio,
    Mas nó, que en esto no hay malicia,
    Si yó prendado estoy, no es de ese marmol,
    Es de un ser animado á quien imita,
    Es sí, de una figura encantadora
    Que al vivo representa ésta esculpida.
    Hállese en qualquier parte esta figura,
    Séa qualquier el cuerpo en quien asista,
    Y qualquiera la mano executora,
    Mi corazon sus votos la encamina,
    Si causa mi delirio solamente

El discernir su hermosa gallardía
Si es delito el que me rinda á ella
Nada á mi noble espíritu íntimida.

Afectuosamente.

¡Qué voráz fuego sale de esta estatua,
Que abrasa mis sentidos, y me obliga
A volver á entregarla el alma toda! . . .
¡Ah! ella se queda yerta y fria,
Mi triste corazon por sus hechizos
Salir quiere del pecho á darla vida. . . .
Muera, pues, Pigmalion el infelize,
Y su adorable Galatéa viva.
Sea yo para amarla siempre ótro
Y vease mi fé correspondida.

Fuera de sí.

¡Amor terrible! . . . ¡Amor el mas funesto!
Mi corazon todo el enfierno abriga. . . .
¡Oh Dioses! á quien no se esconden nunca
Las pasiones que nuestro pecho agitan,
¡Quántos prodigios por menores causas
De vuestro gran poder el hombre admira!
Sed justos con mi pecho y este objeto,
Mereced la oblacion que se os dedica.

Pateticamente.

Y tu suprema esencia que te ocultas
A los sentidos y en el pecho brillas,
Alma del universo, y existencia
De todo ser, tu que eres la harmonía
De cuerpos y elementos, fuego dulce,
Venus celeste, sacra y peregrina,
Venus por quien todo se conserva,
Y siempre está en reproduccion continua;
¿Qué se ha hecho tu equidad, y los auxîlios
De la rara virtud que comunicas?
¿Qué de las leyes de naturaleza
En la ardiente pasion que me domina?
¿Qué se ha hecho aquel calor tan vigoroso
Que en mi vano deseo introducias?
¿Internado en mi pecho esta tu fuego,
Y un mortal yelo en este marmol fixas?
Demas, tengo la vida que á el le falta;
No espero, no, prodigios este dia,
Y si los hay del juicio humano exceden
El orden de las cosas hoy se mira
Muy trastornado, y ultrajado se halla

El vigor de naturaleza misma.
A su poder las leyes restituye,
El curso restablece con que giran
Y esparce hoy con igualdad perfecta
Tu grande influxo y proteccion divina;
Al complemento de las cosas faltan
Dos séres, esta llama se divida
Que abrasa el uno sin que aníme al otro:
A mi súplica atiende, pues tu misma
Por mi mano formaste estos hechizos
Que solo esperan sentimiento y vida,
Quitame la mitad, dásela toda,
Estoy contento como en ella viva.
¡Tú que recibes cultos obsequiosos
Que los mortales todos te dedican,
Y á quien no honra aquel que nada siente,
Tu gloria aumenta con tus obras mismas!
Salva el sonrojo de la naturaleza,
Sí, el baldon que la resulta evita
De que este perfectísimo modélo
Sea imagen de cosa que no exîsta.

Quedase abatido un rato, y al volver en sí, dice blandamente.
        ¡Qué inesperada calma!
Quando mi sangre ardía
En una mortal fiebre,
Mis miembros imprevisto aliento aníma.
        Corriendo por mis venas,
De virtud exquisita,
Va un balsamo muy suave
Causandome esperanza y alegria.
Tambien siento se infunde
En mi ya nueva vida,
Que asi el conocimiento
De nuestra dependencia tranquiliza.
        Por infelíz que sea
Un mortal, se le alivian
Todas las inquietudes,
Si invoca á las Deidades con fé viva.
        Pero esta confianza
Queda desvanecida,
Para aquellos que tienen
Deseos necios, locas fantasías.
        En un estado semejante al mio
Todo se implora, de oir nadie se digna,
Aun es mayor delirio que el deseo,
La esperanza que el logro facilita.

Con este desvario avergonzado,
Ni á contemplar me atrevo á quien me hechiza.
Si quiero levantar los tristes ojos
A este objeto fatal, siento á su vista,
Una nueva inquietud, un nuevo espanto,
Y una opresion que respirar me priva.

Ironicamente.
¡Anímate infelíz! mira tu obra,
Tu atencion toda en esta estatua fixa.

Repara que se anima la estatua.
¡Qué veo Dioses! ¡ó que se me figura!
¡El color veo de las carnes mismas!
¡Moverse el cuerpo y en sus ojos fuego!
¡Esto solo faltaba á mis desdichas!

Cree que el movimiento de la estatua es efecto de su imaginacion enardecida.
¿Infelíz Pigmalion que te sucede?
¡Al extremo llegó tu fantasía!
Te dexa la razon, como el ingenio,
No sientas el perderla, pues perdida,
Libertará á tu fama del oprobio.
Para el que adora un marmol es gran dicha
Llenarse de visiones y rarezas
Hasta el ultimo instante de su vida.

Vuelve á mirar la estatua, y al notar que baxa los escalones, se arrodilla y levanta los ojos al cielo.
¡Oh Dioses! . . . ¡Oh Venus! . . . ¡Oh prestigio,
De una llama de amor la mas activa.

Galatéa tentandose á sí propia.
Yó.

Pigm. ¡Yó!

Galatéa volviendo á tentarse.
Esto es yó.

Pig. ¡Oh encantadora
Ilusion que ya llenas de delicias
Mis oidos! . . . ¡Ah! nunca me abandones.

Galatéa dando algunos pasos y tentando otra estatua.
Esto no es yo.

Galatéa dá vuelta al obrador con la vista, Pigmalion la observa atentamente, ella llega á ponerle una mano sobre el ombro, él se la toma, la arrima á su pecho, y se la besa; al mismo tiempo dice ella dando un suspiro:
    ¡Esto si es yó!

Pigm. Sí, Divina
    Galatéa; si, amable y dulce objeto;
    Sí, obra la mas perfecta y la mas digna
    De mi corazon, mis manos y los dioses,
    Mi ser todo está en tí, y toda mi dicha,
    Penderá desde hoy únicamente,
    En ser yo todo túyo, en ser tú mia.

I

BIBLIOGRAPHY OF SPANISH TRANSLATIONS OF THE WORKS OF J. J. ROUSSEAU[1]

Library holdings are referred to as follows:

B   Boston Public Library.
BG   Bibliothèque Publique de Genève.
BGU Biblioteca Pública del Estado, Guadalajara, Mexico.
BM   British Museum.
BMun Biblioteca Municipal, Madrid.
BN   Biblioteca Nacional, Madrid.
BNB   Biblioteca Nacional, Bogotá, Colombia.
BNBA Biblioteca Nacional, Buenos Aires.
BNC   Biblioteca Nacional, Santiago, Chile.
BNE   Bibliothèque de Neuchâtel.
BNM   Biblioteca Nacional, Mexico.
BNP   Bibliothèque Nationale, Paris.
BNPe Biblioteca Nacional, Lima, Peru.
BNU   Biblioteca Nacional, Montevideo, Uruguay.
BO   Biblioteca del Estado, Oaxaca, Mexico.
BSE   Secretaría de Educación Pública, Mexico.
G   Biblioteca Municipal, Guayaquil, Ecuador.
JRS   In possession of compiler.
LC   Library of Congress.
LCP   Library Company, Philadelphia.
MP   Biblioteca de Menéndez y Pelayo, Santander.
NYP   New York Public Library.
PS   Library of the American Philosophical Society, Philadelphia.
TU   University of Texas, Austin, Texas.

I. DISCOURS SUR LES SCIENCES ET LES ARTS (1750)

1. *Discurso sobre si el restablecimiento de las ciencias y de las artes ha contribuído al mejoramiento de las costumbres.*

In *El Contrato social* . . . Traducción española de Everardo Velarde (Paris, n.d. [1910?], pp. 1–35. See No. 62.

2. *Las ciencias y las artes en relación con las costumbres.* Versión española por Edmundo González-Blanco. Anotada y revisada

---

[1]The bibliographical data concerning copies in the British Museum, the Bibliothèque Nationale, Paris, and the Biblioteca Nacional, Madrid, were generously collected by Prof. R. H. Williams of Brown University while a research fellow of the National Council of Learned Societies in 1931–1932; the details concerning the copies in the National Libraries of Chile and Colombia were furnished by their respective librarians.

conforme a la última edición francesa. Madrid, Tipografía de José Yagües, n.d. [1918?]. 185 pp. 16°.   BN, JRS

Contents: "Advertencia del traductor," signed at Luanco, Asturias, August 5, 1915, 5–15; *Discurso*, 17–58; "Carta a Grimm," 59–74; "Carta al rey de Polonia," 75–102; "Ultima respuesta a Bordes," 103–133; "Carta sobre una nueva refutación del *Discours*, hecha por un académico de Dijón," 135–141; and "Notas del traductor y del autor," 143–185.

3. *Discurso sobre si el restablecimiento de las ciencias y de las artes ha contribuído al mejoramiento de las costumbres.*

In *El Contrato social* . . . Traducción española de Everardo Velarde (Paris, n.d. [1926]), pp. 1–35. See No. 68.

4. *Discurso sobre las artes* . . . Madrid, Espasa-Calpe, n.d.

Listed in *Catálogo general de Literatura—Espasa-Calpe* [Mexico, 1933], p. 61, under heading of "Filosofía (Ensayos)."

II. Discours sur l'origine et les fondements de l'inégalité parmi les hommes (1755)

5. *Discurso sobre el origen y fundamentos de la desigualdad entre los hombres*, por J. J. Rusó, ciudadano de Ginebra. En Charleston. Año MDCCCIII. xxiii + 192 pp. 16°. Signatures: [1]–2⁴ in 16s; A–P⁵ in 12s.   BNM

"Preliminar del traductor," [iii]–xxiii; "A los manes de Juan Jacobo Rusó," [Signed Neufchâtel, 1779, Du Peyrou], [1]–6; "A la república de Ginebra" [Signed Juan Jacobo Rusó. En Chamberi, a 12 de Junio, 1754], 7–32; "Prefacio," 33–44; *Discurso*, [45]–135; "Notas," [136]–192.

Translator was apparently an American as he refers to "nuestra América" [pp. viii and x]. He praises the philosophers who laid the foundations for American independence; mentions the death of Louis XVI and the campaigns of Napoleon and his generals; but there is no evidence in his preliminary statement that the edition is antedated.

6. *Discurso sobre el origen y los fundamentos de la desigualdad de condiciones entre los hombres.* Por J.-J. Rousseau. Puesto en castellano por M———. Madrid, en la imprenta de José del Collado, 1820. xvi + 200 pp. 12°.

BM, BN, JRS, LCP

7. *Discurso sobre el origen y los fundamentos de la desigualdad de condiciones entre los hombres.* Gerona, imp. de Oliva, 1820. xvi + 200 pp. 12°.   Palau²

8. *Discurso sobre el origen y los fundamentos de la desigualdad entre los hombres.* Traducido por M———. Valencia, 1821. 289 pp. 16°.   BNC

---

²Palau y Dulcet, Antonio, *Manual del librero hispano-americano.* Barcelona, 1926. 8 vols. Hereafter referred to as Palau.

9. *Discurso sobre el origen y los fundamentos de la desigualdad de condiciones entre los hombres.* Por J.-J. Rousseau. Puesto en castellano por M——. Revisto y corregido. Madrid, en la imprenta de José del Collado, 1822. [xii] + 200 pp. 12°.

BNP

"Prefacio," i–x; "Advertencia sobre las notas," xi–xii; *Discurso,* 1–142; "Notas," 143–200.

The translator of Nos. 6–9 was José Marchena y Ruiz de Cueto.

9ª. *Discurso sobre el origen y fundamentos de la desigualdad de condiciones entre los hombres; puesto en castellano, por M——, revisto y corregido.* Paris, Rosa, 1822, in –18.

Quérard, *La France Littéraire,* VIII, Paris, 1836.

10. *Discurso sobre el origen y los fundamentos de la desigualdad de condiciones entre los hombres.*

Described on fly-leaf of *Emilio* (Paris, en casa de Tournachon-Molin, 1824), vol. V, as "Nueva edic. corr., en–18 con retr.," under "Libros españoles que se hallan en casa del mismo librero." Most of the works listed were prohibited in Spain. See No. 77.

11. *Discurso sobre el origen y los fundamentos de la desigualdad entre los hombres.* 1 vol. 32°.

Listed in *Catálogo de los libros que existen en la Biblioteca pública del Estado* (Guadalajara, 1874), p. 454.

12. *Memoria sobre el origen de la desigualdad entre los hombres,* por Rousseau.

Advertised on p. 144 of *El Contrato social* (Barcelona, 1868). See No. 56.

13. *Origen y fundamento de la desigualdad entre los hombres.* Memoria presentada a la Academia de Dijón por Juan Jacobo Rousseau. Traducida de la edición de Dresde, MDCCLV, por I. López Lapuya. Madrid, López y Cía., editores, 1886. 176 pp. 16°.

BNM

"Cuatro palabras al lector [Signed Madrid, October 20, 1886], [5]–14; "Advertencia del autor," 15; "Dedicatoria," 17–33; "Prefacio," 35–44; *Discurso,* 45–135; "Notas," [137]–176.

14. *Discurso sobre el siguiente tema propuesto por la Academia de Dijón; ¿Cuál es el origen de la desigualdad entre los hombres? ¿Está ella autorizada por la ley natural?*

In *El Contrato social,* Paris [1910], pp. 35–185. Translation of Everardo Velarde. See No. 62.

15. *Origen y fundamento de la desigualdad entre los hombres.* Traducida de la edición de Dresde, MDCCLV por I. López Lapuya. Prólogo de Carlos Malagarriga. Madrid, Francisco Beltrán. Librería española y extranjera, n.d. [1915?]. 206 pp. 8°.

BN, JRS

"Advertencia del Editor," 5–8; "Prólogo," 9–17; *Discurso,* 18–161, "Notas," 162–206.

16. [Traducción del *Discours sur l'origine de l'inégalité parmi des hommes.*]

Mentioned in *Las ciencias y las artes*, Madrid, [1918?], p. 6, as "traducción ya hecha, pero cuya publicación me han obligado a retrasar exigencias editoriales muy atendibles." On p. 12, in referring to the same work González Blanco adds: "ya traducido, . . . y que en breve saldrá a la luz." The "Advertencia" in which these statements occur is dated August 5, 1915, and signed by Edmundo González Blanco. From the opening sentence (p. [5]), this writer had evidently undertaken the translation of "las obras sociales de Rousseau, principalmente las de carácter popular."

17. *Discurso sobre el origen de la desigualdad entre los hombres.* La traducción del francés ha sido hecha por Angel Pumarega. Madrid, Calpe, 1923. (Colección universal, Nos. 859–860, in Vol. XCII.) 190 + [1] pp. 8°.

BN, BNM, JRS

["Nota del traductor"], 5–7; 8 blank; Epigraph from Aristotle's *Politics*, [9]; 10 blank; "Advertencia del autor sobre las notas," [11]; 12 blank; "Dedicatoria," 13–28; "Prefacio," [29–[37]; 38 blank; *Discurso*, [39]–135; 136 blank; "Notas del autor," 137–190; "Indice," [191].

18. *Discurso sobre el origen y los fundamentos de la desigualdad de condiciones entre los hombres.* Traducido por Camaposada. Barcelona, Sopena, n.d. BN

19. *Discurso sobre el siguiente tema propuesto por la Academia de Dijón: ¿Cuál es el origen de la desigualdad entre los hombres? ¿Está ella autorizada por la ley natural?*

In *El Contrato social* (Paris, [1926]), pp. 35–185. See No. 68.

III. LA NOUVELLE HÉLOÏSE (1761)

20. *Julia o La nueva Heloísa;* ó Cartas de dos amantes habitantes de una ciudad pequeña al pie de los Alpes. Recogidas y publicadas por J. J. Rousseau. Traducidas del Francés al Castellano, con notas del traductor en los asuntos que miran á la religión, y á la moral. En Bayona, en la imprenta de Lamaignere, calle de Port-Neuf. Año 1814. 4 vols. 16°.

JRS [Vol. IV only]

Vol. IV [439 + 2 pp.] contains the fifth and sixth part. At the end of text are two numbered pages headed "Fe de erratas." They are preceded by this note: "No es de extrañar, que en una imprenta donde ninguno entendía el castellano, se hayan cometido muchas faltas."

This translation is marked by omissions of many words, phrases, and chapters; the notes are largely a defense of the church and its teachings, and criticisms of Rousseau's comments on religious matters. The general tone is so far from that of Marchena as to bar the possibility that the translation is his, unless he was trying to secure its publication in Spain, which seems improbable.

21. *Julia, ó La nueva Heloísa; ó Cartas de dos amantes habitantes de una ciudad pequeña al pie de los Alpes: recogidas y publicadas por J. J. Rousseau. Traducidas del francés al castellano, con notas en los asuntos que miran a la religión y a la moral. Por A.B.D.V.B. Segunda edición, corregida y aumentada con las dos cartas, y todo lo demás que se había suprimido en la primera edición.* Burdeos, en la imprenta de Don Pedro Beaume, 1820. 4 vols. 12°. (Signed in 12s) 19 x 11 cms. [Láminas according to Palau.]

BNP [Vols. I–II only]

Vol. I, "Prólogo" of Rousseau, i–viii; "El traductor," ix–x; text, 285 + [1] pp; Vol. II, 388 + [6] pp.

The translator has not been identified.

22. *Julia, o La nueva Heloísa; ó Cartas de dos amantes habitantes de una ciudad pequeña al pie de los Alpes: recogidas y publicadas por J. J. Rousseau. Traducidas del francés al castellano, con notas en los asuntos que miran a la religión y la moral. Por A.B.D.V.B. Segunda edición, corregida, y aumentada con las dos cartas, y todo lo demás que se había suprimido en la primera edición.* Madrid, 1820. 4 vols. 24°.

JRS

Vol. I, "Prólogo de Rousseau," i–viii; "El Traductor," [ix–x]; [xi–xii] blank; text, 1–293 pp.; Vol. II, 394 pp.; Vol. III, 236 pp.; Vol. IV, 419 pp.

In his introductory remarks the translator states that the first twenty-two letters were translated originally by a friend who has won fame through his translation of *El Citador* of Pigault-LeBrun.

23. *Julia, ó la Nueva Heloysa, cartas de dos amantes habitantes de una ciudad chica, a la falda de los Alpes, recogidas y publicadas por J. J. Rousseau; traducidas por J. Marchena. Con láminas finas.* Tolosa, Imprenta de Bellegarrigue, 1821. 4 vols. 12°. 12 engraved plates. B, BNP, BNM, JRS

Vol. I, "Prólogo," v–viii; text, 1–279; 280 blank; "Indice," 281–290; Vol. II, 390 pp.; Vol. III, 232 pp.; Vol. IV, 442 pp.

There are no notes of the translator, but those of Rousseau are included. In Vol. IV, 413–435, "Los Amores de Milord Eduardo Bomston."

24. *Julia, ó la nueva Heloísa, cartas de dos amantes habitantes de una ciudad chica, a la falda de los Alpes, recogidas y publicadas por J. J. Rousseau. Traducidas por Dr. M. V. M. (sic). Con láminas finas.* Madrid, por Dⁿ. Benito Cano, 1822. 4 vols. 12°. 19 x 11 cms. Engraved plates. BNP

Vol. I, viii + 291 + [1] pp.; Vol. II, 392 pp.; Vol. III, 252 pp.; Vol. IV, 445 + [1] pp.

A reprint from the Tolosa, 1821, edition. Contains also "Los amores de milord Eduardo Bomston."

25. *Julia, ó la nueva Heloísa*, cartas de dos amantes habitantes de una ciudad chica, a la falda de los Alpes, recogidas y publicadas por J. J. Rousseau. Traducidas por Dr. M. V. M. (*sic*). Con láminas finas. Versalles, en la imprenta francesa y española, 1823. 4 vols. 12°. Vol. III, 252 pp.; Vol. IV, 445 pp.

B, [Vols. III–IV]

After comparing this edition with that of Tolosa, 1821, James L. Whitney noted: "These translations appear to be identical.[3]

26. *Palau* cites an edition of Madrid, 1822, in 3 vols. 8°.

26ª. *Julia, o la Nueva Heloísa . . .* traducida por D. M. V. M. Versailles, de la imp. de Jacob, 1824. 4 vols. in –4.

Quérard, *La France Littéraire*, VIII, Paris, 1836.

27. A translation of *Julia* is credited to Félix Enciso y Castrillón.[4]

28. *Julia, ó la Nueva Heloísa*, trad. por J. Marchena. Barcelona, 1836.

Described in *Catalogue* of Alex Jullien, Geneva, No. 85, 1933, item 2156, as "6 fig. 3. vol. in—16, baz."

29. *Palau* cites an edition of Barcelona, Sauri, 1836. 1 vol. 8°.

30. *Palau* says same edition circulated with title page of Barcelona, Tauló, 1836.

30ª. *Julia, ó la nueva Heloísa, cartas de dos amantes habitantes de una ciudad chica, á la falda de los Alpes, recogidas y publicadas por J. J. Rousseau;* traducidas por J. Marchena. Adornada con 6 láminas finas. Barcelona, librería nacional de D. M. Sauri, 1836.

12°. 2 engravings in Vol. I. viii, 428 pp.

On verso of title page: Imprenta de José Tauló, calle del Hospital, num. 60.

Details from Burstein, who has only Vol. I.

30ᵇ. *Julia, ó la nueva Eloísa, cartas de dos amantes habitantes de una ciudad chica á la falda de los Alpes, recogidas y publicadas por J. J. Rousseau,* traducidas por J. Marchena, Barcelona, 1836. Imprenta y librería de D. M. Sauri. Madrid, Viuda de Razola; tres tomos en 8° con 6 láminas.

Listed in *Boletín bibliográfico español y estrangero*, Vol. II, 305. Madrid, 1841.

30ᶜ. *Julia ó la nueva Eloísa, cartas de dos amantes habitantes en una pequena ciudad en la falda de los Alpes; recogidas y*

---

[3] *Catalogue of the Spanish library . . . bequeathed by George Ticknor to the Boston Public Library* (Boston, 1879), p. 312.

[4] Juan Hurtado y J. de la Serna and Angel González Palencia, *Historia de la literatura española* (Madrid, 1932), p. 932.

publicadas por Juan Jacobo Rousseau. Traducidas por J.
Marchena, y adicionadas únicamente en esta edición, con la
vida y retrato de su autor. Barcelona, 1837; imprenta y
libreriá de don Francisco Oliva, editor. Madrid, librería de
Cuesta, un tomo en 8° mayor.

Listed in *Boletín bibliográfico español,* Vol. I, p. 44. Madrid, 1840.

31. Also circulated with title page of Oliva, 1837. 3 vols. 8°.
[Palau.]

32. *Julia, ó la nueva Heloísa,* por Juan Jacobo Rousseau; puesta en
castellano por D. José Mor de Fuentes. Barcelona, Imprenta
de A. Bergnes, calle de Escudellers, núm. 26, 1836–1837. 4
vols. 8°. Engraved frontispiece [portrait of Rousseau].
JRS

Vol. I, "Prólogo," v–vii; viii blank; "Prólogo segundo," ix–xl;
text, 1–248 pp.; Vol. II, 5–331 pp.; Vol. III, 5–199, "Erratas del
tomo segundo," [200]; Vol. IV, text, 1–343 pp.; "Los amores de
milord Eduardo Bomston," pp. 345–363; "Carta de [Rousseau a M.
Montmorenci, 1760], pp. 364–366.

Palau says this edition has 12 plates.

33. Same as above, Barcelona, Oliva, n.d. 8°. marquilla. [Palau.]

34. *Julia, ó La Nueva Heloísa,* Cartas de dos amantes habitantes
de una pequeña ciudad, a la falda de los Alpes. Recogidas y
publicadas por Juan Jacobo Rousseau; traducidas por J.
Marchena. Barcelona, Imprenta y librería de Oliva, Calle
de la Platería, 1836. xx + 410 pp. Engraved frontispiece.
BM, JRS

Frontispiece is same as Bergnes, 1836, edition; added title page
bears engraving the reverse of plate 1 in Tolosa edition; below:
Barcelona, Librería de D. Francisco Oliva, 1837.

"El editor," v–vii; viii blank; "Vida de Juan Jacobo Rousseau"
[from Oliva's *Diccionario histórico y biografía universal de hombres
célebres*], ix–xviii; "Prólogo," xix–xx; text in double columns, pp.
1–402; "Los amores de milord Eduardo Bomston," pp. 403–410.

In a two-paged "Prospecto," bound in at end, *Julia* is announced as
the eighth of the "Colección de Novelas" issued by Oliva, and described as "1 tomo 8 marquilla."

35. *Julia o La Nueva Eloísa.* Cartas de dos amantes coleccionadas
y publicadas por J. J. Rousseau. París, Casa editorial Garnier
Hermanos, n.d. [1920?]. 2 vols. 8°. JRS

On cover at head of title: "J. J. Rousseau"; below: "Biblioteca de
autores célebres." On end cover: Paris, "Imp. de Marcel Fesson,
10–20."

Vol. I, [v]–xxxiv + 512 pp.; Vol. II, 524 pp.

This translation differs from the 1814, the Marchena, and the Mor
de Fuentes. The translator may have been Alvaro Gil, who made
other Rousseau translations for Garnier around 1890.

IV. Le contrat social (1762)

36. *El contrato social, ó Principios del derecho político.* Segunda edición. Londres. Año de 1799. 12°. xvi, 332 pp.   JRS
"Advertencia del traductor," iii–xvi; text, 1–326; contents, 327–332. Signatures a, A–T4.

"La traducción de *El Contrato Social* por D. Alonso Arango Sierra, la cita el canónigo D. Carlos González Posada en su obra *Memorias históricas del Principado de Asturias,* tomo I, Tarragona, 1794 [*sic*]. Menciónala asimismo Fuertes Acevedo en su *Bibliografía asturiana,* con el epígrafe *La ley natural,* agregando que fué vertida al castellano *á instancias del Conde de Campomanes.*"—Somoza de Montsoriú, Julio, *Inventario de un Jovellanista* (Madrid, 1901), 198.

"En el catálogo de manuscritos de la Biblioteca de Menéndez Pelayo aparece (número 49) como probablemente suya [Santiváñez] una traducción del *Contrato Social* (Londres, 1799). No me parece verosimil esta hipótesis, dado que Santiváñez no estuvo jamás en Londres, y sobre todo, que en 1799 hacía ya cinco años que había muerto. Lo de Londres es menos concluyente, porque en aquella época . . . abundan las portadas falsas."—Núñez de Arenas, M., "Don Vicente María Santiváñez. Un madrileño en la revolución francesa," in *Revista de la Biblioteca, Archivo y Museo,* II (1925), 375.

Although Menéndez y Pelayo scouts at the idea, *Estudios de crítica literaria,* 3a. serie (Madrid, 1920), III, 314, it is possible that Marchena, since he translated all of Rousseau's other important works, was also the translator of this version. The views expressed in the "Advertencia del traductor" are entirely in accord with those expressed by him in other works.

37. *El Contrato social o Principios del derecho político.* Londres, año de 1799.   MP
"Ms. en 4° de 464 páginas, copiado indudablemente del impreso, con mucha pulcritud y limpieza."—Somoza de Montsoriú, *Inventario de un Jovellanista,* 164.

The extracts the compiler has had copied from the manuscript, namely the "Advertencia del traductor," portions of Bks. I, II, and IV, and the "Notas," correspond entirely with those of the printed copy.

38. "Por estudio privado tradujo el Dr. José María Vargas en 1809 el *Contrato Social de Rousseau.*"—Blanco, J. F., and Azpurúa, Ramón, *Documentos para la Historia de la Vida pública del Libertador* (Caracas, 1875), I, 236.

39. *El contrato social.* Por J. J. Rusó. Charleston, [?].
This title was given me by Professor Marden shortly before his death in 1932. He had clipped the item from a bookseller's catalogue and sent it to Professor Christian Gauss, who has since been unable to locate it. He writes as follows:

"I have no doubt whatever that there is a Spanish translation of the *Social Contract* whose title page announces it as published in Charleston, South Carolina. . . . The title page was probably false title page, and the edition had probably been printed in Spain or Spanish America. . . . The attribution to Charleston was a blind to mislead the censor. The date as I recall was given as about 1800, . . . [but] the edition was probably antedated." Personal letter to compiler, Princeton University, October 28, 1932. In an earlier note to Dr. Marden, Professor Gauss stated that as he recalled the item, the printer's name was Black.

40. *Del Contrato social o principios del derecho político.* Obra escrita por el ciudadano de Ginebra Juan Jacobo Rousseau. Se ha reimpreso en Buenos-Ayres para instrucción de los jovenes americanos. Con superior permiso. En la Real Imprenta de Niños Expósitos. Año de 1810 . . . [Petit in 4º. viii + 92 pp. BG.]

8º. 66 pp., according to Palau. "Prólogo," 1–viii, signed by Mariano Moreno.

Pp. viii, 1–92 (In 8s, A–I, K,L,M–2 only; new title page; pp. 1–66 (Signatures N–T (8 p.) V, X (1 leaf only). Issued in two *entregas*, each with same title page.   BNBA complete. UT pt. 1 only.

Best copy in the Biblioteca Nacional, Buenos Aires, has autograph of Mariano Balcarcel, Octubre de 18[?]. Last two figures trimmed off in binding.

"El editor a los habitantes de esta America" [1]–[vi]. Signed "Dr. Mariano Moreno."

"Harto significativo es que Mariano Moreno, al publicar el *Contrato Social*, no necesitara traducirlo—según suele decirse—pues se valió, al reeditarla en Buenos Aires, de una traducción española que ya circulaba en la Península."—Rojas, Ricardo, *La Literatura argentina* (Buenos Aires), V, 861.

"La traducción no era de Moreno—ni tampoco de Jovellanos, como lo afirma el doctor López . . . fué . . . una reimpresión de la versión española que se esparció por Asturias en 1801. . . ." Groussac, P., "Escritos de Mariano Moreno," in *Crítica literaria*, 251.

"Tal reimpresión—que como lo sugiere la palabra, no es traducción de Moreno, sino una edición española utilizada a ese objeto."—Ricardo Lavene—*La Revolución de Mayo y Mariano Moreno*, II (B. A., 1925), 205.

A comparison of the text of Nos. 40 and 36 reveals that the former was not printed from the latter. If it was actually a reprint, it must have been from the Charleston or some other as yet unknown edition.

41. *El Contrato social, ó Principios del derecho político:* por Juan Santiago Rousseau, Ciudadano de Ginebra. En Valencia, por José Ferrer de Orga, Año de 1812. 280, [xxx] pp. 8º. BN, HS, JRS. Signatures, A–U3.

On verso: "Esta nueva traducción del *Contrato social* es propiedad del editor." Text, 1–280; "Notas" [i]–[xxiii]; [xxiv] blank; "Indice," [xxv]–[xxix]; "Erratas" [xxx].
Translator had the 1799 edition at hand and followed it largely. Two of the notes, Nos. 3 and 21, are taken bodily from that edition.

42. *"Contrato social ó Principios del derecho político* (Queda omitido el tratado de religión en todas sus partes). *Foederis s*[*sic*] *equas Dicamus leges.* Aenid. XL [*sic*]. Habana, oficina de D. Antonio José Valdes. (S.a.) En 8°., 132 ps."
"En menuda impresión. Es una de las mejores impresiones de la Isla. La portada no lleva año, pero no pudo ser antes de 1813 ni muy posterior porque en aquel año abrió su imprenta Valdés y los sucesos posteriores son de todos sabidos. Cita de Bachiller." [y Morales, Antonio. *Apuntes para la historia de las letras y de la instrucción pública en la isla de Cuba.* (Habana, 1859–61, 3 v.) III, 153].
"El Centinela de la Habana de 16 de enero de 1813 manifiesta que acaba de imprimirse esta obra. V. el núm. de Febrero de 1813." Cited by Carlos M. Trelles, *Bibliografía cubana del siglo XIX,* Mantanzas, 1911, I (1800–1825), 110–111.

43. *Principios del derecho político,* traducidos del francés al castellano. En Valencia, por José Ferrer de Orga, Año de 1814. [v], 318, [1] pp. Signatures 1–20.   LC, JRS
Same translation as the Valencian edition of 1812, but the notes from the 1799 edition are not included nor is Chap. VIII, Bk. IV. The notes are at the bottom of the page instead of at the end, as in the 1812 edition.

44. *Cartas sobre la obra de Rousseau titulada: Contrato social,* en las que se vacía todo lo interesante de ella, y se suprime lo que puede herir la religión católica apostólica romana. Por el ciudadano Valentín de Foronda. Coruña: en la oficina de Don Antonio Rodríguez. Año de 1814. 228 pp. 8°.   JRS
Signatures: B in 8s, C–F, F–I, K–U, X–Dd in 4s.
"Me dice que la célebre obra de Rousseau titulada *Contrato Social* le parece algo confusa, que desea aprovecharse de lo bueno que contiene, y que me estimará se la presente de un modo más perceptible. . . . He suprimido la multiplicada división de artículos, . . . unas veces he cambiado toda la frase, y otras no; unas veces he traducido literalmente, y otras con libertad, . . . unas veces he suprimido palabras, y otras he substituido las que me han parecido más cabales. . . . Todo el libro primero . . . he vaciado en la primera carta . . . en los demás libros que reduzco también a cartas, particularmente en la cuarta hai tambien varias supresiones. . . ." [Carta próloga (pp. 5–6), dated Feb. 15, 1814, at Coruña.] As a result of this publication Foronda was imprisoned from 1814 to 1820. As all copies were ordered destroyed, existing copies are rare.[4a]

[4a]Hidalgo, D. *Diccionario general* I, (Madrid, 1859), 344.

45. *El Contrato social, ó Principios del derecho político.* Par [*sic*]
J.-J. Rousseau. Lyon, Librería de Cormon y Blanc. 1819.
228 pp.   NYP
"Impr. de Kindelem, a Lyon. In-18 de 6 feuilles et demie"—
Dufour, Th., *Recherches Bibliographiques*, No. 183.[5]
Translation corresponds exactly with that of 1799, except that typo-
graphical and linguistic errors have been corrected. Chapter VIII of
Bk. IV is included.

46. *El Contrato social, ó Principios del Derecho político.* Por J.-J.
Rousseau. Nueva edición, revista y corregida. Madrid, en la
oficina de José del Collado, 1820. 240 pp.   NYP, BGU
Translation is the same as the 1799 and 1819 editions, but further
errors in both have been corrected. Chap. VIII of Bk. IV is included.

46ª. *Principios del derecho político, traducidos del frances al castellano.* [Quotation] Libro Primero. Madrid: Imprenta de
Repullés, 1820. 47, índice, [48]; 68; 103, verso blank; 85 pp.
16°. 9½ by 14. Binder's title "Rousseau. Derecho público."
                                                             JRS
Same translation as the Valencian editions. Two of the notes from
the 1799 edition are included, but note 20, Bk. III, p. 37, which corresponds with note 21 of the Valencian and that on p. 161 of the 1799
edition, is abbreviated to end with the sentence "Oh Jovino, Jovino!
Tú solo mereces el homenage de todo buen español."

47. *El Contrato social; ó Principios del derecho político,* por J.-J.
Rousseau. Madrid, Librería de Ramos, 1821. [ii] + 224 +
[4] pp. 12° signed in sixes. 15 x 10 cms.   BG, BNP
On verso of title page: Se hallará en Lyon, Librería de B. Cormon
y Blanc.
In reality the printer was J. M. Boursy in Bordeaux.

48. *"El Contrato social. . . . Madrid, 1821. 1 v. pa. 16°."*
Listed in *Catálogo de los libros que existen en la Biblioteca pública
del Estado* (Guadalajara, 1874), 454.

49. *El Contrato social, ó Principios del derecho político.* Por J.-J.
Rousseau. Nueva edición, revista y corregida. Filadelfia:
en la imprenta de M. Carey e Hijos. 1821. Text, [3]–178;
Tabla de los libros y capítulos, [179]–180.   BNC, LCP
Reprinted exactly from Collado's 1820 edition. Title page of LCP
copy—the gift of Mrs. Isaac Lea—bears proofreader's corrections.

50. *El Contrato social, ó Principios del derecho político.* Por J.-J.
Rousseau. Nueva edición, revista y corregida. Filadelfia:
en la imprenta de H. C. Carey & I. Lea. 1822. 180 pp.   B
With the exception of title page, whole is reprinted from same type
as 1821 edition.

---

[5]*Recherches bibliographiques sur les œuvres imprimées de J.-J.
Rousseau. . . . Paris, 1925. 2 vols. Hereafter referred to as Dufour.

51. *Teoría del pacto social,* [con una] advertencia preliminar, sacada de las obras del Sr. Martínez de Marina. 124 pp. 4°.
                                                                        BNM, PS, TU
In *El Fanal del imperio mexicano o Miscelánea política estractada y redactada de las mejores fuentes,* por el autor del *Pacto Social* para inteligencia de esta obra . . . (México, en la nueva imprenta de L.L. H.H. Morán, año de 1822), I, 164–288. [Verso of Signature 21–1 to 36–2.]

The translation begins without title or heading with Bk. I, Chap. II, paragraph III, "La familia es el primer modelo de las sociedades políticas." Bk. II, Chap. V and Chap. VII from Judaic Law on, Bk. IV, Chap. VIII, and note 12, with reference to Calvin, are omitted. Rousseau's name occurs only in the headings on pp. 199–200 and on p. 203.

The translation corresponds exactly with the edition of Madrid, 1820. In the "Prospecto" of *El Fanal,* [I, i–vi] the purpose of the publication of *El Contrato Social* is explained by the editor and publisher, Francisco Severo Maldonado.

52. *"Contrato Social,* 1 vol. en–18."

Listed among "Libros españoles que se hallan en casa del mismo librero," in *Emilio* (Paris, 1824), vol. V, fly-leaf vii. See No. 77.

53. *El Contrato social, ó Principios del derecho político,* por J.-J. Rousseau. Paris, en la librería hispano-francesa de Rosa, calle de Montpensier, no. 5, 1827 [On verso of half-title, Bruxellas, Imprenta de J. Wodon. Calle de las Piedras, No. 1137.] 243 pp. 12°.   JRS

Apparently a reprint of the Lyon, 1819, edition, as errors found in that are reproduced.

54. *El Contrato social, ó Principios del derecho político,* Nueva edición. Londres, 1832. 16°. viii, 247 pp.   JRS

Translation, "Advertencia" and notes correspond with the 1799 London edition.

55. *El Contrato social, ó sea Principios del derecho político.* Por J.-J. Rousseau, ciudadano de Ginebra. Traducido del francés. [On verso]: Barcelona. En la imprenta de los Herederos de Roca, año 1836. 194 pp. 16°.   JRS

Apparently a new Spanish version. Name of translator not given.

56. *El Contrato social, ó sea Principios del derecho político,* por, Juan Jacobo Rousseau, Ciudadano de Ginebra. . . . Barcelona, Establecimiento tipográfico-Editorial de Manero, Ronda del Norte, 128. 1868. 144 pp. 16°.   JRS

On cover at head of title: Biblioteca revolucionaria. Below: "Folleto núm. 3." Text, pp. 5–140; "Folletos publicados," pp. 141–144.

On p. 144, among "Folletos publicados" and "En prensa": *"Memoria sobre el origen de la desigualdad entre los hombres,* por Rousseau, and *Obras políticas* por el mismo."

The translation is that of the Barcelona, 1836, edition.

57. *El Contrato social* por J. J. Rousseau traducido del francés por J. M. Madrid, Librería de Antonio Novo, 1880. 204 pp. 16°. 17 cm.   BSE, JRS
On verso of title page: "Aurelio J. Alaria, impresor."

58. *El Contrato Social.* Filadelfia, 1882 [*sic*].
Cited in *Catálogo alfabético de la Biblioteca del Estado.* (Oaxaca, 1887), p. 33.
This may be the 1822 edition of Carey and Lea.

59. *Del Contrato Social.* Traducción de Anton'o Zozaya. . . . Madrid, Dirección y Administración Plaza del Progreso, 3, 2°., 1883. 206 pp. 32°.   BNM, JRS
At head of title: "Biblioteca económica filosófica. Volúmen X. Juan Jacobo Rousseau," On verso of title page: "Madrid, Imp. de R. Angulo, San Vicente Baja, 63."
"Rousseau—Noticia biográfica," signed "A. Z." pp. [5]–7. [in this the dates of publication of the var'ous works mentioned are largely incorrect.] Text, 9–203; "Indice," 205–206.

60. *El pacto social, o principios del derecho político.* Traducción y notas de A. Redondo Orriols. Madrid, 1884. x, 191 pp. 16°. (Biblioteca universal, Vol. XCIII.)   BN
"El traductor a los lectores," v–vii; "Preliminar," ix–x; Text, 11–191.

61. *Del Contrato social.* Traducción de Antonio Zozaya. . . . Segunda edición. Madrid, Dirección y Administración Plaza del Progreso. 3, 2°., 1887. 204 pp. 32°.   BN, JRS, BNBA
On verso of title page: "Madrid, 1887. Imp. de R. Angulo, San Vicente, 76." At head of title: "Biblioteca económica filósofica. Volúmen X. Juan Jacobo Rousseau."
"Rousseau—Noticia biográfica," signed "A. Z.," pp. [5]–7. [In this the dates of publication of the various works mentioned are still largely incorrect.] Text, [9]–202; "Indice," [203]–204.

62. *El Contrato social o Principios de derecho político.* Traducción española de Everardo Velarde. Prólogo de C. Rodríguez. Paris, Garnier Hermanos, n.d. [1910?]. 349 pp. 19 cms.
                                                    BSE, BNBA, BNPe
For further details, see No. 68.

63. *El Pacto social.* . . . Traducción de Antonio Redondo Orriols. Madrid, 1911. 191 pp. 16°.   BNC

64. *El contrato social.* Traducido por el Dr. Doppelheim. Barcelona, Sopena, n. d.   BN
In a letter from Barcelona, July, 1933, Luis Aznar states: "Sopena no tiene de Rousseau ninguna edición de *Contrato Social.* Hace unos 20 años imprimió solamente, sin ponerla aquí a la venta, una edición para *El Diario Español* de Buenos Aires; pero sin quedarse ningún ejemplar."

65. *Del contrato social.* Fragmentos. Barcelona, Casa editorial. Publicaciones de la escuela moderna, [1917]. 93 + [2] pp.

JRS

At head of title: "Biblioteca popular. Los grandes pensadores. Juan Jacobo Rousseau." Below: "Volúmen XV—Segunda serie." "Noticia biográfica," signed "C. L.," pp. [5]–8; text, [9]–93; "Noticia bibliográfica," [95].

66. *Contrato social.* La traducción del francés ha sido hecha por Fernando de los Ríos. Madrid, Calpe, 1921. 190 pp. 16°. (Colección universal, Nos. 469–470, Vol. CXII.)

BN, BNC, BNM, BNU

At head of title: "Rousseau." On verso: "Tipográfica renovación (C.A.), Larra 6 y 8, Madrid."

[Prólogo], signed Fernando de los Ríos Urruti, pp. [5]–7; text, [9]–187; "Indice," [189]–190.

67. *El Contrato social o sea Principios del derecho político*, por Juan Jacobo Rousseau, Ciudadano de Ginebra. . . . Barcelona, Casa editorial Maucci, n.d. 223 pp. 8°.

JRS

On cover: Potrait of Rousseau [that of Maurice Quentin de la Tour in Museum of Geneva].

"Not cia biográfica," signed J. Brissa, pp. 5–9; Text, 10–219; "Indice," 221–223.

Translation is same as Barcelona, 1836.

68. *El Contrato social o Principios de derecho político.* Traducción española de Everardo Velarde, Adjunto a la legación de la Républica de Panamá en París. Prólogo de C. Rodríguez. Paris, Casa editorial Garnier Hermanos, n.d. [Imp. H. Turgis, 1926.] xvi, 333 [1] pp. 16°.

JRS

At head of title: "J. J. Rousseau."

"Advertencia del traductor," signed December 31, 1909, pp. v–vii; "Prólogo," ix–xv [signed Paris, January, 1910]; Discursos, 1–184; text of *Contrato Social*, 185–333; "Indice," [335].

69. *Contrato social.* La traducción del francés ha sido hecha por Fernando de los Ríos. Madrid, Espasa-Calpe, 1929. 200 pp. 16°. (Colección universal, Nos. 469–470, Vol. CXII.)

BN, JRS, BNBA

["Prólogo"], signed Fernando de los Ríos Urruti, pp. 5–7; text, 9–197; "Indice," 198–200.

70. *El pacto social o Principios del derecho político.* Traducción y notas de Antonio Redondo Orriols. Madrid, Imp. de Librería y casa editorial de Hernando (S. A.), 1931.

191 pp. 32°.

JRS

At head of title: "Biblioteca Universal. Colección de los mejores autores antiguos y modernos, nacionales y extranjeros, tomo XCIII." "El traductor a los lectores," pp. v–vii; "Preliminar," ix–x; text. 11–191.

70ª. *Contrato social.* La traducción del francés ha sido hecho por Fernando de los Ríos. Espasa-Calpe. Madrid, 1934. 200 pp. (Col. Universal, 469–470.) JRS
At head of title: Rousseau.

70ᵇ. *El contrato social o sea principios del derecho político por* Juan Jacobo Rousseau ciudadano de Ginebra. Buenos Aires-Montevideo-Santiago de Chile, Editorial Fé, n.d. [c. 1937]. 223 pp. 13 by 18 cms. JRS
On cover: Portrait of Rousseau [that of Maurice Quentin de la Tour.]
"Noticia biográfica" signed J. Brissa, pp. 5–9; text, 10–219; "Indice," 221-223.
Translation is same as Barcelona, 1836. Whole issue is a reprint of Maucci, Barcelona, n.d.

V. ÉMILE (1762)

71. *Emilio ó De la Educación,* por J. J. Rousseau; Traducido por J. Marchena. [Quotation.] Burdeos, en la imprenta de Pedro Beaume, Librero, Allées de Tourny, nº. 6, 1817.
3 vols. 8º. NYP, JRS
Vol. I, "Prólogo," pp. i–vi; text [bks. 1–2], 7–300; Vol. II [bks. 3–4], 444 pp.; Vol. III [bk. 5], 288 pp.
Cover of Vol. II faced with military order dated Bordeaux, March 15, 1817; that of Vol. III, with order for the execution of Etienne Lalande.
Apparently this is the edition described by Dufour, No. 210, as Burdeos, 1817, 2 vols.
72. Edition of Paris, Alexis Eymery, 1819. 4 vols. Large 8º. Listed in the catalogue of Cánovas del Castillo. [Palau.]
There is a copy in BNP, but bibliographical details were not sent.
73. *Emilio, ó De la Educación,* por J. J. Rousseau; traducido por J. Marchena. Segunda edición. [Quotation.] Burdeos, en la imprenta de Pedro Beaume, Librero, Allées de Tourny, No. 5, 1821. 3 vols. 8º. JRS
Vol. I, "Prólogo," pp. 1–6; text [bks. 1–2], 7–333; Vol. II, 492 pp.; Vol. III [bk. 5], [5]–325 pp.
Lacks the "frontispice de Cochin et 8 planches de Moreau" described in *Le Bouquiniste genevois,* No. 46, librairie Juillien, Geneva (February, 1928), No. 35685 as "3 Vol. in –12."
74. *Emilio, ó De la educación.* Por J.-J. Rousseau. Traducido por J. Marchena. Nueva edición. [Quotation.] Madrid, Imprenta de Alban y Compañía, 1821. 2 vols. 8º. 18.5 x 12 cms.
Signatures 1–24 by eights. BM, BNP, G Vol. I only
Vol. I, vi + 389 + [1] pp.; "Prólogo," pp. i–vi; Vol. II, 371 + [1] pp.
75. Burdeos, 1822. 3 vols. 8º. [Palau.]

76. Madrid, J. Collado, 1822. [Hidalgo, *Diccionario general*, Madrid, 1867.]

77. *Emilio, ó De la educación*, por J. J. Rousseau; Traducido nuevamente y aumentado de *Emilio y Sofía o Los Solitarios*, con una Tabla de Materias, por Rodríguez Buron. París, En casa de Tournachon-Molin, Calle de Savoie, No. 6, 1824. 5 vols. 12°. Frontispiece [portrait of author.]

BNP, BNPe, BNM [Vols. II–V], BNU, JRS [Vol. V]

On verso of half title: "Paris, en la imprenta de A. Bobée, calle de la Tableterie, No. 9."

Vol. I, frontispiece, portrait, xii + 415 pp.; Vol. II, 328 pp.; Vol. III, 296 pp.; Vol. IV, 308 pp.; Vol. V, 297 pp.

Vol. V contains last of bk. 5, pp. 1–99; *Emilio y Sofía*, 100–210; "Tabla de las materias," 211–297. At end, list of Spanish books for sale by same bookseller; among them the following works of Rousseau:

Nueva Heloïsa . . . nueva edición, 4 vols. en–12, con 78 herm. lám.

Contrato (el) Social, 1 vol. en–18.

Discurso sobre el origen . . . nueva edic. corr., en–18 con retr."

BNM copy lacks these fly leaves.

The translation is that of Marchena, revised and emended. Cf. "Prólogo," I, ix.

77ª. "El mismo Marchena publicó en Tolosa el año 1821 una traducción en cuatro tomos, tamaño de 8°, que fué reimpresa en Barcelona el año 1834"—Blanco y Sánchez, Rufino, *Bibliografía pedagógica de obras escritas en castellano o traducidas a este idioma*, (Madrid, 1907–12. 5 vols.), Vol. III, 525.

78. *Emilio*. Madrid, 1850. Publicada en *Las Novedades*. [Palau.]

79. *Emilio*. Madrid, 1850. Published as a separate. [Palau.]

80. *Emilio*, por J. J. Rousseau. Edición ilustrada con 27 grabados, publicada en el folletín de *Las Novedades*. Madrid, Imprenta del Semanario y de la Ilustración, a cargo de D. G. Alhambra, Jacometrezo 26, 1855. 315 pp. 4° (signed in 6s). 27 engravings.

BNM, JRS

Running title on verso of odd-numbered pages: "Folletín de las Novedades." Text in double columns.

Nos. 78–80, to which Palau refers as the translation of Ruiz de Cueto, were in reality translated by Marchena, whose name was José Marchena y Ruiz de Cueto.

80ª. *Emilio o la educación*, por J. J. Rousseau.

In volume 6 of *Eco de los folletines*. Archivo escogido y económico de obras amenas e instructivas de todos los tiempos y de todos los países. Madrid, 1854–56. Imp. del *Semanario é Ilustración*, despacho de *Las Novedades*.

Cf. D. Hidalgo, *El bibliógrafo español y estranjero*, I (Madrid, 1857–59), 147–48.

81. *Emilio*, por J. J. Rousseau. Novísima traducción de D. J. M.
Madrid, Campuzano hermanos, 1872. 2 vols. 8".
[Palau.]
82. *Emilio*, por J. J. Rousseau. Novísima traducción de D. J. M.
Administración Librería de Antonio Novo, Jacometreza, 51,
1879. 2 vols. 8".   BNU, JRS
On verso of title page: Imprenta de Campuzano hermanos, Ave
María, 17.
Vol. I, [3]–339 pp.; Vol. II, [3]–319 pp.
The Marchena translation.
83. *Emilio, o la educación*. Traducción de Ricardo Viñas. París,
Garnier Hermanos, 1896. 2 vols. 8".
BM, BN, BNM, NYP
84. *Emilio o La educación*. Traducción de Ricardo Viñas. París,
Garnier Hnos. n.d. 2 vols.   BNM
Ms. note on title page: "Ballescá, October, 1912." Probably the
donor and date of acquisition.
85. *Emilio o La Educación*. [Quotation from Seneca in original
and in Spanish translation of Fernández Navarrete.] Ver-
sión española con un retrato y autógrafo del autor, revisada
y corregida según las mejores ediciones originales con notas,
ilustraciones y prólogo de Rafael Urbano. Madrid, Daniel
Jorro, editor, 1916. 2 vols. 8". frontispiece. [Portrait of Rousseau from the Maurice-Quentin de La Tour portrait in the
Museum of Geneva.]   BNB, BN, BNM, JRS, NYP
On verso of title page: "Tipolit. L. Faure, Alonso Cano, 15 y 17."
At head of title: Biblioteca científico-filosófica.
Vol. I, "Juan Jacobo Rousseau" [Prólogo del traductor], pp.
[vii]–xix; "Prefacio," 1–6; text, 7–421; 422 blank; "Indice," 423;
Vol. II, text, 386 pp., 387 blank; "Indice," 388.
Notes of the translator are numerous and generally explanatory
of the text.
86. Reprint of Ricardo Viñas edition. París, Garnier, 1916. 2
vols. 8".   BN
87. *Emilio o la Educación*. Traducción de Ricardo Viñas. París,
2 vols. 12".   BNC
88. *Emilio*. Traducción de D. J. M. Barcelona, Casa editorial
Maucci, n.d. [after 1921]. 2 vols. 8".   JRS
On cover: Portrait of Rousseau in colors. At head of title: "J. J.
Rousseau." Printed on very cheap paper. Reprint of Marchena translation. On verso of title page: Paragraph on Rousseau by Matilde
de Noailles. Vol. I, text, pp. [5]–400; Vol. II, [7]–405.
88ª. *Antología de Rousseau*. Selección e introducción de María
Luisa Navarro de Luzuriaga. Madrid, Publicaciones de la
"Revista de Pedagogía" 1931. 110 p.   BNC
La vida, pp. [5]–9, Las ideas, 9–15; Indice, [16]: Text, 17–110.

At head of title: La Pedagogía clásica.

Selections from *Emile* that bear on (1) la primera educación; (2) segunda educación; (3) la educación activa; (4) resultados de la educación; (5) la educación ulteriór; (6) recapitulación. *La Revista de Educación* was established in 1922 to reflect "el movimiento pedagógico contemporáneo. . . ."

89. *Emilio o la Educación*. Traducción de Ricardo Viñas. París, Garnier, n.d. 2 vols. 8°. Librería Robredo, Mexico. On last fly-leaf: "Imp. de H. Turgis, 1–28."

90. *Emilio o Sobre la educación*. Madrid, Librería Bergua, n.d. [1932]. 2 vols. 16°.   JRS

On verso of title page: Versión castellana de Juan España . . . Avila, Tipografía y encuadernación de Senén Martín. On back cover: Biblioteca de Bolsillo No. 17.

Vol. I, "J. J. Rousseau," pp. 5–8; "Prefacio," 9–13; 14 blank; text, 15–355; "Indice," [356].

Vol. II, text, pp. 5–323; "Indice," [324].

The translation ascribed to Juan España is in reality that of Marchena.

90ᵃ. *Emile*, por J. J. Rousseau.

Listed on back cover of No. 70ᵇ. Clearly a South American edition, probably a reprint of the Barcelona edition of Maucci [after 1921].

VI. PYGMALION (1771)

91. *El Pigmalión*, del Sr. Juan Jaime Rousseau, traducido del francés en italiano por el Sr. Abate D. Manuel Lassala, y ahora al español por un amigo suyo, con todas las escenas líricas propias de dicho Sr. Abate en verso de arte mayor.

This translation, made by Eusebio de Canas at Valencia, 1783, was based on the Lassala version which appeared in a volume entitled *Ormasinda. Tragedia. Con alcune scene liriche*, one of which was "Pimmalione del Sig. Giangiacomo Rousseau." Bologna, 1783. Of the Spanish version Justo Pastor Fuster [*Biblioteca valenciana* (Valencia, 1827–1830), II, 330] says: "Todas estas piezas en un tomo en 4° manuscrito, original tengo en mi poder." See also Carlos Sommervogel, *Bibliothèque de la compagnie de Jésus* (Paris, Brussels, 1893), IV, col. 1544. The Italian translation of Lassala is not listed by Mario Schiff in "Editions et traductions italiennes des Oeuvres de Jean-Jacques Rousseau," in *Revue des Bibliothèques*, 1907, 183–216, and 1908, 9–39.

92. *Pigmalión*. Versión parafrástica, en metro castellano endecasílabo, escena lírica, original francés, representada en 1788. Cádiz, en la imprenta de D. Juan Jiménez Carreño.

Listed but not printed in Adolfo de Castro, *Sainetes de D. Juan González del Castillo* con un discurso sobre este género de composiciones (Cádiz, 1846), IV, p. lx; and also in Cano's edition of

Obras completas de Don Juan Ignacio de González del Castillo
(Madrid, 1914).
93. *"Pigmalión.* Escena lírica, traducida del francés al castellano
  por D. Juan Diego Roxo. Papel en 4° de 12 p. En Madrid,
  por Antonio Fernández, 1788."—*Memorial literario,* XIII
  (Feb., 1788), 294.
93ª. *Pigmalión.* Poema Lírico. Puesto en verso [por] D. Francisco
  Durán.
  Full text from *Memorial Literario,* Jan., 1788, on pp. 265–273.
94. *Pigmalión.* Monólogo patético traducido de [*sic*] francés
  libremente, y aumentado en verso castellano por D. F. M. N.
                                                          BN, BMun
  The translator was probably the indefatigable Francisco Mariano
Nipho.
  On the copy in the Biblioteca Municipal, Madrid, is the approval
of the censor, Santos Díez González, dated Jan. 6, 1793.[6]
94ª. *Pigmalión.* Monólogo Patético. Traducido y puesto en verso.
  Por D. F. M. N.—Colophon: En Valencia, por José Ferrer
  de Orga, Año 1813. 14 p.   BNBA
  P. 1, Note by the translator concerning the three Pigmalions of
history and fable: (1) Pigmalión rey de Chypre; (2) Pigmalión,
Rey de Tyro; and (3) Pigmalión, the sculptor who became enamoured
of a statue he had made.
  P. 2. Text begins: ¡Por más que las medito atentamente nada
dicen que adule a mi deseo!
95. *Pigmalión,* escena lírica puesta libremente en verso castellano
  por Don F. Durán. Tercera edición, corregida. Madrid,
  1816. 4°.   BM

VII. Les Pensées (1763)

96. *Pensamientos* de Juan Jacobo Rousseau, ciudadano de Ginebra;
  ó sea el espíritu de este grande hombre en sus obras filosóficas,
  morales y políticas. Traducido del francés al español con
  algunas notas por el ciudadano Santiago de Alvarado y de
  la Peña. Madrid, Imprenta de D. M. de Burgos, 1822–1823.
  2 vols. 16°.   JRS
  Vol. I, "El traductor a los lectores de esta obra," pp. [5]–14;
"Pensamientos de J. J. Rousseau," 15–289; "Indice," [290]; "Erratas,"
[291–292].
  Vol. II, Text, beginning with "Placeres," pp. [5]–295; "Noticia de
la vida y escritos de Juan Jacobo Rousseau," [296]–313; "Erratas
advertidas," [314]; "Indice," [315–316].
  Text agrees with the *Receuil de Prault* described by Dufour, No.
280.

---

  [6]Subirá, José, "Los 'melólogos' de Rousseau, Iriarte y otros
autores, in *Revista de la Biblioteca, Archivo y Museo,* V (1928), 142.

97. *Pensamientos* de Juan Jacobo Rousseau, ciudadano de Ginebra; ó sea el espíritu de este grande hombre en sus obras. Burdeos, 2 vols. in 12". Dufour, No. 337, quoting Quérard.

98. *Pensamientos* de Juan Jacobo Rousseau, ciudadano de Ginebra; ó sea el espíritu de este grande hombre en sus obras filosóficas, morales, y políticas. Traducido del francés al español con algunas notas por el ciudadano Santiago de Alvarado y de la Peña. Madrid, Burgos, 1824. 2 vols. 8". BNC

99. *Los Pensamientos* de J.-J. Rousseau, traducidos del francés por D. Mario Laugier. Marsella, en casa de Laugier hermanos y compañía, fabricantes de papel . . . 1826.

2 vols. 12". BNE, BNP, JRS
Vol. I, [iv] + 223 + [1] pp.; Vol. II, [iv] + 176 + [4] pp.
No introduction or notes. Text begins: Dios. Cuanto más me esfuerzo en contemplar . . .; ends: que no conduce a sus lectores al bien?

Translation is based on the *contrefaçon* of the *receuil de Prault*.

99ᵃ. *Pensamientos, ó sea el Espíritu de este gran hombre en sus obras filosóficas.* 1 vol. en 12.

Listed in *Catalogue of Spanish Books* imported by George R. Lockwood, late Roe Lockwood. February, 1861. New York.

VIII. LETTRE A BEAUMONT (1764)

99ᵇ. *Carta de Juan Jacobo Rousseau vecino de Ginebra a Juan Montillet, arzobispo, y Senor de Autho Prunedo de la Gratia Novem populania*, etc. Ms. Neufcastel, 15 de marzo, 1764. Vol. I, 111. 8 fols. 188b–189b.

"Es traducción de la impresa en francés. Trata de la condenación del *Emilio* y ataca a los jesuitas."—Zarco Cuevas, Eusebio Julián: *Catálogo de los manuscritos castellanos de la Real Biblioteca del Escorial* (Madrid, 1924), 2 vols. II, p. 41, No. 4.

IX. LES CONFESSIONS (1782–1789)

100. *Las Confesiones.* Versión española de E. Lorenzo Oliveres. Barcelona, Sociedad Literaria—editorial Guttemberg, calle del Consulado, núm. 19, 1869. ii, 879, [2] pp. 15 by 22 cms.

"Prólogo del traductor," [i]–ii, text [3]–879; list of engravings, [881].

On fly-leaf, "Obras de J. J. Rousseau ciudadano de Ginebra." Engraved cover title. At head: Obras del espíritu humano libre. In middle, Mayence 1450; above, bust of Gutenberg with letter in the semicircle. At head of title, Biblioteca Guttemberg. p. [881] lists 4 engravings inserted at pp. 111, 129, 570 and 604.

100ᵃ. Also described in *Catalogue* of L'Arsin, April, 1931, No. 518, as "in 4 enq."

p. [881] lists 4th engraving at p. 605.

According to Palau, this edition has portrait and engravings.

101. *Las confesiones.* Versión española de E. Lorenzo Oliveres. Barcelona, Administración, Riera de S. Juan, núm. 3, p. 1°., 1870. 11, 879 + [2] pp. 4°. Engraved cover, frontispiece and 4 plates. JRS

Fly-leaf, cover title, verso of title pages agree with 1869 edition. Cover title: "Obras del espíritu humano libre."

At head of title: Biblioteca Guttemberg [*sic*]. J. J. Rousseau.

On verso of title page: "Esta traducción es propiedad del editor."

101ᵃ. Another copy, found in Santiago, Chile, of which all pages before [3] of text are missing, has first signature set with different type and varies in line setting.

Frontispiece, portrait of Rousseau by Sadurni. "Prólogo del traductor," pp. 1–2; text, 3–879; list of engravings [881].

102. *Las confesiones* de J. J. Rousseau. Versión castellana por Alvaro G. Gil. París, Garnier, 1889. 4°. BNM

103. *Las confesiones.* Versión castellana por Alvaro G. Gil. París, Garnier Hnos., [1907–1910]. 2 vols. 12°. BNM

Vol. I, 415 p.; [at end, 265.10.07].

Vol. II, 375 p.; [at end, 266.10.10].

104. *Las confesiones.* Traducción de Alvaro G. Gil. París, Garnier, 1911. 2 vols. 12°. BNC

105. Same. n.d. 2 vols. 8°. [Palau.]

106. *Las confesiones.* [Quotation.] Versión española, revisada, corregida, con ilustraciones, notas, prólogo y epílogo de Rafael Urbano. Madrid, Daniel Jorro, editor, 23, Calle de la Paz, 1923.

2 vols. 8°. Frontispiece [portrait of Rousseau] and engravings. BN, BNB, JRS

At head of title: Biblioteca científico-filosófica; below: Juan Jacobo Rousseau.

On verso of title page: "11, 834—Faure, Abascal, 21—Madrid."

Vol. I, "J. J. Rousseau y las confesiones," pp. [vii]–xix; text, 1–367; "Apéndices e ilustraciones," 370–386; "Indice," [387]–388.

Vol. II, text, pp. [7]–511; "Epílogo e ilustraciones," [513]–524; "Indice," [525]–526; "Rousseau en España," 522–524.

Urbano states [II, 523] that he is following the Oliveres translation of 1870. In his preface (I, [xix]) he adds that "un ilustre profesor" has announced another translation of the *Confesiones* to be issued shortly.

107. *Las confesiones.* La traducción del francés ha sido hecha por Pedro Vancés. Madrid, Calpe, 1925. 2 vols. 16°.

BNC, BNM, JRS

At head of title: Rousseau.
On cover: Vol. I, Colección universal, Nos. 987–990; Vol. II, Nos. 991–994. [These volumes when bound form Vol. CXI of the Colección Universal.]
Vol. I, text, pp. [5]–534; "Indice," [535].
Vol. II, text, pp. [5]–484; "Indice," [485].
Apparently this is the edition described by Palau as Madrid, Calpe, 1922–1926. 2 vols. 16°.

X. LES REVERIES DU PROMENEUR SOLITAIRE (1782)

108. *Reflexiones de un paseante solitario.* Traducción de José A. Luengo. Valencia, Prometeo, n.d. [1916?]. 198 + [1] pp. 8°.
BN, JRS
109. *Reflexiones de un paseante solitario.* Valencia, Sempere, n.d. 8°.
[Palau.]

II

Works Bearing on the Diffusion of Rousseau's Ideas

Alamán, L. *Historia de México.* . . . Mexico, 1849-1852. 5 vols.
Alarcos, Emilio. "El abate Marchena en Salamanca," in *Homenaje ofrecido a Menéndez Pidal.* Madrid, 1925.
Alcalá Galiano, Antonio. *Historia de la literatura española, francesa, inglesa é italiana en el siglo XVIII.* Lecciones pronunciadas en el Ateneo de Madrid. . . . Madrid, 1844.
Alcázar Molina, Cayetano. *Los hombres del reinado de Carlos III, Don Pablo de Olavide.* . . . Madrid, 1927.
Almeida, Teodoro de. *Armonía de la razón o teología natural . . . contra las absurdas opiniones de los filósofos del día.* Madrid, 1798.
—— *El hombre feliz independiente del mundo y de la fortuna; o Arte de vivir contento en qualesquier trabajos de la vida.* Obra escrita en portugués . . . traducida y exornada . . . por el Dr. D. Benito Ertaun de Riol. Madrid, 1790. 3 vols.
Almodóvar, Pedro de Góngora y Luján, duque de. *Década epistolar sobre el estado de las letras en Francia.* Su fecha en París, 1780. Madrid, 1781.
Altamira y Crevea, Rafael. *Cosas del día—Crónicas de literatura y arte.* Valencia, 1908.
—— *Historia de España.* Barcelona, 1911. 4 vols.
[Alvarado, Francisco.] *Cartas inéditas del filósofo rancio dirigidas [a] . . . Francisco J. Cienfuegos.* Madrid, 1846.
—— *Carta crítica del filósofo rancio en que continuó la impugnación del dictamen del Sr. Gordillo . . . que establece los bases del pacto al gusto de los filósofos de moda.* Cádiz, 1811.

Alvarez de Cienfuegos, N. "Poesías," in *Poetas líricos del siglo XVIII*, in *B.A.E.*, LXVII.

"El Amigo de la Verdad." *Folleto contra los filosofistas españoles, amigos de Rousseau*, formados por ellos mismos y por su maestro. Madrid, 1815.

Amunátegui, M. L. *La crónica de 1810*. Santiago, 1876–1899. 3 vols.

——— *Ensayos biográficos*. Santiago de Chile, 1893–1896. 4 vols.

——— *Los precursores de la independencia de Chile*. Santiago, 1909. 3 vols.

——— *Vida de D. Andrés Bello*. Santiago, 1882.

Amunátegui Solar, Domingo. *Bosquejo histórico de la literatura chilena*. Santiago, 1915.

——— *Los primeros años del Instituto nacional, 1813–1835*. Santiago, 1889.

Andrés, Juan. *Origen, progresos y estado de toda la literatura*. Madrid, 1784. 8 vols.

Annales de la Société J.-J. Rousseau. Geneva, 1905–   . 24 vols. to date.

Antón del Olmet, Fernando de. *El cuerpo diplomático español en la guerra de la independencia*. Madrid, n.d. 6 vols.

Aranda to Floridablanca, Paris, December 8, 1786. A.H.N. Estado, Legajo 2850. MS.

Argentina. Biblioteca Nacional. Lista de los libros del Deán Funes. MS. No. 689.

Arteaga, Estevan de. *Investigaciones filosóficas sobre la belleza ideal*. Madrid, 1789.

——— *La Rivoluzione del teatro musicale italiano*. . . . Bologna, 1783. 2 vols.

Arteta, Antonio. *Tratado metódico para la educación física e intelectual de los niños*. Valencia, n.d. [c. 1800].

La Aurora de Chile. Santiago de Chile, 1812-1813.

[Bachaumont,   .] *Mémoires secrets*. . . . London, 1777–1789. 36 vols.

Bachiller y Morales, Antonio. *Apuntes para la historia de las letras y de la instrucción pública en la Isla de Cuba*. Habana, 1859–1861. 3 vols.

Ballexerd, Jacques. *Dissertation sur l'éducation physique des enfants depuis leur naissance jusqu'à l'âge de puberté*. Paris, 1762. Spanish translation: *Crianza física de los niños desde su nacimiento hasta la pubertad*. Madrid, 1765.

Baquijano, José. *Elogio del excelentísimo Sr. D. Agustín de Jáuregui y Aldecoa* . . . pronunciado en el recibimiento que como a su Vice-Patrón, le hizo la real Universidad de S. Marcos el día XXVII de agosto del año de 1781. 82 pp.

Baretti, Joseph. *A Journey from London to Genoa, through England, Portugal, Spain, and France*. Third edition. London, 1770. 4 vols.

Bassa, José. *Soberanía del pueblo, cartas con honores de discurso.* . . . Lérida, 1815.

Beaumont, Christóval de. *Instrucción pastoral.* Traducida del francés. Valencia, n.d.

Bertrand, J. J. A. "Goethe en Espagne," in *Mélanges d'histoire littéraire générale et comparée offerts à Fernand Baldensberger*, I (Paris, 1930), 39-53.

La Biblioteca. Buenos Aires, 1896–1898. 8 vols.

Blanchard, Jean-Baptiste. *L'École des Mœurs.* Lyon, 1782. Spanish translation: *Escuela de costumbres, ó reflexiones morales é históricas, sobre las máximas de la sabiduría* . . . traducida al Castellano por D. Ignacio García Malo. Madrid, 1786. 4 vols.

Blanco, José Félix (ed.). *Documentos para la historia de la vida pública del Libertador de Colombia, Perú y Bolivia.* . . . Caracas, 1875–1878. 14 vols.

Blanco y Crespo, J. M. *Letters from Spain.* London, 1822.

Blanco y Sánchez, Rufino. *Bibliografía pedagógica de obras escritas en castellano o traducidas a este idioma.* Madrid, 1907–1912. 5 vols.

Bocanegra, Francisco Alejandro. *Declamación oportuna contra el libertinaje del tiempo que en forma de carta pastoral dirigió a su rebaño el Ill. sñr. D. Francisco Alejandro Bocanegra, arzobispo y señor de Santiago.* Madrid, 1794.

Bonilla y San Martín, Adolfo. "El Pensamiento de Espronceda," in *La España moderna*, CCXXXIV (1908), 69–101.

Bosch, Mariano G. "Luis Ambrosio Morante . . .," in *Boletín de la Academia argentina de letras*, III (1935), 123–172.

Bourgoanne, Chevalier de. *Travels in Spain,* containing a new, accurate, and comprehensive view of the present state of that country. Translated from the French of the third edition. Paris, 1803. In Pinkerton, John, *A General Collection of the Best and Most Interesting Voyages and Travels in all the World.* . . . London, 1809.

Brackenridge, H. M. *Voyage to South America in 1817-1818.* London, 1820. 2 vols.

Bradsher, Earl L. *Matthew Carey, Editor, Author and Publisher.* New York, 1912.

Cabarrús, Francisco. "Cartas sobre los obstáculos que la naturaleza, la opinión y las leyes oponen a la felicidad pública," in *B.A.E.*, LXII, 552–568.

Cadalso, Joseph. *Cartas marruecas.* Isla de Leon, 1820.

—— *Obras.* Madrid, 1803. 4 vols.

Campe, Heinrich. *El nuevo Robinson, historia moral, reducida a diálogos para instrucción y entretenimiento de niños y jóvenes de ambos sexos* . . . traducida al castellano por D. Tomás de Iriarte. Madrid, 1789. 2 vols.

Campos, Ramón. *De la desigualdad personal en la sociedad civil.* Paris, 1823.

Caraccioli, Louis-Antoine. *Religión del hombre de bien.* Translated by Francisco Nipho. Madrid, 1779.

Carmena y Millán, Luis. *Crónica de la ópera italiana en Madrid.* Madrid, 1878.

Cartas sobre la nobleza o el Emilio desengañado. . . . Traducidas del francés. Santiago, 1814.

Catálogo alfabético de la Biblioteca del Estado. Oaxaca, 1887.

Catálogo de los libros que existen en la Biblioteca pública del Estado. Guadalajara, 1874.

Catholic Church. *Indice último de los libros prohibidos y mandados expurgar para todos los reynos y señoríos del católico rey de las Españas.* . . . Madrid, 1790.

———— *Suplemento* . . . *que contiene los libros prohibidos* . . . *hasta el 25 de agosto de 1805.* Madrid, 1805.

Ceballos y Mier, Fernando de. *La falso filosofía o el Ateísmo, Deísmo, Materialismo, y demás nuevas sectas, convencidas de crimen de estado.* . . . Segunda impresión. Madrid, 1775–1776. 6 vols.

Cejador y Frauca, J. *Historia de la lengua y literatura castellana.* Madrid, 1915–1922. 14 vols. Vols. V–VI concern this period.

El Censor. Madrid, 1781–1786. 7 vols.

Chile. Archivo nacional. Testimonio de la causa criminal formada contra Dn. Antonio Vergne y Dn. Antonio Gramuset franceses. 1781. Real Audiencia, 1644. Archivo criminal, Legajo 14.

Churchman, P. H. "The Beginnings of Byronism in Spain," in *Revue hispanique*, XXIII (1910), 333–410.

———— "Espronceda, Byron and Ossian," in *Modern Language Notes*, XXIII (1908), 13–16.

Cogollor, Roque Antonio de (pseud.). *Los Aldeanos críticos, ó Cartas críticas sobre lo que se verá,* in *B.A.E.*, XV, 367–386.

Colección de ideas elementales de educación para el uso de una academia de maestros de primeras letras y padres de familias. Sevilla, 17[82]–1784.

Colección de las particularidades de la vida y muerte de un pretendido filósofo moderno. Escrito en francés, por un autor anónimo . . . traducido al castellano por el Dr. D. M. M. Madrid, 1796.

Coloma, Luis. *El Marqués de Mora.* Madrid, n.d.

Colombia. Biblioteca nacional. *Catálogo de las obras existentes en la biblioteca nacional.* Bogotá, 1897.

Colomer, Juan Estevan. *Oír, ver y callar, y el mayor monstruo del mundo.* Madrid, 1781.

Coriche, Christóval Mariana. *Oración vindicativa del honor de las letras y de los literatos.* Puebla, Mexico, 1763.

Correo de Madrid. Madrid, 1787–1791. 6 vols.

Correspondance générale de J.-J. Rousseau. Paris, 1924–1934. 20 vols.

Cotarelo y Mori, E. *Iriarte y su época.* Madrid, 1897.

Cueto, Leopoldo A. de, [Marqués de Valmar]. "Don José María Queypo de Llano, Conde de Toreno," in *Galería de españoles célebres contemporáneos,* III (Madrid, 1843).

———— *Poetas líricos del siglo XVIII,* in *B.A.E.,* LXI, LXIII, and LXVII.

Danvila y Collado, M. *El poder civil en España.* Madrid, 1885–1886. 6 vols.

———— *Reinado de Carlos III.* Madrid, 1893–1896. 6 vols.

Desdevises du Dezert, G. "Un réformateur au dix-huitème siècle, Don Miguel Antonio de la Gándara," *Revista de archivos, bibliotecas y museos,* XIV (1906), 274–293.

Diario de Madrid. 1788–1813. 19 vols. (broken file)

Discursos mercuriales. Madrid, 1755–1756. Edited by Juan Enrique de Graef.

Doblado Leucadio (pseud.). See Blanco y Crespo, J. M.

Documentos escogidos del archivo de la casa de Alba. Madrid, 1891.

Donoso, Ricardo, *Hombres e ideas de antaño y hogaño.* Santiago de Chile, 1936.

Dufour, Théophile. *Recherches bibliographiques sur les œuvres imprimées de J.-J. Rousseau.* Paris, 1925. 2 vols.

El Español. London, 1812–1814. 8 vols. Edited by Blanco White.

El Espíritu de los Mejores Diarios. Madrid, 1787–1791. 11 vols.

Eximeno, Antonio. *Del origen y regla de la música.* Translated by Francisco A. Gutiérrez. Madrid, 1796. 3 vols.

Exposición sumaria del nuevo método de instrucción elemental de Enrique Pestalozzi. . . . Suplemento a la Gaceta de Madrid del viernes 29 de agosto de 1806. Havana, 1807.

El Fanal del imperio mexicano o miscelánea política, extractada y redactada de las mejores fuentes por el autor del *Pacto Social,* para inteligencia de esta obra, es decir, de la única forma de gobierno digna de los seres inteligentes y libres. México, 1822. 2 vols. [Francisco Severo Maldonado, editor.]

Farinelli, Arturo. *Il romanticismo nel mondo latino.* Turin, 1927. 3 vols.

Feijóo y Montenegro, B. G. *Cartas eruditas y curiosas. . . .* Madrid, 1781. 5 vols.

Fernán Núñez, Conde de. "Carta de Dn. Carlos de los Ríos XXII señor y VI conde de Fernán Núñez a sus hijos," in Morel-Fatio, A., *Études sur l'Espagne,* 2nd Ser. (Paris, 1906), 324–325. First published in Paris in 1791.

Fernández Almagro, Melchor. *Orígines del régimen constitucional en España.* Barcelona, 1925.

Fernández de Lizardi, José Joaquín. *El Pensador mexicano*, 1812–1814.
—— *El Periquillo Sarniento*. Mexico, 1830–1831. 5 vols.
—— *La Quijotita y su prima*. Mexico, 1831–1832. 4 vols.
—— *El Unipersonal de Agustín de Iturbide*. Mexico, 1823.
Fernández de Moratín, Leandro. *Obras póstumas*. Madrid, 1867. 3 vols.
Fernández Valcarce, Vicente. *Desengaños filosóficos*. Madrid, 1787–1788. 4 vols.
Ferrer del Río, Antonio. *Historia del reinado de Carlos III*. Madrid, 1856. 4 vols.
La Filósofa por amor, o cartas de dos amantes, apasionados y virtuosos. Las da a luz D. F. de Toxar. Salamanca, 1799. 2 vols.
Floridablanca, Conde de. *Obras originales . . . y escritos referentes a su persona*. Colección hecha por Antonio Ferrer del Río. Madrid, 1867. In *B.A.E.*, LXIX.
Forner, Juan Pablo. *Discursos filosóficos sobre el hombre*. Madrid, 1787.
—— *Oración apologética por la España y su mérito literario*. Madrid, 1786.
—— *Poetas líricos del siglo XVIII*, in *B.A.E.*, LXIII.
—— *Preservativo contra el ateísmo*. Sevilla, 1795.
Foronda, Valentín de. *Cartas sobre los asuntos más exquisitos de la economía-política, y sobre las leyes criminales. . . .* Tercera edición. Pamplona, 1821. 2 vols.
Funes, Gregorio. "Memoria sobre la agricultura," MS. No. 7956 in Biblioteca Nacional. Buenos Aires.
Fuster, Justo Pastor. *Biblioteca Valenciana*. Valencia, 1827–1830. 2 vols.
Gaceta de Buenos Aires. 1810–1812.
Giaffe, F. *Le Drame en France au XVIIIᵉ siècle*. Paris, 1910.
Gándara, Miguel Antonio. *Apuntes sobre el bien y el mal de España*. Madrid, 1762. Reprinted in *Almacén de frutos literarios inéditos de los mejores autores*, León de Francia, 1804.
García Velloso, Enrique. *Historia de la literatura argentina*. 4th edition. Buenos Aires, n.d.
García Villasana, Francisco T. *Refutación de la obra titulada: "Voz de la naturaleza sobre el origen de los gobiernos."* Madrid, 1821.
Gaullier, E. H. *Études sur l'histoire littéraire de la Suisse française, particulièrement dans la seconde moitié du XVIIIᵉ siècle*. Genève, 1856.
Gil y Zárate, Antonio. *De la Instrucción pública en España*. Madrid, 1855. 4 vols.
Godoy, Manuel de, Príncipe de la Paz. *Cuenta dada de su vida política*. Madrid, 1856–1858. 6 vols.

González Palencia, Angel. "Nuevas noticias bibliográficas del abate Hervás y Panduro," in *Revista de la biblioteca, archivo y museo*, V (1928), 345–359.

—— "Pedro Montengón y su novela *El Eusebio*," in *Revista de la biblioteca, archivo y museo*, III (1926), 343–365.

Grimm, Fr. M., etc. *Correspondance littéraire, philosophique et critique par Grimm, Diderot, Raynal, Meister.* . . . Paris, 1877–1882. 16 vols.

Groussac, Paul. *Crítica literaria.* Buenos Aires, 1924.

Gutiérrez, Juan María. *Origen y desarollo de la enseñanza pública superior en Buenos Aires.* Buenos Aires, 1915.

Hahn, G. P. R. *Basedow und sein Verhältniss zu Rousseau.* Leipzig, 1885.

Hartmann, Ernst. *Jean-Jacques Rouseaus Einfluss auf Joachim Heinrich Campe.* Neuenburg, W. Pr., 1904.

Hartzenbusch, Eugenio. *Apuntes para un catálogo de periódicos madrileños.* . . . Madrid, 1894.

Hayes, Francis C. *Rousseau in Spain.* M. A. Thesis. Columbia University, 1930. Unpublished.

Heredia, José María. "Ensayo sobre el carácter de J. J. Rousseau, su *Julia* y sus *Confessiones*," in *Miscelánea, periódico crítico y literario*, II (México, 1830), 33–44.

Hernández Morejón, Antonio. *El triunfo de la razón.* . . . Madrid, 1814.

Hernández y Dávalos, J. E. *Colección de documentos para la historia de la guerra de independencia de México.* Mexico, 1877–1882. 6 vols.

Hervás y Panduro, Lorenzo. *Historia de la vida del hombre.* Madrid, 1789–1805. 7 vols.

Hidalgo, Dionisio. *El bibliógrafo español y estranjero.* Madrid, 1857–1859. 3 vols.

Holland, Elizabeth Lady. *The Spanish Journal of Elizabeth Lady Holland.* London, 1910.

Iguíniz, Juan B.: "Apuntes biográficos del Dr. D. Francisco Severo Maldonado," in *Anales del museo nacional de arqueología, historia y etnología*, III, 131–154. Mexico, 1911.

Iriarte, Tomás de. *Guzmán el Bueno: soliloquio ú escena trágica unipersonal con música en sus intervalos.* Madrid, 1791. See Cotarelo y Mori, *Iriarte y su época.*

—— *Lecciones instructivas sobre la moral, la historia y la geografía.* Madrid, 1791.

—— *Poema de la Música.* Madrid, 1779.

Isla, José Francisco de. *Obras escogidas del Padre José Francisco de Isla*, in *B.A.E.*, XV.

Istel, Edgar. *Die Entstehung des deutschen Melodramas.* Berlin, 1906.
——— *Jean Jacques Rousseau als Komponist seiner lyrischen Scene "Pygmalion."* Leipzig, 1901.
——— "La Partition originale du *Pygmalion* de J. J. Rousseau," in *Annales de la Société Jean-Jacques Rousseau,* I (1905), 141.
Jaudennes, José, and Ignacio de Viar, Philadelphia, July 29, 1795, to Duque de la Alcudia. A.H.N., Estado, Legajo 3896. Madrid.
Josephson, Matthew. *Jean-Jacques Rousseau.* New York, 1931.
Journal économique; ou Mémoires, notes et avis sur l'agriculture, le commerce. . . . Paris, 1751–1753.
Jovellanos, G. M. de. *Diarios (Memorias íntimas), 1790–1801.* Madrid, 1915.
——— *Obras* . . ., in *B.A.E.,* XLVI and I..
Korn, Alejandro. *Influencias filosóficas en la evolución nacional.* Buenos Aires, [1937?].
Lafinur, Juan C. *Curso filosófico dictado* . . ., 1819. Biblioteca Nacional, Buenos Aires, MS. No. 127.
Langle, Jérôme C. [Fleuriau, Marquis of.] *Voyage de Figaro en Espagne.* St. Malo, 1784.
Lasala y Collado, Fermín. *La separación de Guipúzcoa y la paz de Basilea.* Madrid, 1895.
Lassala, Manuel. *Ormesinda. Tragedia. Con alcune scene liriche.* Bologna, 1783.
Latassa y Ortín, Félix de. *Bibliotecas antigua y nueva de escritores aragoneses.* . . . Zaragoza, 1884–1886. 3 vols.
Latorre, Germán. "Separación del virreinato de Nueva España" in *Revista de archivos, bibliotecas y museos,* Año XVIII, Vol. XXXI (1914), 131–152, 210–220.
Lavene, Ricardo. *La Revolución de mayo y Mariano Moreno.* Buenos Aires, 1925. 3 vols.
Leguía, J. G. *Manuel Lorenzo de Vidaurri.* Lima, 1935.
Llorente, J. A. *Historia crítica de la Inquisición en España.* . . . Madrid, 1822. 10 vols.
Macdonald, Frederika. *Jean Jacques Rousseau.* New York, 1906. 2 vols.
Maine, Henry. *Ancient Law.* New York, 1871.
Mancini, J. *Bolívar y la emancipación de las colonias españolas desde los orígenes hasta 1815.* Paris, 1914.
Marchena, José. *Lecciones de filosofía moral y eloquencia.* . . . Burdeos, 1820. 2 vols.
——— *Obras literarias.* . . . Sevilla, 1892–1896. 2 vols.
Marín, Joseph. *La Sabiduría del siglo convencida de necedad, o Elogio de un sabio en lo mismo que ignoró. Díxolo en la* . . . Universidad de Salamanca el día 15 de Julio de 1777 en honra del difunto Doctor D. Francisco Lorenzo Agudo de Pedraza. . . . Barcelona, [1777].

304 ROUSSEAU IN THE SPANISH WORLD BEFORE 1833

Medina, J. T. *Catálogo breve de la Biblioteca Americana que obsequió a la nacional de Santiago.* Santiago, 1926–1931.

────── *Historia del tribunal del santo oficio de la Inquisición de Chile.* Santiago, 1890. 2 vols.

────── *Historia del tribunal del santo oficio de la Inquisición de Lima (1569–1820).* Santiago, 1887.

────── *Historia del tribunal del santo oficio de la Inquisición de México.* Santiago, 1905.

────── *Historia y bibliografía de la imprenta en el antiguo virreinato del Río de la Plata.* La Plata, Buenos Aires, Londres, 1892. Pt. 3: *La imprenta en Buenos Aires, 1780–1810.*

────── *La imprenta en Bogotá.* Santiago, 1904.

────── *La imprenta en Caracas (1808–1821).* Santiago de Chile, 1904.

────── *La Imprenta en la Puebla de los Angeles.* Santiago de Chile, 1908.

────── *Tribunal del santo oficio de la Inquisición de las provincias del Plata.* Santiago, 1899.

Meléndez Valdés, J. "Poesías" in *Poetas líricos del siglo XVIII,* in *B.A.E.,* LXIII.

El Memorial literario, instructivo y curioso de la corte de Madrid. Madrid, 1784–1791; 1793–1797; 1801–1808.

Memorie del Giacobinismo estratti dall'opere de Gian Jacopo Rousseau. Ferrara, 1800.

Méndez Bejarano, Mario. *Historia política de los afrancesados.* Madrid, 1912.

Menéndez y Pelayo, M. *Estudios de crítica literaria.* Tercera serie. Madrid. Vol. III (1920); Vol. V (1908).

────── *Historia de las ideas estéticas en España.* 3rd edition. Madrid, 1923. Vols. V–VI.

────── *Historia de los heterodoxos españoles.* Madrid, 1917–1932. Vols. VI–VII.

Mercure de France. Paris, 1750–1755.

El Mercurio de Chile. Santiago de Chile, 1822.

Mercurio histórico y político. Compuesto del Mercurio del Haya y de otras noticias. Madrid, 1751–1778.

Mérimée, Paul. *L'influence française en Espagne au dix-huitième siècle.* Paris, 1936.

Mexico. Archivo general. *Precursores ideológicos de la guerra de independencia.* Mexico, 1929–1932. 2 vols.

Mexico. Biblioteca nacional. *Catálogos de la Biblioteca nacional de México,* formados por el Director José M. Vigil. Biblioteca Nocturna. Mexico, 1897.

[Mier, José S.] *Historia de la revolución de Nueva España.* Londres, 1813.

Mill, James. "Letter to Spanish Americans by One of Their Compatriots in Philadelphia (Juan Pablo Vizcardo y Guzmán)," in *Edinburgh Review*, January, 1809, pp. 277 ff.

Miranda, Francisco. *Archivo del General Miranda.* Caracas, 1929–1933. 13 vols.

Mitre, Bartolomé. *Historia de Belgrano y de la independencia argentina.* 6th edition. Buenos Aires, 1902–1913. 4 vols.

Monitor araucano, El. Santiago, 1813. 2 vols.

Monteiro, Ignacio. *Ars critica rationis dirigendae.* Venice, 1778.

Montengón, Pedro. *Eudoxia, hija de Belisario.* Madrid, 1793.

——— *Eusebio.* Madrid, 1786–1787. 4 vols.

Morel–Fatio, A. "Grands d'Espagne et petits princes allemands au XVIIIᵉ siècle," in *Études sur l'Espagne.* Deuxième série. Paris, 1906.

[Moreno, Mariano]. *Doctrina democrática de Mariano Moreno.* Buenos Aires, 1915. Edited by Ricardo Rojas.

——— *Escritos.* Buenos Aires, 1896. Edited by Norberto Piñero.

Moreno, Manuel. *Vida y memorias del doctor Mariano Moreno.* London, 1812.

Morf, H. "Pestalozzi en España," in *Boletín de la institución libre de enseñanza*, XI (1887), 20–22, 52–54, 86–89, 115–123.

Morley, John. *Diderot and the Encyclopaedists.* London, 1886. 2 vols.

——— *Rousseau.* London, 1915. 2 vols.

Moses, Bernard. *The Intellectual Background of the Revolution in South America, 1810–1824.* New York, 1926.

Muñoz, Juan Bautista. *Juicio del Tratado de educación.* Madrid, 1778.

Muzzarelli, Alfonso. *L'Emilio disingannato.* Siena, 1783. 4 vols.

——— *Continuazione dell'Emilio disingannato, o sia confutazione del Contratto sociale di Gian Jacopo Rousseau.* Foligno, 1792. 2 vols.

Narganes de Posada, Manuel Josef. *Tres cartas sobre los vicios de la instrucción pública en España, y proyecto de un plan para su reforma.* Madrid, 1809.

Nipho, Francisco Mariano. *Diario extranjero. Noticias importantes y gustosas para los verdaderos apasionados de artes y ciencias.* Madrid, 1763.

Nohl, L. *Mozarts Briefe.* Salzburg, 1865.

Nombela, Julio. *Impresiones y recuerdos.* Madrid, 1914. 4 vols.

Nonnotte, Claude François. *Diccionario antifilosófico, o comentario y correctivo del Diccionario Filosófico de Voltaire, y de otros libros que han salido a luz en estos últimos tiempos contra el cristianismo.* Traducido al español por D.A.O.D.Z.B. [Madrid], 1793. 3 vols.

Núñez de Arenas, M. "Don Vicente María Santiváñez. Un madrileño en la revolución francesa," in *Revista de la biblioteca, archivo y museo*, II (1925), 372–403.

306 ROUSSEAU IN THE SPANISH WORLD BEFORE 1833

Oliver, Miguel Santos. *Los españoles en la revolución francesa.* Primera serie. Madrid, 1914.

El oráculo de los nuevos philósofos, M. Voltaire, impugnado y descubierto en sus errores por sus mismas obras. Traducidos al español por el R. P. Mro. Fr. Pedro Rodríguez Morzo. Madrid, 1769–1770. 2 vols.

Palau y Dulcet, Antonio. *Manual del librero hispano-americano.* Barcelona, 1926. 8 vols.

Paz y Melia, A. *Catálogo de los papeles de Inquisición.* Madrid, 1914.

Peers, A. E. "The Influence of Young and Gray in Spain," in *Modern Language Review*, XXI (1926), 404 ff.

———— "La influencia de Chateaubriand en España," in *Revista de filología española*, XI (1924), 351–382.

Pellissier, Robert E. *The Neo-Classic Movement in Spain during the XVIII Century.* Stanford University, 1918.

Pelliza, Mariano A. *Monteagudo, su vida y sus escritos.* Buenos Aires, 1880. 2 vols.

El pensador matritense. Barcelona, n.d. Edited by José Clavijo y Fajardo.

Pérez y López, Antonio Xavier. *Principios del orden esencial de la naturaleza.* . . . Madrid, 1785.

Picot, Michel (ed.). *Mémoires pour servir à l'histoire ecclésiastique pendant le dix-huitième siècle.* Paris, 1853–1857. 7 vols.

Plan, P. P. *J.-J. Rousseau raconté par les gazettes de son temps.* Paris, 1912.

Posada, Eduardo, and Ibáñez, Pedro M. *El precursor.* Bogotá, 1903.

Pozzi, Cesáreo. *Saggio di educazione claustrale.* . . . Madrid, 1778.

Proceso de Nariño. Cadiz, 1914.

Puglia, Santiago Felipe. *El desengaño del hombre.* . . . Filadelfia, 1822.

Quintana, Manuel José. *Obras completas de Quintana,* in *B.A.E.,* XIX.

Raynal, G. *Historia política de los establecimientos ultramarinos de las naciones europeas.* Translated by the Duque de Almodóvar. Madrid, 1784–1790. 5 vols.

Recueil de toutes les pièces qui ont été publiées à l'occasion du Discours de M. J.-J. Rousseau sur cette question proposée par l'Académie de Dijon pour le Prix de l'année 1750. Gotha, 1753.

Reflexiones políticas sobre la legalidad y legitimidad del Congreso nacional, o Cortes extraordinarias establecidas en la isla de León en 1810. Madrid, 1820.

Río, Angel del. "Algunas notas sobre Rousseau en España," in *Hispania*, XIX (1936), 105–116.

Riva Agüero, José de. "Don José Baquijano de Beascoa y Carrillo de Córdoba, tercer Conde de Vistaflorida en el Perú," in *Revista de archivos, bibliotecas y museos*, XLVI, 465–483; XLVII, 68–86.

[Rivera, Agustín.] *Paralelo entre el "Contrato Social" de Juan Jacobo Rousseau y el Sermón del Ilmo. Sr. D. Antonio Joaquín Pérez* . . . predicado en el púlpito de su catedral en pro del Plan de Iguala el día 5 de agosto de 1821. . . . Lagos, [1894].

Robertson, W. S. *The Life of Miranda.* Chapel Hill, 1929. 2 vols.

Rodríguez Solís, E. *Espronceda, su tiempo, su vida, y sus obras.* Madrid, 1883.

Rojas, R. *La literatura argentina.* Buenos Aires, 1924–1925. 8 vols.

Rousseau, F. *Règne de Charles III d'Espagne.* Paris, 1907. 2 vols.

Rousseau, J.-J. *Correspondance générale.* Paris, 1924–1930. 20 vols. Edited by Théophile Dufour and P. P. Plan.

——— *La nouvelle Héloïse.* Nouvelle édition publiée d'après les manuscrits et les éditions originales avec des variantes, une introduction, des notices et des notes. Paris, 1925. 4 vols. Edited by Daniel Mornet.

——— *Oeuvres complètes.* Paris, 1885–1901. 13 vols. Vols. I–II, 1898; Vols. III–IV, 1901; Vols. V–VI, 1901; Vols. VII–VIII, 1885; Vols. IX–X [1902]; Vols. XI–XII, 1887; Vol. XIII, 1887.

Saint-Pierre, B. *La Vie et les Ouvrages de Jean-Jacques Rousseau.* Paris, 1907.

Samaniego, Félix María. *Obras críticas* . . . precedidas de unos estudios preliminares escritos por Julián Apráiz. Bilboa, 1898.

——— *Obras inéditas o poco conocidas del insigne fabulista Don Félix María de Samaniego.* Victoria, 1866.

Schiff, Mario. "Editions et traductions italiennes des œuvres de Jean-Jacques Rousseau," in *Revue des Bibliothèques*, 1907, pp. 183–216; 1908, pp. 9–39.

Ségur, Comte de. *Mémoires ou souvenirs et anecdotes.* Paris, 1825.

Semanario patriótico de España. Cadiz, 1809–1811. 4 vols. Edited by Manuel José Quintana.

Sempere y Guarinos, Juan. *Ensayo de una bibiloteca española de los mejores escritores.* Madrid, 1785–1789. 6 vols.

Silva, Francisco María de (pseud.). See Almodóvar, duque de.

Silva, Tadeo. *Los apóstoles del diablo.* Santiago, 1822.

Real Sociedad Bascongada de los Amigos del País. *Extractos de las juntas generales celebradas* . . . *en la villa de Bilboa por Julio de 1790.* Victoria, 1790.

Solórzano, Atilano de Ajo. *El hombre en su estado natural.* Cartas filosófico-políticas. . . . Valladolid, 1819.

Sommervogel, Charles. *Bibliothèque de la Compagnie de Jésus.* Paris, 1890–1900. 9 vols.

Somoza de Montsoriú, Julio. *Las amarguras de Jovellanos.* Gijón, 1889.

—— *Inventario de un jovellanista.* Madrid, 1901.

Sonneck, O. G. *Catalogue of Opera Librettos Published Before 1800.* Washington, 1904.

Spain. Cortes. *Diario de las discusiones y actas de las cortes.* Cádiz, 1811–1823. 70 vols.

—— *Discusión del proyecto de decreto sobre el Tribunal de la Inquisición.* Cádiz, 1813.

Spell, J. R. "The Educational Views of Fernández de Lizardi," in *Hispania,* IX (1926), 259–274.

—— "An Illustrious Spaniard in Philadelphia—Valentín de Foronda," in *Hispanic Review,* IV (1936), 136–140.

—— "*Pygmalion* in Spain," in *Romanic Review,* XXV (1934), 395–401.

—— "Rousseau's 1750 *Discourse* in Spain," in *Hispanic Review,* II (1934), 334–344.

—— "A Tentative Bibliography of Spanish Translations of the Works of Rousseau," in *Hispanic Review,* II (1934), 134–152.

Subirá, José. "La escena trágica 'Policena,' " in *Revista de la biblioteca, archivo y museo,* V (1928), 360–364.

—— "Los 'Melólogos' de Rousseau, Iriarte y otros autores," in *Revista de la biblioteca, archivo y museo,* V (1928), 140–161.

Torres Amat, Félix. *Seis cartas a Irénico, en que se dan claras y distintas ideas de los derechos del hombre y de la sociedad civil,* y se desvanecen las del contrato que se finge como origen o fundamento necesario de toda soberanía. . . . Por D. Macario Padua. Barcelona, 1817.

Trelles, Carlos M. *Bibliografía cubana del siglo XIX.* Matanzas, 1911–1915. 8 vols.

Urquijo, Julio de. *Los amigos del país.* San Sebastián, 1929.

—— *Menéndez Pelayo y los caballeritos de Azcoitia.* San Sebastián, 1925.

[Valdés, Antonio José.] "Apología del cristianismo de Rousseau," in *Ideas de los caracteres conque principia la imprenta de D. Antonio José Valdés.* Habana, 1813.

Vargas Ugarte, Rubén. "Juan Pablo Vizcardo y Guzmán, 1747–1798," in *Boletín del museo bolivariano,* Año I, No. 4 (December, 1928), pp. 74–93.

Vélez, Rafael de. *Apología del altar y del trono.* Madrid, 1818. 2 vols.

—— *Preservativo contra la irreligión, o los planes de la filosofía contra la religión y el estado realizados por la Francia para subyugar la Europa, seguidos por Napoleón en la conquista de España, y dados a luz por algunos de nuestros sabios en perjuicio de nuestra patria.* Cádiz, 1812.

El verdadero filósofo. Havana, 1813-1814.

Vidart, Luis. *La filosofía española.* Madrid, 1866.

Viduarre, Manuel Lorenzo de. *Cartas Americanas políticas y morales que contienen muchas reflexiones sobre la guerra civil de las Americas.* Filadelfia, 1823. 2 vols.

Villaba Hervás, Miguel. *Ruiz de Padrón y su tiempo.* Madrid, 1897.

Vizcardo y Guzmán, Juan. *Lettre aux espagnols-américains.* . . . Philadelphia, 1799.

La voz de la Naturaleza sobre el origen de los gobiernos. . . . Traducida del francés. . . . Tarragona, 1814. 3 vols.

Walton, William. *Present State of the Spanish Colonies.* . . . London, 1810.

Ward, H. G. *Mexico in 1827.* London, 1828.

Warner, James H. "Eighteenth Century English Reactions to the *Nouvelle Héloïse,*" in *PMLA,* LII (1937), 803–819.

———— "The Reaction in Eighteenth Century England to Rousseau's Two *Discours,*" in *PMLA,* XLVIII (1933), 473–487.

Whitney, J. L. *Catalogue of the Spanish Library . . . bequeathed by George Ticknor to the Boston Public Library.* Boston, 1879.

Wouves d'Arges, Pedro, to Conde de Floridablanca, August 16, 1787. A.H.N. Legajo 3889. Expediente 6, Doc. 25. MS.

Zinny, Antonio. *Bibliografía histórica de las provincias unidas del Río de la Plata desde el año 1780 hasta el de 1821.* Buenos Aires, 1875.

INDEX

Authors and titles cited in the footnotes and included in the bibliography are not listed here.

Discours sur l'inégalité, circulation of, 26, 76, 137; criticisms of, 71, 106, 111–12, 148, 213; echoes of, in Spain, 30–1, 53–4, 101, 111, 143, 258; in Spanish America, 240, 242–3, 250, 255; hostility to, in France, 27; in Switzerland, 27; prohibited in Spain, 27; refutations of, 85, 90–1, 96–8, 101–2, 148, 201, 204, 250; translations of, 104, 111, 207, 215, 233.
Discursos literarios, 99.
Discursos mercuriales, 8, 22–27, 34, 36, 300.
Doblado Leucadio, pseudonym, see Blanco y Crespo.
Döbely, José, 182.
Domingo, El, Rodríguez de Arellano's, 126.
Dominicans, 34, 36, 39, 218, 252.
Don Antón el Holgazón, 125.
Doncel, El, Larra's, 259.
Dos Robinsones, Los, 179.
Draco, 43.
Drama, 118.
Du Chasselas [of Troyes], pseudonym of Grosley, Pierre Jean.
Dueling, echoes of Rousseau's views on, 73, 169, 252, 258.
Dupaty [Louis H.E.M.]?, 250.
Dupeyrou, Pierre, 59, 132.
Dupuis, Charles François, 147, 212.
Durán, Francisco, 121, 127.

E

Echevarría, Esteban, 263.
Eco de los folletines, 261.
École de mœurs, L', Blanchard's, 68–9.
Economic views, echoes of Rousseau's, 52.
Economics, 180.
Education, echoes of Rousseau's ideas on, 81, 89, 91, 105, 137, 204, 210; compulsory, 178; elementary, 177–87, 195, 210, 247; higher, 49, 55, 103, 148, 210; methods of, 180, 185–6; moral, 79, 185–6; of teachers, 183; of women, 74–6, 247; physical, 79, 181, 184, 195; professional, 180, 187; public, 60-1, 65, 138, 180–4, 195–6; 210; religious, 79, 89, 91, 204, 214; secondary, 180; secular, 56, 178; technical, 178, 180.

Education, in Argentina, 240; in Basque provinces, 45–8; in Chile, 245; in general, 13; in Italy, 80; in Mexico, 247; in Spain, 32, 46–7, 55, 64, 72–76; 79, 153, 177–187, 261; in Spanish America, 130, 229, 240, 245, 247, 255.
Éducation physique des enfants, Ballexerd's, 78–9.
Education, Rousseau's influence on, 13.
Education, works on, 229.
Educational reforms, in Spain, 41, 138, 177, 186, 210; in Spanish America, 42.
Egmont, Comte d', 59.
Eguía, Joaquín de, see Narros, Marqués de.
Elementarwerk, Basedow's, 178.
Elève de la nature, L', Beaurieu's, 63.
Eliot, George, 13.
Eloquence, 69.
Émile, 28, 52, 59; burned in Spain, 36; circulation of copies of, 17, 30, 34, 35, 41, 131, 137, 155, 192; criticisms of, 42, 68–9, 71, 82, 86–7, 107–8, 195, 259; imitations of, 72–6, 261; influence of, 42, 46, 65, 135–7, 204; in Spanish America, 34, 229–30, 246–7, 253, 255; plagiarisms of, 412; prohibition of, 29, 36, 39, 50; quoted, 30, 82, 104; references to, 28–9, 33–4, 149, 165, 200, 234, 253; refutations of, 34, 86–92, 95, 202, 204; teachings of, 32, 68, 72–6, 78–80, 95, 105, 131; translations of, 32, 208, 261; works influenced by, 41–2, 64, 72–80, 82–3, 246–7, 261, 264.
Emilio disingannato, L', Muzzarelli's, 81.
Emilio, El, 261.
En alabanza de un carpintero Alfonso, Cienfuegos', 160–1.
Enciso y Castrillón, Félix, 257.
Encyclopedia metódica, 226–7.
Encyclopédie, subscribers to the, in Spain, 46, 147; in Spanish America, 136, 220.
Encyclopedists, 68, 147, 149, 189, 251, 260.
Enderica, Manuel, 219–220.